TEACHER'S RESOUR

THE AFRICAN AMERICAN EXPERIENCE

A HISTORY

WITH AN INTRODUCTION BY
Henry Louis Gates, Jr.

CONSULTANTS

Sharon Harley
University of Maryland

Stephen Middleton
North Carolina State University

Charlotte Stokes
Alexandria, Virginia, Public Schools

GLOBE BOOK COMPANY
A Division of Simon & Schuster
Englewood Cliffs, New Jersey

ABOUT THE COVER ARTIST

Ed Butler, a graduate of the Philadelphia College of Art, is a prominent African American graphic artist and illustrator. Among his various honors are the Society of Illustrators Merit Award and the American Institute of Graphic Artists 50 Best Books Award.

ABOUT THE COVER

For the cover design, Butler has juxtaposed two symbols—African kente cloth and the American flag. Kente cloth is a traditional West African fabric created by stitching narrow, handwoven strips of material together. These two symbols illustrate the dual roles of African roots and American culture in the lives of African Americans.

Cover Art Ed Butler, Butler/Udell

Maps and Graphs Keithley and Associates

Printed in the United States of America. 2 3 4 5 6 7 8 9 10 95 94 93 92

ISBN: 0-8359-0409-1

GLOBE BOOK COMPANY
A Division of Simon & Schuster
Englewood Cliffs, New Jersey

CONSULTANTS

Henry Louis Gates, Jr., is currently W.E.B. Du Bois Professor of the Humanities at Harvard University and has taught at Duke, Cornell, and Yale. Gates received his Ph.D. from Cambridge University, England. He has written widely on African American issues and has a special interest in African American literature. He has received many awards and prizes, among them the American Book Award in 1989.

Sharon Harley is Associate Professor of Afro-American Studies and History at the University of Maryland. She received her Ph.D. from Howard University. She has conducted extensive research in African American women's history, focusing on the history of women workers.

Stephen Middleton is Assistant professor of History at North Carolina State University. He received his Ph.D. from Miami University, Ohio. His particular field of interest is the history of African Americans in pre-Civil War Ohio, an area in which he has written and edited many articles and books.

Charlotte M. Stokes is Teacher Specialist for Social Studies in the Alexandria, Virginia, City Public Schools and worked on the lesson plans for *The African American Experience.* She received degrees in history at the University of Chicago and North Carolina A&T State University. Stokes has helped develop and implement new social studies curricula in the Alexandria schools.

REVIEWERS

Dr. Chapman W. Bouldin, Jr.
Instructional Teacher Leader
Social Studies Department
Brashear High School
Pittsburgh, Pensylvania

Lawrence D. Broughton
Instructor, African American History
North Chicago Community
High School
North Chicago, Illinois

Booker T. Coleman, Jr.
Director, Social Studies/
Multicultural Education
Community School District 9
Bronx, New York

Mildred Fryer
Department Head, Humanities
Snowden International High School
Boston, Massachusetts

Cleotha Jordan
Consultant, African/African
American History
High School Development Center
Detroit, Michigan

Subira Kifano
Teacher Advisor
Language Development Program
for African American Students
Los Angeles Unified School District
Los Angeles, California

Barbara G. Moses
Curriculum Coordinator
School District of Philadelphia
Philadelphia, Pennsylvania

Thandiwe M.C. Peebles
New York City Board of Education
Brooklyn, New York

Margaret Pulley-Johnson
Supervisor of Social Studies (K–12)
New Orleans Public Schools
New Orleans, Louisiana

Gladis M. Twyman
Coordinator, Social Studies
Coordinator, African American
Curriculum Infusion Project
Atlanta Public Schools
Atlanta, Georgia

Edna J. Whitfield
Social Studies Supervisor
St. Louis Public Schools
St. Louis, Missouri

Charles A. Williams II
Assistant Director of Social Studies
Newark Board of Education
Newark, New Jersey

TABLE OF CONTENTS

Writing Workshops

AN INTRODUCTION TO

THE AFRICAN AMERICAN EXPERIENCE

I entered the first grade in West Virginia in 1956, two years after the famous *Brown* v. *Board of Education* Supreme Court decision that put an end to *de jure* segregation in America's public schools. Despite the fact that West Virginia's school system integrated so very quickly, our text books did not. Even the West Virginia History courses, so avidly taught by our civic-minded instructors determined to instill in us an intense pride in our state, barely touched upon the historical experiences and struggles of black Americans. In so doing, the books glossed over the fact that West Virginia came into the Union in 1863 precisely because of the presence of the Negro and the existence of slavery in the nation. Despite this fact, the students in our school system rarely encountered even *one* black face in any of our history textbooks.

When I was in the eleventh grade, I was leafing through our American history textbook on the first day of school. I liked to skim the final chapters of our history and geography textbooks, because we almost never reached these pages during the course of the academic year. There, in a very brief section entitled "The Achievements of Negro Americans"—just before the appendices, charts, and maps—I encountered the serene and self-confident countenance of a magnificently elegant and intelligent-looking black man. I can never forget his portrait. He looked to be in his mid-fifties, and he was dressed in a three-piece, pinstriped suit, his gold watch chain just visible near the bottom of the frame. How intelligent he looked! This man was a scholar, I said to myself. I hurriedly searched for his name: "William Edward Burghardt Du Bois," the caption read, "author of *The Souls of Black Folk* and the founder of the NAACP."

To say that I was startled is to say almost nothing at all. I was *mesmerized*. The year was 1966, and the Civil Rights Movement was near its peak. Almost each evening for the past several years, my parents and I had watched African Americans engaging in protest marches in an attempt to end segregation. Hungry for more and more knowledge about the Civil Rights Movement, political and social leaders in the black community, and great moments in the black history, I began to search as diligently as I could for *any* facts about the Negro and our history. But in the textbooks that we used in our school system, there were none. Encountering Du Bois's face (and the one paragraph of description in our textbook), however, led me to begin a quest to discover the facts of black history in this country. Unfortunately, however, my high school and its textbooks were not of much help.

High school students today, I am pleased to be able to say, need not confront the dilemma that I faced a quarter of century ago. Readers of this textbook, *The African American Experience,* are able to trace the development of African American culture from its complex origins in Africa to the new forms that it took as it blended with European and native American cultural elements in the Americas. The history of the oppression of Africans and African Americans—first as slaves, and then as the victims of legal segregation and discrimination—is charted in great detail in this volume. But the many wonderful and compelling achievements that persons of African descent have made, individually and collectively, as creators and bearers of culture and the arts in the United States are here as well.

For who can imagine an "American" culture without the myriad contributions of African Americans? The accomplishments and struggles of black Americans are fundamental to the very meaning of the United States itself. Until the facts of the African

American experience are known by every high school and elementary student in this country, we will not be able even to begin to realize the true promise of the United States. When these facts are known, the dream of creating a common public "American" culture out of the many multicolored strands of the people from throughout the world who have shaped this nation may come to pass. It is, in part, to assist in bringing about this great goal that the authors of *The African American Experience* have written this book.

The Roman writer Cicero once noted that a people without a written history are a people destined to remain in the infancy of civilization. Precisely to *keep* African Americans ignorant of their great historical past, many people either denied that blacks had a major part in creating this nation or asserted that the achievements of individual blacks were not important enough to be honored as important historical events. Individual black historians such as George Washington Williams, Carter G. Woodson, Rayford W. Logan, Mary Frances Berry, John W. Blassingame, John Hope Franklin, Nell Painter, and of course, W. E. B. Du Bois himself fought against this deprivation or denial of black history. But it is only in the recent past that junior and senior high school textbooks have begun to face this challenge squarely.

The African American Experience brings vividly to life the joys and triumphs, the frustrations and disappointments, of persons of African descent. The story opens on the continent of Africa in 3200 B.C. and goes on to describe the great kingdoms of West Africa between A.D. 500 and A.D. 1600. It depicts the dreadful era of human slavery and the determined battles to abolish it that culminated in the Civil War. It also traces the next century of sustained struggle as disfranchised freed slaves and their descendants fought to win full equality of citizenship in this great Republic.

Using the thoughts, words, and feelings of black people themselves—as expressed in music, art, literature, speeches, and all sorts of formal documents—the authors of this textbook have brought the history of millions of black Americans vividly to life. To read this book is to be transported into the vital black past, and to be made to feel what it was like to be, as Du Bois put it, at once "a Negro *and* an American." Even its charts, graphs, and maps are easily readable and handsomely done. In addition, this Teacher's Resource Manual provides effective strategies for making the best use of the text.

I only wish that my own generation had been able to use such a textbook. Thank goodness that my own children will never be forced to wonder if African Americans had a history.

Henry Louis Gates, Jr.
W. E. B. Du Bois Professor of the Humanities
Harvard University

INTRODUCING THE PROGRAM

The African American Experience: A History is designed to meet the needs of students and teachers. The many features in the student text and the Teacher's Resource Manual will aid students to read, comprehend, and think critically about the African American experience. The structure of the text and the lesson plans enable teachers to use the program either as the core text in an African American history course or as a supplement in a United States history course. The correlation (p. 1 of this Manual) shows ways to use the text in the latter instance. As Dr. Henry Louis Gates says in his introduction, "The accomplishments and struggles of black Americans are fundamental to the very meaning of the United States itself."

FEATURES OF THE STUDENT TEXT

Organization

Each unit of the student text opens with a the six-page section called *The Big Picture*. It sets students in time and place with an overview of the events and people to be studied in the unit. A two-page timeline provides a visual cue for events in the unit.

Each chapter within a unit has a time box called "Snapshot of the Times" that relates to the unit timeline and provides even more details. Each chapter within a unit provides specific information about how Africans (to 1776) and African Americans (since 1776) participated in that period. The emphasis throughout the text is on people acting and on the actual stories and words of Africans and African Americans. The writing style is narrative rather than expository. Students will be there as Prince Whipple rows across the Delaware on that snowy Christmas Eve in 1776; they will be there as African Americans feel the elation of emancipation and then the disappointment and despair of Reconstruction; they will be there as Rosa Parks begins the Civil Rights Movement.

A six-page list in the student text provides sources for all excerpts quoted in the text as well as a jumping-off point for research. The primary source materials are presented as written, with abridgements made only to eliminate extraneous material. If dialect was used in the original source, it has been retained. Difficult words are followed by synonyms or definitions within brackets.

Incorporated Biographies

Many history books isolate the accomplishments of individuals in tinted boxes set apart from the main text. *The African American Experience* incorporates biographies of people—ordinary and extraordinary—within its running narrative. Photographs of the individuals are included wherever possible to help students "see" them as real people.

Galleries

Too many history texts turn the discussion of the arts and sciences into laundry lists of people and their works. *The African American Experience* departs from this approach in two ways. For the discussion of the arts and sciences in the late 19th century and during the Harlem Renaissance, galleries provide photographs of key figures; explore the significance of those figures in the development of the arts, sciences, and technology; and cite representative works with reasons for their importance. For the arts of the 1950s and later, certain key individuals and their works are discussed in detail in the narrative.

Focus On . . . and Close Up

The African American Experience ends each chapter with a "Focus On . . ." feature. Each one highlights some aspect of the chapter by making a past-to-present connection, by showing the African American experience in a global context, or by emphasizing the arts or education. The feature appears at the end of the chapter so that the flow of student reading will not be interrupted.

The chapter study section called "Close Up" provides a variety of review materials, higher-level thinking activities, and skills instruction and practice. The exercises help students with their understanding of the important people, places, and events of a chapter as well as with the chronology of events discussed. A section entitled "What Would You Have Done" asks students to put themselves in someone else's place and analyze how they would have acted. This is a powerful tool in helping students develop empathy. Many of the exercises call for students to develop paragraphs, letters, advertisements, and other written communication. The final section in each "Close Up" provides instruction and practice in one of 34 skills. The activity sheets in this Manual provide additional practice in important history skills.

Points of View

Two "Points of View" features (pp. 250–51 and 380–81) add to students' understanding of content and are positioned on the text pages so that reading of the narrative is not interrupted. An introduction describes the outlooks of two individuals before they speak for themselves in primary source material. Critical thinking questions then help students analyze the issue discussed.

Maps, Charts, Graphs, and Illustrations

The illustration program uses a variety of maps, charts, graphs, photographs, lithographs, woodcuts, and so on, to help the African American experience come alive for students. The illustration program also serves a teaching purpose. Every map, chart, and graph and many of the other illustrations have questions within captions that require students to read and analyze the illustration. All answers are provided in the lesson plans in this Manual.

The Artist's View

A four-color art section called *The Artist's View* shows representative works of art by African and African Americans. Ancient African works of art, folk art, and professional art from the 19th and 20th centuries are presented with informative captions. A special set of lesson plans in this Manual (pp. 108–113) gives background on the pieces and the artists, as well as teaching suggestions and cooperative learning projects.

TEACHER'S RESOURCE MANUAL

Each component of the Teacher's Resource Manual was developed with the twofold use of the text in mind—as a core text in an African American history course or as a supplement in a U.S. history course. The first section of the manual provides a chart showing how *The African American Experience* can be used as a supplement in U.S. history courses (pp. 1–4).

Incorporating Language Arts and the Writing Process

The next section is a discussion of ways to integrate language arts, especially prereading strategies, into the teaching of history (pp. 5–9). In addition to this opening essay, the Manual also includes a discussion on the use of the writing process in history classes (pp. 257–258), evaluation guides for assessing student writing (pp. 259–61), and a four-page "Writing Workshop" for each unit (pp. 262–301). The listing of resources in chapter lesson plans indicates where the "Writing Workshops" may be used. To help students in preparing and writing a report based on research, a "Checklist for Writing a Research Paper" has been included (pp. 302-303).

Lesson Plans

The largest portion of this Manual details lesson plan suggestions for teaching *The African American Experience* (pp. 10–107). Each unit of lesson plans begins with an overview page describing the major concept of the unit and listing unit content themes. The overview also includes a cooperative learning project for the unit.

The lesson plans for *The Big Picture* include a theme statement, an overview of the content, strategies for using the "African American Speaks" quotation in the student text as well as the timeline, a "Focus Activity," and teaching strategies for each section. If the text is used as a supplement, this organization into separate strategies for sections allows the teacher to use just those portions of *The Big Picture* that he or she needs for the curriculum. The teacher may also find that in such a situation, he or she could omit *The Big Picture* because the core text has enough information to set the stage. If this is the case, the teacher would move immediately to the lesson plans for the chapters, picking and choosing as the course demands.

After an "Overview" of the chapter, a "Focus Activity" for the chapter, and a list of materials that may be used in developing chapter lessons, the lesson plans for each chapter are then divided by section. Each section lesson plan provides an objective tied directly to the teaching strategy. Many strategies contain primary source material as the springboard for the lesson. Many sections also contain an "Historical Sidelight," with additional information about a person, event, or topic from that text section.

The lesson plans for the chapters are followed by six pages of lesson plans for *The Artist's View* (pp. 108–13).

Evaluation

A Testing Program (pp. 124–87) with Answer Key (pp. 188–96) provides a three-page Unit Test for each unit, which may be used either as a pretest or as a posttest, and a one-page test for each chapter. The tests include matching, multiple choice, short-answer, and essay questions. All answers are provided in the Answer Key, including guidelines for evaluating the essays.

Activity Sheets

Each chapter has an Activity Sheet of one or two pages (pp. 197–247). These sheets provide additional historical information as well as skill instruction. Primary sources, maps, charts, and graphs are used as vehicles for developing student understanding of content and skills. In addition, Chapters 23 and 34 each contain an extra activity sheet for use with the "Point of View" feature. A complete Answer Key (pp. 249–56) is provided.

Resources

A 12-page "Directory of Books, Audiovisual Materials, and Community Resources" provides ideas for research and for additional resources for presenting the African American experience. Each entry is annotated. The community section lists museums and centers dedicated to African American studies in many U.S. cities.

Geography

A one-page chart "Using Maps with *The African American Experience*" (p. 304) provides suggestions for emphasizing the five themes of geography in teaching the African American experience. This is followed by outline maps (pp. 305–308) of the world, Africa, the eastern United States, and the entire nation.

CORRELATIONS TO COURSES IN UNITED STATES HISTORY

The chart below is intended as an aid for teachers using *The African American Experience* to supplement a course in United States history. The chart shows common divisions of year-long history courses and the parts of the book that apply to those divisions.

AFRICA BEFORE THE SLAVE TRADE (before 1500s)				
Unit Opener	**Chapter**		**Special Features**	
Unit 1 *The Big Picture*	Chapter 1 Chapter 2 Chapter 3	Egypt, Kush, and Axum Great Empires of West Africa The West African Heritage	Chapter 1 Chapter 2 Chapter 3	Focus On: Rediscovering Meroë Focus On: Choosing Islam Focus On: African Folktale *The Artist's View* A1–A4
THE AGE OF EXPLORATION (1000s–1500s)				
Unit Opener	**Chapter**		**Special Features**	
Unit 2 *The Big Picture:* Face to Face in Africa, The Start of the Slave Trade, Black Gold for the Americas	Chapter 4	The Atlantic Slave Trade	Chapter 4	Focus On: West Africa Today
THE ESTABLISHMENT OF EUROPEAN COLONIES (1500s–1700s)				
Unit Opener	**Chapter**		**Special Features**	
Unit 2 *The Big Picture:* The English Colonies in North America, The Issue of Slavery	Chapter 4 Chapter 5 Chapter 6	The Atlantic Slave Trade The West Indies, First Stop for Africans Africans in the Thirteen Colonies	Chapter 5 Chapter 6	Focus On: The Caribbean Today Focus On: Looking for *Roots*
AMERICAN COLONIAL LIFE (1500s–1700s)				
Unit Opener	**Chapter**		**Special Features**	
Unit 2 *The Big Picture:* The English Colonies in North America, The Issue of Slavery	Chapter 6 Chapter 10 Chapter 11	Africans in the Thirteen Colonies Section 1: The Early Years of Slavery Section 1: Early Slave Rebellions	Chapter 7 Chapter 9 Chapter 11	Focus On: Volunteer Chasseurs Focus On: New Orleans Traditions Focus On: Revolt in Jamaica
THE ESTABLISHMENT OF THE UNITED STATES (1760s–1780s)				
Unit Opener	**Chapter**		**Special Features**	
Unit 3 *The Big Picture*	Chapter 7 Chapter 8 Chapter 11 Chapter 15	The American Revolution: Liberty for All? Forging a New Constitution Section 2: The Prosser Conspiracy Section 3: The Vesey Conspiracy Section 1: The Search for Religious Equality	Chapter 15	Focus On: A Church Named Bethel *The Artist's View* A6–A7

EXPANSION AND REFORM IN THE NEW NATION (1790s–1850s)				
Unit Opener	**Chapter**		**Special Features**	
Unit 3 *The Big Picture:* Defending the Nation, Expanding the Nation	Chapter 9	Expanding the Nation	Chapter 10	Focus On: Slave Narratives Abroad
	Chapter 12	Free Africans in the North and South	Chapter 8	Focus On: The World Questions Slavery
	Chapter 13	Abolitionists	Chapter 13	Focus On: The Other Civil War
Unit 4 *The Big Picture*	Chapter 15	Section 1: The Search for Religious Equality	Chapter 14	Focus On: Leading the Way to Canada
		Section 2: Joining the Antislavery Battle	Chapter 15	Focus On: A Church Named Bethel *The Artist's View* A6–A7

BUILDUP TO CIVIL WAR (1800s–1860s)				
Unit Opener	**Chapter**		**Special Features**	
Unit 4 *The Big Picture:* Cash Crops in the Midwest, Cotton in the South, Internal Trade in Enslaved African Americans	Chapter 10	Section 2: African Americans in the Cotton Kingdom	Chapter 10	Focus On: Slave Narratives Abroad
	Chapter 11	Section 2: The Prosser Conspiracy	Chapter 8	Focus On: The World Questions Slavery
		Section 3: The Vesey Conspiracy	Chapter 13	Focus On: The Other Civil War
		Section 4: "Old Nat's War"	Chapter 14	Focus On: Leading the Way to Canada
Unit 5 *The Big Picture*	Chapter 12	Free Africans in the North and South	Chapter 16	Focus On: St. Louis Courthouse
	Chapter 13	Abolitionists		
	Chapter 14	Escaping from Slavery		
	Chapter 15	Section 2: Joining the Antislavery Battle		
	Chapter 16	The Road to the Civil War		

THE CIVIL WAR AND RECONSTRUCTION (1860s–1870s)				
Unit Opener	**Chapter**		**Special Features**	
Unit 6 *The Big Picture*	Chapter 17	The Civil War and the End of Slavery	Chapter 17	Focus On: The Making of *Glory*
	Chapter 18	The Promise and Failure of Reconstruction	Chapter 18	Focus On: Making a Federal Case

WESTWARD EXPANSION (1840s–1880s)				
Unit Opener	**Chapter**		**Special Features**	
Unit 6 *The Big Picture:* Going West	Chapter 19	Miners, Farmers, and Cowhands	Chapter 19	Focus On: The Buffalo Soldiers

INDUSTRIALIZATION OF THE UNITED STATES (1870s–1910s)				
Unit Opener	**Chapter**		**Special Features**	
Unit 7 *The Big Picture*	Chapter 20 Chapter 21 Chapter 22	African Americans in the New South Living in a Jim Crow World Advances in Education, the Arts, and Science	Chapter 21 Chapter 22 Chapter 22	Focus On: Tuskegee Today Focus On: The Wizard of Tuskegee *The Artist's View* A7–A9 Gallery of African American Writers and Artists Gallery of African American Scientists and Inventors

EARLY TWENTIETH CENTURY CHANGE AND REFORM (1900s–1940s)				
Unit Opener	**Chapter**		**Special Features**	
Unit 8 *The Big Picture*	Chapter 23 Chapter 24 Chapter 24	The Civil Rights Struggle Section 1: Leaving Home Section 2: African American Urban Culture	Chapter 20 Chapter 23	Focus On: Populist Movement Focus On: The NAACP Today Points of View: Washington and Du Bois

THE UNITED STATES AS A WORLD LEADER (1900s–1920s)				
Unit Opener	**Chapter**		**Special Features**	
Unit 8 *The Big Picture:* The Progressive Era, World War I, The Home Front, The Aftermath of War	Chapter 24	Section 3: World War I: Opportunities and Setbacks		

AMERICA BETWEEN THE WORLD WARS (1910s–1940s)				
Unit Opener	**Chapter**		**Special Features**	
Unit 8 *The Big Picture:* The Roaring Twenties, The Great Depression, The New Deal **Unit 9** *The Big Picture*	Chapter 25 Chapter 26 Chapter 27	Black Nationalism Harlem Renaissance The Great Depression and Another War	Chapter 24 Chapter 25 Chapter 27 Chapter 26	Focus On: Jazz in the 1920s Focus On: Pan Africanism Focus On: WPA Writers and Artists *The Artist's View* A8–A14 Gallery of African American Writers Gallery of African American Musicians and Performing Artists Gallery of African American Artists

WORLD WAR II, THE COLD WAR, AND KOREA (1940s–1950s)				
Unit Opener	**Chapter**		**Special Features**	
Unit 9 *The Big Picture:* World War II, The Truman Years, The Eisenhower Years	Chapter 28	World War II and African Americans	Chapter 28	Focus On: Women in the Military

CHALLENGES AT HOME AND ABROAD (1940s–1970s)				
Unit Opener	**Chapter**		**Special Features**	
Unit 10 *The Big Picture:* Changing Attitudes Toward Civil Rights, The Nixon Years, Changes in the Supreme Court, Economic Downturn, The Reagan Years	Chapter 29	Gains and Losses in the Postwar Years	Chapter 12	Focus On: Enterprising Executives
	Chapter 30	The Battle for Civil Rights	Chapter 18	Focus On: Making a Federal Case
	Chapter 31	New Directions in the Civil Rights Movement	Chapter 26	Focus On: Rock 'n' Roll
	Chapter 32	Marching Off to Vietnam	Chapter 29	Focus On: Celebrating Excellence
			Chapter 30	Focus On: Separate Is Not Equal
			Chapter 31	Focus On: Singing for Freedom
			Chapter 32	Focus On: Remembering Vietnam *The Artist's View* A14–A15

AFRICA AND AMERICA TODAY (1970s–1990s)				
Unit Opener	**Chapter**		**Special Features**	
Unit 10 *The Big Picture*: I Have a Dream	Chapter 33	Agenda for Change	Chapter 4	Focus On: West Africa Today
	Chapter 34	Crossing New Frontiers	Chapter 6	Focus On: Looking for *Roots*
			Chapter 21	Focus On: Tuskegee Today
			Chapter 23	Focus On: NAACP Today
			Chapter 33	Focus On: What's in a Name?
			Chapter 34	Focus On: An Educational Heritage
			Chapter 17	Focus On: The Making of *Glory*
				Points of View: Woodson and Lowery

INTEGRATING THE LANGUAGE ARTS INTO THE TEACHING OF HISTORY

In recent years educators have become increasingly aware of the need to integrate the language arts into other subject areas. Usually when people think of the language arts, they think of reading and writing, but listening and speaking are equally important. Listening and speaking, like reading and writing are essential elements in the communication of knowledge.

THE READING PROCESS

Every kind of reading material, no matter what the content area, has peculiarities that must be identified and mastered by the reader. History, for instance, has a specialized vocabulary, its own logic of organization, and its own kind of sentence structure.

An added complication is the fact that students also bring a wide variety of skills to the task of reading history materials. Every teacher has faced the problem of having students who read quickly and with excellent comprehension sitting in the same class with students who struggle to decode text.

As you know, prior experience is a significant factor in the comprehension of text; it is often more important than the student's ability to decode individual words. Since experience varies so much from student to student, it is important to have students share their understandings with each other—and correct their misunderstandings—before approaching the text. This sharing of information and perceptions is easily accomplished by using graphic organizers.

GRAPHIC ORGANIZERS

Graphic organizers are diagrams that illustrate the connections among ideas. Such organizers may take many forms, such as semantic maps, webs, time lines, and idea clusters. The point is to create a visual display of the associations or properties of topics. For instance, suppose that students are about to read a chapter from *The African American Experience* that discusses the ancient civilizations of northeastern Africa. Most students have limited knowledge of these civilizations. In order to prepare students to understand the chapter, you can help them share what knowledge they have in an idea cluster.

The students create an idea cluster by listing all the words and images that come to their minds when they hear the name of a topic, in this case, *Egypt*. You write these ideas on the chalkboard as the students share them. One advantage of this technique is that all students are able to participate in, and learn from, this activity. As the students dictate their ideas, you will have an opportunity to introduce and use in context any unfamiliar vocabulary that the students will encounter in the text. Through discussion, you are also able to correct any information students may have that is incorrect or inaccurate.

A typical idea cluster might look like this:

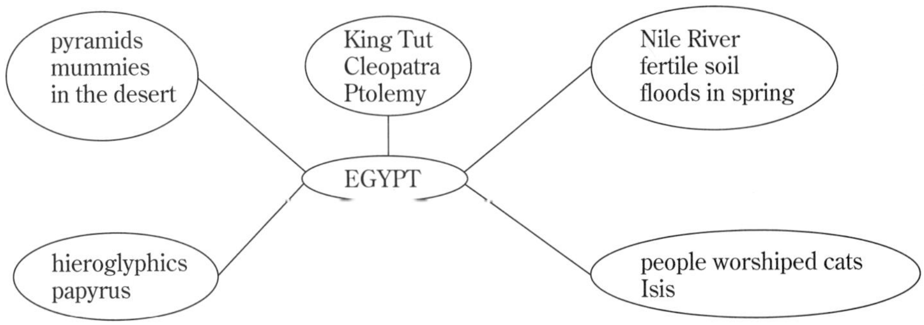

pyramids
mummies
in the desert

King Tut
Cleopatra
Ptolemy

Nile River
fertile soil
floods in spring

EGYPT

hieroglyphics
papyrus

people worshiped cats
Isis

Or like this:

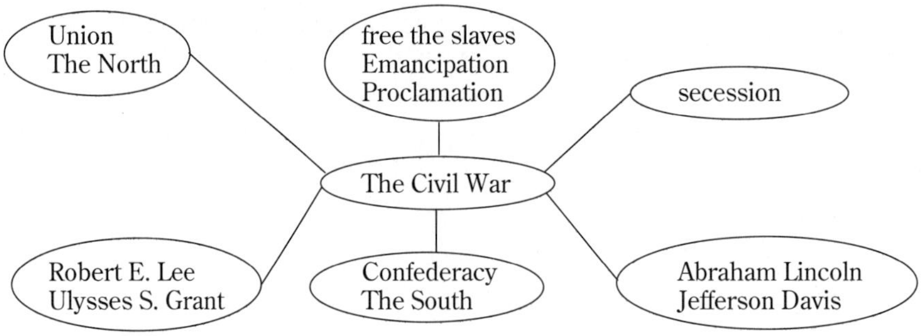

Such diagrams are pictures of the collective knowledge of the group about the topics. In order to develop the diagrams, the students had to reach into their experiences and generate meaning. As they read the chapters, and learn additional relevant details, they can add to their graphic organizers, which then become visual representations of their new learning.

PREDICTION GUIDES

Another way of directing students' attention and building needed background information is the use of prediction guides. A prediction guide is merely a series of statements that you write concerning the material that students are about to read. The statements are written so that thinking is stimulated at the literal, interpretive, and applied levels.

Example:

Literal — The people of Kush lived in ancient Africa.

I agree ________ I disagree ________

Inferential — Rich deposits of iron ore gave the Kushites an advantage over neighboring peoples.

I agree ________ I disagree ________

Applied — Iron enabled the Kushites to produce ample quantities of food and to conquer neighboring peoples.

I agree ________ I disagree ________

As the students respond to these statements, they are predicting what they will read. (The prediction guides should not be graded for accuracy.) This prereading focus gives students the chance to read with a purpose as they judge their preconceptions and change their ideas.

Vocabulary is another factor in understanding content-area material. All of the research that has been done in the area of language acquisition reveals that unfamiliar words should always be taught in context if students are to retain their meaning. One way to teach new vocabulary is to give the students sentences in which the words are used in context and then require the students to infer the meaning of the words. After the students have completed their inferences, they check their dictionaries for the correct meanings.

Example:

I felt nervous about standing so close to the escarpment, but the view of the valley was spectacular.

I think that the word escarpment means ______________________________.

Dictionary definition:______________________________________.

SILENT READING

It is often necessary to focus the students' attention as they read. In *The African American Experience*, the text itself provides purpose-setting questions to direct the reading experience. These questions appear at the beginning of each section of the chapter. Discussion should always follow silent reading. It is important that the students be asked to provide information and opinions, and they should always be required to substantiate their opinions by reading pertinent text aloud. In whole-class lessons, it is important that students be encouraged to discuss their answers with one another as well as with you.

Another method of guiding silent reading encourages students to pose their own questions about events and ideas in the text. In this method, you preview the chapter with the students. Together, you examine the visuals that appear in the chapter. In discussing these images, you are giving the students a chance to predict what they are going to read. You may also wish to mention some key ideas or events that will be covered in the text.

In another method, you would divide the class into small discussion groups of five or six students and ask them to list questions about the text. Turning section heads into questions is a good study technique. Next, have students read to find the answers to their own questions.

META-COGNITIVE SKILLS

Students who have difficulty reading text need to be taught comprehension monitoring skills. Reading teachers refer to these as skills as metacognitive. This term means that students must develop awareness of themselves as readers. They must learn to think about how they process the text. Such students read aloud portions of the text that are difficult for them to decode and interpret during independent reading. They explain why portions of the text were hard to understand and demonstrate how they worked with the text to create meaning. Working with these students to recognize problems of text interpretation, you can lead them to identify their own strategies for getting meaning from print. As they deal with their reading difficulties, these students benefit from using alternative sources of knowledge, particularly listening and speaking.

LISTENING

In this "information age" much of what the students learn comes from listening. They listen constantly to the radio and the television. However, this is usually passive listening in which they are being entertained. They are not listening for information, and often the information from the radio that they actually retain is incomplete or inaccurate. Ask any student about a current controversial public issue, and you will frequently discover that the issue is poorly understood, at best.

To a great extent this lack of listening comprehension can be attributed to the fact that few students are taught *how* to listen. Most Americans come from cultures that have rich oral traditions. Yet this emphasis on oral learning has been eclipsed by the availability of print materials. In our eagerness to teach students how to read, we have neglected to teach them how to listen.

One method to use to teach listening skills to your students is to read to a section of connected text to your class daily. After reading to them, ask your students to summarize what they have heard. If they are typical, the information in their summaries will be disappointing at first. Once they begin to listen for who, what, when, where, why, and how—with a purpose, that is, they will be able to report the content of what you have read more and more accurately.

SPEAKING

Just as the development of listening skills has been neglected, so the development of speaking skills has been given little attention. Of course, most social studies classrooms are filled with discussion. However, the same students often seem to do most of the talking. Often the less articulate students sit silently. Frequently, a student who talks freely and comfortably with his or her peers stands up in front of a classroom filled with those very same peers and gasps, stammers, and utters many "uh's" and "uhm's."

Speaking in front of a group just does not seem safe to many people. That is why creating an environment in which students feel safe to speak is so important in the development of speaking skills. The first step in creating such an environment is to limit the number of people in the audience. Extremely inarticulate students may need to be paired with a single partner at first. Gradually, as the student becomes more confident, the number of auditors may be increased.

The most nonthreatening situation for listening and speaking is the cooperative learning group. In this situation, all the students are equal. Properly monitored, a cooperative learning group can be effective in turning a fearful speaker into a confident one. The key to teaching the reluctant speaker is structure. Whereas being called upon to speak extemporaneously on some issue to the whole class might cause reactions of terror in some students, the task of reporting a piece of discrete and limited information to a small group does not seem so threatening. You can arrange the group assignments with this in mind. After a while, the student with stage fright will grow more confident and can be given more challenging assignments.

WRITING

The writing process has been treated elsewhere in this teacher's manual (see pp. 257–58). However, writing should be an important part of every social studies lesson. Students learn to write the same way they learn to play the piano—by practicing. Just as practicing makes better pianists, it makes better writers.

Writing also makes better readers. One way to increase your students' comprehension of written text is to make them write about a passage before they read it. This is a particularly effective way to prepare your students to read difficult primary source material. Students often struggle to read material written in previous centuries. Quite often the vocabulary is beyond them and the content does not seem relevant to their own lives. Writing is the way to make the connections for them.

Suppose, for example, that your students are about to read an excerpt from the autobiography of Frederick Douglass. This is challenging text, so it is advisable to work with the students to create an idea cluster. Since the text concerns Douglass's experiences as an enslaved young African American in 19th century Baltimore, the students should try to think of what their feelings and experiences might be if they were in the same situation.

The resulting idea cluster might look like this:

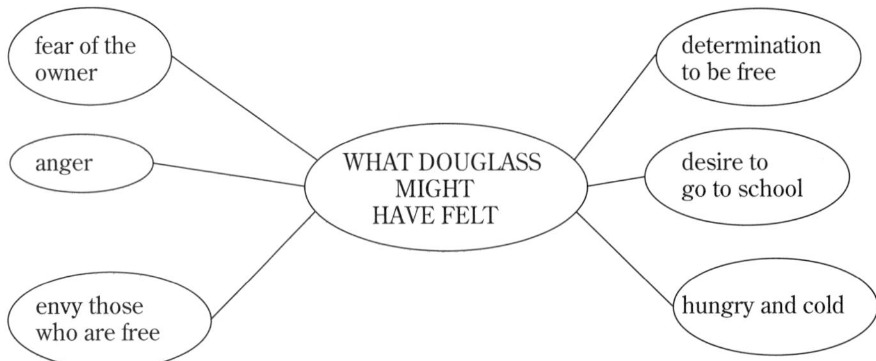

As soon as the students have finished listing ideas, have them take out a piece of paper and write very quickly what sort of experiences they think they will read about in the life of Frederick Douglass. Tell the students that they will not receive a mark for their brief essay and that they should not worry about spelling or punctuation, since this is "not for publication."

Be certain that everyone writes something down on paper. The important thing about this assignment is that it be strictly stream- of-consciousness; it is designed to get the students past the writer's block that is often caused by fear of writing something inaccurate or "dumb".

After the students have been writing for two or three minutes at the most, tell them to put down their pens. Ask if anyone in the group wants to share what he or she has written. You will find many students eager to share their efforts. Write their predictions about the Douglass autobiography on the chalkboard. Tell the students that they should now read the text to verify the accuracy of their predictions. After the students have finished reading the text (this may be done silently or aloud), refer to the list of predictions on the chalkboard and discuss with the class which of their predictions were accurate.

This entire activity will take only ten or fifteen minutes of class time. But it will yield obvious dividends in reading comprehension, student interest, and student participation in learning.

UNIT 1 The African Homeland (pp. 2–31)

UNIT THEME

The African continent is the birthplace of humankind and home to some of the world's oldest civilizations.

UNIT CONCEPTS

- Over a period of millions of years, the descendants of the first humans spread out from Africa.
- The growth of farming along the banks of the Nile contributed to the growth of Egypt, one of the world's great ancient civilizations.
- Egypt lay at the crossroads of continents, and its cultural influence extended beyond Africa into areas that are now parts of the Middle East, Asia, and southern Europe.
- Egyptian civilization influenced and was influenced by African peoples to the south, particularly the Kushites.
- For nearly 1,000 years, three West African empires—Ghana, Mali, and Songhai—produced cultural achievements that rivaled or outshone those of Europe.
- Islamic conquerors brought a new religion to West Africa, but native African religious practices remained strong.
- West Africans of the 500s–1500s had a rich and varied cultural heritage that would form the basis of the culture that would be developed by enslaved Africans in the Americas.

UNIT OVERVIEW

Unit 1 describes in broad terms the African homeland, from the origins of the first humans to the emergence of great African civilizations—Egypt, Kush, Axum, and the empires of West Africa. *The Big Picture* and the three chapters in the unit describe: (1) the orgins of humankind in Africa and the emergence of Egypt as well as as of Kush and Axum, (2) the growth of sophisticated West African empires, and (3) West African culture on the eve of the Atlantic slave trade.

For many years, courses in world history and world cultures have separated the study of Egypt from that of the rest of the African continent. Using religion as one determinant, many historians and cultural geographers have tied Egypt to the Middle East. However, Islam was not introduced into sub-Saharan Africa until the A.D. 1000s and much of West Africa was converted. Today, Islam continues to be a dominant religious force in the region.

COOPERATIVE LEARNING ACTIVITY

The following cooperative learning activity can be used for alternative assessment after study of the unit has been completed.

At the end of the unit, divide the class into groups, and assign each group a part in organizing an African festival. Request that one group plan and prepare a menu of African foods. Have another group collect pictures or draw posters depicting African arts. Direct a third group to find recordings of African music to play. Ask students to try to wear something African influenced—clothing, jewelry, and so on—on the day of the festival. Before the day of the festival, set aside one class period for a joint planning session with all groups. Accept new ideas that students may have come up with during their research. In evaluating the groups' work, consider the extent of their research, their creativity in preparing their contributions, and how well they cooperated in completing their task.

Unit 1 THE BIG PICTURE (pp. 3–7)

Theme

Human history began and early civilizations developed in Africa.

Overview

The Big Picture opens with a geographic look at Africa, highlighting the continent's size and diversity. Then it moves on to a discussion of the work of Louis and Mary Leakey, who discovered evidence that has led most anthropologists today to conclude that the first humans appeared in Africa. Over millions of years, early humans moved out of Africa and their descendants populated the rest of the world.

The Big Picture then describes how, between 10,000 B.C. and 3500 B.C., people in parts of Africa, Asia, the Middle East, and the Americas developed farming—one of the great revolutions in human history. Some of the world's earliest farming villages arose in Egypt along the banks of the Nile. African American historian W.E.B. Du Bois called Egypt "the first great experiment in human civilization." Monumental architecture, systems of writing and mathematics, irrigation, and medicine were some of the achievements of ancient Egypt.

Over thousands of years, Egypt's influence spread. Its location on the northeastern edge of the continent made it one of the most cosmopolitan cultures of the ancient world. Within Egypt's boundaries, peoples from Asia, Africa, and parts of southern Europe mingled.

Europeans knew of Egypt, and the Greeks and Romans eventually conquered it. But they knew little of the other great African cultures. To the south of Egypt lay Kush and the Christian kingdom of Axum. To the west lay three great empires—Ghana, Mali, and Songhai. Most of the ancestors of today's African Americans came from West Africa.

Objectives

- To understand that the human race had its beginnings in Africa.
- To use a timeline to write a summary of some of Africa's contributions.
- To use a map to evaluate the factual accuracy of statements about Africa's geography.
- To write news stories about key events in Africa's early development.
- To compare developments in Africa with those elsewhere from 5000 B.C. to A.D. 1500.

Introducing *The Big Picture*

Call on a volunteer to read aloud the quotation in "An African American Speaks" on student text p. 3. Ask students what role in history Bennett assigns to Africans. (*the first people on Earth*) Make sure students understand the word benefactor (*one who aids or contributes to another*). Then focus student attention on the unit title. Based on the quotation ask how Bennett might retitle the unit. (*possibility: Africa—Birthplace of Humankind*)

Using the Timeline

Divide the class into three groups. Assign one group the period 500,000–2500 B.C. Assign the second group the period 2500 B.C.–A.D. 400, and the third group, A.D. 400–1600. Have each group select the event from its period that it considers most important. The groups should then report on their choices and the reasons for them.

Teaching *The Big Picture*

1. Interpreting a Map. Have students, working in pairs, make up statements to test their partners' knowledge of Africa's geography. Assign "The African Landscape" (pp. 3–4), and then refer students to the map on student text p. 3. Ask them to use the map to determine if each of the following statements is true or false. If a statement is false, have students explain reasons for their answer.

- Africa is made up mostly of jungles and tropical rain forests. (*false: desert and savanna*)
- The Sahara is larger than the Kalahari. (*true*)
- The equator cuts Africa roughly in half. (*true*)

2. Writing News Stories. Assign sections from "Birthplace of Humans" up to and including "The New Kingdom" (pp. 4–7). While students read, copy the following headlines on the chalkboard or an overhead transparency:

- Two-Million-Year Old Human Found in Africa
- Farming Revolution Shakes Up the World
- Dynastic Rule Comes to Egypt
- Egyptians Announce a Golden Age
- Egypt Rocked by Asian Invaders
- Greeks Issue Challenge to Egypt

Divide the class into six groups. Direct each group to write a news article to accompany one of the headlines. To help students design their articles, you might distribute copies of a local newspaper. Call on volunteers to read their news articles aloud. Bind the articles together in a newsletter.

3. Using Prior Knowledge. Have students recall from previous courses in world history developments that were occurring in other parts of the world between 5000 B.C. and A.D. 1500. You might draw six columns on the board and label them Europe, Asia, the Middle East, North America, South America, and Africa. If necessary, distribute to students copies of world history texts or other books that have timelines of world history to assist them in them in identifying such events.

Review and Practice

Assign "Taking Another Look," p. 7.

Answers to Questions in Captions (pp. 3–7)

(p. 3) one quarter; less than a quarter (p. 6) ensured rich soil, reliable supply of water for crops (p. 7) uses of medicine, paper, scientific principles, etc.

Answers to Taking Another Look (p. 7)

1. rain forest, savanna, desert, Great Rift Valley, escarpment, plateau **2.** Anthropologists found skull and tools nearly 2 million years old. **3.** Farming enabled settlement, freeing time for other activities. **4. Critical Thinking** advent of farming, interest in science, trading, conquest, adaptability

Chapter 1 Egypt, Kush, and Axum (pp. 8–15)

Overview

Egyptian accomplishments dazzled the ancient world. Architecture such as the pyramids attested to the wealth and power of the Egyptian pharaohs. Egypt's location in the northeastern corner of Africa made it the crossroads of many cultures. Through trade and conquest, Egypt came in contact with peoples along the Mediterranean, southwestern Asia, and northwestern Africa. The Egyptians also pushed south along the Nile, seeking to conquer the gold-producing region of Nubia. But the Nubian kingdom of Kush had its own dreams of glory. In the 700s B.C., the Kushites conquered Egypt. Although their reign over Egypt lasted only about 80 years, Kush built an empire south of Egypt that lasted nearly 800 years. Kushite influence rested upon iron-making and control of trading routes to the Red Sea. In A.D. 350, the neighboring kingdom of Axum seized control of these routes and broke Kush's power. Christianity followed along these routes, and King Ezana proclaimed Axum a Christian nation. Present-day Ethiopians are still predominantly Coptic Christians.

Resources

Chapter 1 Activity Sheet: Using a Timeline (p. 197)
Chapter 1 Test (p. 127)
Outline Map: Africa (p. 306)

Focus Activity

Refer students to the photograph on text p. 8. To give students an idea of scale, tell them that a human standing at the base of the Sphinx would reach to the paw. Then assign the chapter introduction on pp. 8–9. Ask them why stone-cutting crews would take pride in their work. (*bringing honor to the pharaoh*) Have them suggest qualities a civilization must have to produce monumental works like the pyramids and list them on the chalkboard. (*possible inclusions: engineering skills, mathematical skills, economy that would free workers from simply producing food, etc.*) As students read the chapter, have them add examples of accomplishments that demonstrate each of the qualities.

Teaching Section 1: The Mingling of African Cultures (pp. 9–11)

Objective

- To use a map to describe the location of Egypt and Kush.

Historical Sidelight

Looking to Nubia. When Ramses II took power in 1279 B.C., Egypt's borders reached to the Fourth Cataract of the Nile. Ramses set out to expand them by conquering Syria and Nubia. Nubia provided Egypt with gold, labor, and exotic materials—ebony, ivory, and more. To impress the Nubians with Egypt's power, Ramses built his grandest monument—Abu Simbel—on a pink sandstone bluff overlooking the Nile in what is today Sudan. Here Ramses ordered four 67-foot statues of himself carved into the rock. He had workers cut a temple 160 feet into the hillside. On a nearby bluff, he built another monument to his favorite wife, Nefertari, who was a black African.

Developing the Section

Interpreting a Map. Tell students that location indicates where a place exists in relation to other places. To help students describe the locations of Egypt and Kush, refer them to the map on text p. 9. Then ask the following questions:

Where was Egypt situated in Africa? (*northeastern corner*) Along what bodies of water did

Egypt lie? (*Mediterranean Sea, Nile River, Red Sea*) Why might Egypt's location have encouraged trade? (*Water routes gave Egypt access to peoples along the Mediterranean, the Arabian Peninsula, and northern Africa.*) What kingdom lay south of Egypt? (*Kush*) How did the location of Kush help protect it from Egypt? (*The cataracts of the Nile acted as a barrier.*)

Review and Practice

Assign "Taking Another Look," p. 11.

Answer to Question in Caption (p. 9)

located along bodies of water that facilitated movement among them

Answers to Taking Another Look (p. 11)

1. to punish Nubia for aiding Hyksos' invasion of Egypt, to gain control of Nubia's wealth **2.** Kushite rule was similar to that of Egyptian pharaohs. **3. Critical Thinking** **admiration:** art and technological advances; **hatred:** murder of king, enslavement of Kushites, forcible rule, wealth and power at Kushite expense

Teaching Section 2: An Empire Built on Iron (pp. 11–12)

Objective

- To state reasons Kush remained isolated from non-African peoples.

Developing the Section

Historical Speculation. Read aloud the opening quotation in the "Focus On" feature on text p. 14. Point out that this quotation might sound like a description of Egypt. But it actually describes the ancient city of Meroë—capital of Kush. Have students read the rest of the feature. Then, using the geographic description of Africa in *The Big Picture* (p. 3–7) and the map on p. 9, ask students to speculate on why so few non-Africans ever saw Meroë. (*Most students will mention the cataracts along the Nile, lack of inland rivers, and so on.*)

Review and Practice

Assign "Taking Another Look," p. 12.

Answer to Question in Caption (p. 11)

evidence of Egyptian influence, part of little remaining evidence of Meroë

Answers to Taking Another Look (p. 12)

1. beyond reach of Egypt, near iron ore deposits, fertile land, convenient caravan stop for trade with ports on Red Sea **2.** Iron ploughs increased food production; iron spears used to seize and then protect trade routes. **3. Critical Thinking** Kush adopted Egyptian religion, artistic styles and content; Egypt's wealth came from Kushite gold mines.

Teaching Section 3: A Christian Empire in Africa (pp. 12–13)

Objective

- To evaluate a quotation about Axum's reasons for attacking Kush.

Historical Sidelight

The First Arab Prayer Caller. In the early 600s, an Arab merchant visited Axum and bought an African named Bilal. The trader took Bilal to the city of Medina, where he sold him to a disciple of Muhammad. Both Bilal and the disciple dreamed that Allah [God] wanted them to summon the followers of Muhammad to prayer. The two rushed to Muhammad, who agreed that the dreams were indeed messages from Allah. Because Bilal had a deep, resonant voice, Muhammad decided that he should deliver the first calls to prayer. Thus an African slave became the first *muezzin*, or caller to prayer in what is now the Middle East.

Developing the Section

Interpreting a Primary Source. Read aloud King Ezana's explanation for attacking Kush.

> Twice and thrice they [the Kushites] had broken their solemn oaths, and had killed their neighbors without mercy, and they had stripped our deputies and messengers whom I sent to enquire into the raids, and had stolen their weapons and belongings. And as I had warned them, and they . . . refused to cease from their evil deeds . . . , I made war on them.

Ask students why Ezana says he attacked Kush. (*Kushites had raided Axum, humiliating Ezana's deputies and messengers.*) Then ask students to think about what they already know of Kush and to suggest other reasons that might have led Ezana to march into Kush. (*desire to control African trade along the Red Sea, desire to seize wealth*) Have students read more of Ezana's account on text p. 12. Does it support their speculations? (*yes*)

Review and Practice

Assign "Taking Another Look," p. 13.

Answers to Taking Another Look (p. 13)

1. conquest and trade **2.** overthrew Kush, converted Axum to Christianity **3. Critical Thinking** Port of Adulis was a gateway for trade.

Extending the Chapter

Investigating the Past. Divide the class into three groups. Then assign each group to research one of the following topics for a presentation to be titled "The Glories of Ancient Egypt": art, architecture, hieroglyphics. Encourage students to find pictures and descriptions of historic sites and works that still exist. Have volunteers from each group present their findings in the form of oral reports using whatever visual aids they find to enliven their presentations.

Looking Ahead

After students have read "Looking Ahead," p. 13, refer them to the map of Africa on p. 3. Ask them to suggest geographic factors that might have influenced the development of empires in West Africa. (*the Sahara or Atlas Mountains, both of which acted as barriers to Europe; large stretches of savanna for farming*)

Answers to Close Up (p. 14)

The Who, What, Where of History

1. Olduvai, Tanzania, East Africa **2.** steep cliff **3.** high, flat ground **4.** move from one area to another **5.** ruling family **6.** ancient Egyptian rulers **7.** Africa south of Sahara desert **8.** Asian invaders of Egypt; ruled for 200 years **9.** Meroë **10.** Axum **11.** Egypt **12.** King Ezana

Making the Connection

1. Mural shows influence of other cultures on Egyptian art. **2.** Egyptians took control of Kush. **3.** Assyrian iron swords and armors were superior to Kushite bronze weapons.

Time Check

1. Hyksos **2.** A.D. 350

What Would You Have Done?

1. ironworker: could make weapons, help trade industry; **farmer:** could grow food, feed population **2. Leakeys:** discovery of humans' origins; **archaeologists:** find new facts about Meroë

Thinking and Writing About History

1. Iron ploughs make preparing soil easier; farmers can plant and grow more crops. **2.** center of Kushite Empire, located 100 miles south of present-day Khartoum, iron manufacturing center, rich trading center, pyramids, Egyptian and southern African influence in art **3 a.** competent people will help you govern; judge people by actions **b.** by actions, so he wouldn't discriminate against people **c.** evaluated people by their actions, not by appearance or wealth; would have been tolerant of differences **d.** might discuss tolerance, delegation of authority; should show understanding of facts about Africa in chapter

Building Skills

1. Physical Features of Africa, Ancient Kingdoms of Africa **2.** Physical Features of Africa, West African Empires **3.** Ancient Kingdoms of Africa

Chapter 2 Great Empires of West Africa (pp. 16–23)

Overview

From the A.D. 500s–1600, three great trading empires arose in West Africa—Ghana, Mali, and Songhai. Their wealth and social organization easily equaled the struggling kingdoms of medieval and early modern Europe. But geographic barriers prevented Europeans from knowing of these lands firsthand. It was not until the 1300s and the pilgrimage to Mecca by a West African king named Mansa Musa, that the area appeared on European maps. Mansa Musa, however, was only one name in a rich West African history. His empire of Mali had replaced the earlier kingdom of Ghana. Yet another empire, Songhai, would succeed Mali. The power and might of Songhai would reach into Europe itself.

Resources

Chapter 2 Activity Sheet: Reading A Map (p. 198)
Chapter 2 Test (p. 128)
Outline Map: Africa (p. 306)
Unit 1 Writing Workshop: A Paragraph (pp. 262–65)

Focus Activity

After students have read the chapter introduction on text pp. 16–17, divide the class into small groups. Then assign each group to study the map and caption on p. 17. Direct students, based on this information, to write short news bulletins describing European reactions to the startling news of Mansa Musa's *hajj*. Remind students that Europeans had no idea that the great kingdoms of West Africa existed. Also, Europeans in the 1300s had scant geographic knowledge. Call on a volunteer from each group to deliver its group's bulletin to the class.

Teaching Section 1: The Empire of Ghana (pp. 17–19)

Objective

- To use a map to describe the geographic location of Ghana.

Developing the Section

Interpreting Maps. Have students find Ghana on the map on text p. 17. Ask them why Ghana might have grown up along the banks of the Niger. (*the importance of water to farming and trade*) In what direction did trade routes run out of Ghana? (*north/south*) What geographical barrier did traders encounter? (*the Sahara*) What people probably acted as intermediaries between Ghana and the rest of the world? (*Moroccans*) Ask students to suggest what nation in Europe was probably the first to learn of the goods of West Africa. (*Spain*)

Review and Practice

Assign "Taking Another Look," p. 19.

Answer to Question in Caption (p. 17)

Mali, Ghana, Songhai

Answers to Taking Another Look (p. 19)

1. lay across trade routes between sources of salt and sources of gold **2.** Almoravids took control of Ghana forcing acceptance of Islam; struggle weakened Ghana which fell to invaders from Mali **3. Critical Thinking** could charge import and export taxes, attain more wealth, strengthen armies

Teaching Section 2: The Empire of Mali (pp. 19–20)

Objective

- To write ads promoting the attraction of Timbuktu for scholars and students.

Historical Sidelight

Gold Crash in Cairo. When Mansa Musa entered Cairo, Egypt, he handed out gold to nearly everyone. So much gold flooded around Cairo that Egyptian gold coins became nearly worthless. According to one contemporary at the time, it took Egypt 12 years to recover from the gold crash of 1324.

Developing the Section

Writing Advertisements. Refer students to the picture of Timbuktu on text p. 20. Then read aloud the following description of the city by Arab traveler Leo Africanus:

> In Timbuktu, there are numerous judges, doctors, and clerics, all receiving good salaries from the king. He pays great respect to men of learning. There is a big demand for books in manuscript. . . . More profit is made from the book trade than from any other line of business.

Next, divide the class into small groups. Have half the groups write advertisements to run in Arab newspapers recruiting professors for the University of Sankore. Have the other groups write advertisements to attract Arab students to the university.

Review and Practice

Assign "Taking Another Look," p. 20.

Answer to Question in Caption (p. 20)

Mansa Musa

Answers to Taking Another Look (p. 20)

1. Mansa Musa brought back the best and brightest Arabs to create a center of learning, culture, and trade. **2.** foreign raiders attacked cities; local rulers broke away to set up own kingdoms; revolt in mid-1400s **3. Critical Thinking** story of Sundiata; Mali's conversion to Islam; growth of Timbuktu

Teaching Section 3: The Empire of Songhai (pp. 20–21)

Objective

- To write travel logs of a caravan journey from Gao to Cairo.

Historical Sidelight

African Scholar. One of the most famous writers of Timbuktu was Ahmad Baba. Born in 1556, Ahmad Baba wrote many works on Islamic law and a biographical dictionary of Muslim scholars. The *ulama*, or scholars, of West Africa still use some of his works. When Moroccan armies poured into Timbuktu in 1591, Ahmad Baba refused to bow to their rule. Fearing his influence, the Moroccans took Ahmad Baba in chains to Marrakesh. From his prison cell, Ahmad Baba continued to protest foreign rule of his country. As a result, some West Africans claim Ahmad Baba as one of the first spokesmen for African nationalism.

Developing the Section

Writing a Travel Log. Divide students into pairs. Based on information in this section, details in the photo on text p. 21, and travel routes on the map on p. 17, have students write entries in a travel log about a caravan journey from Gao to Cairo.

Review and Practice

Assign "Taking Another Look," p. 21.

Answers to Taking Another Look (p. 21)

1. leaders resented his practice of traditional Songhai religion; disliked his willingness to allow conquered people to retain non-Muslim beliefs and practices **2.** expanded empire through military conquests, reformed system of laws and taxation **3. Critical Thinking** A Moroccan army of 4,000, using the harquebus,defeated a force of over 28,000. The possessor of new technology has a military advantage over its adversary.

Extending the Chapter

Doing Library Research. Divide the class into five groups, and assign each group to research one of the following West African empires or peoples in the 1200s to 1500s: Kanem-Bornu empire, Hausa states, Ibo, Yoruba, and Edo. Have students present their findings in short oral reports.

Looking Ahead

After students finish reading "Looking Ahead," p. 21, write the date 1492 on the chalkboard. Ask what the significance of this date is in U.S. history. (*year that Columbus landed in the Americas*) Why was that event signficant to the history of West Africa? (*opened the way for the trans-Atlantic slave trade*)

Answers to Close Up (pp. 22–23)

The Who, What, Where of History

1. ruler of Mali in early 1300s; known for *hajj* and enlarging and building Timbuktu **2.** believer in religion of Islam **3.** pilgrimage to Muslim holy city of Mecca **4.** holy war **5.** trade in salt and gold conducted without speaking **6.** founder of Islam **7.** storytellers who memorized and passed down the history of their people **8.** founder of Mali **9.** fierce emperor of Songhai **10.** Mali

Making the Connection

1. Ghanaians traded gold from the south for salt from North Africa, growing rich in the process. **2.** When Almoravids invaded Ghana forcing acceptance of Islam, Ghana weakened and fell.

Time Check

1. Askia rules in Songhai. **2.** 14th century

What Would You Have Done?

1. gold: valuable, beautiful; salt: substance necessary for desert survival and to flavor and preserve food **2.** trader: travel, excitement, possibilities for acquiring wealth; griot: interesting knowledge, respect of people, self-expression, preserve history

Thinking and Writing About History

1. reports should discuss Mansa Musa's procession and answer: who—Mansa Musa and 60,000 people; what—a hajj, a caravan; when—A.D. 1324; where—from Mali, through Chair, to Mecca; why—to make a pilgrimage **2.** Letters should mention architecture of Timbuktu, universities, manuscripts in Greek, Latin, and Arabic, scholars who lived and taught there, lively trade.

Building Skills

Empire	Dates	Founder	Major Religion	Source of Wealth
Ghana	300s–1325	Soninke	local religions, after 1000 Islam	gold-salt trade; slave trade
Mali	1235–1468	Sundiata	Islam	gold-salt trade; slave trade
Songhai	1400s–1591	sons of king of Gao	Islam	gold-ivory trade
All three kingdoms obtained wealth through gold.				

Chapter 3 The West African Heritage (pp. 24–31)

Overview

Because many peoples with different languages and customs lived in West Africa, a diversity of cultures developed. Yet, amid the diversity, certain common patterns emerged. The extended family played a central role in the lives of most West African peoples. All activities—from birth to death—carried religious meaning. West Africans lived in a spirit-filled world, and they celebrated that world in music, dance, and the arts. Although they were familiar with slavery, no experience had prepared West Africans for the slavery that enveloped them in the Americas. To survive, West Africans clung to traditions that reminded them of their homes on the African continent. The traditions that they managed to preserve in the face of terrible hardships formed the basis of what would one day become African American culture.

Resources

Chapter 3 Activity Sheet: Interpreting a Primary Source (p. 200)
Chapter 3 Test (p. 129)
Lesson Plans for *The Artist's View* (p. 108)
Unit 1 Test (pp. 124–126)

Focus Activity

Open the chapter by asking students to think of examples that show the influence of African culture in the United States today. Conduct a three-minute brainstorming session. As students read the chapter, have them modify the list.

Teaching Section 1: West African Families (pp. 25–26)

Objective

- To analyze West African society.

Historical Sidelight

Expert Weavers. By A.D. 1000 many West African peoples became known for their skill at weaving and dying cotton cloth for clothing. When Portuguese merchants landed in West Africa in 1450, they found cotton cloth of a higher quality than anything available in Europe—the kente cloth shown on the cover and in *The Artist's View*.

Developing the Section

Categorizing. Using the "Building Skills" activity on p. 3 as a base, talk students through this section. Draw the table on the chalkboard or duplicate and distribute it to students. Have students read the section and then call on volunteers to fill in column 1.

Review and Practice

Assign "Taking Another Look," p. 26.

Answer to Question in Caption (p. 26)

more eyes to keep watch

Answers to Taking Another Look (p. 26)

1. to repay family for loss of woman's labor **2.** elders, farmers and craftworkers, slaves **3. Critical Thinking** No, slaves were still considered inferior to owners.

Teaching Section 2: West African Religious Practices (pp. 26–27)

Objective

- To understand that most African peoples lived in a spirit-filled world.

Developing the Section

Analyzing a Secondary Source. Read aloud the following description of African beliefs from *Black Odyssey*, by Nathan Irvin Huggins:

> The force of life that tied person to person and to all time past linked a person as well to all things. The force that moved through him moved through the plants of the field, trees, animals, and even stones. Spirits dwelt in each thing and imparted [gave] to it special meaning.

Tell students that Huggins described African religion as a "seamless web." Divide students into small groups and have each prepare a paragraph explaining what they think Huggins means. Have the recorder from each group read its paragraph aloud. Be sure students see that most Africans believed that all objects—animate and inanimate—possessed a spiritual force and that this force bound life together.

Review and Practice

Assign "Taking Another Look," p. 27.

Answers to Taking Another Look (p. 27)

1. believed in Creator, many goddesses and gods; spirits in all things, ancestor worship **2.** believed souls survived death and could protect and aid the living **3. Critical Thinking** Answers should deal with religion as center of society.

Teaching Section 3: Other West African Traditions (pp. 27–29)

Objective

- To draw conclusions about West African civilizations based on selected artifacts.

Historical Sidelight

Government Without Kings. The Ibo people in what is now Nigeria developed a system of government that had no visible rulers. Instead, the Ibo thought of themselves as one extended family. Family compounds formed the center of local government. In each compound, all adult men had an equal say in decision-making. When a compound grew too large for every male to participate in government, part of the family would split off and start a new compound. Iboland was thus made up of hundreds of clans, or "big families" as they were known.

Developing the Section

Drawing Conclusions. Divide the class into groups, and tell them to pretend they are archaeologists who have just uncovered artifacts of an ancient West African civilization: a shred of cloth similar to the fabric shown in the picture on text p. 28 and the three works of art shown on text pp. 26, 27, and 29. Ask students what conclusions they can draw about the people who fashioned these objects.

Review and Practice

Assign "Taking Another Look," p. 29.

Answer to Question in Caption (p. 28)

weddings, births, harvests, deaths, etc.

Answers to Taking Another Look (p. 29)

1. music played central role in life and religion **2.** created kente cloth and items from leather, ivory, wood, gold, silver, copper, and bronze **3. Critical Thinking** music, dance, and art—all part of religious practice, ritual

Extending the Chapter

Researching African Culture. Divide the class into groups. Assign each group to research one of the following topics about West Africa: art, dance, music, folktales. Have students present their findings through oral reports, illustrations, and/or audio or videotape. The students researching folktales, for example, might prepare dramatic readings on tape.

Looking Ahead

After students have read "Looking Ahead," p. 29, ask them to think about how their lives would be changed if their families suddenly moved to a city a thousand miles away. What things would they want to take with them? What or whom would they miss? Lead them to appreciate the shock that Africans faced when captured and taken to a distant land.

Answers to Close Up (pp. 30–31)

The Who, What, Where of History

1. present-day Nigeria and Benin **2.** parent, unmarried children, married sons and their families, sometimes grandparents, aunts, uncles, and cousins **3.** payment by groom's family to bride's family to compensate for the loss of her labor **4.** moon goddess **5.** farmer who grows crops for his own use only **6.** praying to deceased relatives for aid **7.** type of music in which a leader sings and people sing back to him **8.** brilliantly colored cotton cloth

Making the Connection

1. Groom's family gained an extra worker; bridewealth compensated bride's family for loss of her labor. **2.** Daily life *was* religious life, and community was a religious community.

What Would You Have Done?

1. Examples: cotton—could weave beautiful cloth; metals—could make sculptures and useful items; wood—could make sculptures and do carpentry **2. craftworkers:** could create useful items, works of art, or both; **farmers:** could grow food to feed your own family as well as others

Thinking and Writing About History

1. West Africans danced to celebrate important occasions such as birth, marriage, and death, all of which were also religious events; entire community participated in the dancing **2.** Head is detailed and meticulously crafted. **3.** Rhythm of West African music adopted for reggae, jazz and blues; African art influenced modern artists, including Picasso. **4.** good—allows different people to use land, encourages cooperation; bad—could cause conflict among users.

Building Skills

Tradition	West African	African American
Family	extended; children important	children important
Marriage	polygyny	monogamy
Work	mostly farmers	various professions
Society	class system: elders, farmers and craftworkers, captives, slaves	no distinct classes
Religion	part of all aspects of life; belief in many gods and goddesses	separate aspect of life; belief in one God
Music	plays a role in religion; used to mark important occasions	plays a role in religion; used mainly as entertainment
Stories	traditional stories often have morals; handed down by griots	traditional stories often have morals; handed down in books, television,etc.
Art	made by craftworkers; each people had own special craft	made by artists; anyone can make any type of art

UNIT 2 Africans in the Americas (pp.32–63)

UNIT THEME

The forced movement of millions of enslaved Africans to the Americas is one of the pivotal events in world history.

UNIT CONCEPTS

- The European discovery of the Americas turned the African slave trade into big business.
- The slave trade robbed West Africa of valuable human resources and brutalized the human beings forced to endure the Middle Passage.
- Many Europeans justified slavery through the theory of racism.
- Enslaved Africans and their descendants helped shape the cultures of many nations in the Western Hemisphere.
- Africans took part in the founding of all 13 English colonies.
- The enslavement of Africans in the United States became one of the most critical issues in the nation's history.

UNIT OVERVIEW

Unit 2 traces the development of the Atlantic slave trade and its effects on Africans and Europeans. *The Big Picture* and the three chapters in the unit explore (1) the economic roots of slavery in the Americas and the part that racism played in creating such an inhuman system, (2) the role of Africans in building thriving colonies in the Americas, and (3) how, as slavery became increasingly important to the economic well-being of Britain's North American colonies, a growing body of laws confined Africans to the status of slaves.

In teaching this unit, you might mention to students that enslaved Africans who came to the Americas had strong identities as members of specific groups. They thought of themselves as Ibos, Yorubas, Mandingos, or any of the other dozens of peoples who lived in West Africa. Slave traders, however, tried to strip them of their identities. They referred to Africans by the color of their skin; Portuguese slave traders called Africans *negro*, for "black." This term slipped into English usage as Negro. Some people called the Africans "colored," as in the French *gens de couleur* for "people of color." Africans, however, often clung to their names—both as individuals and as a people—as an act of defiance. Ask students why it was so important for enslaved Africans to keep their names. You might also ask students to consider why the phrase "black is beautiful" became one of the battle cries of the Civil Rights Movement of the late 1960s. Because of its origin, the term black was replaced by *Afro American* for a time in the 1970s and, more recently, by *African American*.

COOPERATIVE LEARNING ACTIVITY

The following cooperative learning activity can be used for alternative assessment during and after the study of this unit.

As part of an ongoing assignment thoughout the unit, direct students to make up a book entitled "African Founders of the Americas." Divide the class into four groups, and assign each group one of the following regions: New England, Middle Colonies, Southern Colonies, and Spanish colonies north of Mexico. Each group should prepare one- or two-page illustrated entries on individuals who played important roles in the development of each region. Students may focus on individuals mentioned in the text or do research to find others. At the end of the project, bind the entries together in a book for class display. In evaluating student contributions, consider thoroughness of research and clarity of writing style.

Unit 2 THE BIG PICTURE (pp. 33–37)

Theme

The Atlantic slave trade and the institution of slavery based on race played important parts in the development of European colonies in the Americas.

Overview

The Big Picture explores the development of slavery as an outgrowth of European political and economic expansion after the Crusades. This opening of the African slave trade changed the history of three continents.

The Portuguese brought the first Africans to Europe in the 1400s as slaves. The African-European slave trade might have remained small, but as the Spanish and Portuguese colonized the Americas after 1492, a labor shortage developed in the new colonies. Other European nations began to deal in Africa's "black gold," the profitable trade in human beings.

The sugar plantations of the Caribbean set the pattern for slavery elsewhere in the Americas. Slave ships sailing under many flags carried millions of enslaved Africans to the West Indies. Europeans' belief in white superiority enabled them to justify the cruelties of slavery. The conflicts between slavery and the ideal of Christian charity and, in the case of the English, the ideal of liberty, were largely ignored.

Slavery spread to all 13 of England's mainland colonies. But it became most entrenched in the Southern Colonies, many of which adopted the plantation style of agriculture used in the Caribbean. During the 1600s, slavery crept into the colonial legal system and was a major exception to white colonists' demands for freedom.

Objectives

- To use a picture and a quotation to develop empathy for what it meant to be a slave.
- To use a timeline to compare actions.
- To use historical imagination to describe the first meeting between the Portuguese and West Africans.
- To analyze an eyewitness account of the first European episode in the African slave trade.
- To interpret a picture showing the economic activities of African slaves working on an indigo plantation.
- To draw an economic map of the 13 English colonies in North America.
- To summarize the issue of slavery at the start of the 1700s.

Introducing *The Big Picture*

Refer students to the picture on student text p. 32, and the quotation in "An African American Speaks" on p. 33. Then write the following incomplete statement on the chalkboard: "To be a slave meant to ______________________________."
Have students, working individually or in small groups, finish the statement on a sheet of paper. You might encourage them to write several versions of the statement. Then, call on volunteers to share their statements with the class.

Using the Timeline

Divide the class into small groups. Have each group select three events on the timeline that show how Africans took leading roles in the settlement of the Americas. Then have them select three other events that show efforts by Europeans to limit the rights of Africans. Ask students how, if they had been Africans in the Americas during the 1600s, they would have resisted slavery.

Teaching *The Big Picture*

1. Using Historical Imagination. Assign "Expanding the Horizons of Europe" and "Face to Face in Africa" on student text pp. 33–34. Then divide the class into small groups. Have half the groups write diary entries on the first meeting between the Portuguese and West Africans from the West African point of view. Have the other half write dialogues expressing the Portuguese reaction. Call on volunteers from each group to read their diary entries or dialogues aloud.

2. Analyzing a Quote. After students have read "Start of the African Slave Trade" on text pp. 34–35, tell them that an advisor to Prince Henry named Gomes Eanes de Zurara witnessed the first sale of Africans as slaves in Europe. Read aloud the following selection from his first-hand account:

> Some kept their heads low and their faces bathed in tears, looking upon one another; others stood groaning, . . . looking up to the heights of heaven. . . . The mothers clasped their . . . children in their arms and threw themselves flat on the ground with them, receiving blows with little pity for their own flesh, if only they might not be torn from them.

Then ask students to speculate on how such scenes might have affected European observers. Have the students turn to the timeline on student text pp. 34–35, and ask them what events shown there helped spur the growth of slavery. (*Columbus arrives in the Americas; first Africans arrive in the Americas as slaves; Virginia recognizes slavery as legal.*)

3. Interpreting a Picture. After students have read "Black Gold for the Americas," question them about the picture on student text p. 36. What does it depict? (*indigo plantation in the West Indies*) What would be the main costs in using slave labor? (*the purchase price of slaves; providing the slaves with housing, clothing, and food*) Why would slavery be most profitable in warm climates? (*because longer growing seasons allowed slaves to work year round rather than for only part of the time*)

4. Drawing a Map. Divide the class into groups, and distribute the outline map of Eastern North America, p. 307 of this manual. Assign students to read "The English Colonies in North America" on text pp. 36–37. Assign students to draw picture symbols on their outline maps illustrating economic activities in New England, the Middle Colonies, and the Southern Colonies. They might use a ship, for example, to illustrate New England's sea trade. Display the completed maps around the classroom for students to use while they study the unit.

5. Writing a Summary. After students have read "The Issue of Slavery" on text p. 37, have them write a short paragraph summarizing colonial attitudes toward slavery in the 1600s and early 1700s. When they have finished, call on volunteers to read their summaries aloud.

Review and Practice

Assign "Taking Another Look," p. 37.

Answers to Taking Another Look (p. 37)

1. wanted Asian goods, but couldn't take land routes from Muslims **2.** slave trade yielded high profits **3.** worried about making a living, had troubles with Great Britain **4. Critical Thinking** plantations were main part of Southern economy, demanded great deal of labor; African slaves were the most practical and profitable solution for European's labor needs

Chapter 4 The Atlantic Slave Trade (pp. 38–45)

Overview

At first, Europeans tried to solve their labor shortage in the Americas by enslaving the people who already lived there. But when European diseases wiped out the Native American population in some areas, Europeans turned to West African slaves. By the 1600s, slave-trading had become a big business, complete with "slave factories" along the West African coast and slave-trading companies to run them. The brutal trade in human beings and the inhumanity of the Middle Passage cost millions of West Africans their lives. Although some West African rulers tried to resist slavery, the guns and greed of slave traders won out. In the 1600s and 1700s, Europeans robbed Africa of its people. In the centuries ahead, they would seize the continent itself.

Resources

Chapter 4 Activity Sheet: Explaining Illustrations (p. 201)
Chapter 4 Test (p. 133)
Outline Map: The World (p. 305)
Unit 2 Writing Workshop: A First-Person Narrative (pp. 266–69)

Focus Activity

Assign the chapter introduction on student text pp. 38–39. Then ask students to imagine the following situation: Las Casas regrets his decision to enslave Africans and rushes *History of the Indies* to press in 1550. Next, divide the class into groups. Have each group prepare a review of Las Casas's book from one of the following points of view: a plantation owner in the West Indies, a Portuguese slave trader, the king of Spain, a Spanish conquistador. Call on volunteers to read the reviews aloud. Ask the students if the spread of African slavery to the Americas was inevitable. (*Student responses should indicate an awareness of the economic incentives behind the slave trade.*)

Teaching Section 1: Slave Raids in West Africa (pp. 39–40)

Objective

- To speculate on reasons why Africans took part in the slave trade.

Historical Sidelight

Antislavery Protest. In 1526, King Nzinga Mbemba of the Bakongo state of Kongo wrote a letter to the king of Portugal. He had accepted the Roman Catholic religion and even the name priests conferred upon him at baptism—King Affonso. But Affonso wrote of his people, "it is our will that in these kingdoms of Kongo there should not be any trade in slaves nor any market for slaves." When the Portuguese king ignored the letter, King Affonso appealed directly to the pope. Roman Catholic rulers, however, convinced the pope that African slaves would spur the growth of Roman Catholic colonies. So he, too, ignored Affonso.

Developing the Section

Analyzing a Picture. Refer students' attention to the picture on student text p. 39. Ask who is leading the slave coffle. (*African slave traders*) How are the captives shackled together? (*by heavy logs at the neck and ropes at their arms*) What weapons are the slave traders carrying? (*axes, sticks, and guns*) Ask students why they think Africans might have enslaved their own people. (*economics, political rivalries, old feuds, etc.*)

Review and Practice

Assign "Taking Another Look," p. 40.

Answers to Taking Another Look (p. 40)

1. Slave traders overran villages. **2.** quartered there until they were loaded onto ships **3. Critical Thinking** All wanted a share of the slave trade profits; none wanted to be enslaved.

Teaching Section 2: The Middle Passage (pp. 40–42)

Objective

- To analyze a former slave's description of the Middle Passage.

Historical Sidelight

The African Kingdom of Palmares. In 1605, African slaves on the northeastern corner of present-day Brazil fled bondage. They marched as a group into the wilderness to form their own kingdom known as Palmares. The Africans elected rulers and set up a government similar to those in West Africa. Palmares held out until 1694, when an army sent from Portugal destroyed it.

Developing the Section

Analyzing a Quote. To develop among students a sense of what the Middle Passage was like, read aloud the following description written by Olaudah Equiano.

> When I was carried on board I was immediately handled and tossed up, to see if I were sound, by some of the crew. I was now persuaded that I had got into a world of bad spirits, and that they were going to kill me. . . .
>
> I was soon put down under the decks. There, with the stench [smell] and crying together, I became so sick and low that I was not able to eat. . . . But soon, to my grief, two of the white men offered me something to eat. On my refusing, . . . one of them held me fast . . . , while the other flogged me severely.

Ask students how Equiano viewed the whites. (*as bad spirits full of cruelty*) How did the whites treat Equiano? (*They tossed him about like merchandise and flogged him when he refused to eat.*) Have students speculate on what the results of such treatment might be among the Africans. (*sickness, death, anger, mutiny*)

Review and Practice

Assign "Taking Another Look," p. 42.

Answers to Taking Another Look (p. 42)

1. inhuman conditions, corporal punishment **2.** threw themselves overboard, refused food and medicine, mutinied **3. Critical Thinking** journey either broke their spirits and made them more resigned to accepting enslavement or enraged them, made them more determined to fight back against those who enslaved them

Teaching Section 3: West Africa After the Slave Trade (pp. 42–43)

Objective

- To design a diagram depicting the cycle of economic dependence created by the slave trade.

Developing the Section

Drawing a Diagram. After students have read the section, have them restudy "Effects on the West African Economy." Divide the class into three groups and have each prepare a diagram illustrating the economic cycle created in West Africa by the Atlantic slave trade. Each group should draw its diagram on the chalkboard for a review and critique by the entire class.

Review and Practice

Assign "Taking Another Look," p. 43.

Answers to Taking Another Look (p. 43)

1. loss of population, local warfare spread, increased cycle of economic dependence **2.** Cheap goods exchanged for slaves stunted development of manufacturing or other commerce. When demand for slaves declined Africa was left help-demand for slaves declined Africa was left helpless. **3. Critical Thinking** made it easier for them to treat the Africans poorly, only humans deserve human treatment, to participate in trade must view Africans as property

Extending the Chapter

Illustrating an Idea. Divide the class into groups of 4 or 5 students. Tell them to imagine that they are the editors and art directors for Olaudah Equiano's story, *The Interesting Narrative of the Life of Olaudah Equiano, or Gustavus Vassa.* Kidnapped from Benin when he was eleven in 1745, he was taken to the Americas. He was a slave on a Virginia plantation and then a servant to a British naval officer and finally to a Philadelphia merchant. He bought his freedom and moved to England where he became involved in the antislavery movement. Have each group design a cover for Equiano's book including the title, author, and an illustration as well as a blurb on the back cover that will encourage people to read it.

Looking Ahead

Focus on the quotation in "Looking Ahead," p. 43, by asking how the quotation contrasts with what students have learned about West African cultures. (*Most students will note the sophistication and complexity of the societies mentioned in Unit 1.*) Ask what hardships they think Africans would face upon landing in the Americas. (*Answers should indicate awareness of difficulties that Africans faced in adjusting not only to bondage but to life on a strange continent among strange people.*)

Answers to Close Up (pp. 44–45)

The Who, What, Where, of History

1. Portuguese prince, ordered exploration of West African coast in early 1400s **2.** West African coast so named by Portuguese who bought people there **3.** Spanish conquerors of Native Americans **4.** one who exchanged a period of work for passage to Americas **5.** conquistador, priest, opposed enslavement of Native Americans **6.** harbors along West African coast **7.** voyage across Atlantic from Africa to Americas **8.** queen of Matamba, battled Portuguese for 30 years disrupting slave trade

Making the Connection

1. To stop enslavement of Native Americans Las Casas suggested using Africans. **2.** slave trade destroyed order of West African society, caused loss of population and created economic dependence, when demand decreased Africa was vulnerable

Time Check

1. 1502 **2.** 1700–1800

What Would You Have Done?

1. Examples: would not have participated due to moral and economic objections; would have participated to make profit **2. Examples:** end to slave trade within certain radius; reparations for subjects already sold into slavery; guns and other modern weapons **3.** Answers (whether justifying cooperation or refusal) should show understanding of slave ship conditions.

Thinking and Writing About History

1. Letters may discuss immorality of using any people as slave labor while noting positive benefits of switch for Native Americans. **2.** Letters should discuss Quakers' opposition to slavery on moral/religious grounds. **3.** Answers should reflect Middle Passage descriptions in text.

Building Skills

2, 5, 7

Chapter 5 The West Indies, First Stop for Africans (pp. 46–51)

Overview

Instead of turning to sugar suppliers in the warm climates of Asia, Europeans increasingly set up their own sugar factories in the West Indies. So important were these islands that European nations turned the Caribbean into a war zone as nations vied for control of rivals' island possessions. African slaves provided the economic base for the emerging plantation economy of the West Indies. They turned the island's products—sugar cane, dyewoods, cotton, and spices—into hard cash. Slavery itself became big business as Africans brought high prices in the West Indies. The system of slavery that emerged in this region, based on hard labor and racism, became the model for the later plantation system in the 13 English colonies.

Resources

Chapter 5 Activity Sheet: Interpreting a Circle Graph (p. 202)
Chapter 5 Test (p. 134)

Focus Activity

Write the word *Maroon* on the chalkboard. Tell students that some linguists say the word comes from the Spanish *cimarron* for "wild and unruly." Others say it comes from an African word for "men who hide in the mountains." Ask them to speculate on who the term *Maroon* might describe, given its possible origins. (*runaway slaves*) What can they infer about the Maroons of Jamaica based on the "Snapshot of the Times," p. 48? (*that the Maroons successfully resisted British efforts to control them*)

Teaching Section 1: Empires Built on Sugar (pp. 47–48)

Objective

- To interpret statistics on the costs of setting up a Jamaican plantation in 1672.

Historical Sidelight

The Land of Look Behind. In the 1600s and 1700s, British soldiers who dared to enter the Cockpit Country controlled by the Maroons rode back-to-back on mules, constantly on the lookout for ambushes. The soldiers soon dubbed Cockpit Country "The Land of Look Behind."

Developing the Section

Interpreting Statistics. Before students read the section, copy the following figures on the chalkboard. Tell students that the figures represent the money spent by a pair of brothers to set up a plantation in Jamaica in 1672.

Negroes (55)	£1,205
White servants and hired labor	160
Millwork, ironwork, and tools	223
Horses, hogs, and poultry	35
Food and drink	128
Cloth and clothing	21
Furniture for the plantation house	26
Land	21
Taxes and rewards for runaway servants	7
Miscellaneous	32
	£1,858

Help students understand the importance of slavery to the plantation system by asking questions about what the single largest expense was to the plantation owner and what the average price per slave was. (*roughly £21.9 each*) Which was more expensive—slaves or land? (*slaves*) Ask students what conclusion they can draw about the importance of African slaves to the plantation system. (*Most students will conclude that slaves were the basis of the system.*)

Review and Practice

Assign "Taking Another Look," p. 48.

Answers to Questions in Caption (p. 48)

2; enslaved Africans

Answers to Taking Another Look (p. 48)

1. demand for sugar increased the demand for slaves needed to produce it **2.** Africa, West Indies, English colonies, Europe, Great Britain **3. Critical Thinking** **No:** plantation owners made huge amounts of sugar and needed cheap labor to do all the work. **Yes:** more humane treatment of workers would have allowed more of them to survive, decreased demand for slaves.

Teaching Section 2: Patterns of West Indian Slavery (pp. 48–49)

Objective

- To evaluate a point of view on the system of slavery that evolved in the English West Indies.

Historical Sidelight

Slave Codes. In 1661, fear of slave rebellions led the English assembly on Barbados to pass a slave act. The law required slave owners to keep slave cabins under close surveillance, searching them at least twice a month. Africans who left plantations had to carry a ticket from their owner. The law required white colonists to whip or brand any African slave found without a ticket.

Developing the Section

Evaluating a Point of View. Write the following statement by historian Richard S. Dunn, author of *Sugar and Slaves*, on the chalkboard: "The seventeenth-century English sugar planters created one of the harshest systems of servitude in the Western World." Then divide the class into groups. Ask them what evidence from the text supports or refutes this point of view. Allow students time to skim this chapter and earlier ones. Record student responses in two columns on the chalkboard. Ask what additional research might allow them to assess better the accuracy of this statement. (*Students should understand that they might also need to investigate slavery in New Spain, Portuguese Brazil, and so on, to see if West Indian slavery was indeed the harshest form.*)

Review and Practice

Assign "Taking Another Look," p. 49.

Answer to Question in Caption (p. 49)

Cheap labor contributed to large profits for plantation owners.

Answers to Taking Another Look (p. 49)

1. sale to whites, loss of family, poor working conditions **2.** racists denied African slaves human rights **3. Critical Thinking** **Africa:** slaves were war captives, could earn or buy freedom; **West Indies:** captured for trade only, could never overcome status as property

Extending the Chapter

Linking Past to Present. Assign the "Focus On" feature on student text p. 50. Then divide the class into groups of 4 or 5 students to do research on the islands in the West Indies today. Advise students to look for customs or traditions that reflect the island's past connections with Africa or African slavery. Have each group prepare an oral report on the island it chose. Encourage students to enliven their presentations with pictures, music—or even some foods mentioned in the feature.

Looking Ahead

After students have read "Looking Ahead" on student text p. 49, ask them to speculate on economic reasons the English might have allowed the spread of African slavery to mainland colonies.

Answers to Close Up (pp. 50–51)

The Who, What, Where of History

1. runaway African slaves in Jamaica **2.** agricultural products raised for profit **3.** three-legged trade routes beginning in West Africa, crossing to West Indies, ending in English colonies **4.** belief that one race is superior to another **5.** West Indies

Making the Connection

1. Maroons won independence from British; slave owners feared their success would encourage rebellion and took brutal measures to prevent African escape or revolt. **2.** African slaves were needed to grow cane and work in mills

Time Check

1. Puerto Rico **2.** 1655

What Would You Have Done?

1. yes: solidarity with ex-slaves, respect for Maroons' strength; **no:** too risky, would try to leave Jamaica **2.** French or Spanish island; racism not so severe as among the British

Thinking and Writing About History

1. Who—Sir Henry Colt and crew, 20 Spanish ships; What—naval battle; When—Sunday morning, July 1631; Where—aboard Alexander, off coast of St. Christopher Island; Why—Spanish wanted to expel English from Caribbean **2.** Ads should discuss potential for profits. **3.** may advance economic explanations or racist opinions

Building Skills

1. F **2.** D **3.** C **4.** E **5.** A **6.** B
Effect: need for slaves in West Indies decreased; **Cause:** price of sugar dropped. **Effect:** Price of sugar dropped; **Cause:** glut on market due to others' production

Chapter 6 Africans in the Thirteen Colonies (pp. 52–63)

Overview

From the start, Africans played an important role in the history of what is today the United States. They contributed greatly to the success of English North America. Many English settlers in the 1600s accorded Africans a measure of freedom that they would not again enjoy until after the Civil War. In the late 1600s and the 1700s, however, colony after colony restricted the rights of Africans on the basis of color. In the South, slavery became even more firmly entrenched.

Resources

Chapter 6 Activity Sheet: Drawing Conclusions (p. 203)
Chapter 6 Test (p. 135)
Outline Map: Eastern North America (p. 307)
Unit 2 Test (pp. 130–32)

Focus Activity

After students have read the chapter-opening story on text pp. 52–53, divide them into three groups. Direct each group to write a plaque for a historical marker that might appear at either Georgetown, South Carolina, or St. Augustine, Florida. Tell students that their plaques should honor the role of Africans in the settlement of what is now the United States. When students are done, have them share their plaques with the rest of the class. You might repeat this activity with other sites mentioned in the chapter.

Teaching Section 1: Arrival in Jamestown (pp. 53–55)

Objective

- To understand that Africans enjoyed certain freedoms in the 1600s later denied them by law.

Historical Sidelight

Little Stephen. "When smoke hung over the house-tops, and the ladder-rounds were still unbroken," says Zuni legend, "the Black Mexicans came from their abode in the Everlasting Summer." The

Black Mexicans were really only one person—"Little Stephen", or Estevanico as he was known among the Spaniards. He had already trekked across much of what is now the American Southwest and south to Mexico City when he came to the Zuni pueblo in New Mexico in 1539. Estevanico came in search of the Seven Cities of Cibola, fabled cities filled with gold and emeralds. By now, news of white conquerors had spread, and the Zuni distrusted the African who walked with them. Estevancio fell in battle with the Zuni.

Developing the Section

Interpreting Information. Refer students to the "Snapshot of the Times" on text p. 54. Then point out the heading to the right: "Slavery Amid Freedom." Ask students how the items in the "Snapshot" show the dual status of Africans in early colonial history. (*1641 and 1644 entries show Africans had certain freedoms; 1660s, 1663 and 1750 entries show limitations of rights.*)

Review and Practice

Assign "Taking Another Look," p. 55.

Answers to Questions in Caption (p. 55)

five, Middle Colonies

Answers to Taking Another Look (p. 55)

1. voting, owning property, testifying in court **2.** slaves worked for life, had no protection from home country, were easily identified, were in plentiful supply **3. Critical Thinking** easier to justify slavery if racist views are embraced

Teaching Section 2: Africans in the Southern Colonies (pp. 55–58)

Objective

- To compare how African slavery developed in the Southern Colonies.

Historical Sidelight

With a Stroke of the Pen. In an early edition of *Lists of Emigrants to America*, a chronicler entered the names of America's first African family in the following manner: "Athoney Negro: Isabell Negro; and William theire Child Baptised." In a later edition, however, the entry was changed to read: "Anthony, negro, Isabell, a negro, and William her child, baptised."

Developing the Section

Comparing Information. Refer students to the map on p. 55, and ask them to list the Southern Colonies. Write the names on the chalkboard and then ask students how African slavery developed in each. Through discussion, be sure students understand the implications of the Africans' loss of freedom and the institution of *durante vita*.

Review and Practice

Assign "Taking Another Look," p. 58.

Answer to Question in Caption (p. 56)

Europe

Answers to Taking Another Look (p. 58)

1.the tobacco plantation system developed **2.** Africans regarded as property **3. Critical Thinking Maryland:** tobacco business; **Carolinas:** rice business; **Georgia:** gradual development of slavery after significant resistance

Teaching Section 3: Africans in the Middle Colonies (pp. 58–59)

Objective

- To compare slavery in the Middle Colonies with slavery in the Southern Colonies.

Developing the Section

Using Pictures to Compare Information. Refer students to the picture on text p. 59. Have them compare this farm to the diagram of tobacco production on p. 56. Ask why the owners of such farms would have less need for slaves than the owners of tobacco plantations. (*A small-scale farm needed fewer workers than a cash-crop plantation.*) Ask how the climate of the Middle Colonies differed from the climate of the Southern Colonies. (*cooler, with winter seasons*) How might climate affect the economics of slavery? (*more profitable to own slaves where they could work year round*)

Review and Practice

Assign "Taking Another Look," p. 59.

Answer to Question in Caption (p. 59)

Small farms could be worked by owners and their families, with little need for added labor.

Answers to Taking Another Look (p. 59)

1. climate unsuited to plantation system **2.** legalized slavery in New Jersey and New York **3. Critical Thinking** might not have been enslaved because Dutch initially promised freedom

Teaching Section 4: Africans in New England (pp. 60–61)

Objective

- To use a graph to make predictions about the growth of the African American population.

Historical Sidelight

African Medical Advice. In the early 1700s, an outbreak of smallbox swept through New England. Preacher Cotton Mather pressed the colonists to use an experimental inoculation technique against the disease. To bolster his case, Mather called upon Africans who had seen the procedure work in their homeland.The accounts of the procedure given by the Africans so impressed the colonists that Mather won the debate—and saved countless lives.

Developing the Section

Making Predictions. Refer students to the line graph on text p. 61. Ask whether they would expect the growth of the slave population in the South to increase or decrease in the 1790s. (*increase*) Why? (*It had steadily increased since 1690.*) Have them compare this graph with the table on p. 60. Note that the number of Africans brought to the colonies declined during the years 1771–1775 yet the African American population in the South continued to climb. Ask what might account for this great increase. (*birthrate among African Americans*) If the Atlantic slave trade had suddenly stopped in 1800, ask if the students think the trade in slaves in the North American colonies would necessarily have ended. (*Answers should indicate an awareness that slavery was deeply entrenched in the United States by the late 1700s.*)

Review and Practice

Assign "Taking Another Look," p. 61.

Answers to Questions in Captions (pp. 60–61)

(p. 60) 1761–1770, 1731–1740; (p. 61) about 50,000, about 150,000, about 450,000

Answers to Taking Another Look (p. 61)

1. allowed enslavement of people sold to them and captives **2.** economics; climate ruled out plantations, turned to sea trade, which included slave trade **3. Critical Thinking** **Southern:** plantation system called for slavery: **Middle:** climate made slaves impractical; **New England:** terrain and climate made slavery impractical

Extending the Chapter

Interpreting Historical Maps. Divide the students into groups, and have them find maps in historical atlases that show the distribution of the African population in colonial America. Direct students to draw or bring copies of these maps to class. Have them use the maps to determine which region(s) had the largest concentration of Africans. Have each group prepare a brief statement explaining how it thinks this population distribution affected relationships among the colonies.

Looking Ahead

After students have read "Looking Ahead" on student text p. 61, ask them whether they would have supported colonial independence from Great Britain had they been slaves.

Answers to Close Up (pp. 62–63)

The Who, What, Where of History

1. near present-day Georgetown, South Carolina **2.** African who accompanied Spanish explorers throughout southwest **3.** Jamestown **4.** William **5.** Virginia assembly, first legislative assembly in U.S. **6.** indentured servant, arrived in Virginia in 1621, gained freedom, acquired land **7.** indentured servant, landed in Maryland in 1634, completed term of service, elected to General Assembly **8.** for life **9.** John Locke **10.** founder of Georgia

Making the Connection

1. slavery important to colonies with warm climates, crops grew all year, large labor force needed **2.** few slaves in Middle and New England colonies; slaves couldn't work in winter, making them economically infeasible

Time Check

1. 1619 **2.** 1663

What Would You Have Done?

1. Examples: go to a colony where freedmen were allowed, or one that outlawed slavery; go to Africa; organize rebellion **2.** all colonists should start on equal footing, slavery created differences in wealth and status

Thinking and Writing About History

1. San Miguel story—rebelled, set fire to settlement, fate remains a mystery, maybe built new settlement or went to live with Native Americans **2.** J.F. Orange letter—Father, an indentured servant, petitioned Council of New Netherlands for freedom that had been promised him in exchange for helping to build New Amsterdam, received grant of land in present-day Greenwich Village. Protest may make specific note of change from Dutch to British rule and appeal to king to make good on Dutch promises; should support argument with knowledge learned from text

Building Skills

1. a. R b. I c. R
2. a. R b. R c. I
3. a. R b. R c. I

UNIT 3 African Americans and a New Nation (pp. 64–91)

UNIT THEME

The debate over the rights of African Americans increases as the nation fights for independence and begins to expand beyond the Mississippi.

UNIT CONCEPTS

- African Americans fought on both sides in the Revolutionary War, hoping for freedom and equal rights.
- The signers of the Constitution placed national unity above the rights of African Americans and allowed slavery to continue.
- The Haitian Revolution led by Toussaint L'Ouverture played a significant part in events that led to the acquisition of the Louisiana Territory.
- African Americans—free and enslaved—played important roles in the continued growth and expansion of the United States.

UNIT OVERVIEW

Unit 3 focuses on the Revolutionary period and the early years of the Republic. It also looks ahead to the role played by African American Mountain Men—explorers who led the nation westward. The contributions of African Americans to the nation's freedom and expansion underscore the lack of rights given them by the nation they helped to found. *The Big Picture* and the three chapters in the unit describe: (1) how and why African Americans were involved in the buildup that led to the Revolutionary War and in fighting the war, (2) why the debate over the slave trade and slavery during the writing of the Constitution ended in a compromise that allowed both to continue, and (3) how Toussaint L'Ouverture's revolt in Haiti resulted in the Louisiana Purchase and the beginning of the new nation's expansion beyond the Mississippi River.

In teaching this unit, you might point to the use of the term *African American* on student p. 65. The earlier two units referred to peoples of African descent as *Africans*, but the Africans who helped found the nation thought of themselves as Americans, too. Like white Americans, they claimed the United States as their homeland. The term, however, should not indicate to students that free African Americans had the same rights as white Americans. Free males of African descent were permitted to vote in only five Northern states at the time the Constitution was ratified in the late 1780s and early 1790s, but over time this right was limited as were other rights, which students will read about in Unit 4. Slavery continued in Northern states into the 1800s. The Atlantic trade in Africans continued under the Constitution until 1808. You might ask students what it meant to be an African and an American (in the late 1700s and early 1800s) and what it means today.

COOPERATIVE LEARNING ACTIVITY

You may wish to use the following cooperative learning activity for alternative assessment after study of the unit has been completed.

As a wrap-up activity for the unit, divide the class into groups of 4 to 5 students. Tell the students to imagine it is 1821, and President James Monroe is about to deliver his State of the Union address to Congress. Have each group write a State of the Union message from the point of view of African Americans. Their messages should assess the gains and losses for African Americans since the Revolution. Have the recorder from each group read its message aloud. In evaluating student work, consider how convincingly students have expressed the point of view and how accurately they have assessed gains and losses.

Unit 3 THE BIG PICTURE (pp. 66–69)

Theme

The Declaration of Independence and the founding of the new nation bring into sharp contrast the ideals of liberty and the forced enslavement of peoples of African descent.

Overview

The Big Picture traces the start of a long, historic struggle by African Americans to win equal rights with whites. In the 1770s, as colonial protests against British economic policies escalated, some African Americans hoped that the system of slavery might end. When the Declaration of Independence was written stating that "All men are created equal", many African Americans became Patriots.

One by one after the war, Northern states ended slavery, and the Confederation Congress barred slavery in the Northwest Territory. When white delegates to the Constitutional Convention wrote a constitution for the new nation, however, they struck a bargain—the recognition of slavery in exchange for the continued loyalty of the slave holding Southern states.

Ironically, expansion of the nation came, in part, as a result of actions by people of African descent. A revolution in Haiti led by Toussaint L'Ouverture opened the way for the Louisiana Purchase. The United States acquired Spanish Florida in part because of pressure by slave owners to subdue communities of runaway slaves living among the Seminoles. When Great Britain challenged U.S. rights at sea and along its western borders, African Americans helped defend the nation in the War of 1812. African American Mountain Men helped in the exploration and charting of the lands beyond the Mississippi River.

Objectives

- To infer how African Americans may have felt about the outcome of the Revolution.
- To predict future treatment of African Americans in the new United States.
- To draw conclusions about the conduct of African American soldiers during the war.
- To form opinions about African American reactions to the U.S. Constitution.

Introducing *The Big Picture*

Call on a volunteer to read the quotation on p. 65 aloud. Then add the following lines from the same source:

> How much money has been spent and how many lives have been lost to defend their liberty! I must say that I have hoped that God would open their eyes, when they were so much engaged for liberty, to think of the state of the poor blacks, and to pity us.

Ask students when Hammon made this remark and what his status was at the time. (*1787; a slave*) Point out that the American Revolution ended in 1783. Given this fact, ask students what they can infer about the effect of the Revolution on African Americans. (*did not free them*) How would they describe Hammon's feelings about the Revolution? (*Students should detect his disappointment.*)

Using the Timeline

Divide the class into small groups and have them identify three events on the timeline on pp. 66–67 that involve African Americans, either enslaved or free. Ask students to predict how these events might affect the future of African Americans in the United States. Have a volunteer from each group report its predictions to the class. (*Forecasts may be positive or negative.*)

Teaching *The Big Picture*

1. Drawing Conclusions. Assign the sections up to and including "Promises of Freedom" on p. 67. Either write on the chalkboard or distribute copies of the following quotation by Congressman William Eustis, a surgeon in the Continental Army and future governor of Massachusetts.

> The war over, and peace restored, these men [African American veterans] returned to their respective states; and who could have said to them, . . . after having shed their blood . . . in defense of the liberties of the country: "You are not to participate in the rights secured by the struggle [Revolution], or in the liberty for which you have been fighting?"

Ask students to draw conclusions about Eustis' opinion of African Americans' service in the war. (*They served bravely.*) Have students provide evidence to support their answers. (*African Americans shed their blood in defense of liberty.*) Ask students what stand they would expect Eustis to take on the issue of slavery. (*probably oppose it*)

2. Writing an Editorial. Remind students that an editorial expresses a point of view. Then have them review the information in "Debating

Slavery" and "A New Law of the Land" (pp. 67–68). Have students, working in pairs, write editorials expressing African Americans' reactions to the newly adopted U.S. Constitution.

Review and Practice

Assign "Taking Another Look," p. 69.

Answers to Questions in Caption (p. 69)

Ohio and Mississippi rivers, Lakes Superior, Michigan, Huron, Erie; Wisconsin, Illinois, Indiana, Ohio, Michigan, part of Minnesota

Answers to Taking Another Look (p. 69)

1. British offered freedom; Americans were fighting for liberty. **2.** did not abolish slavery, but allowed Congress to end slave trade in 1808 **3.** banned slavery in Northwest Territory **4. Critical Thinking** joined anti-British boycotts, fought in Revolution, fought in War of 1812

Chapter 7 The American Revolution: Liberty for All? (pp. 70–77)

Overview

African Americans took part in the Revolution from the buildup to the war to the British surrender at Yorktown. Some joined the Patriots, believing in the ideals expressed by the Declaration of Independence. Others joined the British, who promised freedom to African American slaves who served with them. Although the Revolutionary War brought independence from Great Britain, it neither ended slavery nor extended equal rights to free African Americans, but the seeds of abolition had been planted. An ugly question nagged at the nation's conscience: How could a nation founded upon liberty deprive some of its peoples of their basic human rights?

Resources

Chapter 7 Activity Sheet: Interpreting a Primary Source (p. 205)
Chapter 7 Test (p. 139)
Outline Map: Eastern United States (p. 307)

Focus Activity

Assign the chapter introduction on student pp. 70–71. Ask students what the story of Prince Whipple shows about the dilemma faced by African Americans during the Revolution. (*Many fought for colonial liberty even though personal liberty was denied to them.*) Have students speculate about reasons why African Americans may have fought in the Revolution. Record student responses on the chalkboard. You may wish to modify the list as students read the chapter, asking them to add or delete reasons.

Teaching Section 1: From Protest to War (pp. 71–72)

Objective

- To show how the Patriots might have used the Boston Massacre for propaganda purposes.

Historical Sidelights

1. Who Was Crispus Attucks? "The first to defy, and the first to die." That was how poet John Boyle O'Reilly described Crispus Attucks. Today, a monument to Attucks stands on the Boston Common. Yet little is known about him. A Framingham slave owner advertised in 1750 for the return of a runaway named Crispus. Many historians think this was Crispus Attucks. Attucks may have been part Native American. He may have escaped capture by working at sea, perhaps on cargo ships bound for the West Indies or on whaling ships. On the evening of March 5, 1770, he sat in a Boston tavern when a fire bell interrupted his supper. He rushed to the front of a mob headed up King Street—and into history.

2. Phillis Wheatley. In autumn 1784, Phillis Wheatley wrote her last poem, "Liberty and Peace." Wheatley had just given birth to her third child and was living in a boardinghouse on the edge of poverty. By the time the poem appeared in December, she was dead at age 31. No stone marked her burial site, but history did not forget her. In 1985, the state of Massachusetts honored her by naming February 1 Phillis Wheatley Day.

Developing the Section

Identifying Propaganda. Write the word *propaganda* on the chalkboard. Then call on students to define the term or look it up in a dictionary. (*spreading ideas or beliefs to support or oppose a cause*) Tell students that the Patriots used the Boston Massacre as propaganda to turn colonists against Great Britain. Divide the class into small groups and have each group write news articles depicting the Boston Massacre and Crispus Attucks' death from the Patriots' point of view. Have each group read its news article to the class and discuss the techniques groups used to sway colonists' opinions. You might also enlarge the discussion by asking how the British might view the same events differently than the Patriots.

Review and Practice

Assign "Taking Another Look," p. 72.

Answer to Question in Caption (p. 71)

died in defense of liberty, became a rallying point for Patriots

Answers to Taking Another Look (p. 72)

1. Intolerable Acts, Boston Tea Party, Boston Massacre **2.** led colonists to defy British in Boston **3. Critical Thinking** **yes:** they were advancing the cause of liberty; **no:** they would not grant freedom to African Americans

Teaching Section 2: Fighting the War (pp. 72–75)

Objectives

- To evaluate an historical interpretation.
- To weigh the pros and cons of African Americans' fighting with the British in the Revolution.

Historical Sidelight

First Regiment of Rhode Island. During the Revolution, African Americans fought alongside white Americans rather than in separate units. The First Regiment of Rhode Island was an exception. When Rhode Island could not supply its quota of white soldiers in 1778, it promised African American slaves their freedom if they volunteered for duty. Some 95 slaves and 30 African American freedmen volunteered. The recruits saw their first fire at the Battle of Rhode Island where they turned back a murderous charge by Hessian soldiers. The regiment served for the entire war.

Developing the Section

1. Evaluating an Historical Interpretation. Refer students to the "Snapshot of the Times" on p. 73. Then read aloud the following statement by African American historian Benjamin Quarles:

> The Negro's role in the Revolution can best be understood by realizing that his major loyalty was not to a place nor to a people, but to a principle. . . . Whoever invoked the image of liberty . . . could count on a ready response from the blacks.

Ask if the events listed in the "Snapshot" tend to prove or disprove Quarles' statement. (*prove*) Why? (*African Americans joined both sides, hoping to win their freedom.*)

2. Weighing Pros and Cons. Have students imagine they are African American slaves who have just learned of the British offer of freedom. On the chalkboard draw a table with two columns, one labeled "Reasons for Joining the British" and the other "Reasons for Not Joining." Have the class as a whole fill in the table, discussing each reason and deciding with whom they would have fought.

Review and Practice

Assign "Taking Another Look," p. 74.

Answers to Taking Another Look (p. 74)

1. showed they could stand up to British troops **2.** feared that British offer of freedom would increase size of their army **3. Critical Thinking** African Americans fought in the Revolution; Americans valued liberty for themselves.

Teaching Section 3: Seeking Liberty (p. 75)

Objectives

- To develop historical empathy for the African Americans who left the United States with the British after the war.
- To discuss the economic reasons the North abolished slavery.

Historical Sidelight

The Colony of Cayenne. Impressed by African Americans' bravery during the Revolution, the Marquis de Lafayette urged George Washington in 1783 to join him in a plan to free African American slaves. "Let us unite in purchasing a small estate," said Lafayette, "where we may try the experiment to free the Negroes, and use them only as tenants. Such an example as yours might render [make] it a general practice." When Washington refused, Lafayette funded a small colony called Cayenne in French Guinea in 1784.

Developing the Section

1. Developing Historical Empathy. Have students in small groups write letters expressing how African Americans may have felt as they left the United States on British ships bound for other lands. Remind students to consider the possible hopes and fears of these former slaves.

2. Discussing an Issue. Discuss with students whether they think economic concerns rather than a concern for liberty led Northerners to free African American slaves.

Review and Practice

Assign "Taking Another Look," p. 75.

Answers to Taking Another Look (p. 75)

1. Some taken to Jamaica, England or Canada and

freed; others returned to owners or sold in West Indies. **2.** helped to end slavery in the North **3. Critical Thinking** kept them from joining British army; African Americans showed bravery.

Extending the Chapter

Designing Timelines. Divide the class into small groups, and assign each group to do research and then create a timeline of important dates for the period from 1768 to 1819. Encourage students to find additional events involving African Americans in such sources as *America in Time, Before the Mayflower,* or *The Negro in the American Revolution*. Post the completed timelines in the classroom for students to examine.

Looking Ahead

Have students read Washington's quotation in "Looking Ahead" on student text p. 75, and ask them to predict what they think will be the topic of the next chapter. (*whether slavery should be ended in the new nation*)

Answers to Close Up (p. 76–77)

The Who, What, Where of History

1. British troops **2.** first colonist killed by British **3.** acts passed by Britain to punish colonists **4.** Phillis Wheatley **5.** colonists who favored independence **6.** Patriots' dumping of tea into Boston Harbor as an act of defiance of British tax **7.** colonists ready to fight the British at a minute's notice **8.** Lexington and Concord, Massachusetts **9.** freedom **10.** colonial army **11.** African American soldier at Bunker Hill **12.** Vermont

Making the Connection

1. British passed Intolerable Acts because of Boston Tea Party **2.** Many African Americans who were inspired by the words of the Declaration of Independence, "All men are created equal", hoped to win freedom.

Time Check

1. 1770 **2.** Declaration of Independence **3.** 1777 **4.** British offer of freedom

What Would You Have Done?

1. Examples: belief in the cause of independence, hope for freedom afterwards **2. fought with the British:** because they offered freedom; **fought with the Patriots:** because they believed in cause of liberty

Thinking and Writing About History

1. Examples: What do you remember about your life in Africa? How did you feel about fighting for freedom while you were a slave? What did you do after you were freed? **2.** may describe intolerable features of slavery; may focus on hopes for the future as a free person

Building Skills

1. The American Revolution: Liberty for All? **2.** Revolution did not bring liberty to all African American slaves. Though there were 60,000 free African Americans by 1790, 700,000 were still enslaved in 1800. **3.** From Protest to War; Fighting the War; Seeking Liberty **4. a.** Sec. 3; **b.** Sec. 1; **c.** Sec. 2 **5. Sec. 1:** Events such as Boston Massacre, Boston Tea Party, and enactment of harsh laws led colonists to stand together against Great Britain. **Sec. 2:** Many were Patriots, many played key roles in battle victories. **Sec. 3:** After the Revolution, British helped nearly 20,000 African Americans to leave the U.S. By 1804, all northern states had passed laws to end slavery; slavery still existed in the South and not all African American Patriots were freed.

Chapter 8 Forging a New Constitution (pp. 78–83)

Overview

After the Revolution, free African Americans soon experienced limits on their liberty. In Northern cities, where most free African Americans lived, they encountered prejudice. In 1787, Richard Allen and Absalom Jones founded the Free African Society in Philadelphia to improve the lives of African Americans. That same year, however, white delegates to the Constitutional Convention made slavery part of the law of the land. The recognition of slavery ensured Southern support of the new government, but it cost hundreds of thousands of African Americans their freedom for almost another century.

Resources

Chapter 8 Activity Sheet: Interpreting a Chart (p. 206)
Chapter 8 Test (p. 140)
Outline Map: Eastern North America (p. 307)

Focus Activity

Assign students the chapter introduction on text p. 78–79. Direct student attention to Banneker's letter to Jefferson. Ask what inconsistencies Banneker points out to Jefferson. (*Jefferson fought a war for independence and yet still allowed slavery to exist within the new nation; Jefferson wrote the words "all men are created equal" yet accepted the unequal treatment of African Americans and was himself a slave owner.*)

Next, ask students how Banneker's life disproved racist arguments in support of slavery. Read aloud the following passage from a letter that accompanied Banneker's 1792 Almanac. Written by James McHenry, former Maryland state senator and delegate to the Constitutional Convention, it says in part, "I consider this Negro as a fresh proof that the powers of the mind are disconnected with the color of the skin."

Teaching Section 1: African Americans Organize (pp. 79–80)

Objective

- To use a poem to appreciate African American courage demonstrated during the yellow fever epidemic of 1793.

Historical Sidelight

Free African Schools. In 1787, African Americans in New York City opened the first Free African School. The school received aid from the city and state, thus becoming a forerunner of New York's public school system. The New York example inspired Prince Hall in 1787 to petition the Massachusetts legislature to provide equal schools for African Americans. The legislature turned down his request but, in 1789, African American parents in Boston opened a school in Hall's home. In Philadelphia, Richard Allen opened a similar school. These two schools trained many of the leaders of the abolition movement.

Developing the Section

Analyzing a Poem. To help students evaluate African American courage demonstrated during the yellow fever epidemic in Philadelphia, read the following description of the epidemic by poet Philip Freneau aloud:

> Hot, dry winds forever blowing,
> Dead men to the grave-yards going:
> Constant hearses,
> Funeral verses;
> Oh! What plague there is no knowing!

Ask what images Freneau uses to describe the effects of the epidemic. (*"dead men to the grave-yards going," "constant hearses," "funeral verses"*) Why might white Philadelphians have been surprised by the willingness of free African Americans to fight the plague? (*Through discussion, encourage students to review the examples of prejudice cited in the text.*)

Review and Practice

Assign "Taking Another Look," p. 80.

Answers to Taking Another Look (p. 80)

1. to promote self-help **2.** to work for freedom; to educate African Americans; to help the sick, widows, fatherless children **3. Critical Thinking** would have supported the letter, or maybe even co-signed it

Teaching Section 2: Compromises Over Slavery (pp. 80–81)

Objectives

- To write letters expressing African American hopes for a new plan of government.
- To use historical imagination to speculate how the history of African Americans might have been different if Britain had won the Revolutionary War.

Historical Sidelight

"A Man Ahead of His Times." In 1791, Robert Carter III, one of the wealthiest men in Virginia, stunned his neighbors by filing a deed to free some 500 of his slaves. He set up a schedule that emancipated 15 slaves each year for 21 years. Carter's descendants tried to overturn the deed, but failed. In 1991, the African American governor of Virginia, L. Douglas Wilder, issued a proclamation honoring Carter's accomplishment.

Developing the Section

1. Understanding Point of View. Have students read the first paragraph in the section. Then divide the class into 13 groups, one for each state in the Union in 1787. Tell each group to write a letter that African Americans might have sent to delegates to the Constitutional Convention. Remind students of the large number of enslaved peoples in Southern states. Have volunteers read their letters aloud and construct a master list of demands on the chalkboard.

2. Developing Historical Imagination. Have students read the "Focus On" feature, student text p. 82. Ask how the history of African Americans might have been different if the United States had lost the Revolutionary War.

Review and Practice

Assign "Taking Another Look," p. 81.

Answers to Taking Another Look (p. 81)

1. allowed slavery and slave trade to continue; counted each slave as three-fifths of a person **2.** wanted to ensure support from Southern states **3. Critical Thinking** **yes:** there had to be a solid union; **no:** slavery should not have been allowed to continue

Extending the Chapter

Reenacting History. Divide the class into three groups. Have one group do research about the emotional debates over slavery at the Constitutional Convention. One source they might use is *Miracle at Philadelphia* by Catherine Drinker Bowen. The group should report on its findings in either a report or a skit recreating the debates. The second group should write a petition to Congress asking for changes in the new federal Constitution. The petition should be based on research about the continuance of slavery in the United States and the lack of other rights for African Americans under the new government. The third group, representing women, Native Americans, and other disfranchised Americans (men lacking certain property qualifications) should do research and then write a petition listing the rights they expect under the Constitution.

Looking Ahead

Assign "Looking Ahead," student text p. 81. Ask what economic developments in the United States in the late 1700s and early 1800s might have caused the debate over slavery to heat up. Why?

Answers to Close Up (pp. 82–83)

The Who, What, Where of History

1. African American who wrote an almanac, criticized Jefferson's stand on slavery, helped survey Washington, D.C. **2.** African American self-help organization **3.** book of weather forecasts and astronomical information **4. and 5.** founders of Free African Society **6.** end of slavery **7.** meeting at which delegates wrote the U.S. Constitution **8.** Philadelphia **9.** system dividing power between national and state governments **10.** first new U.S. territory; includes present-day Ohio, Indiana, Illinois, Michigan, Wisconsin, and part of Minnesota

Making the Connection

1. Free African Society helped plague victims impressing many whites and inspiring them to join the abolition movement. **2.** Delegates compromised on slavery to gain votes for Constitution. **3.** Northwest Ordinance banned slavery in Northwest Territory.

Thinking and Writing About History

1. Advertisements should mention the benefits of working to help one another. **2.** Letters should show an understanding of the disappointment felt at the failure of the Constitution to abolish slavery.

Time Check

1. the adoption of the Articles of Confederation **2.** 1789

What Would You Have Done?

1. yes: consistent with ideal of liberty for all; **no:** danger of losing Southern support **2.** Slavery was illegal in both places; Philadelphia offered opportunities and pleasures of a large city; Northwest Territory offered opportunities of open land and natural resources.

Building Skills

1. first sentence **2.** third sentence

Chapter 9 Expanding the Nation (pp. 84–91)

Overview

A slave revolution in Haiti helped change the course of U.S. history. Led by Toussaint L'Ouverture, the rebels showed that Africans could successfully challenge a European power such as France. The loss of Haiti convinced Napoleon to sell the entire Louisiana Territory to the United States. With this purchase, a vast territory was opened to settlement by whites and to the possible expansion of slavery.

The United States was also expanding southward. The acquisition of Florida is not often attributed in textbooks to the desire of Southern slave owners to destroy the safe haven for runaways among Seminoles in Florida, but this was a major reason for the purchase.

The chapter also discusses the contributions of Jean Baptiste Point Du Sable, and his Native American wife Catherine, to the founding of Chicago, of the African American slave York to the Lewis and Clark expedition, and of Mountain Men like African American James Beckwourth.

Resources

Chapter 9 Activity Sheet: Explaining a Map (pp. 207–208)

Chapter 9 Test (p. 141)
Outline Map: The United States (p. 308)
Unit 3 Writing Workshop: Writing About Geography (pp. 270–73)
Unit 3 Test (pp. 136–38)

Focus Activity

Read the following prediction made by a Northern delegate to the Constitutional Convention: "Slavery will be but a speck in our country." Point out that the delegate was referring to the effect that he thought the Northwest Ordinance would have. Refer students to the map on text p. 85. Ask if students think Southern states would be willing to accept a ban on slavery in these lands. (*probably not*) Why or why not? (*Southerners could easily expand into lands along their western borders; unlike the Northwest Territory, the southern location of some of the lands offered a climate suitable for growing crops such as tobacco or cotton.*)

Teaching Section 1: Increasing the Nation's Size (pp. 85–86)

Objective

- To analyze a primary source opinion of Toussaint L'Ouverture.

Historical Sidelight

The Bravest. A Flathead explained how his people viewed York: "Those brave and fearless, the victorious ones in battle, painted themselves in charcoal. So the black man, they thought, had been the bravest in the party." After the expedition ended, York returned home with Clark. Legend says he later went to live with Native Americans, but most historians agree that York settled with a wife in Kentucky. There he ran a wagon service between Nashville, Tennessee, and Richmond, Virginia, until his death.

Developing the Section

Analyzing a Quote. Read aloud the following remark made by an observer in the late 1800s:

> [A]ll of Indian Territory, all of Kansas and Nebraska, Iowa and Wyoming, Montana and the Dakotas, and most of Colorado and Minnesota, and all of Washington and Oregon states, came to us as the indirect work of a despised Negro. Praise, if you will, the work of Robert Livingston [minister who arranged the sale] or a Jefferson, but today let us not forget our debt to Toussaint L'Ouverture, who was indirectly the means of America's expansion by the Louisiana Purchase of 1803.

Based on information in the text, ask students why the speaker might have credited the purchase to Toussaint. (*The Haitian revolt led Napoleon to sell the territory.*) What was the long-range result of the sale? (*U.S. expansion*) Then focus on the words "despised Negro." Ask why white Americans in the 1800s might have seen Toussaint in this way. (*Some students may cite racism, while others may mention fears that the example of Toussaint would inspire African Americans to rebel.*)

Review and Practice

Assign "Taking Another Look," p. 86.

Answers to Question in Caption (p. 85)

Montana, Nebraska, Iowa, Kansas, Missouri, Oklahoma, Arkansas; parts of North Dakota, South Dakota, Wyoming, Minnesota, Colorado, New Mexico, Texas, Louisiana

Answers to Taking Another Look (p. 86)

1. worn out by revolt in Haiti, gave up the idea of a North American empire **2. a.** Lands west of the Mississippi became known to inhabitants of the east; opened Louisiana Territory to settlement. **b.** provided food; traded with Native Americans for supplies **3. Critical Thinking** might have made owners treat African American slaves better because they feared similar revolt

Teaching Section 2: Securing Independence (pp. 87–88)

Objectives

- To evaluate a primary source recruiting African American volunteers into the War of 1812.
- To write news stories on key topics in the War of 1812 and the steps leading to U.S acquisition of Florida.

Historical Sidelight

A Veteran Returns to Arms. In 1775, William Flora braved British fire to defend a bridge over the Elizabeth River in Virginia. The rest of the Virginia militia retreated, while Flora stood his ground. He eventually pulled back, but not before removing a huge plank from the bridge. Flora's bravery earned him his freedom, and he later bought the freedom of his wife and children. When Virginia recruited soldiers for the War of 1812, a gray-haired Billy Flora presented himself for duty.

Developing the Section

Writing a News Story. Divide the class into six groups. Assign each group one of the following topics to write a news story about: African

American sailors in the War of 1812, African American soldiers at the Battle of New Orleans, flight of African American slaves into Florida, start of the Seminole Wars, United States purchase of Florida. Suggest that students write an attention-getting headline for their articles and use a "hook," or an interesting opening sentence, to make readers want to read on. Have volunteers from each group read the group's news story to the class.

Review and Practice

Assign "Taking Another Look," p. 88.

Answers to Taking Another Look (p. 88)

1. Battle of Lake Erie, Battle of New Orleans, fortifying Philadelphia against the British **2.** could be free there **3. Critical Thinking** Seminoles sympathized with African American slaves.

Teaching Section 3: Looking Westward (p. 89)

Objective

- To recognize historical prejudice in past presentations of Beckwourth.

Historical Sidelight

Beckwourth's "Fame". In 1855, journalist T.D. Bonner interviewed James Beckwourth in San Francisco and the next year published a biography about him. It never mentioned Beckwourth's African ancestors, and sketches in the book made Beckwourth appear white. Nearly a century later, Hollywood repeated the error. In the 1951 movie *Tomahawk,* a white actor played the role of Beckwourth.

Developing the Section

Recognizing Prejudice. Read aloud the "Historical Sidelight" about Beckwourth. Ask students how prejudice and/or ignorance among some white Americans affected the treatment of Beckwourth's role in history. (*led Bonner and Hollywood producers to attribute Beckwourth's accomplishments to a white.*) How does an accurate presentation of Beckwourth help reduce prejudice? Lead students to understand the importance of showing that people of many groups have helped shape our nation's history.

Review and Practice

Assign "Taking Another Look," p. 89.

Answers to Taking Another Look (p. 89)

1. The Beckwourth Pass is named for him. **2. Critical Thinking** It was a life of great freedom—and adventure.

Extending the Chapter

Interviewing the Explorers. Divide the class into panel members and newspaper reporters. Panel members should assume the roles of Jean Baptiste Point Du Sable, Catherine Du Sable, Thomas Jefferson, York, William Clark, Sacajawea, and James Beckwourth. Each panel member should do research about his or her character in order to be able to answer questions. Divide the rest of the class into seven groups and assign each group to do research and write questions to ask one panel member.

Looking Ahead

Have students read "Looking Ahead," student text p. 89. Ask what predictions they might make about the effect of the Louisiana Purchase on the slave trade in the United States.

Answers to Close Up (pp. 90–91)

The Who, What, Where, of History

1. Jean Baptiste Point du Sable **2.** leader of slave revolt in Haiti **3.** 1803 U.S. purchase of Louisiana Territory from France **4.** accompanied Lewis and Clark **5.** Battle of New Orleans **6.** Florida **7.** take over **8.** African Americans who lived with Seminoles **9.** fur trappers and explorers

Making the Connection

1. When his troops in Haiti were unable to defeat revolutionaries, Napoleon gave up plan for a great empire in North America and sold Louisiana Territory. **2.** runaway slaves fled to Florida, receive-help from Seminoles; slave owners demanded government action; U.S. fought Seminoles and African Americans in Florida, risking war with Spain; bought Florida from Spain

Time Check

1. purchase of Florida **2.** 1815

What Would You Have Done?

1. Responses should show understanding of the rigors and uncertainties of the expedition. **2. yes:** want to fight for liberty and defeat British; **no:** shouldn't have to fight for liberty for others

Thinking and Writing About History

1. Du Sable was born in Haiti, educated in France, a sea captain, started a trading post on the site of Chicago, etc. **2. pros:** freedom, excitement, chance to make important discoveries; **cons:** danger, unknown areas, loneliness

Building Skills

2, 4

UNIT 4 Free and Enslaved (pp. 92–127)

UNIT THEME

Africans, and their descendants, forge a culture that allows them to endure—and even defy—a system designed to strip them of their basic dignity and rights as human beings.

UNIT CONCEPTS

- African Americans resisted slavery by creating a culture that reflected their African origins.
- Enslaved African Americans relied upon the extended family and their religious beliefs to provide comfort.
- The South—the Cotton Kingdom—grew wealthy from African American slave labor.
- Enslaved African Americans used a variety of methods including rebellions to resist slavery.
- Although few in number, free African Americans disproved the arguments in favor of slavery.

UNIT OVERVIEW

Unit 4 recounts the story of a culture that survived all efforts to destroy it. The unit tells of African American slaves who found dignity in their African past and it depicts the spiritual comfort found by African Americans—both enslaved and free—within their families, churches, and the African American community. *The Big Picture* and the three chapters in this unit describe: (1) the culture forged by slaves in the Cotton Kingdom, (2) the rebellions by African Americans who sought to tear down the slave system by force, and (3) the free African Americans whose day-to-day lives and accomplishments undermined the racist arguments used to justify slavery.

In teaching this unit, you might point out to students that the first generation of enslaved Africans dreamed of returning to their homeland. By the 1700s and 1800s, however, the descendants of Africans knew freedom lay only in death or in an end to the system of slavery itself. Some African American slaves tried to end the system through armed rebellion, but it proved impossible against a white majority. Other African Americans resisted bondage by maintaining African culture traits and by melding these into a new cultural heritage. Discuss with students how preservation of a culture can be a form of protest. To start student discussion, remind them that enslaved Africans often secretly gave African names to their children. These names sometimes were passed down from generation to generation. In Unit 10 students will read about modern use of such names.

COOPERATIVE LEARNING ACTIVITY

The following cooperative learning activity can be used for alternative assessment after study of the unit has been completed.

At the end of the unit, review the material in "African Americans in the Cotton Kingdom" on text pp. 102–107. Then divide the class into groups of about 4 to 5 students each. Have each group prepare a presentation describing the culture that Africans and African Americans developed under slavery. Encourage students to use both pictures and written materials to present their research. Among the items they might present are spirituals and folktales. In evaluating group presentations, consider the accuracy of the material and the evidence of research beyond the assigned reading.

Unit 4 THE BIG PICTURE (pp. 93–97)

Theme

The economic and physical growth of the United States produced conditions that locked the institution of slavery more firmly in place.

Overview

The Big Picture highlights two key themes in U.S. history during the early 1800s—expansion and sectionalism. The nation was moving westward beyond the Mississippi, and improved systems of transportation and communication sped the movement of people, goods, and ideas, thus spurring economic growth. Farm goods from the Midwest and manufactured goods from the Northeast flowed back and forth by canal and railroad.

Two developments of the time had particular impact on the lives of African Americans. The invention of the cotton gin helped the South produce huge supplies of raw cotton, while development of the factory system allowed the North to turn much of that cotton into cloth.

Despite this growth, sectional differences were at work that would, in time, tear the nation apart. The factory towns of New England were growing into industrial cities as immigrants from Europe, especially Ireland, provided the labor to run the machines. Many German immigrants, on the other hand, moved to the Midwest to farm. Few immigrants headed into the South where slaves dominated the labor force and the economy was still firmly based on agriculture. As cotton became the major crop in the South, the region increasingly grew apart from the rest of the nation, which barred slavery, and Southerners became increasingly defensive of the "peculiar institution."

Objectives

- To recognize the achievements of African Americans in spite of their enslavement.
- To write a letter assessing the state of the nation at the start of the 1800s.
- To design posters showing improvements in transportation and communication.
- To draw illustrated economic maps of the nation in the mid-1800s.
- To analyze mathematically the size of the slaveholding population of the South.

Introducing *The Big Picture*

Call on a volunteer to read "An African American Speaks" on text p. 93 aloud. Discuss what Ellison means when he refers to African Americans' experiences as one of the great triumphs of the human spirit. Ask for evidence that will support students' opinions.

Using the Timeline

Divide the class into small groups, and have each group select a different event on the timeline. Make sure that each group's choice is different. Have each group explain how the event it selected might have affected lives of African Americans in the early to mid-1800s.

Teaching *The Big Picture*

1. Writing a Speech. After students have read "From Colonies to Nation" and "The United States in 1800" (p. 93), tell them to imagine they are President-elect Thomas Jefferson, who was a prolific letter writer. Have them imagine they are Jefferson writing to a friend in 1801 just before Jefferson takes office. Students should assess both past accomplishments of the nation and challenges ahead. Review Jefferson's thoughts on slavery in Unit 3.

2. Designing Posters. Assign the sections "Improved Transportation" and "Improved Communication" on pp. 93–94. Then divide the class into small groups, and direct each group to design a poster advertising one of the following: a steamboat company on the Mississippi, a barge service on the Erie Canal, a railroad line running from Detroit to Chicago, a telegraph company offering service from Washington, D.C. to Richmond, Virginia. As a wrap-up activity, ask students which business activities probably used the labor of African American slaves and which others may have benefited from such labor.

3. Drawing an Illustrated Map. Assign the sections from "The Growth of Factories in the Northeast" up to and including "The Internal Slave Trade" on text pp. 94–96. Based on information in these sections, have students, working individually or in small groups, draw an illustrated economic map of the United States in the mid-1800s. (Use the outline map on p. 308 of this manual as the base map.) Students might begin by designing a key to explain the various pictures or symbols they will use on the map. For example, a cotton boll might stand for cotton and a person for slave labor, a smokestack might stand for factories, a plough for farming, and so on.

4. Mathematics and History. Have students read "Southern Slave Owners" on text p. 97. Then work with them to analyze the figures in the section. Ask them what percentage of whites owned slaves. (*8 million divided by 385,000 = .04*) How many slave owners had more than 20 slaves? (*385,000 x .12 = 46,200*) What percentage of all slave owners owned more than a hundred slaves? (*3,000 divided by 385,000 = .008%*) Encourage speculation on why Southerners as a whole supported slavery when the number of slave owners was so small.

Review and Practice

Assign "Taking Another Look," p. 97.

Answer to Question in Caption (p. 96)

By allowing the rapid cleaning of large quantities of cotton, the gin encouraged cotton production.

Answers to Taking Another Look (p. 97)

1. transportation easier due to steamboats, better roads, canals, railroads **2. a.** corn, wheat **b.** cotton **c.** Midwest—family run; South—slave labor **3.** cotton gin allowed farmers to grow larger crops, increased demand for slaves to work land **4. Critical Thinking** South became dependent on income from cotton production; factories might have varied the South's economic base, but with cotton alone there was no potential for continued economic growth.

Chapter 10 The Tyranny of Slavery (pp. 98–109)

Overview

Slave traders and slave owners tried to strip Africans of their identities. They robbed them of their names, kept them in strange quarters, fed them strange foods, and forced new religions on them. But the resolve of enslaved Africans proved strong. They secretly used their African names and, in the privacy of slave quarters, they turned to activities that reminded them of their homeland. Over time, their captors picked up bits and pieces of this culture—a word here and there, a dance, a food—and without knowing it, were touched by the people they sought to dominate. Later generations of African Americans showed the same toughness of spirit. Gathering strength from their extended families and their religious beliefs, they clung to dreams of liberty.

Resources

Chapter 10 Activity Sheet: Interpreting a Map (pp. 209–210)
Chapter 10 Test (p. 145)
Outline Map: Eastern United States (p. 307)
Lesson Plans for *The Artist's View* (p. 109)

Focus Activity

Refer students to the "Snapshot of the Times" on p. 100. Then review the definition of cause and effect. (*A cause is an event that makes something happen; it answers the question "why." An effect is the outcome or result of an event.*) Ask what event in the "Snapshot" explains why so many slaves worked in cotton fields by 1860. (*invention of the cotton gin*) What was one of the effects of the Congressional ban on slavery? (*a boom in the internal slave trade*) Based on the "Snapshot," what causes can students offer for the kidnapping of Solomon? (*Congressional ban on the African slave trade and a booming internal slave trade made it profitable to sell African Americans—free or enslaved.*)

Teaching Section 1: The Early Years of Slavery (pp. 99–102)

Objective

- To use evidence from pictures to form hypotheses about slave life.

Historical Sidelight

Gullah. Africans along the Georgia–South Carolina coast developed their own dialect known as Gullah. To whites it sounded like gibberish, but to the speakers of Gullah it was a way of keeping whites out of their world. They gave African pronunciations to many English words, and put English words together to form equivalents of African expressions: "sweet mouth" for flatter, "day clean" for dawn, and "a-beat-on the iron" for mechanic. Gullah also included some 4,000 words from more than 20 West African languages. As late as the 1940s, African Americans on the Carolina Sea Islands used Gullah as their primary language.

Developing the Section

Using Pictorial Evidence. Refer students to the pictures on pp. 98 and 101. Then read aloud the section-opening question: What was life like for enslaved Africans from 1619 to the early 1800s? Ask students to respond to this question based on the two photos. Record their responses on the chalkboard. Modify the list as students work their way through the section.

Review and Practice

Assign "Taking Another Look," p. 102.

Answers to Taking Another Look (p. 102)

1. songs, crafts, dances, foods, words **2.** dancing, singing, family life, religion **3. Critical Thinking** viewed themselves as Israelites, suffering persecution to be freed by benevolent God

Teaching Section 2: African Americans in the Cotton Kingdom (pp. 102–107)

Objective

• To organize self-teaching lessons on the life of African American slaves in the Cotton Kingdom.

Historical Sidelight

Tarkars. The African slave trade continued illegally long after Congress officially ended the practice in 1808. The last slave ship landed in the United States in 1859. The 116 Africans aboard the *Clotide* became known as "Tarkars," because of the name given to the language they spoke. When interviewers spoke to the nine survivors of the *Clotide* in 1913, they still spoke fluent Tarkar.

Developing the Section

Self-Teaching. Divide the class into groups of 4 to 5 students, and assign each group one or more of the subsections in this section. Tell each group to organize a short lesson in which they teach the rest of the class about information in the subsection(s). Advise students to make full use of any graphics in the section that they might use to illustrate this lesson. Each group should make up questions for a student-generated section test.

Review and Practice

Assign "Taking Another Look," p. 107.

Answers to Questions in Captions (pp. 103–104)

(p. 103) S.C., Va., Miss.; (p. 104, top) numbers are large but would include plantation owners, factory owners, factory workers, people who wore cotton goods, etc.; (p. 104, bottom) 1820

Answers to Taking Another Look (p. 107)

1. Paragraphs should mention long work hours, little break or food and severe punishment. **2.** reliance on extended family, strengthened religion **3. Critical Thinking** Owners may have thought slaves were plotting rebellion and escape.

Extending the Chapter

Researching Primary Sources. Divide the class into groups of 2 or 3 students each. Then direct each team to find at least one eyewitness account of life under slavery written by a former African American slave. Direct students to prepare short presentations entitled "In Their Own Words." One student from each group should serve as the narrator, setting the stage for each reading. The other student(s) should give a dramatic reading of the account(s). After each group's presentation, ask the class to explain what they have learned about slavery from the reading(s).

Looking Ahead

After they have read "Looking Ahead," p. 107, ask students to explain what they think the last sentence means: "The Cotton Kingdom contained within itself the seeds of its own destruction, and its end loomed on the horizon."

Answers to Close Up (pp. 108–109)

The Who, What, Where of History

1. African American slave, escaped and wrote autobiography **2.** forms of language particular to group or region **3.** places where slaves lived **4.** free African American, kidnapped and sold as slave, later wrote autobiography **5.** whites who supervised slaves' field work **6.** secret religious services held by African American slaves in woods **7.** overseers' assistants, often African American slaves **8.** band of cotton-growing states from Georgia to Texas **9.** defiant/religious songs composed and sung by African American slaves

Making the Connection

1. To resist owners, African American slaves developed pronunciations and sayings that had secret meanings. **2.** When the African slave trade closed and the Cotton Kingdom rose, slavery became big business and slave families were broken apart by sales. African American slaves relied on extended families for support. All slaves helped care for children because parents could be sold. **3.** Slaves saw themselves as Israelites, enslaved by wicked masters.

Time Check

1. invention of cotton gin **2.** 1808

What Would You Have Done?

1. could earn more for owner as craftsperson than fieldhand; owner could rent out skilled worker **2.** may describe horror of plantation conditions and rage at loss of freedom

Thinking and Writing About History

1. Examples: selling of family members, physical punishment, no pay for labor, long hours in fields, any cruelty mentioned in text **2.** Suggest to students that they look for African American folktales and spirituals in the library before beginning to write their own. **3.** Preacher would not want to address the difficult question of African American enslavement.

Building Skills

1. Slave owners did not want to lose money by spending any more than they had to to meet basic needs of slaves, so they kept them as cheaply as they possibly could. **2.** African slaves did many things that helped them remember better times in Africa.

Chapter 11 Armed Resistance to Slavery (pp. 110–19)

Overview

Enslaved Africans had resisted their bondage from the earliest days of the slave trade. Some planned rebellions aboard slave ships; others took their own lives rather than submit to their captors. Once in the Americas, thousands of enslaved Africans fled to live among Native Americans. Southern Colonies passed tough slave codes to control African Americans, but the laws did not stop them from taking up arms against their oppressors. From New England to the Carolinas, individual African Americans—enslaved and free—planned for their freedom. Southerners tried to crush even the desire for freedom with brutality, but even guns, whips, and branding irons could not stop the growing resistance among African American slaves.

Resources

Chapter 11 Activity Sheet: Recognizing Cause and Effect (p. 211)
Chapter 11 Test (p. 146)
Outline Map: Eastern United States (p. 307)

Focus Activity

Assign students the chapter-opening story on pp. 110–11. Ask them to whom Walker addressed his appeal. (*to both enslaved African Americans and the whites who held them in bondage*) What advice did he offer to each group? (*slaves: to fight if necessary; whites: to free African Americans in good will or face violence*)

Teaching Section 1: Early Slave Rebellions (pp. 111–13)

Objective

• To create a list of arguments to refute a slave owner's description of slave life.

Historical Sidelight

The Great Negro Plot. During New York City's "Great Negro Plot" of 1741, authorities used bribery and torture to force confessions. Between May 11 and August 29, more than 30 people went to their death, including several whites who helped the African Americans. To this day, historians debate whether a plot actually existed. The incident confirmed the belief among white colonists that African slaves would go to any length to rebel.

Developing the Section

Organizing Arguments. Write the following remark by a Virginia slave owner on the chalkboard: "A merrier being does not exist on the face of the globe, than the Negro slave of the United States." Then divide the class into groups of 4 to 5 students each. Have each group organize a list of arguments to refute this point. Encourage students to skim earlier chapters for additional facts. Have the groups read their lists aloud and discuss each point.

Review and Practice

Assign "Taking Another Look," p. 113.

Answers to Questions in Captions (p. 111–12)

(p. 111) Slave discontent was not confined to South; slaves in the North may have been less tightly controlled; (p. 112) Runaway slaves built a fort in Florida for their protection. This inspired other African slaves to revolt and join them.

Answers to Taking Another Look (p. 113)

1. New York City; Hartford, Connecticut; Gloucester County, Virginia; Long Island, New York; Stono River, Charleston, S.C. **2.** passed slave codes **3. Critical Thinking** They wanted to limit access to antislavery writings, and limit communication among slaves.

Teaching Section 2: The Prosser Conspiracy (pp. 113–14)

Objective

• To appreciate the difficulty enslaved African Americans faced in considering whether to join a bid for freedom.

Historical Sidelight

Slave Mutiny. A famous African mutiny took place in 1839. In that year, a group of enslaved Africans seized the *Armistad* and killed their captors. As they headed back to Africa, a U.S. naval vessel intercepted them. Abolitionists hired former President John Quincy Adams to defend the Africans. Adams won the case, and the Africans returned to their homeland in victory.

Developing the Section

Weighing Pros and Cons. Divide the class into cooperative learning groups. Tell students to imagine that they are Henrico County slaves who have just learned of plans for a slave rebellion. On a sheet of paper, have each group list the pros and cons of joining the rebellion. Direct each group, using its list, to reach a consensus on whether to join the rebellion. Call on a member from each group to report reasons for the decision. Allow dissenting members time to present their opinions to the class.

Review and Practice

Assign "Taking Another Look," p. 114.

Answers to Questions in Captions (p. 114)

6; 5

Answers to Taking Another Look (p. 114)

1. an African American state in Richmond, Va. **2.** Bible, identification with Israelites **3. Critical Thinking** viewed himself as fighter for liberty

Teaching Section 3: The Vesey Conspiracy (pp. 114–15)

Objective

- To use a map to draw conclusions about the effectiveness of slave codes in crushing the spirit of freedom.

Historical Sidelight

Shelter in Mexico. In the 1800s, word of a safe haven in Mexico reached some enslaved African Americans in the Cotton Belt. In 1824, Mexico had abolished slavery. In 1857, it included an antislavery clause in its constitution. Mexican authorities offered runaway slaves guns and land in border states such as Tamaulipas and Coahuila. The Mexicans also threw open their doors to hundreds of Seminoles forcibly removed from Florida.

Developing the Section

Working with a Map. Refer students to the map on p. 114. Ask them where the Vesey Conspiracy was uncovered. (*South Carolina*) What other rebellion had already taken place there? (*Stono Uprising*) When did the Vesey Conspiracy take place? (*1800*) When did the Stono Uprising take place? (*1739*) What conclusion can the students reach about the effectiveness of slave laws passed after the Stono Uprising? (*They failed to crush the desire for freedom among African Americans.*) Next, tell students that in 1800 African Americans in South Carolina far outnumbered whites. Have them speculate on actions white Carolinians might have taken when they discovered the Vesey Conspiracy.

Review and Practice

Assign "Taking Another Look," p. 115.

Answers to Taking Another Look (p. 115)

1. both sought to overthrow state capitals **2.** the legislature limited rights of free African Americans **3. Critical Thinking** would not have been effective, private discussions would continue

Teaching Section 4: "Old Nat's War" (pp. 115-117)

Objective

- To interpret a slave song about Nat Turner and the fate of slavery.

Developing the Section

Interpreting a Song. Read aloud or duplicate and distribute copies of the following:

You mought [might] be rich as cream
And drive you coach and four-horse team.
But you can't keep de world from moverin' round
Nor Nat Turner from gainin ground.
And your name it mought be Caesar sure.
And got you cannon can shoot a mile or more,
But you can't keep de world from moverin' round
Nor Nat Turner from gainin ground.

Ask students how the song depicts Turner. (*as a hero*) What does the song say about the power of slave owners? (*Despite their wealth and power, they cannot stop the world from changing; they cannot stop an African American rebel such as Turner "from gaining ground."*) Ask students what the existence of a song like this indicates. (*that Turner had become a figure of hope after his death and that African American slaves still had a desire for freedom even if it meant violence*)

Review and Practice

Assign "Taking Another Look," p. 117.

Answer to Question in Caption (p. 116)
The revolt upset their view that African American slaves were happy and caused fear that other slaves would revolt.

Answers to Taking Another Look (p. 117)
1. mission from God, no elaborate plan or large numbers **2.** strengthened slave codes heightened enforcement **3. Critical Thinking** showed whites that slaves hated their enslavement; showed that African Americans could organize

Extending the Chapter
Writing a Newsletter. Divide the class into groups, and assign each group one of the sections in this chapter. Have each group design and write a front-page for a newspaper based on the section. Tell students to include at least one of each of the following on their front-page: a hard-news story telling a straight-forward account of events, a feature article giving a human interest or anecedotal side to events, an editorial expressing an opinion on an event, a political cartoon also expressing an opinion on an event, and an obituary for one of the rebels mentioned in the section. After students have completed their spreads, post them for display.

Looking Ahead
Encourage students to speculate on why free African Americans might have posed the biggest threat to the slave system. Lead them to understand that the daily lives and accomplishments of free African Americans sent a powerful message to the world.

Answers to Close Up (pp. 118–19)

The Who, What, Where of History
1. former slave, wrote *Appeal* **2.** first African American newspaper **3.** laws limiting slaves' rights **4.** New York City **5.** slave rebellion near Stono River, Charleston, South Carolina **6.** planner of rebellion in Henrico County, Virginia, 1800 **7.** New Orleans **8.** planner of rebellion in Charleston, S.C., 1832 **9.** leader of rebellion in Southampton County, Virginia, 1832

Making the Connection
1. codes passed after revolts as an attempt at prevention **2.** King offered fugitives freedom in Spanish Florida; provided arms **3.** L'Ouverture's uprising inspired Prosser's rebellion.

Time Check
1. Nat Turner's rebellion **2.** 1658 **3.** 1829

What Would You Have Done?
1. carry Appeal: oppose slavery, believe in free speech; **ban Appeal:** believe in slavery, fear for own safety **2. Examples:** refuse to try case on personal grounds; follow law strictly in sentencing slave; sentence slave to prison, but not to death **3.** might express horror over deaths, but support Turner's cause; might condemn both cause and use of force

Thinking and Writing About History
1. Provide students with some short book reviews to look at for format and style. **2.** paper would condemn rebellion; probably advocate stricter slave codes **3.** might mention that rebellion frightened whites, showed that uprisings were possible, encouraged slaves to fight **4.** might inspire further action with better planning; might discourage further action due to basic failure of attempt and loss of lives

Building Skills:
Sec. 1: Early Slave Rebellions; Where did slave rebellions take place in the late 1600s and 1700s? New York City; Hartford, Conn; Gloucester Cty. Va; Long Island, N.Y.; Stono River, S.C. **Sec. 2:** The Prosser Conspiracy; What was Gabriel Prosser's daring plan? Gabriel Prosser planned a slave uprising to create an African American state in Virginia. **Sec. 3:** The Vesey Conspiracy; How did the Vesy conspiracy further prove African Americans' willingness to resist slavery? Vesey planned to take over Charleston in 1832, but he was betrayed by an informer. **Sec. 4:** "Old Nat's War"; Why was it said that no Southerner before the Civil War could ever forget Nat Turner? Nat Turner's rebellion panicked white Southerners and inspired African American slaves.

Chapter 12 Free African Americans in the North and South (pp. 120–27)

Overview
Living in the shadow of slavery, free African Americans faced discrimination and legal limits on their liberty. In the North, free African Americans also encountered economic competition from a flood of immigrants who not only worked cheaply but were white. Hiring of unskilled white immigrants over skilled African Americans made the deep-rooted prejudice of white society clear. Some African Americans supported a colonization move-

ment to Africa. But the bulk of African Americans refused to leave their homeland—or their enslaved brothers and sisters. Instead, a growing number of free African Americans began to raise their voices in angry protest against slavery.

Resources

Chapter 12 Activity Sheet: Making Inferences (pp. 212–13)
Chapter 12 Test (p. 147)
Unit 4 Test (p. 142)
Unit 4 Writing Workshop: A Letter to Persuade (pp. 274–77)

Focus Activity

Assign the chapter-opening story on pp. 120–21. Ask students what Prince's experiences abroad revealed to her. (*the extent of prejudice in the U.S.*) Why do you think there was little prejudice against African Americans in Russia at the time? (*Students may suggest that Russia did not practice slavery by race.*) You should point out that at this time Russian peasants were caught in the system of serfdom that severely limited their freedom. As a follow-up activity, have students write letters that Prince might have sent to her husband about her return to Boston.

Teaching Section 1: Neither Slave Nor Free (pp. 121–23)

Objective

• To speculate on reasons for the hardships free African Americans faced.

Historical Sidelight

Across the Continent. Twenty-six of the original founders of Los Angeles claimed African parentage. Maria Rita Valdez, for one, owned Rancho Rodeo de Las Anguas, known today as Beverly Hills. Another person of African descent, Francisco Reyes, owned much of the San Fernando Valley. In the 1790s, Reyes was appointed mayor of Los Angeles. He thus became one of the first African public officials in what is now the United States.

Developing the Section

Historical Speculation. Refer students to the "Snapshot of the Times" on p. 122. Ask how the arrival of European immigrants might have affected the ability of African Americans to find jobs (*limited it*) What other changes might have occurred? (*More difficult to find housing*) Record student speculations on the chalkboard. Have students modify the list as they work through the section. Ask how they think the immigrants might have viewed free African Americans.

Review and Practice

Assign "Taking Another Look," p. 123.

Answer to Question in Caption (p. 121)

Number of enslaved African Americans grew more quickly.

Answers to Taking Another Look (p. 123)

1. could not travel freely, no trial by jury, no vote, no testimony against whites, no freedom of assembly **2.** Immigrants competed for jobs. **3. Critical Thinking** paid taxes, had few rights

Teaching Section 2: A Fragile Freedom (pp. 123–25)

Objective

• To plan an agenda for change that an African American mutual-aid society might have followed in the 1850s.

Historical Sidelight

Fraunces Tavern. In 1762, a free African named Samuel Fraunces bought an old Dutch mansion on the corner of Broad and Pearl streets in New York City. Here he opened what became known as Fraunces Tavern. Within a short time, the tavern became a popular meeting place for New Yorkers. In 1768, state officials met at the tavern to organize the New York Chamber of Commerce. In 1774, the Sons of Liberty gathered to plan the "New York Tea Party." At the end of the Revolution, George Washington summoned his officers to the tavern for an emotional farewell. Today, Fraunces Tavern is a national historic site.

Developing the Section

Planning an Agenda. Divide the class into groups of 4 or 5 students. Tell students to imagine they are members of a newly formed African American mutual-aid society in the 1850s. Next, direct students to brainstorm the various programs they think the society should support. After students have compiled their lists, have them determine which *two* programs they think would *most* help African Americans. Call on recorders from each group to read their programs and give reasons for their choices.

Review and Practice

Assign "Taking Another Look," p. 125.

Answers to Taking Another Look (p. 125)

1. paid money and established schools despite risk **2.** felt solidarity with slaves, felt U.S. was home **3. Critical Thinking** some might be relatives or friends; sympathy due to own experience of slavery

Extending the Chapter

Comparing Past and Present. Assign students the "Focus On" feature on p. 126. Then divide the class into teams. Have half the teams do research on famous African American business leaders prior to emancipation. Each team should choose one person to present an oral report about. Some people are already mentioned in the text. For other possibilities, refer students to *The Shaping of Black America* by Lerone Bennett, Jr., *From Slavery to Freedom,* by John Hope Franklin and Alfred A. Moss, Jr., or *The Negro in the Making of America* by Benjamin Quarles. Have the other teams do research on prominent African American business leaders today and choose one person to present. Suggest they use the *Readers Guide to Periodical Literature* to locate articles in such publications as *Black Enterprise* or *Ebony.*

Looking Ahead

After students have read "Looking Ahead," p. 125, have them discuss ways they would have protested slavery in the mid-1800s. Remind them to be aware of the historical context, that is, such protest entailed great risks. Record student answers on the chalkboard to evaluate as students work through the next unit.

Answers to Close Up (pp. 126–27)

The Who, What Where of History

1. African American entrepreneur, invented device for handling sails, built sail-making factory **2.** unjust treatment based on color or religion **3.** people who risk money to earn profit **4.** owned a shipping business **5.** people who wanted slavery abolished **6.** Liberia

Making the Connection

1. Employers preferred to hire less skilled white immigrants **2.** Southerners were anxious to remove free African Americans.

Time Check

1. 1817 **2.** Over 400,000

What Would You Have Done?

1. would stay in Boston because of health and work for end to discrimination; would leave, set up dressmaking business in area with warmer weather and less prejudice **2.** build libraries, schools, hospitals; fund antislavery publications or movements; any philanthropic act is appropriate answer **3. would take part:** escape discrimination, start over; **would not take part:** because of friends, relatives, connection with America **4.** South Carolina: better economic chances; New York: fewer limits on free African Americans

Thinking and Writing About History

1. plays should indicate fears of being sold into slavery, should show understanding of conditions for African Americans **2.** should include date, goal of Colonization Society, call for free African Americans to attend meeting

Building Skills

In northern cities, free African Americans banded together in organizations to help one another in a variety of ways.

UNIT 5 Challenges to Slavery (pp. 128–59)

UNIT THEME

Taking advantage of the national spirit of reform, abolitionists wage an increasingly vocal campaign to end slavery.

UNIT CONCEPTS

- The urge to perfect U.S. society led reformers in the mid-1800s to fight one of the nation's greatest evils—slavery.
- Both African American and white abolitionists played important roles in the struggle against slavery.
- The antislavery movement helped women recognize their own lack of rights within U.S. society.
- Former African American slaves added strong, new voices to the abolitionist movement as they brought their stories to audiences across the nation and in Europe.
- Thousands of African American slaves risked great danger by fleeing to freedom, many on the Underground Railroad.
- African American churches became vital forces for change, providing freedom of expression for African Americans and forums from which to launch the antislavery crusade.

UNIT OVERVIEW

Unit 5 tells the story of the abolitionist movement from the point of view of African Americans—those whose fate depended upon the crusade's success. *The Big Picture* and the three chapters in the unit describe: (1) the African Americans who helped reshape the antislavery movement, (2) the Underground Railroad and the African Americans who ran it, and (3) the founding of African American churches and their role in the antislavery movement.

In teaching this unit, you might note the role of African Americans in broadening the meaning of liberty in the United States in the last 150 years or more. Mention that the abolitionist movement of the mid-1800s triggered the women's suffrage movement. During the Civil Rights Movement of this century, African Americans introduced ideals and tactics that other minority groups soon adopted. By the 1970s, a rights explosion had hit the nation, involving a number of ethnic groups, women, the aged, and the mentally and physically challenged. Ask students to discuss how the nation's history might have been different if proslavery forces had managed to silence the abolitionists.

COOPERATIVE LEARNING ACTIVITY

The following cooperative learning activity can be used for alternative assessment after study of the unit has been completed.

For decades, abolitionists—African American and white alike—delivered brilliant and impassioned speeches against slavery. At the end of the unit, divide the class into groups and have each group locate one of these speeches. Each group should duplicate its speech to distribute to the rest of the class. Each group should also prepare the following three-part presentation: (1) an introduction placing the speech in its historical framework, (2) a dramatic reading of the speech, and (3) a panel discussion of the speech's meaning. During the discussion, other members of the class should ask questions of the panel members. In evaluating student work, consider the organization of the activity and the accuracy and depth of the analysis of the historical context and meaning of the speech.

Unit 5 THE BIG PICTURE (pp. 129–33)

Theme

The spirit of reform that gave rise to the abolitionist movement swept the nation in the early 1800s.

Overview

The Big Picture explores the spirit of reform that spread across the nation in the early to mid-1800s. The progress and expansion of the young republic led many Americans to believe that perfection might be within their reach. Reformers aimed to rid the nation of a host of evils—drunkenness, mistreatment of prisoners and the mentally ill, and lack of a public school system among others. The impulse to perfect society brought reformers face to face with the issue of slavery.

For years, many Americans had hoped slavery would gradually disappear or at least remain confined to the South. The Northwest Ordinance of 1787 had barred slavery from territories north of the Ohio River, Congress had ended the Atlantic slave trade in 1808, and state after state in the North had prohibited slavery. But the acquisition of new lands to the west and the invention of the cotton gin made the institution of slavery even more important to the economy of the South.

By the mid-1800s, reformers struggled with how they might end the injustice of slavery without ending the Union itself. At first, the mostly white reformers favored a gradual end to slavery through moral persuasion. Soon, however, more radical abolitionists began to call for an immediate end to slavery. African American abolitionists played an important role in bringing the issue to public attention. As abolitionist attacks on slavery increased, slave owners became more insistent in its defense. By the 1850s, arguments over the slave system threatened to divide the nation.

Objectives

- To use a quotation to assess the spirit of abolitionism.
- To use a timeline to categorize events.
- To develop a campaign to influence public opinion in support of reform.
- To debate the pros and cons of the colonization movement.
- To express opinions on *The Liberator* and *Uncle Tom's Cabin*.
- To analyze the connection between the abolition movement and the women's movement.

Introducing *The Big Picture*

Call on a volunteer to read aloud the quotation from "An African American Speaks" on text p. 129. Ask students how Douglass says freedom must come. (*through agitation*) Does he believe change is inevitable? (*probably*) Why? (*The analogies he uses are of natural processes, implying that the desire for freedom is natural.*) Discuss with students whether agitation necessarily involves violence. Ask if they think there was much chance of an end to slavery without violence. (*probably not*)

Using the Timeline

Direct students to study the timeline on text pp. 130–31. Have them practice their categorizing skills by suggesting three or four titles under which entries on the timeline could be grouped. (*possible categories: religion, abolition movement, efforts to limit freedom for slaves, etc.*) Write the categories on the chalkboard and have volunteers write in events in the proper columns.

Teaching *The Big Picture*

1. Influencing Public Opinion. After students have read "The Spirit of Reform" and "Reform Movements" on text pp. 129–30, divide them into four groups. Then assign each group one of the following topics: temperance, improved treatment of the mentally ill, prison reform, universal public education. Tell students to imagine it is the mid-1800s, and they are in charge of a campaign to influence public opinion in favor of these programs. Then have students develop a poster, brochure, speech, eyewitness testimony, or any other device that might help win support for their cause. Allow each group 15–30 minutes to present its campaign to the entire class.

2. Conducting a Debate. Assign "Early Antislavery Efforts" on pp. 130–31. Then select two teams to debate the following topic: *Resolved*—That the best hope of liberty for African Americans lies in Africa. (Additional information on the topic can be found in Chapter 12.) While the debating teams formulate their arguments, direct the rest of the class to draw two columns on a piece of notebook paper. Tell them to record the *pro* aguments in one column and the *con* arguments in the other. After the debating exercise, assemble a master chart on the chalkboard.

3. Expressing an Opinion. After students have read "William Lloyd Garrison and the

Abolitionist Movement" on pp. 130–32, divide them into teams. Assign half the teams to express their opinion of the first issue of *The Liberator* from one of the following points of view: a gradualist, an abolitionist, a Southern slave owner, a free African American. Opinions can be expressed either in the form of a letter to the editor (in this case, Garrison) or in the form of a political cartoon. Assign the other teams to write book reviews of Harriet Beecher Stowe's *Uncle Tom's Cabin* from the same points of view mentioned above. When the teams have completed their assignments, have them share their work with the rest of the class.

4. Analyzing an Historical Document. Before assigning "The Women's Movement" on pp. 132–33, read aloud or distribute copies of the following selection from the Seneca Falls *Declaration of Sentiments:*

> The history of mankind is a history of repeated injuries and usurpations on the part of man toward woman, having in direct object the establishment of an absolute tyranny over her. To prove this let facts be submitted to a candid [impartial] world.
> He has never permitted her to exercise her inalienable right to the elective franchise.
> He has compelled her to submit to laws, in the formation of which she had no voice.
> He has withheld from her rights which are given to the most ignorant and degraded men—both natives and foreigners.

Ask students what right the Declaration says has been denied to women. (*the franchise, or right to vote*) How has denial of this right led to the oppression of women? (*forced them to submit to laws in which they had no voice*) Why might the abolition movement have influenced women to write the *Declaration of Sentiments?* Lead students to understand that as women spoke against the oppression of enslaved African Americans, they recognized their own lack of rights.

Review and Practice

Assign "Taking Another Look," p. 133.

Answer to Question in Caption (p. 132)

brought the issue of slavery to the attention of a huge audience

Answers to Taking Another Look (p. 133)

1. promote women's rights, end drunkenness, change prisons, increase availability of education, end slavery **2.** abolitionists demanded immediate end to slavery; gradualists looked for slow, orderly end **3. Critical Thinking** Women gained the right to vote, to own property, etc.; education became widely available through public schools.

Chapter 13 Abolitionists (pp. 134–43)

Overview

With the growth of slavery in the Cotton Belt, abolitionism took on a militant spirit. African American and white abolitionists demanded an immediate end to slavery. Not all antislavery advocates, however, agreed. Bitter debates raged over whether the movement should be moderate or radical, violent or nonviolent. Men within the movement also split over whether they should support the disfranchised women in their call for suffrage. Amid the quarreling, new voices captured the nation's attention. African Americans—including runaway slaves—spoke out not only for an end of slavery, but for full equality for African Americans under the law.

Resources

Chapter 13 Activity Sheet: Comparing and Contrasting Primary Sources (p. 214)
Chapter 13 Test (p. 151)

Focus Activity

Assign the section-opening story on pp. 134–35. Ask students to explain the purpose of the Philadelphia meeting. (*coordinate the activities of African American and white abolitionists*) How did the delegates try to accomplish this goal? (*formed the American Anti-Slavery Society; drafted the Declaration of Sentiments*) What did the *Declaration* demand? (*liberation of the more than 2 million enslaved African Americans*) As a follow-up activity, direct groups of students to design flyers announcing formation of the society.

Teaching Section 1: New Directions (pp. 135–36)

Objective

- To use a chronology of events in order to speculate on ways African Americans tried to end slavery.

Historical Sidelight

Youthful Abolitionists. From the start, abolitionists appealed to the young. They published schoolbooks and monthly magazines such as *The Slave's Friend*. These publications contained hymns, pictures, and anecdotes on the evils of slavery. The effort was not without its effect. Starting in 1830, both African American and white children began creating antislavery societies of their own. In 1833, for example, young people of both sexes formed the Juvenile Garrison Independent Society in Boston. Similar societies soon appeared in other cities throughout the North.

Developing the Section

Historical Speculation. Read aloud the chapter question, "How did African Americans work to end slavery in the United States?" Then refer students to the "Snapshot of the Times" on text p. 136. Ask what preliminary answers they can give to the question based on this list of events. (*formed antislavery societies, held antislavery conventions, spoke out, called for slave revolts*) List student answers on the chalkboard. As they work their way through the section, have students modify or add to the list. This activity may be repeated at the end of each section in the chapter.

Review and Practice

Assign "Taking Another Look," p. 136.

Answers to Questions in Caption (p. 137)

because he supported freedom for African American slaves; racism, economic worries

Answers to Taking Another Look (p. 136)

1. formed Female Anti-Slavery Society and network of women's antislavery societies **2.** conflict between radicals and moderates, advocates of nonviolence and advocates of force **3. Critical Thinking** Citizens who are denied their rights feel solidarity with one another.

Teaching Section 2: New Voices (pp. 137–39)

Objective

- To write news stories about anti-abolitionists' efforts to stop Frederick Douglass from speaking.

Historical Sidelight

Independence Day, August 1. For African Americans in the mid-1800s, Independence Day fell on August 1. It was on that date in 1834 that the British Parliament declared an end to slavery in the British West Indies. Emancipation was to take place over several years, with the last slaves to be freed officially on August 1, 1838. In the years following 1838, African Americans in the United States held special August 1 celebrations until they had their own independence day to celebrate—January 1, 1863, the date Abraham Lincoln announced the Emancipation Proclamation.

Developing the Section

Writing a News Story. Have students, working individually or in small groups, write news stories to accompany the picture on p. 138. Have half the class write their stories from the perspective of a newspaper in the South, the other half from the perspective of *The Liberator*. Stories should include headlines, datelines, bylines, and interesting lead sentences. The most important facts—who, what, how, and why—should be in the first paragraph. Call on volunteers to read their stories aloud.

Review and Practice

Assign "Taking Another Look," p. 139.

Answer to Question in Caption (p. 138)

feared his ideas might lead more African Americans to demand freedom and rights

Answers to Taking Another Look (p. 139)

1. to abolish slavery, let women to play a more active role in abolitionism **2.** (four of the following) Frederick Douglass, Henry Highland Garnet, Sojourner Truth, Mary Ann Shadd, Mary Bibb, Sarah Redmond **3. Douglass:** called for justice for all oppressed; **Truth:** championed women's rights **4. Critical Thinking** Douglass implies U.S. is endangered by injustice toward its citizens. This may be interpreted as a threat or a moral criticism.

Teaching Section 3: Taking Action (pp. 140–41)

Objectives

- To interpret the message contained in an abolitionist poster.

Developing the Section

Analyzing a Poster. Refer students to the poster entitled "Ladies' Department" on p. 140. Ask them to whom the poster is directed. (*white women*) What rights are denied to enslaved African American women? (*the rights of motherhood, including the right to claim their own children*) Refer to the words above the woman's head:

"Am I not a Woman and a Sister?" Ask how slave owners viewed enslaved African Americans. (*viewed them as property*) What point does the poster make? (*the humanity of slaves*) Ask students what message they think abolitionists wanted to send to white women through this poster. (*Enslaved African American mothers are women just like you.*)

Review and Practice

Assign "Taking Another Look," p. 141.

Answers to Taking Another Look (p. 141)

1. Writers composed antislavery poems, pamphlets, newspaper stories; mutual-aid societies raised funds to support antislavery causes, set up legal committees for runaways. **2.** demanded that African Americans be equal citizens under law **3. Critical Thinking yes:** would have frightened whites into abolishing slavery; **no:** would only have caused whites to make harsher laws inhibiting rights of African Amercans

Extending the Chapter

1. Designing Posters. Divide the class into small groups. Then have each group design a poster announcing the appearance of one of the following speakers: Henry Highland Garnet, Frederick Douglass or Sojourner Truth. Advise students that the poster should try to appeal to both African Americans and whites.

2. Preparing Biographies. Divide the class into small groups and instruct each one to prepare a biography of one of the abolitionists discussed in this chapter. Groups should find a picture of the figure they have selected, as well as an extract from that person's speeches or writings. The reports should be presented orally to the class as a whole. Be sure students clearly indicate in their report why the person was significant to the abolitionist movement.

Looking Ahead

After students have read "Looking Ahead," p. 141, ask them to speculate on the risks faced by runaway slaves. What risks were faced by African Americans who helped runaways ?

Answers to Close Up (pp. 142–43)

The Who, What, Where of History

1. member of Female Anti-Slavery Society of Philadelphia; principal of school for African Americans **2.** radical white abolitionist, founder of *The Liberator* **3.** novel about slavery by Harriet Beecher Stowe **4.** statement of liberation for African Americans drawn up by American Antislavery Society **5.** aggressive **6.** leading African American abolitionist **7.** first great woman abolitionist

Making the Connection

Women abolitionists, often denied an equal role in the antislavery movement, began working for women's rights as well.

Time Check

1. 1833 **2.** 1837

What Would You Have Done?

1. Answers should show a grasp of major reform movements. **2. Garrison:** morally opposed to violence; weapons cannot force people to change their minds. **Critics:** violence necessary; slave owners would never voluntarily give up slaves.

Thinking and Writing About History

1. may mention gross injustice of slavery, harm to society as a whole; economic harm **2.** might describe Douglass, mention his skill as an orator, strength of his message **3.** Business necessity cannot justify a moral wrong.

Building Skills

4

Chapter 14 Escaping from Slavery (pp. 144–51)

Overview

The Underground Railroad was the pathway to freedom for thousands of African American slaves fleeing the South. Slave owners brutally punished or even killed slaves caught fleeing or helping others to flee, but African American slaves fled nonetheless. They followed the "drinking gourd" (Big Dipper) north and passed along word of safe stopping points on the way. These stopping points formed stations on the Underground Railroad. Abolitionists provided moral and financial support to the conductors who ran the railroad, but the driving force behind the railroad was the courage of daring African Americans such as Harriet Tubman who risked their lives to deliver others from slavery.

Resources

Chapter 14 Activity Sheet: Recognizing a Point of View (p. 216)

Chapter 14 Test (p. 152)
Outline Map: Eastern United States (p. 307)
Unit 5 Writing Workshop: Taking a Stand (pp. 278–81)

Focus Activity

Assign the chapter-opening story about Ellen and William Craft on pp. 144–45. Ask what motivated Ellen to plot the couple's escape. (*her desire to have a child that would not be sold away from her*) Why did the Crafts have more freedom than many enslaved African Americans in the South? (*They lived in a city, and their owners hired them out.*) Why might the couple have escaped the notice of white slave owners so successfully? Lead students to understand that few slave owners credited slaves with the intelligence or daring to risk such an openly public escape.

Teaching Section 1: Path to Freedom (pp. 145–48)

Objective

- To analyze how African American slaves may have planned their escapes.

Historical Sidelight

Naming the Pathway to Freedom. Many stories surround the naming of the Underground Railroad. One of the most widely accepted credits the name to a Kentucky slave owner. In 1831, the slave owner pursued an African American slave named Tice Davids all the way to the Ohio River. Here Davids disappeared without a trace leaving the slave owner to remark that his slave must have "gone off on an underground road." The term soon was applied to the system for aiding runaways.

Developing the Section

Analyzing a Plan. Divide the class into small groups. Have each group study the map on p. 147 and choose a route on the Underground Railroad. Then have students plan their escape. Caution them to take into account the following: clothing or disguise, food, method of travel, time of travel, ultimate destination, and contingency plan if spotted by slave catchers. Have the recorder from each group read the plan that the group decides on.

Review and Practice

Assign "Taking Another Look," p. 148.

Answers to Questions in Captions (p. 145–47)

(p. 145) that slavery was so terrible that some slaves would use any means to gain freedom (p. 147) no fugitive slave laws or slave catchers there

Answers to Taking Another Look (p. 148)

1. might be killed or crippled **2.** had "tracks" (roads, rivers, trails), "stations" (homes), "conductors" (abolitionists) **3. Critical Thinking yes:** want to help slaves become free because slavery is morally wrong; **no:** too much risk to self and family's safety, must obey law, even if distasteful

Teaching Section 2: A Woman Called Moses (pp. 148–49)

Objectives

- To decode the meaning of a spiritual sung by Harriet Tubman as she planned escapes.
- To write speeches Tubman might have given to abolitionist audiences.

Historical Sidelight

Tickets from Overseas. Some of the "tickets" for runaways on the Underground Railroad were paid for by donations from antislavery societies in Great Britain. Women ran a large number of these societies, and they freely sent money to their antislavery sisters in the United States. According to the estimates of Jermain W. Loguen, his Fugitive Aid Society in Syracuse, New York, received some $400 a year between 1855 and 1860 from the British antislavery societies.

Developing the Section

1. Decoding a Spiritual. Tell students that Harriet Tubman used to visit a plantation's slave quarters to alert African Americans that she was there to help them escape. She would sing a song like the following. Have students listen carefully as you read the lyrics. Then ask them what information about the planned escape is contained in the song. (*an escape is planned; will leave in the morning; possibly meet across a nearby river*)

When that old chariot comes,
I'm going to leave you,
I'm bound for the promised land.
Friends I'm going to leave you.

I'm sorry friends, to leave you,
Farewell! oh, farewell!
But I'll meet you in the morning,
Farewell! oh, farewell!

I'll meet you in the morning
When you reach the promised land;
On the other side of the Jordan,
For I'm bound for the promised land.

2. Writing a Speech. Assign students, working individually or in small groups, to write speeches that Tubman might have given to abolitionist audiences. The speeches should include an account of Tubman's early life, her decision to run away, and her purpose in joining the Underground Railroad. Allow time for students to deliver their speeches to the entire class.

Review and Practice

Assign "Taking Another Look," p. 149.

Answers to Taking Another Look (p. 149)

1. went to William Still for help in rescuing her family; led sister, nieces, brother, two other men to freedom **2.** had a $40,000 reward on her head **3. Critical Thinking** flagrant and continuous defiance; any escape increased likelihood of others

Extending the Chapter

Writing Biographies. Assign groups of students to research conductors on the Underground Railroad other than Tubman and Still. Some names are mentioned in the chapter and others can be found in such sources as *We Are Your Sisters,* edited by Dorothy Sterling, and *Black Abolitionists,* by Benjamin Quarles. Have students present their findings in biographies similar to those used in the text.

Looking Ahead

After students have read "Looking Ahead," p. 149, encourage them to speculate on reasons why African Americans may have formed their own churches. (*Most students will probably suggest reasons centering on prejudice.*)

Answers to Close Up (pp. 150–51)

The Who, What, Where of History

1. enslaved African Americans who escaped by disguising themselves as a planter and servant **2.** slave who escaped by having himself shipped North in a crate **3.** Big Dipper **4.** network of roads, homes, and abolitionists; helped guide escaping slaves to freedom **5.** Quaker founder of the Underground Railroad **6.** African American "president" of Underground Railroad **7.** former African American slave who returned South 19 times to help over 300 slaves to freedom

Making the Connection

Fugitive Slave Law made it a crime to help escaping slaves; Underground Railroad operated in secret to protect slaves and those who helped them escape

Time Check

1. 1830s–1860s **2.** the end

What Would You Have Done?

1. bravery, outdoor survival skills, cleverness, intense desire for freedom **2. help:** slavery is morally wrong and helping slaves worth the risk; **not help:** could not be of help to slaves or own family if in prison or homeless

Thinking and Writing About History

1. might show Crafts rebuffing offers of assistance or invitations to socialize, overhearing conversations about slavery and reacting to those conversations **2.** Answers should show understanding of the secret code of Underground Railroad.

Building Skills

1. 2, 3, 4 **2.** 2, 5, 6 **3.** grandfather's stories, memoirs; oral history helpful in telling story, check primary and secondary sources

Chapter 15 African American Churches: Agents for Change (pp. 152–59)

Overview

At first, African Americans worshiped in white churches, accepting the places assigned to them. But in 1787, church officials at the St. George Methodist Episcopal Church humiliated African American worshipers. The incident led Richard Allen and Absalom Jones to start the first independent African American church in the nation. Over time, African American churches provided more than spiritual shelter. They also gave African Americans a forum in which to speak out freely. In the mid-1800s, African American churches joined the antislavery battle.

Resources

Chapter 15 Activity Sheet: Using a Map and Time Chart (p. 217)
Chapter 15 Test (p. 153)
Unit 5 Test: Challenges to Slavery (p. 148–50)

Focus Activity

Assign the chapter-opening story on student pp. 152–53. Ask students to speculate on the opportunities African American churches afforded former slaves that might have been denied them in white churches. (*place in which to learn to read; place to speak their minds freely; haven from prej-*

udice) How did an African American church help Frederick Douglass begin his career as an abolitionist? (*Pastor James first noticed Douglass' talent for public speaking in church.*)

Teaching Section 1: The Search for Religious Equality (pp. 153–55)

Objectives

- To write a letter explaining reasons for building the Mother Bethel Church.
- To analyze how discrimination by white churches denied African Americans certain basic freedoms.
- To analyze the effectiveness of separate churches as a tool for promoting African American progress.

Historical Sidelight

Methodism. The Methodist religion was brought to the United States by George Whitefield. During the Second Great Awakening in the 1730s, Whitefield spread the Methodist message throughout the colonies. That message contained a condemnation of slavery. In 1743, John Wesley made an antislavery position a part of the church's *General Rules*. Because of this stand, many free and enslaved African Americans converted to Methodism. By the late 1700s, however, policies had changed. It was a Methodist church that forced Richard Allen to sit in restricted pews.

Developing the Section

1. Writing a Letter. Have students, working individually or in small groups, compose a letter that Richard Allen might have written to Methodist Church officials to explain his reasons for forming Bethel Church. Remind students that Allen did not set out to establish a separate denomination. Call on volunteers to read their letters aloud.

2. Analyzing an Issue. Working with the class as a whole, have them write a statement explaining why discrimination in white churches denied African Americans both freedom of religion and freedom of assembly. You might read the 1st Amendment of the Constitution as a way to begin the activity.

3. Analyzing an Issue. Discuss with the class whether they think separate churches made it more difficult for African Americans to achieve equality. They should consider the pros and cons of separatism for both African Americans and the society at large.

Review and Practice

Assign "Taking Another Look," p. 155.

Answers to Taking Another Look (p. 155)

1. mistreated in white churches **2.** gave them place to worship without discrimination **3. Critical Thinking** fewer restrictions on African American activities in North; independent churches provided freedom to organize protests

Teaching Section 2: Joining the Antislavery Battle (pp. 155–57)

Objectives

- To recognize the prejudice and intimidation that African American churches faced because of their involvement in the antislavery movement.
- To design posters asking people to support the free-produce movement.

Historical Sidelight

African American Women and Religion. In Africa, women played important religious roles as queens, priests, healers, midwives, and diviners. Women continued to take part in religious ceremonies both in the Caribbean and in sections of Latin America where African influences remained strong. But in the slave quarters in the United States, African women ran into prejudice from both white and African American male preachers. Nonetheless, some African American women would not be denied their religious calling. When Jarena Lee demanded that Richard Allen license her as a minister, he refused, but allowed her to hold prayer meetings. Some women left African American churches entirely. Rebecca Cox Jackson and Rebecca Perot found a haven among the sect known as the Shakers. Jackson founded a largely African American Shaker sisterhood near Philadelphia.

Developing the Section

1. Recognizing Key Ideas. Assign students to read the opening paragraph of this section. Then ask them if they think police would have taken similar action in a white church. (*probably not*) Call on volunteers to explain their responses. Lead students to an understanding of the lack of rights extended to African Americans, especially in slave-trading centers such as Washington, D.C. Through discussion, help students appreciate the courage displayed by African American congregations in working to end slavery.

2. Designing Posters. Assign students, working individually or in small groups, to design posters urging people to support the boycott of goods made with African American slave labor. Advise students that the posters should appeal to both African Americans and whites.

Review and Practice

Assign "Taking Another Look," p. 157.

Answers to Taking Another Look (p. 157)

1. In many states, only white ministers could preach to African American congregations; African American preachers had to be approved by white ministers. **2.** meeting place for abolitionists, made donations to fund abolitionist meetings, provided safe haven for runaways, acted as stations on Underground Railroad **3. Critical Thinking Allen:** discrimination should not be tolerated; **Douglass:** must stay in white churches in order to fight prejudice rather than just avoiding it

Extending the Chapter

Local History. Assign the "Focus On" feature on p. 158. Then call on groups of students to research the histories of local African American churches. Suggest that students contact the current pastor or minister for information that might be used in an oral report. Additional sources of information include the local history section of the local library, the state historical society, and the local chapter of the NAACP.

Looking Ahead

After students have read "Looking Ahead," p. 157, ask them whether they think it was still possible in the late 1850s for the nation to compromise over the issue of slavery. Ask if they think abolitionism made civil war inevitable.

Answers to Close Up (pp. 158–159)

The Who, What, Where of History

1. former African American slave, became an American Methodist Episcopal Zionist minister **2.** founder of Mother Bethel African Methodist Episcopal Church **3.** founder of St. Thomas Free African Church **4.** Philadelphia **5.** religious group **6.** African American minister and antislavery agent

Making the Connection

African American ministers used their pulpits to speak out against slavery and inspired others to do the same.

Time Check

1. 1787 **2.** 29 **3.** about 14

What Would You Have Done?

1. might do nothing at time of service, but would withdraw from the church; support Jones in setting up African American church; write letters of protest **2.** should remain in racially mixed churches to protest discrimination there; should found separate churches to protest treatment in white churches and support antislavery activities by providing a meeting place **3.** Point out that Quakers did not integrate their own schools; suggest full rights of participation for African Americans in Quaker institutions.

Thinking and Writing About History

1. provided a place to worship, assemble freely, organize antislavery protests, support antislavery movement financially, help runaway slaves **2.** Plaque should state when church was founded, tell about the Underground Railroad activities, and list abolitionists who spoke there.

Building Skills

1. Racially mixed churches often did not treat African Americans equally. **2.** African American churches offered many different forms of support to the antislavery movement.

UNIT 6 Hope for a New Way of Life (pp. 160–205)

UNIT THEME

The Civil War ends the institution of slavery, but prejudice and inequality characterize the treatment of recently freed African Americans.

UNIT CONCEPTS

- After 1850, conflict replaced compromise as the method for dealing with African American enslavement, and civil war resulted.
- At the beginning of the Civil War, President Abraham Lincoln fought to preserve the Union rather than to abolish slavery.
- Congress passed the 13th, 14th, and 15th Amendments to the Constitution to ensure equality for African Americans, but prejudice prevented the full application of these laws.
- Newly freed African Americans used their freedom to reestablish their families, set up and make use of schools, build churches, and attempt to earn their livings as free people.
- As Reconstruction ended, a bleak period of economic and political repression and segregation began.
- Despite the failed promises of the Civil War and Reconstruction, African Americans continued to play important roles in the nation's growth and expansion.

UNIT OVERVIEW

Unit 6 traces the failure of national compromise over the issue of slavery in the 1800s and the eventual outbreak of the Civil War. The war ended African American enslavement, but new issues developed as African Americans began the long struggle to win their full civil rights. *The Big Picture* and the four chapters in the unit describe: (1) the causes and some of the events leading to the Civil War, (2) the Union's shift toward African American emancipation as a goal of the war and the efforts of African Americans to help win the war, (3) the triumphs and failures of Reconstruction, and (4) the role of African Americans in settling the territories beyond the Mississippi.

In teaching this unit, you might underscore the fact that most white Americans in the North saw the Civil War as a struggle to preserve the Union. Only during the war did Lincoln change the aims of the Union to include abolition of slavery. The war, however, was not fought for racial equality for African Americans. In fact, in the post–Civil War years, many white Americans in the North and South put up obstacles to equality. The most critical barriers were the restrictions on African Americans' voting rights. You might ask students to discuss why voting rights are an important guarantee of equality, while noting that these rights did not extend to women at this time—African American or white.

COOPERATIVE LEARNING ACTIVITY

The following cooperative learning activity can be used for alternative assessment after study of the unit has been completed.

At the end of the unit, divide the class into three groups. Have each group prepare oral and visual reports on the following decades: 1850–1860, 1860–1870, 1870–1880. Each report should begin with the words, "It is 18–, and the nation now faces a great test." The first group will focus on the buildup to the Civil War; the second group, on the Civil War and the start of Reconstruction; and the third group, on the unfulfilled promises of Reconstruction and African Americans' beyond the Mississippi. Suggest that students use the unit timeline and the "Snapshot of the Times" in each chapter as guides to key events to include. Allow one class period for each group to present a series of mini-reports on its decade. In evaluating the reports, consider the organization of each group's presentation, its selection of events to be covered, and the amount of research evidenced.

Unit 6 THE BIG PICTURE (pp. 160–65)

Theme

After the Civil War ended slavery, Reconstruction held out the promise of full civil rights to African Americans, but ultimately failed to deliver on this promise.

Objectives

- To use a primary source to understand how enslaved African Americans saw freedom.
- To use a timeline to predict events.
- To analyze whether the Civil War was inevitable.
- To write news stories showing various reactions to the Emancipation Proclamation.
- To chart the successes and failures of Reconstruction.
- To understand the difficulties for newly freed African Americans in deciding whether to head west and settle in new territory.

Overview

The Big Picture describes the buildup to the Civil War. In the early 1800s, a series of crises erupted over the issue of slavery. The Missouri Compromise of 1820 and the Compromise of 1850 proved only temporary resolutions to the question of whether slavery should be permitted to expand in the nation. By the late 1850s, hopes for continued compromises vanished as people in the North increasingly demanded an end to slavery, while Southerners hotly defended the institution and pressed for its expansion into new territories. The Republican Party was organized as an anti-slavery party and, when its candidate, Abraham Lincoln, won the presidency in 1860, the Southern states seceded and the Civil War began.

At first, Lincoln sought to reunite the Union rather than to end slavery. But as fighting dragged on, he made abolition a goal of the war. The war now became a moral crusade for the North. More practically, Union armies now accepted thousands of African Americans into their ranks.

After the war, the battle of Reconstruction began. Radical Republicans took control of Congress seeking to punish the South and to ensure that the defeated states granted full rights to newly emancipated African Americans. As part of their efforts, they gained passage of the 13th, 14th, and 15th Amendments to the Constitution. The Radicals lost their hold on Congress and the nation turned its attention to other problems, ending Reconstruction in 1877. African Americans were left to face a hostile white South and a North that had lost interest in enforcing new laws protecting the rights of African Americans. By the late 1800s, Southern states had begun to restrict the freedoms of African Americans. In the face of this repression, some African Americans moved out to the Great Plains as settlers. Others went to California and Colorado looking for gold and silver while some became cowhands.

Introducing *The Big Picture*

Before assigning *The Big Picture,* write the word *freedom* on the chalkboard. Ask how free African Americans might have defined the term. (*Most students will probably suggest definitions that involve equality.*) How might enslaved African Americans have defined the term? (*probably an end to bondage, to being sold, to being separated from family, to being whipped*)

Using the Timeline

Have students study the unit timeline on pp. 162–63. Ask when the Civil War started. (*1861*) How many years did it take before Lincoln issued the Emancipation Proclamation? (*2 years*) How many years passed before he accepted African Americans into the Union armed forces? (*2 years*) Was abolition Lincoln's primary goal in the war during the years 1861–1863? (*probably not*) Why or why not? What events on the timeline show a change in the North's position? (*Emancipation Proclamation; passage of the 13th, 14th, and 15th Amendments, the civil rights acts*)

Teaching *The Big Picture*

1. Analyzing an Issue. Assign sections up to and including "Lincoln" (pp. 161–63). Then ask students to think about the following question: Was the Civil War inevitable? Record and discuss student responses on the chalkboard. Based on comparison of these arguments, ask students to suggest solutions that might have avoided war.

2. Writing a News Story. After students have read "The Emancipation Proclamation" on pp. 163–64, tell them to imagine they are reporters from one of the following regions: the Union states, the Confederate states, the border states, or the organized territories of the Great Plains. Have students, working individually or in small groups, write news stories announcing Lincoln's action. Each story should have a headline, dateline, byline, and an interest-grabbing first sentence. Remind students that the stories should answer as many of the reporter's questions as possible: *who? what? where? when? why?* and *how?*

3. Organizing Information on a Chart. Direct students to draw a chart with two columns on notebook paper. One column should be labeled "Accomplishments of Reconstruction" and the other "Shortcomings of Reconstruction." Then assign students to read "The Reconstruction Years," "The White Reaction," and "The End of Reconstruction," pp. 164–65. Have students fill in their charts based on information from their reading. Ask volunteers to read their charts as the basis of a discussion about how successful Reconstruction was for African Americans. You might return to this discussion at the end of Chapter 18.

4. Making a Decision. Assign "Going West" on p. 165. Tell students to imagine they are newly freed African American slaves who have just heard news of available farmland on the Great Plains. They are considering whether to move there. They know the route is dangerous because roving bands of whites have threatened the lives of any former African American slaves who attempt to "desert" the South. Have students discuss whether they would make the journey, taking into account the danger and their ties to the South.

Review and Practice

Assign "Taking Another Look," p. 165.

Answers to Questions in Captions (pp. 161–65)

(p. 161) to set up a boundary north of which slavery would be banned; Missouri, Maine (p. 165) 13th; 14th

Answers to Taking Another Look (p. 165)

1. Missouri Compromise: admitted Missouri as slave state, Maine as free; **Compromise of 1850:** admitted California as free, former Mexican lands would vote; **Kansas-Nebraska Act:** repealed Missouri Compromise **2.** larger population, 92 percent of factories, 70 percent of railroads, almost all the nation's iron, coal and copper **3.** gave North moral reason to fight; encouraged African American slaves to run away, damaging Southern economy **4. Critical Thinking** find gold, escape oppression, begin new life

Chapter 16 The Road to the Civil War (pp. 166–75)

Overview

The period of compromise over the issue of slavery ended in the 1850s. The Fugitive Slave Law of 1850 brought slave catchers into the North itself. Escaped African Americans no longer felt safe short of Canada. The story of Anthony Burns, that is recounted in this chapter, is an example of the legal system at this time and of the anger of antislavery advocates. In its decision in the *Dred Scott* case, the Supreme Court overturned the Missouri Compromise. In outrage, abolitionist John Brown declared that the time for talk had ended. He took up arms and attempted to organize a rebellion of enslaved African Americans at Harpers Ferry, Virginia. The outpouring of Northern sympathy at Brown's subsequent hanging convinced many Southerners that the time had come to part from the Union.

Resources

Chapter 16 Activity Sheet: Summarizing a Primary Source (pp. 219–20)
Chapter 16 Test (p. 157)

Focus Activity

Assign the chapter introduction on pp. 166–67. Recall how the Free African Society had helped battle the yellow fever epidemic in Philadelphia in 1793 (pp. 79–80). Then point out how Dr. Martin Robison Delany also helped both African Americans and whites during the cholera epidemic. Review, too, the voices of abolition mentioned in Unit 5. Then call on a volunteer to do a dramatic reading of Delany's speech on p. 167. Ask if Delany was more in the tradition of William Lloyd Garrison or Henry Highland Garnet. (*Garrison called for nonviolent change; Garnet for armed rebellion*) If students have difficulty answering, have them skim through Chapter 13 to review.

Teaching Section 1: Challenges to the Fugitive Slave Law (pp. 167–69)

Objective

- To analyze reaction to the Anthony Burns case.

Historical Sidelight

Sending in the Marines. In 1854, it took four platoons of U.S. Marines, one battalion of artillery, and 22 militia companies to remove Anthony Burns from Boston. It cost the federal government $40,000 to return one enslaved man to the South. Burns was the last fugitive enslaved African American to be caught in Massachusetts.

Developing the Section

Analyzing an Illustration. Refer students to the illustration on text p. 168. Point out that the scene takes place in Boston and involves the capture of runaway African American slave Anthony Burns. Ask students what details in the painting show the potential for violence. (*the raised fist of one of the figures, the presence of troops*) What effect might such a scene have on abolitionists? (*probably strengthen resolve to end slavery*) What effect might it have on others—slave owning Southerners, those with no opinion on slavery? (*seem justified to slave owners, the undecided might turn against slavery*)

Review and Practice

Assign "Taking Another Look," p. 169.

Answers to Taking Another Look (p. 169)

1. authorized federal marshals to capture and return them to slavery, denied those arrested the right to testify in self-defense **2.** passed personal liberty laws, forbidding enforcement of Fugitive Slave Law, guaranteed fair trials for captured runaways **3. Critical Thinking** Moral wrong can't be justified by any law; if a law is wrong, it should be changed, not broken.

Teaching Section 2: The Dred Scott Case, A Test of Slavery (pp. 169–71)

Objective

- To analyze a statement by Frederick Douglass on the effect of the *Dred Scott* decision.

Historical Sidelight

The Harriet Scott Decision. Around 1835, Dred Scott traveled with his owner Dr. John Emerson to Fort Snelling in Missouri. Here he met a young enslaved woman named Harriet Robinson. Scott proposed marriage. Harriet "belonged" to one of the largest slave owners in the area, Lawrence Taliaferro. A justice of the peace, Taliaferro not only agreed to the marriage, but performed the civil wedding ceremony himself. He then sold Harriet to Emerson so that the Scotts could be together. In 1846, *both* Scotts filed for their freedom in separate cases. Each case made its way through the courts, and there might also have been a "*Harriet Scott* decision" if lawyers had not agreed to combine the two cases in 1850.

Developing the Section

Analyzing a Quotation. Focus attention on the statement by Frederick Douglass on p. 171. Ask students how Douglass described the *Dred Scott* decision. (*as monstrous*) How did he advise opponents of the decision to respond? (*cheerfully*) Why? (*because the decision was a necessary step in the overthrow of slavery*) Then have students discuss whether they agree with Douglass. That is, did the Scott case indeed help advance the antislavery cause? Why or why not?

Review and Practice

Assign "Taking Another Look," p. 171.

Answers to Taking Another Look (p. 171)

1. had lived in a free state and a free territory and was therefore free **2.** right to hold slaves was a property right; Missouri Compromise ruled unconstitutional **3. Critical Thinking** supported idea of slaves as property

Teaching Section 3: John Brown's Raid (pp. 171–73)

Objective

- To recognize bias in a painting.

Developing the Section

Recognizing Bias. Explain to students that a painting, like an editorial, can be used as a means of expressing or swaying opinion. Then refer students to the painting on p. 173. Ask students what opinion they think the artist has of Brown. (*shows him as a martyr and a hero*) How does the artist communicate his view? (*Brown's kindly appearance, the African American mother holding her child up to Brown*) How might Southerners react to such a painting? (*with anger*) If this painting were your only source of information on Brown, would you have an accurate representation of history? (*probably not*) Why? Lead students to understand that there were many opinions of Brown. It is the job of historians to understand and interpret all of these views. You might enlarge the discussion by having students turn to Horace Pippin's painting of a similar scene in *The Artist's View*, p. A12.

Review and Practice

Assign "Taking Another Look," p. 173.

Answer to Question in Caption (p. 173)

Brown's kindly expression, affection of mother and child for Brown

Answers to Taking Another Look (p. 173)

1. victory over slavery by violent uprising **2.** hoped-for uprising never occurred, Brown and followers caught and killed; seizure of arsenal encouraged others, enraged South **3. Critical Thinking hero:** combatting evil of slavery; **enemy of the state:** Brown was a criminal who broke laws, attempted murder.

Extending the Chapter

Planning a Campaign. Remind students that 1860 was a presidential election year. (See *The Big Picture.*) Then list the candidates for office on the chalkboard: Republican Abraham Lincoln, Southern Democrat John C. Breckinridge, Northern Democrat Stephen A. Douglas, and Constitutional Unionist John Bell. Assign groups of students to research each candidate. Have them design campaign posters and speeches in support of each candidate. Allow time for each group to show its posters and deliver its speeches.

Looking Ahead

Focus students' attention on the first sentence in "Looking Ahead," p. 173. Discuss whether students believe that slavery could have been compromised away, that is, whether enough compromises could have been reached that would have allowed slavery to continue indefinitely.

Answers to Close Up (pp. 174–75)

The Who, What, Where of History

1. 1820 law that forbade slavery north of line drawn across the Louisiana Purchase, excepting Missouri **2.** allowed California to enter Union as free; in other former Mexican lands, settlers would vote on slavery **3.** 1850 law, allowed federal marshals to hunt runaway slaves and return them to slavery **4.** runaway slave whose capture in Boston stirred protest **5.** forbade northern state enforcement of Fugitive Slave Law, guaranteed African American fugitives fair trial **6.** Congress cannot deprive a citizen of property; slaves are property—not citizens and can't sue in court; Missouri Compromise unconstitutional **7.** led attack on federal arsenal in Harpers Ferry, Virginia

Making the Connection

1. Northern states passed personal liberty laws to prevent enforcement of the Fugitive Slave Law. **2.** Scott had lived in territory the Missouri Compromise declared free, so he claimed freedom.

Time Check

1. 1850 **2.** capture of Anthony Burns

What Would You Have Done?

1. yes: because slavery was morally wrong; **no:** because law prohibited it **2. obeyed:** without law there is chaos; **disobeyed:** fugitive slaves deserve their freedom

Thinking and Writing About History

1. Letters might mention Fugitive Slave Law, fear of being kidnapped and sent South, Anthony Burns. **2.** should discuss raid, comments by Brown while he was going to his hanging, comments by crowd

Building Skills

1. Martin Delany's address in Pittsburgh; Anthony Burns's letter; Frederick Douglass's comment on the *Dred Scott* decision; letter from Brooklyn women to John Brown **2.** a, c, f, g, h, i; Explanations should show understanding of definition of primary source.

Chapter 17 The Civil War and the End of Slavery (pp. 176–87)

Overview

When the Civil War began, Lincoln saw saving the Union rather than ending slavery as the war's goal. He feared losing the support of the border states and Northerners who opposed abolition, so Lincoln delayed freeing African American slaves. By 1863, however, the Union cause needed a moral and military boost. Lincoln found the answer in the Emancipation Proclamation in which he announced the freeing of African American slaves in Confederate-held territory. Although the document was limited in scope, African Americans rejoiced that the federal government had taken a step toward ending slavery.

More than 200,000 African Americans joined the Union armed forces. Many more worked behind Union lines. Meanwhile, thousands of slaves fled the South, further weakening its economy and its ability to resist Union armed forces. By 1865, the Union had won a complete victory.

Resources

Chapter 17 Activity Sheet: Understanding Points of View (p. 221)

Chapter 17 Test (p. 158)
Outline Map: Eastern United States (p. 307)

Focus Activity

Assign the chapter-opening story on pp. 176–77. Then ask students to find the names of some of the members of the 54th Massachusetts Infantry on the Civil War Honor Roll on p. 182. (*William H. Carney, Peter Vogelsang*) Have students use information in these two sources to write an account of the attack on Fort Wagner.

Teaching Section 1: On the Road to Ending Slavery (pp. 177–79)

Objective

- To interpret a map showing the application of the Emancipation Proclamation.

Historical Sidelight

Running the Underground Railroad. Thousands of Union soldiers found themselves trapped behind Confederate lines or in disease-infested prisons in the South. Those lucky enough to escape often took shelter in the cabins of African American slaves who helped the soldiers escape the South by putting them on the Underground Railroad.

Developing the Section

Interpreting a Map. To help students better understand the Emancipation Proclamation, refer them to the map on text p. 179. Ask if the Emancipation Proclamation ended slavery everywhere. (*no*) Would it have freed a slave in Maryland? (*no*) Where *did* the Emancipation apply? (*areas controlled by the Confederate States of America*) Did the federal government have the authority to enforce it there? (*no*) Ask students why, despite such limitations, African Americans greeted the Emancipation Proclamation with joy. Lead students to understand that the document held the promise of liberty for millions of African Americans.

Review and Practice

Assign "Taking Another Look," p. 179.

Answers to Questions in Caption (p. 179)

Tex., La., Ark., Miss., Ala., Fla., Ga., Tenn., Va.; in parts of La., Ga., S.C., N.C., and Va. under Union Control

Answers to Taking Another Look (p. 179)

1. wanted war to be fought primarily to end slavery **2.** freedom for all slaves in areas in rebellion against Union **3. Critical Thinking** Even partial victory over slavery was significant.

Teaching Section 2: On the Home Front (pp. 179–81)

Objective

- To form generalizations about the experiences of African American slaves and former slaves on the home front.

Developing the Section

Forming Generalizations. Remind students that generalizations are broad conclusions based on many related facts. (If necessary, review the "Building Skills" lessons on pp. 143, 151.) Then divide the class into teams of 4 to 5 students each. Have the teams draw up a list of at least four valid generalizations about the effect of the Civil War on African American slaves and former slaves.

Review and Practice

Assign "Taking Another Look," p. 181.

Answer to Question in Caption (p. 180)

contrabands

Answers to Taking Another Look (p. 181)

1. ran away, refused to work or submit to punishment, demanded wages, seized and destroyed property, gave information to Union army **2.** laborers, cooks, teamsters, mechanics, nurses, ambulance drivers, gave information to Union army **3. Critical Thinking** Former slaves may have drained army's resources and had little military training; Some Union officers may have held racist views.

Teaching Section 3: On the War Front (pp. 181–85)

Objective

- To gather evidence of African American behavior in combat to refute justifications of slavery.

Developing the Section

Gathering Evidence. Open the section by writing the following statement by a Confederate senator on the chalkboard: "If a black man can make a good soldier, our whole system of government is wrong." Remind students that many Southerners justified slavery on the basis of racist views—that African Americans were inferior to whites. As students read through the section, have them write down examples of actions by African Americans that prove the Confederate "system of government is wrong."

Review and Practice

Assign "Taking Another Look," p. 185.

Answers to Taking Another Look (p. 185)
1. political reasons, enlisting African Americans would antagonize border states and encourage them to join Confederacy **2.** Union battlefield defeats, desperate need for soldiers **3. Critical Thinking** bravery, willingness to fight to end slavery, discrimination, similarity of circumstances to life as slave, issue of white leadership

Extending the Chapter

Preparing a Civil War Newsletter. Divide the class into groups to design a Civil War newsletter. One group should be responsible for news stories; another for front page feature articles to accompany some of the news stories; and the third, for an editorial page with a political cartoon, letters to the editor, and an editorial on Union treatment of contrabands. Have each group lay out its articles on a large piece of newsprint.

Looking Ahead

After students have read "Looking Ahead," p. 185, have them prepare a list of priorities for the newly freed African Americans. Ask the class to select the five most important items that former slaves might need to built their new lives.

Answers to Close Up(pp. 186–87)

The Who, What, Where of History
1. African American regiment of Union army **2.** Abraham Lincoln **3.** leave the Union **4.** liberation **5.** Missouri, Kentucky, Maryland, Delaware **6.** freed all African American slaves in Confederate states **7.** ran away, refused to work or submit to punishment, seized and destroyed property, gave information to Union, demanded wages **8.** former slaves who fled to the Union side **9.** laborers, cooks, nurses, ambulance drivers

Making the Connection
1. Lincoln feared that freeing slaves would drive border states into the Confederacy. **2.** The Union lost many men and needed more soldiers.

Time Check
Richmond, Virginia

What Would You Have Done?
1. yes: fight slavery, prove African Americans make good soldiers; **no:** would not get equal treatment, opposed to war **2. yes:** feel antislavery support of government, resistance safer now; **no:** fear of consequences if Union lost and slavery continued **3. yes:** showed Lincoln wanted to end slavery; **no:** proclamation didn't free all slaves

Thinking and Writing About History
1. fight slavery, earn salary, prove worth of African American soldiers **2.** Answers should show accurate knowledge of person selected. Plaque should include dates and acts of valor.

Building Skills
1. opinions **2.** bravest, heroism unsurpassed **3.** don't know **4.** could research primary source accounts of battles or check well-documented secondary sources **5. Stanton:** because he had nothing to gain by letter; **abolitionist paper:** might be a more biased source

Chapter 18 The Promise and Failure of Reconstruction (pp. 188–97)

Overview

The Civil War ended slavery, and many African Americans believed that the postwar period known as Reconstruction would see them enter the mainstream of U.S. life. Congress set up a Freedmen's Bureau to aid enslaved African Americans, passed the 13th, 14th, and 15th Amendments, and instituted policies in the South that gave African Americans the chance to participate in politics. But the promises of Reconstruction proved short-lived. By 1877, hostile white Southerners were passing new laws designed to keep African Americans in a status little better than enslavement.

Resources

Chapter 18 Activity Sheet: Comparing and Contrasting Maps (pp. 222–23)
Chapter 18 Test (p. 159)
Outline Map: Eastern United States (p. 307)
Unit 6 Writing Workshop: Reporting Facts (pp. 282–85)

Focus Activity

Write the chapter title on the chalkboard. Then direct student attention to the "Snapshot of the Times" on p. 190. Ask what event preceded Reconstruction. (*formation of Southern white secret societies*) What event ended it? (*return of white Democrats to power in former Confederate states*) Ask what students infer to be the "failure" of Reconstruction. (*inability to break the political hold of whites on the South*) What events help explain the "promise" in the chapter title? (*election of African American officials, Freedmen's schools, new Southern state constitutions*). Point out that the chapter also discusses economic promises and failures.

Teaching Section 1: Changes in Family Life, Religion, and Education (pp. 189–91)

Objective

- To set priorities for the tasks facing African Americans once slavery had ended.

Historical Sidelight

After the War. At the end of the Civil War, Harriet Tubman turned her house into the Home for Indigent and Aged Negroes. She married a formerly enslaved veteran named Nelson Davis in 1869. She died in Auburn, N.Y., in 1913 at age 93.

Developing the Section

Setting an Agenda. Begin the section by reading aloud the following quotation by Frederick Douglass: "Verily [truly], the work does not end with the abolition of slavery, but only begins." Ask students what tasks they think African Americans faced after the end of slavery. Before they read the section, have them suggest things that the federal government, Southern states, and African Americans themselves would have to do to ensure that former slaves were treated fairly and were able to earn a living.

Review and Practice

Assign "Taking Another Look," p. 190.

Answers to Taking Another Look (p. 190)

1. couples were married; men took places as heads of families, did not allow wives to work in fields, disciplined own children **2.** Churches housed schools, social gatherings, and political meetings. Ministers were highly respected in the community. **3.** set up 4,500 schools **4. Critical Thinking** During Reconstruction some 250,000 illiterate former slaves learned to read and write.

Teaching Section 2: New Working Conditions (pp. 191–92)

Objective

- To infer a definition of the term *sharecropper* using the word and a map of a plantation in 1880.

Developing the Section

Write the word *sharecropper* on the chalkboard. Explain that this word describes the employment status of many former African American slaves following the Civil War. Point out the map on p. 191 and, using this diagram and the two main parts of the word *sharecropper* (*share* and *crop[per]*), ask students to speculate on the term's meaning. Record responses on the chalkboard for review when students have completed the section.

Review and Practice

Assign "Taking Another Look," p. 192.

Answers to Questions in Captions (pp. 191–92)

(p. 191, map) to be free of the former slave owner's control (p. 191, picture) They seem eager. (p. 192) They worked for themselves, not an owner.

Answers to Taking Another Look (p. 192)

1. could work where they wished, doing work they chose and earning wages **2.** farmed land that belonged to someone else; bought all supplies on credit and owner of land subtracted amount owed from profits **3. Critical Thinking** **yes:** because he or she was free and not a slave; **no:** he or she was impoverished and debt-ridden

Teaching Section 3: Reconstruction Governments (pp. 192–94)

Objective

- To use a quotation to assess African American understanding of citizenship.

Historical Sidelight

A Mixed Jury. The first jury composed of both African Americans and whites was assembled during Reconstruction to try the case of former Confederate President Jefferson Davis. Shortly after the jury was assembled, the government decided not to press charges of treason and he was released from prison, where he had been held since the end of the war.

Developing the Section

Analyzing a Primary Source. Read aloud the following selection from a declaration issued by an African American convention in Alabama during Reconstruction.

> We claim *exactly the same rights, privileges immunities* [protections] *as are enjoyed by white men*—we ask nothing more and will be content with nothing less. . . . the law no longer knows white nor black, but simply men, and consequently we are entitled to ride in public conveyances, hold office, sit on juries and do everything else which we have in the past been prevented from doing solely on the ground of color.

Ask how the convention defined citizenship. (*equal rights, privileges, protections, and access to public office and services as whites*) Assign students, working in pairs, to write a paragraph explaining how well this standard was met before 1877.

Review and Practice

Assign "Taking Another Look," p. 194.

Answers to Questions in Captions (p. 193)

(bottom) interested in decisions that affected their lives (top) first African American in the Senate

Answers to Taking Another Look (p. 194)

1. abolished property test for voting and holding office, granted vote to adult males **2.** services to African Americans and poor whites through legal aid, medical care, public schools, improved hospitals and institutions; did away with Black Codes; outlawed corporal punishment, reduced capital punishment and penalties for theft **3. Critical Thinking** He educated himself, elevated his own position in society and fought for others.

Teaching Section 4: A Campaign of Terror (pp. 194–95)

Objective

- To discuss ways in which the actions of many white Southerners violated the rights of African American citizens.

Developing the Section

Discussing Rights of Citizens. Have students read the section. Then ask what actions by African Americans angered whites. (*attending school, voting, holding public office*) What did white terrorist groups think was the "place" of African Americans? (*slavery, bottom of society*) Refer the students to the table on p. 165. Ask what amendment the actions of white terrorist groups violated. (*14th*) Divide the class into small groups. Instruct each group to suggest a course of action that might have protected the rights of African Americans. Have them also suggest why that course was not followed.

Review and Practice

Assign "Taking Another Look," p. 195.

Answer to Question in Caption (p. 195)

terrorize African Americans to keep them from voting

Answers to Taking Another Look (p. 195)

1. unable to accept African Americans' freedom and rights **2.** reasonably successful; African Americans stayed away from polls, more white democrats held office, Reconstruction governments fell **3. Critical Thinking** may have sympathized with Ku Klux Klan and White Camelia, or feared their power

Extending the Chapter

Comparing Past and Present. Divide the class into four groups. Assign two groups to research African American members of the House and Senate during Reconstruction. The other two groups should investigate African American members in the House and Senate since 1960. Have each group present its findings in the form of a chart. Besides listing name, party affiliation, state or district represented, and occupation before entering Congress, students should include a brief biography of the member.

Looking Ahead

After students have read "Looking Ahead," p. 195, ask them to speculate on ways African Americans could improve conditions for themselves. Ask students if moving out of the South might have helped. Why or why not?

Answers to Close Up (pp. 196–97)

The Who, What, Where of History

1. period from end of Civil War to 1877 when federal government tried to restore the Union **2.** system in which landlord provides tenants with land and credit against profits from sale of harvest **3.** government agency that assisted former slaves, founded schools **4.** first African American to serve in U.S. Senate **5.** 1870s **6.** racially mixed **7.** laws in Southern states limiting rights of free African Americans **8.** second African American to serve in the U.S. Senate

Making the Connection

1. During slavery African Americans were mostly self-taught. During Reconstruction, freed African Americans went to school at Freedmen's Bureau schools. **2.** Newly freed African American slaves had no land or money and sharecropping seemed to offer a means of support.

Time Check

1. 1865–1877 **2. a.** 13th, 14th, 15th **b.** 13th—freed African American slaves; 14th—gave freed slaves citizenship; 15th—gave freed slaves right to vote

What Would You Have Done?

1. yes: voting is an important part of being a citizen, want to exercise new rights; **no:** fear for safety **2. stay:** need means of support, work until self supporting; **leave:** start new life

Thinking and Writing About History

1. might include legal marriage, reuniting of families, new role of father as head of household, no more field work, taking of surname **2.** laws to build schools, improve legal aid, provide medical care for needy

Building Skills

Examples: political effects: passage of 14th and 15th amendments, election of African Americans to Congress and state offices; **economic effects:** African Americans receiving wages for work, legal aid for the needy; **social effects:** schooling for African Americans, African American men heads of family, surnames

Chapter 19 Miners, Farmers, and Cowhands (pp. 198–205)

Overview

Even before the Civil War ended, African Americans had headed across the Mississippi. Some traveled to the California or Colorado gold fields, either as free African Americans hoping to strike it rich or as slaves working the gold fields for their owners. Others found work herding cattle. But the largest number of African Americans to travel west after the Civil War came in search of land—the key to economic freedom. These were the people known as Exodusters.

Resources

Chapter 19 Activity Sheet: Drawing Conclusions (p. 224)
Chapter 19 Test (p. 160)
Unit 6 Test (pp. 154–56)
Outline Map: The United States (p. 308)

Focus Activity

Have students skim the photographs in the chapter. Ask what occupations these photographs depict. (*farming, gold mining, cattle herding*) Ask what occupation they think most former slaves would choose. (*probably farming*) Why? Lead students to understand that farming was the work that African Americans knew best from their years as slaves. Also point out the connection between freedom and land ownership in the minds of many.

Teaching Section 1: The Gold Rush and After (pp. 199–200)

Objective

- To use a timeline to develop a historical framework for the western gold rushes.

Historical Sidelight

Spreading African American Culture. The free African Americans who headed into California during the gold rush brought their culture with them. The 1850s saw the establishment of African American churches in both San Francisco and Sacramento. They included, among others, an African Methodist Episcopal church—the church originally founded by Richard Allen.

Developing the Section

Developing a Historical Framework. Refer students to the unit timeline on pp. 162–63. Ask when the gold rush took place in California. (*1849*) When was gold and silver discovered in the western territories? (*1850s*) How would these discoveries affect settlement in the West? (*probably speed it up*) Based on other items on the timeline, what relationship did the gold and silver strikes have on the debate over slavery? (*probably added to the debate*) Why? (*raised the issue of statehood for California and whether slavery would be allowed in the western territories as a whole*)

Review and Practice

Assign "Taking Another Look," p. 200.

Answer to Question in Caption (p. 199)

No, most were merchants, barbers, and craftworkers.

Answers to Taking Another Look (p. 200)

1. escape limited opportunity, violence, and racism, search for gold **2.** barbers, merchants, craftworkers, newspaper or restaurant owners **3. Critical Thinking** determination, willingness to work hard, resourcefulness

Teaching Section 2: The Exodusters and the Sodbusters (pp.200–202)

Objective

- To illustrate the vision of the promised land of Kansas held by supporters of the Exodusters.

Developing the Section

Designing Posters. Tell students that "Pap" Singleton circulated posters showing African

American farmers surrounded by livestock and crops in Kansas. Divide the class into small groups, and have each group design a poster illustrating Singleton's vision of Kansas.

Review and Practice

Assign "Taking Another Look," p. 202.

Answer to Question in Caption (p. 201)

economic betterment, escape from repression and discrimination

Answers to Taking Another Look (p. 202)

1. to provide equal economic opportunity **2.** much freer on plains; could travel where, when, and for as long as they pleased; no curfews; less prejudice **3.** better off than they were as sharecroppers; could have their own land **4. Critical Thinking** less tradition of racism west of Mississippi

Teaching Section 3: Cattle Drives and Cowhands (pp. 202–203)

Objective

- To compare and contrast working conditions for sharecroppers and cowhands.

Developing the Section

Comparing and Contrasting. After students have read this section, instruct them to review the information on working conditions for sharecroppers on pp. 191–92. On the chalkboard write the terms *sharecropper* and *cowhand.* Under each job, write *advantages* and *disadvantages*. Have students, using text information and outside knowledge, suggest as many advantages and disadvantages for both jobs as they can.

Review and Practice

Assign "Taking Another Look," p. 203.

Answers to Taking Another Look (p. 203)

1. contrary to history, few African American cowhands portrayed **2. Critical Thinking** came west to escape southern racism; withstood hardships of nature and lived under difficult conditions

Extending the Chapter

Conducting Library Research. Assign groups of students to research the contributions of African Americans to the settlement of the area beyond the Mississippi. Have students present their findings in a series of short oral reports.

Looking Ahead

After students have read "Looking Ahead" (p. 203), call on students to summarize the situation of African Americans in the South in the late 1800s. See if students can reach a consensus on the biggest challenge facing African Americans.

Answers to Close Up (pp. 204–205)

1. California **2.** worked as merchants, barbers, and craftworkers **3.** African American who bought freedom, went to Colorado during Gold Rush, became one of Colorado's richest citizens **4.** African Americans who left South for West **5.** settlers on the Great Plains **6.** Kansas, Oklahoma, and areas farther west and north **7.** leaders of Exodusters in 1879 and 1880 **8.** heroes of common people, celebrated in legends and songs **9.** famous African American cowhand a.k.a. "Deadwood Dick" **10.** Between 1879 and 1880

Making the Connection

1. African American sharecroppers in South saw little hope for opportunity due to Southern prejudice; in West, greater opportunity and less racism **2.** Some African Americans had been brought West as slaves and were herding cattle before emancipation.

Time Check

1. before **2.** after

What Would You Have Done?

1. Exoduster or sodbuster: possibilities for decent family life, chance to be self-supporting; **cowhand:** prefer adventure, perpetual travel **2. separate:** no prejudice, no discrimination; **mixed:** only realistic way to work toward equality

Thinking and Writing About History

1. may mention inexpensive land, all African American communities, lack of racism **2.** should reflect a grasp of material on pp. 202–203

Building Skills

1. a, b **2.** a, c **3.** b, c **4.** a, b, c

UNIT 7 Freedom Without Equality (pp. 206–41)

UNIT THEME

During the post-Reconstruction years, African Americans struggle against segregation laws, lynchings, and efforts to disfranchise them while making progress in business, education, the arts and sciences.

UNIT CONCEPTS

- Poverty, disfranchisement, and the terror of lynchings brought a new form of slavery to African Americans in the New South.
- Jim Crow laws, reinforced by the decision in *Plessy* v. *Ferguson*, created a separate and unequal society.
- Some African Americans such as Ida B. Wells-Barnett fought the world of Jim Crow openly, while other African Americans such as Booker T. Washington favored a less confrontational course of action.
- African Americans entered the field of business in greater numbers and provided a stable base of educated, middle-class citizens.
- The educational, artistic, and scientific achievements of African Americans between 1877 and 1910 were all the more impressive because they were accomplished despite the handicap of segregation.

UNIT OVERVIEW

Unit 7 describes the post-Reconstruction years during which African Americans saw their hopes of equality shattered by the rise of Jim Crow. White supremacists showed little hesitancy in terrorizing and even lynching African Americans who dared to challenge efforts to disfranchise them or to keep them in economic bondage. Amid this hatred, a new generation of African Americans came of age—people determined to forge a place for themselves in the United States. *The Big Picture* and the three chapters in this unit describe: (1) the conditions faced by African Americans in the New South, (2) the response of African American leaders such as Booker T. Washington to prejudice, and (3) the achievements of African Americans during this period.

In teaching this unit, you might copy these signs on the chalkboard:

Whites Only   Negroes and Freight Only   No Blacks Allowed

Tell students that during the late 19th century and well into this century, African Americans saw such signs all over the South and even in parts of the North. Ask students to discuss the effect of such signs on African Americans. Remind students that such signs were a result of the legal policy of segregation. As a precursor to Unit 9, ask students to suggest ways African Americans could resist such policies mandated by state and local laws.

COOPERATIVE LEARNING ACTIVITY

The following cooperative learning activity can be used for alternative assessment after study of the unit has been completed.

To bring closure to the unit, divide students into cooperative learning groups. Tell them to imagine they are part of the curriculum committee for a new African American college being founded in 1900. The students are to set up a program of study for the college. Each group is to decide what disciplines will be taught, such as foreign languages, English, industrial arts, philosophy, and so on, and what courses should be offered within each discipline. Have each group present its curriculum to the class, explaining how its plan will help African Americans succeed. In evaluating each presentation, consider how well students have fit their curriculum within the historical context of the times and how persuasive the arguments are that they use to defend their programs.

Unit 7 THE BIG PICTURE (pp. 207–11)

Theme

The United States entered a period of tremendous growth and expansion toward the end of the 19th century, but African Americans had little share in the increased national wealth.

Overview

The Big Picture explores the benefits and difficulties that accompanied the nation's rapid economic growth in the years 1877–1910. During the post-Reconstruction era, the United States underwent a second industrial revolution as new industries and new forms of business organization appeared. Business leaders grew wealthy and became notable public figures.

Not all citizens shared in the new wealth. Workers organized labor unions to battle for safe working conditions, reasonable working hours, and fair wages. But a flood of immigrants from southern and eastern Europe, willing to work cheaply in order to survive, weakened efforts to unionize.

The large-scale arrival of immigrants hurt African Americans' hopes to escape the agricultural poverty of the South by finding work in the factories of the Northeast and Midwest. Southerners touted a New South with a varied economy based on both agriculture and industry, but in reality, far fewer factories opened in the South than in the rest of the country. Those that did often refused to employ African Americans.

Objectives

- To form inferences about the rights lost by African Americans during the years 1877–1910.
- To use a timeline to analyze the impact of new U.S. technology.
- To write a letter to analyze the impact of new technology.
- To reenact a scene showing the relationship between business and labor in the late 1800s.
- To analyze a description of the ethnic makeup of a voting district in Chicago.
- To infer how African Americans might have responded to the term *New South*.
- To interpret a song about settlement on the Great Plains.

Introducing *The Big Picture*

Refer students to "An African American Speaks" on p. 207. Point out that Reconstruction ended in 1877. Ask how many years had passed by the time Representative Miller spoke (*14*). What rights does he say African Americans have lost, or failed to win, in that time? (*the right to wages for their labor; the right to trial by jury; the right to prevent intruders from entering their homes; the right to prosecute whites for violent crimes committed against them*)

Using the Timeline

Divide the class into groups. Direct them to study the timeline on pp. 208–209. Tell the groups to select two events on the timeline that are connected and prepare a brief paragraph explaining the connection. Students may skim *The Big Picture* and other chapters in the unit for additional information they may need to explain the connection.

Teaching *The Big Picture*

1. Writing a Letter. Assign "The Growth of Industry" on p. 207. Then tell students that many examples of American technical achievement were first exhibited at the nation's Centennial Exposition, held in Philadelphia in 1876. Here, American inventors unveiled the telephone, typewriter, and electric elevator. Divide the class into small groups and ask each to select one of these inventions. Then each group should write a letter home explaining their reactions upon "first" seeing the invention. They should include predictions about how the invention might change the way Americans live or work.

2. Reenacting History. Have students read "The Rise of Big Business" and "Labor and Unions" on pp. 207–209, paying particular attention to the description of working conditions. Then, divide the class into two negotiating teams. One team should represent the owners of a factory. The other team should represent an early union such as the Knights of Labor. Assign union leaders to draw up a list of demands to present to the owners. The team representing the corporation should consider the demands and prepare responses. Remind both teams that the balance of power in negotiations at the time was tipped in favor of big business.

3. Analyzing a Quotation. Assign "Immigration" and "Growth of Cities" on pp. 209–10. Then read aloud the following description of one Chicago voting district during the late 1800s.

> Between Halsted Street and the river live about ten thousand Italians, Neapolitans, Sicilians, and Calabrians. . . . To the south on Twelfth Street are many Germans, and the side streets are given over almost entirely to Polish and Prussian Jews. Further south, three Jewish colonies merge into a huge Bohemian colony. . . . To the north-west are many Canadians. . . . and to the north are many Irish.

Ask students what parts of the world the immigrants came from. (*central, southern, and eastern Europe, Canada, and Ireland*) Why might the immigrants have lived in separate neighborhoods? (*Living together helped immigrants make the transition to U.S. society more easily; result of prejudice and discrimination*) Point out that African Americans were not the only people to live in isolated districts in the North.

4. Making Inferences. After students have read "The New South" on pp. 210–11, ask them to infer how African Americans might have reacted to the term *New South*. Have them imagine they are African Americans living in the South in 1800. Ask them to list things they think would be necessary to make the South truly "new" for African Americans. Compile their suggestions on the chalkboard. Revise and add to the list as the class works through the unit.

5. Interpreting a Song. Read aloud the following lyrics from a popular song sung by settlers heading west of the Mississippi in the late 1800s.

> Come along, come along—don't be alarmed,
> Uncle Sam is rich enough to give us all a farm.

Then assign "Westward Expansion" on p. 211. Ask students whom Uncle Sam represents. (*the federal government*) Where did the government get the land to give away for farms? (*from Native Americans*) What effect did settlement of the Plains have on Native Americans? (*destroyed their way of life and restricted them to confined tracts of land*) Ask students to compare the nation's treatment of Native Americans with that of African Americans.

Review and Practice

Assign "Taking Another Look," p. 211.

Answers to Taking Another Look (p. 211)

1. shift from agriculture to industry, gross national product grew, advent of "big business" and monopolies **2.** number of cities and their populations mushroomed due to immigration **3. Critical Thinking** Some impoverished ethnic groups eventually moved into the middle class; farmers, cattle ranchers, miners benefited from expansion west.

Chapter 20 African Americans in the New South (pp. 212–21)

Overview

The post-Reconstruction years brought continued poverty and the loss of political rights to African Americans living in the South. Jim Crow laws imposed so many restrictions on African Americans that life was not much different than it had been under slavery. Southern whites restricted African Americans to the least desirable and lowest-paying jobs the region had to offer, and moved to silence their political voice by denying them the vote and threatening to lynch any who protested. With the decision in *Plessy* v. *Ferguson*, segregation became part of the law of the land. Some African Americans, however, including Thomas Fortune and Ida B. Wells-Barnett, continued to fight for full citizenship for African Americans.

Resources

Chapter 20 Activity Sheet: Comparing Supreme Court Opinions (pp. 225–26)
Chapter 20 Test (p. 164)
Unit 7 Writing Workshop: Stating Your Case (pp. 286–89)

Focus Activity

Have students study the photographs in the chapter, the "Snapshot of the Times" on p. 213, and the charts on pp. 215 and 216. Then read aloud the chapter-opening question: "Why were the closing decades of the 1800s and the first years of the 1900s a difficult time for African Americans in the South?" Ask students to offer preliminary answers to this question, based on the information in the pictures, charts, and "Snapshot". Record their responses on the chalkboard, and modify or add to the list as students work through the chapter.

Teaching Section 1: Hard Work and More Poverty (pp. 213–14)

Objective

- To gather evidence in support of a description of the South by an African American journalist.

Developing the Section

Gathering Evidence. Have students copy onto a piece of notebook paper the statement by T. Thomas Fortune on p. 213. Assign students, working individually or in small groups, to list evidence from the section that supports Fortune's description of the South. After students have finished, compile a master list on the chalkboard discussing each piece of evidence as you list it.

Review and Practice

Assign "Taking Another Look," p. 215.

Answers to Taking Another Look (p. 215)

1. sharecroppers continuously in debt; industrial jobs dangerous; women working as domestics earned lowest pay of anyone in U.S.; excluded from labor unions; paid less than whites for same work **2.** offered employment as strikebreakers during labor union strikes; convict-lease system provided free labor, decreasing the number of paying jobs **3. Critical Thinking** African Americans were denied rights of citizenship. New immigrants were treated better than African American citizens.

Teaching Section 2: The Land of Jim Crow (pp. 215–18)

Objectives

- To write a letter summarizing the situation facing African Americans in the South in the 1890s.
- To assess the dissenting opinion in *Plessy* v. *Ferguson.*

Historical Sidelight

Lone Voice of Dissent. When the Supreme Court handed down its decision in *Plessy* v. *Ferguson*, Justice John Marshall Harlan issued a blistering dissent. He argued that the "Constitution is color-blind, and neither knows nor tolerates classes among citizens." He went on to predict that "the judgment this day rendered will, in time, prove to be quite as pernicious [wicked] as the decision made by this tribunal [Court] in the *Dred Scott* case." In 1954, the Supreme Court overturned *Plessy* with a unanimous decision in the case of *Brown* v. *Board of Education of Topeka*. Casting a vote in this historic decision was John Marshall Harlan, Jr., grandson of the lone dissenter in the *Plessy* decision.

Developing the Section

1. Writing to Congress. Divide students into small groups and have the groups write letters to their representatives in Congress explaining the situation facing African Americans in the South during the 1890s. At the end of their letters, have students propose one law that they think would help to correct the situation. Call on students to read their letters aloud.

2. Assessing a Court Decision. Read the "Historical Sidelight" entitled: "Lone Voice of Dissent." Ask on what grounds Harlan protested the decision in *Plessy.* (*Constitution was "color-blind" and did not tolerate "classes among citizens"*) Ask students why they think Harlan predicted the ruling would prove as wicked as the decision in the *Dred Scott* case. (*Ruling gave states the right to institute legalized segregation and to pass laws on the basis of color.*)

Review and Practice

Assign "Taking Another Look," p. 218.

Answers to Questions in Captions (pp. 215–16)

(p.215) without the vote and political power, African Americans would be second-class citizens, at mercy of whites (p. 216) racism; fear of blacks gaining power in society

Answers to Taking Another Look (p. 218)

1. poll tax: fee to vote; **property test:** vote given only to property owners; **literacy test:** had to read to vote; **grandfather clause:** waived literacy and property tests for men whose grandfathers were eligible to vote before Civil War; **white primary elections:** primaries from which African American men could be banned because they were not covered by 15th Amendment **2.** denied 14th amendment meant to abolish segregation, allowed "separate but equal" facilities **3. Critical Thinking** 14th Amendment "could not have been intended to abolish distinctions based on color"; questionable interpretation

Teaching Section 3: The African American Response (pp. 218–19)

Objective

- To set priorities for improving the lives of African Americans in the early 1900s.

Historical Sidelight

Colonization Movement—Again. The oppression of the Jim Crow world led some African Americans to reconsider colonization. Edwin P. McCabe proposed an African American colony within the United States. He suggested that Congress turn the Oklahoma Territory, home of many Exodusters, into an African American state.

Developing the Section

Setting Priorities. Tell students that during the early 1900s, African Americans and their white supporters began to organize self-help groups to improve the lives of those trapped in the world of Jim Crow. Then divide the class into small groups, and assign each group to create an agenda for change for one of these groups. Each group should list its top three priorities and the methods it proposes to achieve these goals. Call on the recorder from each group to propose its plan to the class.

Review and Practice

Assign "Taking Another Look," p. 219.

Answers to Taking Another Look (p. 219)

1. petitioned Congress for new civil rights bill, petitioned individual states, boycotted segregated streetcar companies **2.** wrote antilynching editorials for her paper, *Free Speech*; compiled *The Red Record*, a study of lynchings from 1892 to 1895 **3. Critical Thinking** believed cause of equal rights was worth risking safety

Extending the Chapter

Developing Empathy. Divide the class into pairs. One student should take the part of an African American in the Deep South; the other, an African American in the Northeast. Assign students from the South to write letters to their Northern friends in which they describe what it is like to live under Jim Crow. Students from the North should write letters reacting to the situations their friends have described. Call on volunteers to read their letters aloud. You might save the "letters" from Northern African Americans and have students add to them after reading Chapter 24.

Looking Ahead

After students have read "Looking Ahead," p. 219, ask them to discuss whether they would have stayed in the South to fight Jim Crow or whether they would have tried to escape by moving to the Northeast or Midwest. Students may rethink these views after reading Chapter 24.

Answers to Close Up (pp. 220–21)

The Who, What, Where of History

1. system of segregation laws in South **2.** South with variety of crops, decent race relations, growing industry **3.** association of workers formed to protect their rights **4.** work gangs leased out to perform labor without receiving wages **5.** denying rights of citizenship **6.** African American who refused to move from whites-only railroad car **7.** 1896 Supreme Court decision established separate but equal doctrine, limited 14th amendment **8.** murdering by mob action **9.** African American journalist who led anti-lynching campaign

Making the Connection

1. During strikes by white workers employers would offer jobs to African Americans as strikebreakers; ill will between African Americans and whites increased. **2.** Free convict labor decreased the number of paying jobs available.

Time Check

1. 1883 **2.** 1896

What Would You Have Done?

1. would be strikebreaker: feel no solidarity with whites-only union, need job badly; **would not be strikebreaker:** believe it's wrong to engage in union busting, could gain from successful strike **2. leave:** city government refuses to protect personal safety, no equal treatment; **stay:** connections to friends, family, desire to effect change

Thinking and Writing About History

1. The cost of land lease and supplies outweighed available profits from crop sale, and created an inescapable cycle of debt. Some owners cheated sharecroppers. **2.** Descriptions should show understanding of all aspects of daily life that were affected by Jim Crow laws and specifically mention segregated facilities.

Building Skills

1. race **2.** property **3.** Alabama, Florida, Georgia, Louisiana, Mississippi, South Carolina, Tennessee, Texas, Virginia **4.** Alabama, Georgia, Louisiana, Mississippi, North Carolina, Virginia **5.** better chance of voting in 1930 because states had abolished race requirement

Chapter 21 Living in the Jim Crow World (pp. 222–31)

Overview

Should African Americans live with Jim Crow or try to fight it? This became the controversial question for African Americans in the late 1800s and the beginning of this century. Booker T. Washington chose the former. He urged African Americans to pull themselves up by their bootstraps to seize opportunities that lay within their grasp. Washington's accommodation on issues such as segregation and disfranchisement drew criticism from some African Americans, though many still saw him as their spokesman. Washington promoted African American enterprise, believing African American businesses would provide a stepping-stone into the mainstream economy of the nation. Despite obstacles, a small number of African Americans set out to test that belief.

Resources

Chapter 21 Activity Sheet: Analyzing Political Cartoon (p. 227)
Chapter 21 Test (p. 165)

Focus Activity

Assign the chapter-opening story on pp. 222–23. Ask students what approach to change Washington disagreed with. (*protest*) What approach did he favor instead? (*advancement through industrial education, self-help, and business ownership*)

Teaching Section 1: A Strong Leader (pp. 223–27)

Objective

- To infer reasons why Washington might have placed economic improvement ahead of ending Jim Crow.

Historical Sidelight

A Strange Entrance Exam. In 1872, Booker T. Washington arrived at Hampton Institute. His trip had left his clothes so rumpled and worn that Washington feared the teacher would turn him away. After several hours, the teacher told Washington to clean the classroom. She then left him alone. Washington grabbed a dusting-cloth and broom and went to work. When the teacher returned, she inspected the room closely. Finding not a trace of dirt, she said softly: "I guess you will do to enter this institution." As Washington later recalled, "Sweeping that room was my college examination," he wrote, "and never did any youth pass an examination into Harvard or Yale that gave him more satisfaction."

Developing the Section

Analyzing a Quotation. Open the section by reading aloud the following two statements made by Booker T. Washington in the late 1800s.

> The opportunity to earn a dollar in a factory just now is worth [far] more than the opportunity to spend a dollar in an opera.
>
> • • •
>
> There is little race prejudice in the American dollar.

Ask students, based on these two quotations, which goal they think Booker T. Washington would be most likely to tackle first—ending Jim Crow or improving economic conditions for African Americans. (*economic improvement*) Lead them into a discussion of why Washington might have chosen this course. Remind them of the poverty that the vast majority of African Americans faced in the post-Reconstruction years. Ask students if they think that improvement in their economic well-being would have helped African Americans to tear down other barriers to full participation in U.S. society.

Review and Practice

Assign "Taking Another Look," p. 227.

Answers to Questions in Captions (pp. 225–26)

(p. 225) believed that such education offered the best way to increase economic opportunities (p. 226) Fortune

Answers to Taking Another Look (p. 227)

1. practical education in subjects such as farming, carpentry, sewing **2.** social segregation was acceptable, economic integration was essential for advancement **3. Critical Thinking** Washington asked for concessions from whites while making concessions to whites.

Teaching Section 2: African American Businesses (pp. 227–29)

Objective

- To analyze statistics on African American occupations during the years 1890–1930.

Historical Sidelight

Villa Lewaro. In 1916, entrepreneur Madame C. J. Walker built Villa Lewaro in Irvington-on-the Hudson, New York, as a showplace to inspire other African Americans to reach for their dreams. In 1991, A'leila Perry Bundles, Mme. Walker's great-great-granddaughter, started a campaign to turn the mansion into an African American landmark. Backers of the project included Alex Haley, the author of *Roots*, and television personality Oprah Winfrey. Villa Lewaro, explained Ms. Bundles, stands for what her great-great-grandmother termed "the wealth of business possibilities within the race to point to young Negroes what a lone woman can accomplish and to inspire them to do big things."

Developing the Section

Analyzing a Table. To open the section, copy

the following table on the chalkboard or distribute copies to students.

African American Occupations, 1890–1930

Occupation	1890	1910	1930
Agricultural	56%	55%	38%
Domestic service	31%	23%	29%
Manufacturing/ mechanical	7%	13%	19%
Transportation/ trade/clerical	5%	7%	11%
Professional	1%	2%	3%

Ask students what jobs most African Americans held in 1890. (*agricultural, domestic service*) Which two job categories showed the biggest increase between 1890 and 1930? (*manfacturing/mechanical and transportation/trade/clerical*) Which occupational category was the most difficult for African Americans to enter? (*professional*) Ask students what traits they think an African American entrepreneur needed to possess to succeed in the economic climate of the late 1800s and early 1900s. Record student responses on the chalkboard. Modify or add to the list as students work through the section.

Review and Practice

Assign "Taking Another Look," p. 229.

Answers to Taking Another Look (p. 229)

1. food stores, restaurants, drugstores, cigar stores, dry-cleaning establishments, shoe-repair shops, as well as services unavailable to African Americans elsewhere **2.** inexperience, poor business decisions, undesirable locations, competition with white businesses offering lower prices **3. Critical Thinking** more self-help societies to assist African American businesses

Extending the Chapter

Comparing Past to Present. Assign groups of students to investigate local African American-run businesses. Suggest that students contact the Chamber of Commerce or the local chapter of the NAACP for information. Direct the members of each group to contact one such business for information about its founding. Have students share their findings in the form of oral reports.

Looking Ahead

After students have read "Looking Ahead," p. 229, tell them that the late 1800s and early 1900s saw an explosion of African American cultural achievements. Ask students to speculate on why African Americans might have turned to artistic expression amid the repression of Jim Crow. (*As a hint for them, recall how the arts had helped maintain pride in the African American heritage during slavery.*)

Answers to Close Up (pp. 230–31)

The Who, What, Where of History

1. African American leader and founder of Tuskegee Institute **2.** Tuskegee, Alabama **3.** Washington's 1895 speech advocating advancement through job skills as opposed to political protest **4.** organization founded by Washington to promote African American businesses **5.** African American woman who founded a cosmetics company catering to African Americans and amassed a fortune

Making the Connection

White-owned insurance companies often wouldn't insure African American businesses. African American self-help societies set up insurance companies and banks to help African American business people prosper.

Time Check

1895

What Would You Have Done?

1. agree: only by entering middle class through economic achievement will respect of whites be gained, equal citizenship status will follow; **disagree:** full rights guaranteed by Constitution, African Americans should settle for nothing less **2. yes:** Tuskegee could be used as a stepping-stone to other education; **no:** prefer to study subject of interest outside of African American college system if necessary

Thinking and Writing About History

1. should show understanding of Tuskegee's goals and use proper letter form **2. Examples:** If rights are guaranteed by the Constitution, why shouldn't African Americans demand them? Can African Americans hope to achieve true equality if they don't have complete equality in all aspects of American life? Responses should show understanding of Washington quotations in text.

Building Skills

1. 5 **2.** 7 **3.** cannot tell from chart

Chapter 22 Advances in Education, the Arts, and Science (pp. 232–41)

Overview

Freedom brought opportunity to thousands of African Americans who sought to use their talents and intellectual gifts. When white-run governments failed to aid them, African Americans took the initiative and started elementary schools, high schools, and colleges. People began to take notice of breakthroughs by African Americans in the arts and sciences.

Resources

Chapter 22 Activity Sheet: Analyzing a Bar Graph (pp. 228–29)
Chapter 22 Test (p. 166)
Unit 7 Test (pp. 161–63)
Lesson Plans for *The Artist's View* (p. 110)
Outline Map: The United States (p. 308)

Focus Activity

Open the chapter by reading aloud the following selection from a speech delivered to Congress in 1894 by African American Representative George H. Murray.

> We have proven in almost every line that we are capable of doing what other people can do. We have proven that we can work as much and as well as other people. We have proven that we can learn as well as other people. We have proven that we can fight as well as other people. . . . There are still, however, . . . slanderers . . . who claim that we are not equal to others because we have failed to produce inventors.

Refer students to the "Snapshot of the Times" on p. 239, the "Gallery" on pp. 236–37, and the "Focus On" feature on p. 240. Have groups of students complete Murray's speech refuting the charge that African Americans are not inventors. Call on students to read their endings aloud to the class.

Teaching Section 1: Education (pp. 233–38)

Objective

- To interpret a map using statistics on the distribution of African American colleges in the United States.

Developing the Section

Using Statistics to Interpret a Map. Copy the following table onto the chalkboard or distribute copies to students.

Percentage of All African Americans Who Lived in the South	
Year	Percentage
1880	91%
1900	90%
1920	85%
1940	75%
1960	55%

Then refer students to the map and questions in the caption on p. 233. Ask them how the figures in the table help answer the second question raised in the caption. (*prove that most African Americans lived in the South during the late 1800s and early 1900s*) Ask what common background and experiences they think most African Americans who attended these colleges in the late 1800s might have shared. (*Most students or their parents lived under slavery; most had experience with Jim Crow laws.*) What benefits might African American colleges have offered? (*sheltered students from prejudice*) What drawbacks? (*no chance to interact with whites who dominated U.S. society*)

Review and Practice

Assign "Taking Another Look," p. 238.

Answer to Questions in Caption (p. 233)

Southern states, that most African Americans probably lived there

Answers to Taking Another Look (p. 238)

1. literacy rate among African Americans more than doubled **2. Howard:** trained African American doctors, lawyers, engineers; **Spelman:** women's college; **Wilberforce:** trained men for ministry; **Shaw:** one of the first medical schools for African Americans **3. Critical Thinking** allowed them access to higher education, improved career opportunities

Teaching Section 2: The Arts (pp. 238–39)

Objective

- To plan an interview of famous African American musicians, writers, and artists of the late 1800s and early 1900s.

Historical Sidelight

Revival. Ragtime music faded from popularity after World War I. In the 1970s, however, musicians rediscovered ragtime and Scott Joplin. The score of the hit movie *The Sting*, based heavily on Joplin tunes, won an Academy Award. Joplin's opera *Treemonisha* was first produced 60 years after it was written and earned Joplin a posthumous Pulitzer Prize in 1976.

Developing the Section

Conducting Interviews. Divide the class into four groups. Tell the students to imagine they are reporters for one of the African American newspapers started at the turn of the century, such as the *Baltimore Afro-American* (1893), the *Chicago Defender* (1905), or the *Pittsburgh Courier* (1910). Direct student-reporters to prepare five questions they would ask the writers, musicians, and artists in the "Gallery" on pp. 234–35. Questions should exhibit knowledge of the subject drawn from the "Gallery".

Review and Practice

Assign "Taking Another Look," p. 239.

Answers to Taking Another Look (p. 239)

1. highly rhythmic music based on blues **2.** less prejudice in Europe **3. Critical Thinking** Good music appeals to all groups.

Teaching Section 3: Achievements in Science and Invention (pp. 239–40)

Objective

- To write recommendations citing achievements of African American scientists and inventors

Developing the Section

Writing a Recommendation. Point out that Lewis H. Latimer was the only African American member of the Edison Pioneers, a group of scientists and inventors who worked in the Edison laboratories before 1885. Next, tell students to imagine that the Edison Pioneers accept applications for membership from other scientists and inventors of the day. Have students, working individually or in groups, write letters of recommendation for one of the African Americans mentioned in the "Gallery."

Review and Practice

Assign "Taking Another Look," p. 239

Answers to Taking Another Look (p. 239)

1. both African American inventors **2.** rare for African Americans to have science background before higher education available **3. Critical Thinking** **Carver:** 300 uses for peanut, 100 for sweet potato; **Matzeliger:** shoe-lasting machine; **McCoy:** lubricating cup; **Rillieux:** sugar refining; **Woods:** automatic railroad brake

Extending the Chapter

Preparing an Audiovisual Show. Divide the class into groups to find pictures of artistic works, recordings of music, or literary selections of one of the figures in the "Gallery" on pp. 234–35. Have students present their findings to the class.

Looking Ahead

After students have read "Looking Ahead," p. 239, refer them to the criticisms of Booker T. Washington on p. 226. Encourage them to speculate on some new courses of action to improve conditions for African Americans that would depart from Washington's Atlanta Compromise idea.

Answers to Close Up (pp. 240–41)

The Who, What, Where of History

1. Washington D.C. university training African American leaders **2.** type of music based on offbeat rhythms **3.** composer known as Father of the Blues **4.** first important African American writer of fiction **5.** poet and fiction writer, one of the first nationally known African American writers **6.** composer and pianist who brought ragtime to prominence **7.** African American portrait sculptor **8.** scientist who revolutionized agriculture of South

Making the Connection

1. trained African American students for white-dominated professions in which earnings lead to middle class status **2.** call-and-response

Time Check

1. 1872 **2.** 1909

What Would You Have Done?

move: did not want to waste training, loved opera **switch:** because of friends or family ties

Thinking and Writing About History

1. should discuss value of practical education, such as at Tuskegee, or value of professional education, such as at Howard **2.**Questions should demonstrate understanding of achievements.

Building Skills

1. cunning **2.** say one thing and mean another **3.** African Americans, whites **4.** African Americans cannot show whites how they really feel **5.** difficult and stressful lives; always had to disguise feelings

UNIT 8 Protest and Hope in a New Century (pp. 242–99)

UNIT THEME

Frustrated by the slow pace of change, some African Americans begin to press more actively for equality, planting the seeds of the later Civil Rights Movement.

UNIT CONCEPTS

- The failure of Progressive reformers to address the oppression of Jim Crow encouraged African American leaders to search for ways to unite as a political force for change.
- A new generation of African American reformers rejected the accommodation of Booker T. Washington in favor of agitation and protest.
- Under the direction of W.E.B. Du Bois, the NAACP took the issues of lynching and segregation into the legislatures and courtrooms of the United States.
- A combination of natural disasters, white Southern repression, and labor shortages caused by World War I set off a Great Migration of Southern African Americans to cities of the North and Midwest.
- African American soldiers who fought in segregated units during World War I to "make the world safe for democracy" returned home with a strengthened resolve to win equal rights.
- In the 1920s, the black nationalism of Marcus Garvey and the Harlem Renaissance brought a new sense of pride to many African Americans.
- African Americans suffered disproportionately during the Great Depression and many switched their political allegiance to Franklin D. Roosevelt and the Democrats, whose New Deal programs provided the promise of some relief.

UNIT OVERVIEW

Unit 8 recounts the turmoil of the early 1900s as aggressive new African American leaders declared an end to the accommodation of Booker T. Washington. It was an era of tremendous, and sometimes painful, change. *The Big Picture* and the five chapters in this unit describe: (1) the rise of the NAACP and a new era in the historic civil rights struggle, (2) the migration of rural African Americans to the North and Midwest, (3) the beginning of black nationalism, (4) the Harlem Renaissance, and (5) the effects of the Great Depression and the realignment of African American political loyalties during the New Deal.

In teaching this unit, you might write the words *Black* and *Beautiful* on the chalkboard. Then draw a line connecting the two terms. Tell students that this simple diagram represents a key concept in the African American experience that developed from 1900 to 1940. Repeat the advice offered by W.E.B. Du Bois: Look for "beauty in black." Ask why Du Bois considered this connection essential to African American progress. In the following discussion, lead students to understand how prejudice erodes a person's will to succeed and how a positive self-image can counter that effect.

COOPERATIVE LEARNING ACTIVITY

The following cooperative learning activity can be used for alternative assessment after study of the unit has been completed.

At the end of the unit, review the idea of "beauty in black" developed by Du Bois and Garvey. Then divide the class into groups, and have each group prepare a photo montage offering evidence of ways this idea influences African Americans today. Pictures can be clipped from newspapers or magazines or shot in the students' own community. Pictures should be arranged on posters for display throughout the rest of the course. In evaluating group projects, consider the originality of approach and the thematic arrangement of the posters.

Unit 8 THE BIG PICTURE (pp. 243–47)

Theme

The Progressive era, World War I, the economic boom of the 1920s, and the Great Depression of the 1930s profoundly altered life in the United States during the early years of the 20th century and increased African Americans' desires for full rights and participation in society.

Overview

The Big Picture tells the story of the first 40 years of this century. In that time, the United States moved from Progressive idealism to postwar disillusionment, from economic boom to economic bust. As the century opened, reformers were attempting to correct the social problems that resulted from rapid urban growth. They focused on improving slums and corrupt government and on harnessing the power of big business. But Progressives paid scant attention to the problems facing African Americans. The exception was a handful of white reformers who joined with African Americans in founding the National Association for the Advancement of Colored People (NAACP).

World War I ended the Progressive Era and brought major changes for African Americans. Millions left the South to escape Jim Crow and find jobs in the defense industries of the North and Midwest. Over 370,000 African Americans fought in segregated units during the war and came home to a segregated society.

After the war, many people in the United States experienced the benefits of the nation's economic boom. African Americans, however, did not share equally in the new prosperity. In addition, in the South they faced persecution and lynching at the hands of a revitalized Ku Klux Klan. Despite these obstacles, African American artists, writers, and musicians contributed to the period with a stunning outpouring of creativity that was known as the Harlem Renaissance.

During the Great Depression of the 1930s, conditions for many African Americans became nearly unbearable. In these hard times, President Franklin D. Roosevelt's social program offered a glimmer of hope, though Roosevelt at first was slow to extend the benefits of these programs to African Americans. In a historic political realignment, African Americans by the thousands left the Republican party of Lincoln to join the New Deal Democrats represented by Roosevelt.

Objectives

- To compare the strategies by which Booker T. Washington and W.E.B. Du Bois hoped to achieve progress for African Americans.
- To use a timeline to speculate on advances and setbacks for African Americans from 1900–1941.
- To write a speech that a Progressive candidate for office might have delivered.
- To design a poster urging African Americans to support World War I.
- To write letters protesting the treatment of African Americans after World War I.
- To prepare news reports on key events of the Roaring Twenties and Great Depression.
- To infer from a photograph how the Great Depression may have affected the political choices of African Americans.

Introducing *The Big Picture*

Select a volunteer to read from Booker T. Washington's Atlanta speech on text p. 250. Then have another student read from "An African American Speaks" on p. 243. Ask which speaker is more defiant. (*W.E.B. Du Bois*) What evidence supports that answer? (*Focus student attention on the active verbs used by Du Bois: "We went in for agitation"; "We pushed"; "We demanded"; "We urged and pushed"; "We encouraged"; "We studied"; "We declared."*) Briefly review conditions for African Americans in the South after Reconstruction. Ask which approach to change might have best served African Americans living in the rural South at that time. (*probably Washington's approach*) Why? (*brutal repression during the Jim Crow era*)

Using the Timeline

Before assigning *The Big Picture*, have students study the timeline on pp. 244–45. Write the words *Setbacks* and *Advances* on the chalkboard. Ask students to speculate on which entries on the timeline represent advances in the efforts of African Americans to gain equal rights and which represent setbacks in the progress toward that goal. List responses under the appropriate word, making sure that students explain why they assign a particular event to that category.

Teaching *The Big Picture*

1. Writing a Speech. Assign "The Progressive Era" and "Progressive Achievements" on pp. 243–44. Then divide the class into small groups.

Have each group write a campaign speech for a Progressive candidate running for federal or state office to be delivered to African American voters in a Northern city. Be sure students include some of the victories for which a Progressive might have taken credit. Assign at least one group to write a speech from the point of view of an African American candidate. Have the recorder from each group read its speech. Discuss with the class whether they found the arguments convincing.

2. Designing Posters. After students have read "World War I" and "The Home Front" on pp. 244–45, have them design posters urging African Americans to support the war effort. Some posters should urge enlistment in the military. Others should encourage African Americans on the home front to make contributions to the war effort.

3. Writing a Letter to Congress. Based on information in "The Aftermath of War" on p. 245, direct students to write letters to a member of Congress protesting the racial tension underlying the Red Scare. Some letters should be written from the point of view of an African American who served in World War I; others, from the viewpoint of someone who worked in a defense plant.

4. Preparing a News Report. Divide students into small groups, and assign each group one of the following topics: the election of Warren Harding, investment in the stock market, the Harlem Renaissance, the stock market crash of 1929, the election of Franklin D. Roosevelt. Using information from "The Roaring Twenties" and "The Great Depression" on pp. 245–46, have students prepare one-minute news reports for a radio news broadcast. If time allows, you might have students do additional research in U.S. history textbooks used in your school.

5. Interpreting a Photograph. Refer students to the photo on p. 247. Using information from "The Great Depression" and "The New Deal" on pp. 246–47, ask why the homeless called shanty towns "Hoovervilles". (*because Hoover had failed to find a solution to the problems that had created the shanty towns*) Would people in the shanty towns be likely to vote for or against Roosevelt in 1936? (*for*) Why? (*He had started programs to bring about some relief.*)

Review and Practice

Assign "Taking Another Look," p. 247.

Answer to Question in Caption (p. 247)

to mock President Hoover, who many people blamed for failing to take action to relieve the effects of the depression

Answers to Taking Another Look (p. 247)

1. Jane Addams's Hull House, National Consumers League, "good government" organizations, constitutional amendments enacting income tax, suffrage for women, banning alcohol **2.** created government bodies to deal with different aspects of nation's economic problems **3. Critical Thinking yes:** economic boom would be better for everyone; **no:** "normalcy" did not include working for reform

Chapter 23 The Civil Rights Struggle (pp. 248–57)

Overview

In the early 1900s, some African Americans began to question Booker T. Washington's policy of accommodation. Among Washington's most vocal critics was W.E.B. Du Bois. Du Bois called upon exceptional African Americans—the Talented Tenth—to lead the way in a civil rights struggle. To carry his message across the nation, Du Bois helped found the NAACP and its literary arm, the *Crisis*. Articles and editorials in the *Crisis* supported agitation, urging African Americans to attack segregation and lynching in the legislatures and courtrooms of the nation. This young civil rights movement indicated that the impetus for future efforts at gaining equality would come not from whites but from African Americans. The time for change had arrived, said Du Bois, and African Americans should act.

Resources

Chapter 23 Activity Sheet A: Drawing Conclusions (pp. 230–31)
Chapter 23 Activity Sheet B: Recognizing Points of View (p. 232)
Chapter 23 Test (p. 170)

Focus Activity

Assign the chapter-opening story on pp. 248–49. Ask why the incident was significant. (*an African American was openly challenging Booker T. Washington, long accepted as leader*) What did Trotter demand? (*full and immediate equality*) How did this call to action differ from Washington's strategy? (*Washington favored gradual change through economic improvement and power of example.*) How might most whites at the time have viewed Trotter's outburst? (*Answers will probably suggest that most whites favored Washington's tactics. Students might suggest some support for Trotter among the Progressives.*)

Teaching Section 1: W.E.B. Du Bois (pp. 249–51)

Objective

- To analyze how W.E.B. Du Bois viewed the relationship between African Americans and whites.

Developing the Section

Analyzing a Quotation. Read aloud the following selection from *The Souls of Black Folk.* In it, Du Bois explains the goals of individual African Americans such as himself.

> He [the African American] would not Africanize America, for America has too much to teach the world and Africa. He would not bleach his Negro soul in a flood of white Americanism, for he knows that Negro blood has a message for the world. He simply wishes to make it possible for a man to be both a Negro and an American.

Ask students if the passage suggests that Du Bois views differences between African Americans and white Americans as positive or negative. (*positive*) Why? (*because each race has something beneficial to teach the other*) What advice might Du Bois offer to young African American artists, writers, or historians? Lead students to understand that Du Bois urged African Americans to create their own culture based on their unique experience.

Review and Practice

Assign "Taking Another Look," p. 251.

Answers to Taking Another Look (p. 251)

1. Du Bois opposed Washington's belief that cooperating with segregation would lead to civil rights gains and economic progress, advocated peaceful resistance. **2.** Du Bois felt race would be saved by its exceptional, well-educated "Talented Tenth". **3. Critical Thinking** might feel that all African Americans should take part in leadership.

Teaching Section 2: Organizing for Justice (pp. 251–53)

Objectives

- To infer the direction members of the Niagara Movement might take.
- To write press releases that the Committee of Forty might have drafted.

Historical Sidelight

An Epic in Prejudice. In 1915, D.W. Griffith released *Birth of a Nation*, an epic film about the Civil War and Reconstruction. The film stunned audiences with its technical feats—fade-outs, close-ups, and huge battle scenes. It also carried a strong message. Words flashed across the screen describing Reconstruction as a plot to "put the white South under the heel of the black South." White critics praised the film and President Wilson endorsed it saying, "My only regret is that it is all so terribly true." The NAACP condemned the film, and a few Northern states ordered the most outrageously racist scenes cut. But, for decades *Birth of a Nation* stood as a classic cinematic work. Today, it stands as a classic study in extreme racial prejudice.

Developing the Section

1. Making Inferences. Assign students to read the section-opening story on p. 251. Ask what memories Harpers Ferry would call up in the minds of most Americans. (*John Brown's raid*) What does the choice of Harpers Ferry suggest about the course of action favored by members of the Niagara Movement? (*a commitment to forceful, radical change*) What action is called for in the members' pledge? (*persistent, unceasing agitation through sacrifice and work*)

2. Writing a Press Release. Ask students, working either individually or in small groups, to draft a press release that the Committee of Forty might have handed out to reporters at the end of the May 1909 meeting. The statements should include a summary of what happened at the meeting and what the reformers hope that their efforts will achieve in the future.

Review and Practice

Assign "Taking Another Look," p. 253.

Answers to Questions in Caption (p. 252)

to agitate for equality for African Americans; attracted few followers but laid groundwork for the NAACP

Answers to Taking Another Look (p. 253)

1. immediate end to racial discrimination, equal justice, fair housing, full voting rights for African American men **2.** Niagara Movement, Springfield Massacre, National Negro Conference, Committee of Forty meeting **3. Critical Thinking** philosophical differences

Teaching Section 3: The NAACP's Fight for Civil Rights (pp. 253–55)

Objectives

- To identify tactics used by the NAACP in its fight for civil rights.
- To write letters to a member of Congress in support of an antilynching bill.

Historical Sidelight

Legal Action. In 1915, NAACP lawyers went before the Supreme Court to argue a case known as *Guinn* v. *United States*. The issue was a grandfather clause in the Oklahoma state constitution that was used to deny the vote to almost all African American males. In an historic ruling, the Court held that the clause violated the 15th Amendment by restoring "the very conditions the Amendment was intended to destroy." The *Guinn* ruling marked the first major legal victory by the NAACP in its battle for equal rights for African Americans.

Developing the Section

1. Analyzing a Chart. Before students begin the section, refer them to the chart on p. 254. Ask them, on the basis of this table, what tactics the NAACP used to advance the civil rights of African Americans. (*took cases to court, organized parades, opposed appointment of anti-civil rights candidates to the Supreme Court, set up action committees*) Would Booker T. Washington have approved of these tactics? (*not publicly, but remind students he secretly supported some court challenges*) Then assign the section.

2. Writing a Letter to Congress. Have students, working individually or in small groups, write letters to members of the House and Senate urging them to support the 1921 antilynching bill. Call on students to read their letters aloud. Discuss with students possible reasons why the bill was not passed.

Review and Practice

Assign "Taking Another Look," p. 255.

Answers to Question in Caption (p. 254)

filing court cases, organizing protests, forming action committees

Answers to Taking Another Look (p. 255)

1. newspaper ads publicizing racial violence; studies printed about African American living conditions **2.** ads, articles editorials in the Crisis; persuaded Congress to make lynching a federal crime **3. Critical Thinking yes:** injustices against African Americans did, in fact, constitute a crisis; **no:** title of paper was too inflammatory

Extending the Chapter

Designing a Magazine. Divide the class into small groups, and have them prepare a mock issue of the *Crisis*. Assign each group one of the following topics to do research on and write front-page news articles (including stories on Walter White's undercover operation, the increase in NAACP membership, and introduction of an antilynching bill into the House), a full-page ad opposing lynching, feature articles profiling some of the figures mentioned in the chapter, and several short stories and poems (either from the time period or original works by the students). When students have finished, conduct a joint planning session in which students design the layout for the magazine as a whole.

Looking Ahead

After students have read "Looking Ahead," p. 255, have them speculate on some of the issues that concerned the majority of African Americans. To provoke discussion, you might compare the pictures on pp. 255 and 262. Ask them what the photos show about differences between the lives of the people who worked for the *Crisis* and the lives of ordinary African Americans.

Answers to Close Up (pp. 256–57)

The Who, What, Where of History

1. reform movement of the early 1900s that sought to improve city, state, federal governments **2.** publisher of the *Guardian* who opposed Booker T. Washington **3.** African American newspaper **4.** most important leader of African American protest in the first half of the 1900s **5.** Du Bois's term for top 10 percent of educated African Americans **6.** founder of Afro-American League **7.** first president of National Association of Colored Women **8.** 1905 African American protest group, demanded immediate action for equal rights **9.** National Association for the Advancement of Colored People: organization with goal of securing equal rights for all 10. NAACP's magazine

Making the Connection

1. Niagara Movement laid groundwork for the NAACP. **2.** National Negro Conference was organized in response to Springfield Massacre.

Time Check

1. Seven **2.** Five

What Would You Have Done?

1. Answers should show an understanding of the concerns and aims of organizations described in the text. **2.** Students should show an understanding of "Talented Tenth" as a concept and the reasoning behind Du Bois's idea.

Thinking and Writing About History

1. Students should discuss Washington's speech, Trotter's questions, and his arrest. **2.** Answers should include views on education, peaceful resistance versus acceptance, need for leadership by Talented Tenth, pride in cultural heritage.

Building Skills

1. industrial education, accumulation of wealth, conciliation of South **2.** disfranchisement, legal inferiority, withdrawal of aid from universities **3.** cannot be considered equal members of society without equal rights **4.** Student responses should show understanding of the text material describing both points of view.

Chapter 24 The Great Migration (pp. 258–67)

Overview

A series of natural disasters and the outbreak of World War I drew over a million Southern African American sharecroppers North in search of work between 1910 and 1930. The Great Migration was one of the largest internal movements of people in the history of the United States. It brought the African American culture of the rural South into the cities of the Northeast and Midwest. Although African Americans did not share equally in the benefits of democracy, they fought valiantly to defend it in World War I. Yet, even in the war, they faced racism and segregation.

Resources

Chapter 24 Activity Sheet: Interpreting a Map (p. 233)
Chapter 24 Test (p. 171)
Outline Map: The World (p. 305), The United States (p. 308)
Unit 8 Writing Workshop: A Leaflet of Protest (pp. 290–93)

Focus Activity

Assign the chapter-opening story on pp. 258–59. Ask why letters such as the one quoted might attract African American sharecroppers to cities in the North. (*the promise of good wages and freedom from Jim Crow*) Then refer students to the "Snapshot of the Times" on p. 259. Ask what event in the "Snapshot" hinted that African Americans in Northern cities might still face problems arising from racial prejudice. (*1917 race riots*)

Teaching Section 1: Leaving Home (pp. 259–60)

Objective

- To draw political cartoons depicting "Northern fever" among African Americans in the South.

Historical Sidelight

The Boll Weevil. Around 1890, a tiny insect called the boll weevil flew out of Mexico and headed into Texas. From there, it cut a path of destruction across the cotton fields of the South. So devastating were the results of that destruction on the lives of sharecroppers that blues singers composed dozens of songs with the same title—"Ballad of the Boll Weevil."

Developing the Section

Drawing a Political Cartoon. Remind students that political cartoons express opinions and usually appear on the editorial page of a newspaper. Assign students, working individually or in small groups, to design political cartoons entitled "Northern Fever" that might have run in one of the African American newspapers in 1917. As a follow-up activity, you might have students draw another cartoon entitled "Northern Chill" showing the revival of racial tensions in the aftermath of World War I.

Review and Practice

Assign "Taking Another Look," p. 260.

Answers to Question in Caption (p. 260)

Among the advantages that African Americans discovered in the North were better-paying jobs, better schools, better housing, freedom from Jim Crow laws, and services designed for their particular needs.

Answers to Taking Another Look (p. 260)

1. difficulty of sharecropping increased by boll weevil and floods, threat of lynching **2.** availability of jobs due to enlistment and slowed immigration **3. Critical Thinking** Answers should show understanding of poor conditions that sharecroppers faced in South, the lure of opportunity in North, and constraints placed on indebted sharecroppers.

Teaching Section 2: African American Urban Culture (pp. 260–63)

Objective

- To interpret a map showing African American migration during the years 1910–1920.

Developing the Section

Interpreting a Map. Refer students to the map on p. 261. Call on volunteers to answer the question raised in the map's caption. (*New York, Philadelphia, Chicago*) Then point out the remarkable rates of growth in other Northern cities such as Detroit and Cleveland. Ask what problems students think such rapid growth might have created. Record responses on the chalkboard and modify them as students work through the section.

Review and Practice

Assign "Taking Another Look," p. 263.

Answers to Questions in Captions (pp. 261–62)

(p. 261) New York, Philadelphia, Chicago (p. 262) less well clothed and fed, poorer housing and schools

Answers to Taking Another Look (p. 263)

1. crowded and expensive housing in run-down ghettoes **2.** Churches and National Urban League helped find jobs and housing where they were treated fairly. **3. Critical Thinking** **no:** had to live in unbearable conditions; **yes:** substantial freedoms, cohesive communities

Teaching Section 3: World War I: Opportunities and Setbacks (pp. 263–65)

Objective

- To analyze German efforts to encourage African Americans to desert the Allied cause.

Historical Sidelight

Silent Protest. Race riots and lynchings continued during World War I, leading the NAACP to organize a massive silent protest parade. (Refer students to the picture on text p. 248.) Some 10,000 African Americans and their white supporters marched down New York City's Fifth Avenue. First in line were young children dressed in white. They carried signs that read:

> MOTHER, DO LYNCHERS GO TO HEAVEN?
>
> MR. PRESIDENT, WHY NOT MAKE AMERICA SAFE FOR DEMOCRACY?

Developing the Section

Analyzing a Document. After students have completed the section, read aloud the following statement from a brochure distributed among African American troops by the Germans.

> What is Democracy? Personal freedom, all citizens enjoying the same rights socially and before the law. Do you enjoy the same rights as the white people do in America, the land of Freedom and Democracy, or are you rather not treated over there as second-class citizens?

Ask what the purpose of the brochure was. (*to persuade African Americans not to support the Allied cause*) Are the statements in the brochure accurate? (*yes*) Ask students, working in groups, to prepare brochures that explain to German soldiers why African Americans fought for the United States despite the truth of these statements.

Review and Practice

Assign "Taking Another Look," p. 265.

Answers to Taking Another Look (p. 265)

1. trained in segregated camps, often in racist South; served in segregated units, chiefly labor battalions **2.** mined coal, built military vehicles, bought Liberty Bonds, supported Red Cross **3. Critical Thinking** **Civil War:** fighting for freedom; **World War I:** drafted and hoped, by supporting war, to win respect of whites and gain better treatment

Extending the Chapter

Preparing an Illustrated Timeline. Divide the class into groups, and assign each group to do further research on key events during World War I that affected African Americans both at home and abroad. Then direct students to plot these events along an illustrated timeline.

Looking Ahead

After students have read "Looking Ahead," p. 265, write the title of the next chapter on the chalkboard: "Black Nationalism". Ask students to speculate on what this term might mean.

Answers to Close Up (pp. 266–67)

The Who, What, Where of History

1. movement of African Americans North during and after WW I **2.** insect that attacked cotton plants **3.** people forced to move in search of work **4.** section of a city in which members of an ethnic group live **5.** organization founded to gain economic and political rights and provide practical help for African American urban dwellers **6.** founder of the *Defender* **7.** New York City

Making the Connection

1. boll weevils ruined cotton crops in South, many African Americans lost means of income, moved North in search of jobs **2.** State laws made it illegal for indebted sharecroppers to leave fields. **3.** African Americans replaced white workers who were in armed forces

Time Check

1. 1914 **2.** 1915 **3.** 1917

What Would You Have Done?

1. should mention use of churches and other African American gathering places to advertise, emphasize concerns of African American community **2.** **army:** opportunity to go overseas, escape prejudice; **factory:** Jim Crow army distasteful, opposed to war

Thinking and Writing About History

1. **come North:** more work for more pay, no fear of lynching; **stay South:** expensive ghetto housing, family ties **2.** **Examples:** search out new migrant families, help them find housing and jobs; work with unions and factories to get them to train African Americans; raise funds forhealth-care centers and playgrounds; personal gains for friends and associates, racial pride **3.** Students might mention that no whites received sentences. Answers should show a grasp of the facts presented in the text

Building Skills

1. the percentage of farmers who were tenants **2.** Alabama, Georgia, Louisiana, Mississippi, and South Carolina **3.** Connecticut, New Hampshire, Maine, Vermont, and Massachusetts **4.** Tenant farming in the United States in 1930 was most prevalent in the South. **5.** Farm tenancy in the West in 1930 was higher inland than along the coast.

Chapter 25 Black Nationalism (pp. 268–75)

Overview

As World War I ended, race riots broke out and unemployment soared. Hooded members of the Ku Klux Klan marched in the nation's streets, openly proclaiming a reign of terror. Red Summer exploded in 1919 and left hundreds of African Americans injured or dead in 25 cities. Onto this scene stepped Marcus Garvey with his call for racial solidarity, pride in blackness, and celebration of the African heritage. Unlike Du Bois who spoke to the Talented Tenth, Garvey spoke to the millions. His words triggered a movement known as black nationalism. Garvey was in the public eye for only a few years, but the ideas of black nationalism lingered into the 1960s when once again the slogan "black is beautiful" gripped the imagination of African Americans.

Resources

Chapter 25 Activity Sheet: Analyzing a Primary Source (p. 234)
Chapter 25 Test (p. 172)

Focus Activity

Before students read the chapter, have them look at the photographs on pp. 268, 269 and 272. Ask them if they think any of the following words—*proud, strong, self-confident, determined*—would apply to the people pictured. Ask students to suggest other possibilities. Tell students that the people in the photographs on pp. 269 and 272 were followers of the man in the photograph on p. 268, Marcus Garvey. Point out that one of Garvey's aims was to help strengthen characteristics such as those listed above in African Americans. In doing so, he ignited the imaginations of the African American masses in a way no other leader had before him.

Teaching Section 1: The Appeal of Black Nationalism (pp. 269–71)

Objective

- To discover connections between the repression of African Americans and the growth of their interest in the ideas of black nationalism and Pan-Africanism.

Historical Sidelight

Father of Black History. Both W.E.B. Du Bois and Marcus Garvey urged African Americans to study their past, but few African Americans had received enough schooling in the early 1900s to become formal historians. The white historians who told the story of the United States tended to write biased accounts that often did grave injustices to African Americans and their achievements.

Carter G. Woodson, known as the "father of black history," set out to rectify this situation. In 1915, Woodson, who was educated at the University of Chicago, founded the Association for the Study of Negro Life and History. In 1926, he instituted "Negro History Week"; the second week of February. This week includes the birthdate of Abraham Lincoln and the probable birthdate of Frederick Douglass. In the 1960s, African American activists expanded the week into Black History Month. Woodson's pioneering works in African American history are still cited today by African American and white historians alike.

Developing the Section

Making Connections. Write on the chalkboard Garvey's words, "We are descendants of a people determined to suffer no longer." Instruct students to skim through *The Big Picture* for Unit 8, and Chapters 23, 24 and 25. Ask what evidence they find of African Americans suffering in the decade before Garvey's 1920 speech. (*segregation in armed forces, lynchings, loss of wartime jobs, race riots, rebirth of Ku Klux Klan*) Review the text definitions of black nationalism (p. 269) and Pan-Africanism (pp. 270–71) and discuss the connections between the evidence students cited and the growth of these two movements.

Review and Practice

Assign "Taking Another Look," p. 271.

Answers to Taking Another Look (p.271)

1. movement emphasizing ethnic pride, identification with African culture, and self-reliance **2.** International Convention of the Negro Peoples of the World, black nationalism, Pan-Africanism, violence, various legal and political strategies **3. Critical Thinking** **black nationalism:** encouraged self-reliance; **Pan-Africanism:** encouraged those of African descent to unite; **International Convention:** encouraged pride in heritage; **legal strategies:** worked within system; **violence:** demonstrated passion

Teaching Section 2: Marcus Garvey (pp. 271–73)

Objective

- To evaluate the success of Marcus Garvey's programs.

Developing the Section

Evaluating Garvey's Movement. Write the following headings on the chalkboard: "Developing Pride," "Fostering Economic Independence," and "Developing National Independence." After students have read the section, ask them to list the ways that Garvey planned to achieve each of these goals. Record their responses in the proper columns. Then ask students to evaluate the success of each of the items. Ask what they consider to be Garvey's most successful and least successful programs.

Review and Practice

Assign "Taking Another Look," p. 273.

Answers to Taking Another Look (p. 273)

1. founded Black Star Line to develop commercial ties between African peoples the world over **2.** tailored appeal to ordinary African Americans **3. Critical Thinking** chance of self-sufficiency; chance to feel part of a united group of people with common interests; escape from U.S. racism

Extending the Chapter

Preparing Illustrated Reports. Divide the class into small groups. Assign each group to do research and prepare an illustrated report on various aspects of the life of Marcus Garvey. Possible topics for reports include the following: Garvey's life before his arrival in the United States, UNIA's economic programs, plans for African settlement, the Black Star Line, his life after leaving the United States. Display completed reports in the classroom.

Looking Ahead

After students have read "Looking Ahead," p. 273, ask them to speculate on how African Americans might respond if Marcus Garvey reappeared today. Ask if they think his message still has appeal. Why or why not?

Answers to Close Up (pp. 274–75)

The Who, What, Where of History

1. leader of black nationalist movement; president of Universal Negro Improvement Association **2.** movement emphasizing ethnic pride, identification with and study of African history, self-reliance **3.** belief that all people of African descent have common interests and should join in common struggle for freedom **4.** summer of 1919 when many race riots occurred **5.** Universal Negro Improvement Association; organization to help African Americans win equality through economic, political, and cultural independence **6.** steamship company founded by Marcus Garvey to develop commercial ties between African peoples all over world

Making the Connection
When white soldiers came home, they returned to jobs African Americans had held.

Time Check
1. 1920 **2.** 11

What Would You Have Done?
1. might express horror and disgust at number of people killed and at tensions between African Americans and whites **2. Examples:** black nationalism, Pan-Africanism, economic independence for African Americans, need to develop powerful African nation

Thinking and Writing About History
1. create economic, political, and cultural independence for African Americans **2.** might discuss goals of UNIA; should note time and place of meeting, type of event **3.** should note that Garvey died in London, when and where Garvey was born, what philosophies he espoused, organizations he founded, what happened to Black Star shipping line **4. valid:** Garvey's ambitions were admirable and would have been beneficial to African Americans had they been carried out; **invalid:** his plans were not sound and he would never be considered a hero

Building Skills
1. bandwagon **2.** name calling **3.** glittering generalities **4.** testimonial **5.** plain folks **6.** transfer **7.** card stacking

Chapter 26 The Harlem Renaissance (pp. 276–87)

Overview
The Great Migration made Harlem the largest African American community in the United States. In the 1920s, Harlem bristled with excitement. African American writers, actors, and artists produced an unprecedented outpouring of new works. Examples of paintings from this period appear on pp. A8, A9, and A14. This burst of creativity, known as the Harlem Renaissance, focused the attention of white society on the artistic achievements of African Americans for the first time. Although these works caught the eye of white audiences, what was most important was the fact that, for the first time, African Americans in large numbers were dealing with ideas and concerns of the African American community. Thus, the Harlem Renaissance can be seen as an outgrowth of black nationalist concerns.

Resources
Chapter 26 Activity Sheet: Analyzing a Primary Source (pp. 235–36)
Chapter 26 Test (p. 173)
Lesson Plans for the Artist's View (p. 111)

Teaching the Chapter (pp. 276–87)

Objectives
- To interpret a statistical table showing African American migration to New York City in 1930.
- To identify key artistic figures in the Harlem Renaissance.
- To make inferences about the lives of migrants to Harlem from a list of tenant complaints.

Historical Sidelight
Jazz Soviet Style. In the 1920s, the sound of American jazz reached into the Soviet Union. The fact that the Soviet government branded the music as decadent only heightened public fascination. In 1926, the Communist-run government reluctantly opened its doors to a troupe of 35 African American singers, dancers, and jazz musicians from Harlem. Shortly thereafter, Benny Peyton's seven-piece Jazz Kings visited Moscow and dazzled audiences with its improvisation. "The players actually play," said one startled critic, "[without] any written music."

Developing the Chapter
1. Interpreting Statistics. Copy the following table on the chalkboard or onto an overhead transparency.

African American Migrants to New York City (1930)			
Born in	*Numbers*	*Born in*	*Numbers*
VA	44,471	SC	33,765
NC	26,120	GA	19,546
FL	8,249	MD	6,656
PA	6,226	NJ	5,275
Wash.,DC	3,358	AL	3,205
MA	2,329	LA	2,182
OH	1,721	TN	1,592
TX	1,216	KY	1,216
MS	969	Foreign-born*	54,754

*West Indies, other islands in the Caribbean

Ask students how many African American migrants came to New York City in 1930. (*222,850*) From which three states did most of the migrants come? (*Virginia, South Carolina, North Carolina*) What might have drawn so many migrants to the city? (*hope for employment, better housing, better lives, excitment*) How might this population have contributed to the vitality of Harlem? Lead students to see that creativity can be fostered by crosscultural interaction.

2. Identifying Historical Figures. Write the names of the 24 figures listed in the "Galleries" in this chapter on small slips of paper. Distribute one slip to each student in the class. If necessary, duplicate slips. Direct students to develop a series of clues to describe the person they have been given. Each set of clues should end with the question: Who am I? Example: I brought my golden trumpet from New Orleans and turned Chicago jazz upside down. Who am I? (*Louis Armstrong*) Have students play several rounds in pairs, small groups, or as a class.

3. Making Inferences. Tell students that behind its dazzling artistic accomplishments, Harlem had another side, one that showed all the strains of rapid growth. Then read aloud the following list of complaints filed in municipal courts by Harlem tenants: "No improvement in ten years"; "Rats, rat holes, and roaches"; "Very, very cold"; "Air shaft smells"; "Ceilings in two rooms have fallen." From this list of complaints, ask students what they can infer about living conditions in the tenements of Harlem. (*generally rundown, ill-maintained, and so on*) Ask them, based on what they have read in earlier chapters, who they think might have been forced to live in these tenements. (*rural poor who came during the Great Migration*).

Review and Practice

Assign "Taking Another Look," p. 285.

Answers to Taking Another Look (p. 285)

1. NAACP, Urban League: offered cash prizes for writers; **Harmon Foundation:** offered cash prizes for writers and artists, arranged exhibitions of work by African American artists **2.** mixing of blues and ragtime **3. Critical Thinking yes:** music had enormous impact on culture, reached both black and white audiences worldwide; **no:** many African American cultural contributions had impact; **Alternative Title:** Age of Creativity

Extending the Chapter

Preparing an Audiovisual Show. The three "Galleries" in this chapter provide a wealth of ideas for preparing an audiovisual presentation of the Harlem Renaissance. Divide the class into three groups, and assign each group one of the "Galleries". Have them bring in pictures, recordings, and material for readings that they can share with the rest of the class.

Looking Ahead

After students have read "Looking Ahead," p. 285, ask them what effects they think the economic downturn that began in 1929 might have had on Harlem and the Harlem Renaissance.

Answers to Close Up (pp. 286–87)

The Who, What, Where of History

1. the northern portion of Manhattan, New York City **2.** burst of creativity among African American artists during 1920s **3.** sculptor **4.** poet and writer **5.** jazz trumpeter/composer **6.** novelist and anthropologist **7.** mural painter **8.** white charitable organization that offered prizes to African American writers and artists

Making the Connection

1. Harlem was nation's largest African American community; opportunity for financial success in cultural center **2.** jazz started in New Orleans with mixing of blues and ragtime; New York jazz musicians developed skills in clubs and theater

Time Check

1920–1930

What Would You Have Done?

1. yes: make contact with other artists, learn from them, live in cultural center; **no:** prefer rural atmosphere, closeness to friends and family, lack of financial pressure **2.** may include names of businesses mentioned in chapter

Thinking and Writing About History

1. Article should locate Harlem correctly and mention jazz clubs, Strivers' Row, cultural events, etc. **2.** gave voice and attention to African American artists, encouraged diversity **3.** African American immigrants integral to life in United States

Building Skills

1. Euphrates, Congo, Nile, Mississippi; Asia, Africa, North America **2.** yes, showed awareness of African roots **3.** Hughes himself, any African American **4.** to emphasize long span of African history **5.** the breadth and depth of the African (African American) experience contributes to sensitivity and understanding **6.** yes, proud of African contributions to civilization

Chapter 27 The Great Depression and the New Deal (pp. 288–99)

Overview

The Great Depression brought economic despair to millions of Americans, especially to African Americans living in the rural South. Federal and state governments failed to provide relief, and African Americans' efforts at self-help could not overcome the national crisis. The worsening economic situation led African Americans to turn their backs on the Republican party and vote for the Democratic party, which promised them a "new deal" and in 1936, Franklin D. Roosevelt entered the White House. With the help of his Black Cabinet, some federal aid finally reached African Americans. African American leaders kept up the pressure, and in the late 1930s, action by A. Philip Randolph convinced Roosevelt to bar discrimination in many federally funded programs.

Focus Activity

Start a discussion of the double burden that the Great Depression and racial discrimination placed on African Americans by reading the lyrics of a depression-era song; "Discrimination Blues."

> This little song that I'm singing about
> People you all know its true,
> If you're black and gotta work for a living
> Now this is what they'll say to you, they'll say:
> If you're white, you're all right,
> And if you're brown, stick around,
> But if you're black, O brother,
> Get back, get back, get back.

Resources

Chapter 27 Activity Sheet: Interpreting a Chart (p. 237)
Chapter 27 Test (p. 174)
Unit 8 Test (p. 167–69)

Teaching Section 1: Fighting the Great Depression (pp. 289–91)

Objective

- To analyze a newspaper article advising African Americans to prepare for hard times.

Historical Sidelight

The Letter X. In the 1930s, an African American named Elijah Poole became the leader of a religious organization known as the Nation of Islam. Poole changed his name to Elijah Muhammad. He demanded that his followers, known as Black Muslims, substitute an "X" for their surnames. Their true African surnames, said Elijah Muhammad, had been stripped from their ancestors during the days of slavery. He said the Black Muslims would use the letter "X" until white domination was broken.

Developing the Section

Read aloud the following selection from the August 23, 1930, issue of the African American newspaper, the *Chicago Defender:*

> Times are not what they used to be. There is no use shutting our eyes to this fact. Prosperity has gone into retirement. . . . Our advice is for everyone to get something, and hold onto it. Get it in the city if possible, but, failing this, start toward the farm before the snow flies.

Ask what the article reveals about the economy in 1930. (*that prosperity had disappeared*) Ask what problems students think this situation produced for African Americans. (*loss of jobs, inability to pay rent or buy food*) Lead students in a discussion of whether or not African Americans would follow the *Defender's* advice.

Review and Practice

Assign "Taking Another Look," p. 291.

Answers to Taking Another Look (p. 291)

1. Private charities and local relief organizations were overwhelmed and often discriminated against African Americans. **2.** churches became involved in welfare work; National Urban League organized emergency relief committees, set up survival shelters **3. Critical Thinking Hoover:** believe in "trickle down" theory and local action, loyal to Democratic party; **Roosevelt:** intrigued by promise of a new deal

Teaching Section 2: A New Deal for African Americans? (pp. 291–94)

Objectives

- To weigh the pros and cons of the New Deal from the perspective of African Americans.
- To express African American opinion of the Social Security Act.

Developing the Section

1. Weighing Pros and Cons. Write the following slogan on the chalkboard: "New Deal or

Raw Deal?" Then divide the class into small groups and have students draw up a list of pros and cons of the New Deal from the perspective of poor African Americans.

2. Expressing an Opinion. Assign students, working individually or in small groups, to write a letter to the editorial page of the *Crisis* criticizing the Social Security Act. For variety, you might have some students present their opinions in the form of political cartoons.

Review and Practice

Assign "Taking Another Look," p. 294.

Answers to Taking Another Look (p. 294)

1. African American advisers Roosevelt named to departments of federal government **2.** New Deal programs forbade discrimination on basis of race. **3. Critical Thinking** Students should demonstrate understanding of Roosevelt's political concerns as well as those of African American voters.

Teaching Section 3: Gains for African American Workers (pp. 295–97)

Objective

- To draw up a Bill of Rights for African American workers in the 1930s.

Developing the Section

Creating a Labor Bill of Rights. Write the following phrase on the chalkboard: "a Bill of Rights for Negro labor." Ask students to speculate on what this phrase might mean. Do they think African American workers during the 1930s needed such a Bill of Rights? (*probably will say yes*) What rights do they think such a bill might list? (*no discrimination in hiring, equal pay for equal work, etc.*). After students have read the chapter, ask them whether the CIO charter, or Executive Order 8802 protected any of the rights they listed.

Review and Practice

Assign "Taking Another Look," p. 297.

Answers to Taking Another Look (p. 297)

1. AFL leadership ignored African American leaders and segregated members, CIO opened to them, Thurgood Marshall called charter "a Bill of Rights for Negro labor" **2.** barred discrimination in defense industries, government agencies, and work-training programs **3. Critical Thinking** feared it might hurt him politically

Extending the Chapter

Doing Library Research. Remind students that the artistic outpouring by African Americans that began during the Harlem Renaissance did not end in 1929. Assign them to do library research and prepare reports on African American artists of the 1930s. Possible figures to focus on include Ralph Ellison, Richard Wright, Jacob Lawrence, Marion Anderson, Canada Lee, and Ella Fitzgerald.

Looking Ahead

After students have read "Looking Ahead," p. 297, have them speculate on how fighting another war in defense of democracy might affect the lives of African Americans. Point out the gains that African Americans had made under the New Deal. Also, contrast the differing attitudes of Wilson and Roosevelt toward African Americans.

Answers to Close Up (pp. 298–99)

1. period when many people are unemployed; wages, prices, business activity all drop **2.** President at start of Great Depression in 1929 **3.** President elected in 1932; formulated New Deal **4.** First Lady, prominent worker for African American rights **5.** leading African American advisers to Roosevelt **6.** educator, Director of Division of Negro Affairs of National Youth Administration **7.** Public Works Administration: New Deal work program **8.** Works Progress Administration: New Deal Work program **9.** founder and president of Brotherhood of Sleeping Car Porters **10.** Washington, D.C.

Making the Connection

1. Unemployed whites took jobs which usually fell to African Americans. **2.** Both were Republicans. **3.** Unions needed members.

Time Check

1. 1929 **2.** 1932

What Would You Have Done?

1. yes: must use economic power to support one's people; **no:** disapprove of civil disobedience, demonstrations **2. yes:** putting people to work, using African American advisers; **no:** allowing discrimination to continue

Thinking and Writing About History

1. should compare Hoover's hands-off approach to welfare programs to Roosevelt's orientation toward reform and relief efforts **2.** might highlight Randolph's terms for calling off march and Roosevelt's reasons for wanting march called off

Building Skills

1. illiteracy decreasing **2.** South Atlantic, East South Central **3.** more illiteracy in rural areas

UNIT 9 The Civil Rights Revolution (pp. 300–55)

UNIT THEME

African Americans increase their efforts to secure their civil rights, beginning a movement that brings sweeping changes to U.S. society.

UNIT CONCEPTS

- African Americans at home and abroad contributed greatly to the Allied victory in World War II.
- Mechanization of Southern farms threw millions of sharecroppers out of work and set off another African American wave of migration to the North.
- The concentration of African Americans in cities created problems such as overcrowding and crime, but it also gave African Americans a chance to elect more representatives to government.
- The landmark victory in *Brown* v. *Board of Education of Topeka*, overturned *Plessy* v. *Ferguson* and eliminated the legal basis for segregation.
- Martin Luther King, Jr., inspired African Americans to meet violence with nonviolence and emerged as a major leader of the Civil Rights Movement.
- The Civil Rights Movement had an enormous impact on U.S. society and produced deep and lasting changes.
- The rise of the Black Power movement led to splits within the Civil Rights Movement and revived the tradition of black nationalism.
- African Americans who fought in Vietnam were heavily influenced by the ideas of the Civil Rights and Black Power movements.

UNIT OVERVIEW

Unit 9 profiles one of the most far-reaching revolutions that U.S society has ever known—the Civil Rights Movement of the 1950s and 1960s. The movement broke down the legal barriers that had limited the rights of African Americans since the end of Reconstruction. *The Big Picture* and the five chapters in this unit describe: (1) the activities of African Americans in World War II, (2) the setbacks and accomplishments of African Americans in the Cold War era, (3) the shaping of the Civil Rights Movement, (4) the splits that developed within the Civil Rights Movement and its enduring legacy, and (5) the lasting effects of the Vietnam War on the Civil Rights Movement.

In teaching this unit, you might begin by reviewing important turning points in the African American experience. Possible choices include: arrival of the first Africans in the Americas, institution of slavery, acceptance of slavery under the Constitution, the Civil War, emancipation, Reconstruction, and the rise of Jim Crow. Note a continuing theme that has built African American unity: survival in the face of adversity. Then tell students that in the 1950s African Americans standing together finally won the civil rights that the U.S. government and society had long denied them. Call on students to explain how the tradition of self-help prepared African Americans for one of their most important struggles.

COOPERATIVE LEARNING ACTIVITY

The following cooperative learning activity can be used for alternative assessment after study of the unit has been completed.

At the beginning of the unit, tell students that travel guides now direct people to important historic sites in the civil rights struggle. Tell students to keep a running list of the important sites in history mentioned in this unit. At the end of the unit, divide students into groups to prepare their own directories listing the sites and their historical significance. Students should augment the information in the text with additional research and should include photographs or drawings where possible. In evaluating the guides, consider the organization and visual appeal of the piece and clarity of the writing.

Unit 9 THE BIG PICTURE (pp. 301–305)

Theme

As the United States developed into a superpower after World War II, African Americans organized a movement to force the federal government to act on its promise of equal rights for all citizens.

Overview

The Big Picture explores the response of the U.S. government both to pressure arising from conditions abroad and to pressure for change from African Americans at home. The two situations involved the definition and defense of democracy. While the United States presented itself as the model of free government for the world, it became increasingly difficult for African Americans to tolerate injustices within U.S. society. As a result, African Americans returned home from World War II with a new resolve to win their civil rights.

President Harry S. Truman used the power of his office to integrate the military, but he failed to get civil rights legislation past Southern opposition in Congress. His successor, President Dwight D. "Ike" Eisenhower, chose to focus on the Cold War rather than on domestic issues. During the Eisenhower era, the absence of government support convinced many African Americans to take action in the courts and in the streets as the Civil Rights Movement took shape.

Martin Luther King, Jr., emerged as the most visible leader of the Civil Rights Movement in the late 1950s and early 1960s. Constant pressure by King led President John F. Kennedy to propose a comprehensive civil rights package. After Kennedy's assassination, his sucessor, Lyndon B. Johnson pushed the legislation through Congress. Legal segregation ended, but African Americans still had to contend with the de facto segregation that grew out of poverty. Johnson tried to rid the nation of poverty and its attendant problems with his "Great Society" programs, only to see those programs weakened by the nation's growing involvement in the Vietnam War.

As the war dragged on, violence shook U.S society, as antiwar protesters took to the streets, riots erupted in the cities, and assassins claimed the lives of Martin Luther King, Jr., and Robert Kennedy. Dismayed and disheartened, many Americans turned to Republican Richard Nixon. Nixon did not dismantle civil rights laws, but he did little to implement them. As he brought the Vietnam War to a close, both African Americans and whites tried to assess the effects of the changes in their lives and their society.

Objectives

- To define the word *revolution* and determine what a civil rights revolution for African Americans would involve.
- To use a timeline to identify events that may have furthered African American equality.
- To infer, from a primary source, social conditions African Americans faced during World War II.
- To prepare a self-teaching exercise on each of the administrations covered in *The Big Picture.*

Introducing *The Big Picture*

Write the title of the unit on the chalkboard: "The Civil Rights Revolution". Ask students how they would define the word *revolution.* (*a complete or drastic change; the overthrow of a government or social system*) Tell them to consult classroom dictionaries if necessary. Review with students the social conditions that African Americans faced through the 1930s. Then ask students to say what they think a "civil rights revolution" for African Americans would involve. Record the responses on the chalkboard. Refer to and modify them as students work through the unit.

Using the Timeline

Read aloud the statement in "An African American Speaks" on text p. 301. Then refer students to the timeline on pp. 302–303. Ask them to select events from the timeline that might have helped King realize his dreams. Have students give reasons for their choices.

Teaching *The Big Picture*

1. Making an Inference. Open the section by reading the following lines from a sign at the front of a South Carolina bus during World War II.

> Victory demands your cooperation. . . . Avoid friction. Be Patriotic. White passengers will be seated from front to rear; colored passengers from rear to front.

Ask students what inconsistencies the sign reveals. (*African Americans are being asked to help in the war effort, while being assigned to the back of a bus.*) Ask students if they would expect, based on this sign, that conditions for African Americans during World War II would be more similar to or different from what they had been during World War I. (*probably similar*) Ask students what effect signs like this would have on African Americans. (*produce anger, resentment; lower sense of self-esteem*)

2. Self-Teaching. The rest of *The Big Picture* provides an excellent opportunity for a cooperative learning activity. Divide the class into five groups, and assign each group one of the administrations described on pp. 301–305 of *The Big Picture*. The group that takes "The Eisenhower Years, 1953–1961" should also receive "Challenging Segregation." All other groups should receive one subsection each. Distribute or write on the chalkboard the following tasks for each group to complete:

- Prepare a list of main ideas or key facts in the subsection to copy and distribute to the rest of the class.
- Draft a State of the Union message in which your President summarizes his main concerns, including his position on the issue of civil rights.
- Write several short-answer questions for use in a general test on *The Big Picture*.

When students have finished, call on each group in chronological order of administration. Allow the rest of the class time to look over the duplicated information prepared by the group. Then have a volunteer deliver the group's State of the Union message. Encourage members of the class to ask questions at the end of the speech. Repeat the process until all the administrations are covered. Then assemble the student's questions into a general test for self-evaluation. The questions may be answered individually or in small groups.

Review and Practice

Assign "Taking Another Look," p. 305.

Answers to Taking Another Look (p. 305)

1. Korea, Vietnam **2.** Nixon did not try to change civil rights laws of Johnson administration, but was not enthusiastic about enforcing them; cut back on Great Society programs **3. Critical Thinking** Some countries may have lost respect for United States; United States did not have a united population and, therefore, was not as strong as it could have been.

Chapter 28 World War II and African Americans (pp. 306–13)

Overview

During World War II, African Americans fought a "Double-V" campaign. One V stood for victory over the enemy overseas, and the other V stood for victory over prejudice and discrimination in the military and at home. More than one million African Americans served in the war, but they also protested the conditions they faced in the armed forces. Racial discrimination within the U.S. military seemed particularly out of place since the Allies were fighting a racist Nazi enemy. Meanwhile, African Americans on the home front played an important part in the war effort. Large numbers of them left the South to take jobs in defense industries located in the Northeast and Midwest, just as other African Americans had during World War I.

Resources

Chapter 28 Activity Sheet: Interpreting Statistics (p. 238)
Chapter 28 Test (p. 178)
Outline Map: The World (p. 305)

Focus Activity

Assign the chapter-opening story on pp. 306–307. Then divide the class into groups. Have half the groups draw political cartoons or posters celebrating Dorie Miller's heroism under fire. Have the other half draw political cartoons or posters criticizing the Navy's reassignment of Dorie Miller to the ship's mess. Display the various cartoons and posters around the classroom, and use them as springboards to discuss the "Double-V" campaign for African Americans.

Teaching Section 1: In the Armed Forces (pp. 307–309)

Objective

- To compare and contrast the treatment of African American troops in World Wars I and II.

Historical Sidelight

Jim Crow Blood. African American doctor Charles Richard Drew developed a technique for preserving and storing blood that saved countless lives during World War II. Drew also set up Red Cross blood banks that accepted blood donations from the armed forces and directed U.S. efforts to ship blood to the Allies. The Red Cross, however, insisted on segregating the blood of whites from that of African Americans. This policy later led to the death of Drew in 1950 when, bleeding profusely from a car accident, a white hospital turned him away. By the time he reached an African American hospital with "African American blood," he had bled to death.

Developing the Section

Comparing and Contrasting. Have students review the treatment of African Americans in the armed forces during World War I (pp. 263–64). Ask if events between the two wars might have led African Americans to expect better treatment during World War II. (*possibly, citing the New Deal*) Then recount the following story told by Gunnar Myrdal, a Swedish scholar who wrote *American Dilemma*, a classic study of racism in the United States. An African American soldier reportedly told Myrdal in 1944, "Just carve on my tombstone, 'Here lies a black man killed fighting a yellow man for the protection of a white man.'" Ask students if harsh treatment of the African Americans in the military had improved based on this reponse. (*no*) Write two headings on the chalkboard: "Same as World War I", "Different from World War I". As students read the section, have them suggest entries showing the similarities and differences between the two wars in the treatment of African American troops.

Review and Practice

Assign "Taking Another Look," p. 309.

Answer to Question in Caption (p. 307)

still segregated, but more officer training, more chances for combat

Answers to Taking Another Look (p. 309)

1. needed officers to command growing number of African American soldiers **2.** In a time of need 2,500 African Americans volunteered and fought side by side with whites to help turn back Nazi attack. **3. Critical Thinking** Responses will differ but should note that after helping to defend their country, African Americans still were treated as second-class citizens.

Teaching Section 2: On the Home Front (pp. 309–11)

Objective

- To recognize similarities and differences in conditions on the homefront during World War I and World War II.

Developing the Section

Recognizing Similarities and Differences. Refer students to the photos on p. 310. Ask how some African Americans contributed to the war effort at home. (*by producing war equipment used by the military*) Next, assign students to read the section-opening story on p. 309. What treatment greeted some of the African Americans who worked in these war-related industries? (*discrimination*) Remind students that African American workers in defense industries during World War I had also suffered discrimination. Ask if students think that conditions had or had not improved by World War II. What evidence can they find to support their conclusions? (*probably had improved; FEPC in existence during World War II*) What other similarities can students find in conditions on the home front in both wars? (*large-scale African American migration out of the South, race riots in cities*)

Review and Practice

Assign "Taking Another Look," p. 311.

Answers to Taking Another Look (p. 311)

1. defense industries needed workers; African Americans got high-paying, skilled jobs in defense plants, joined unions **2.** defense work available in North **3. Critical Thinking** responses should note competition for employment and housing; difficulty of shift to integrated workplaces and neighborhoods

Extending the Chapter

Identifying Propaganda. Direct students to review the seven propaganda techniques in the "Building Skills" section on p. 275. Remind them that propaganda can be used to promote positive as well as negative causes. Then divide the class into groups, and assign each group to design a poster or brochure promoting African American participation in World War II. Call on each group to share its poster or brochure with the class. Encourage the other students to identify the propaganda techniques used in each piece.

Looking Ahead

After they have read "Looking Ahead," p. 311, ask students to predict some of the post-war challenges facing African Americans after the troops returned home. Record student responses on the chalkboard. Add to or modify the list of predictions as students work through the next chapter.

Answers to Close Up (pp. 312–13)

The Who, What, Where of History

1. African American mess attendant who shot down four planes at Pearl Harbor **2.** Hawaii **3.** playwright who wrote *Black Eagles* **4.** 99th Pursuit Squadron; escorted white bomber crews and destroyed enemy aircraft **5.** commander of Black Eagles, first African American major general **6.** Women's Army Corps **7.** Fair Employment Practices Committee, Roosevelt's task force to end discrimination in defense industries

Making the Connection

1. Many African Americans migrated north to work in defense plants. **2.** FEPC helped many African Americans get jobs in defense plants.

Time Check

1. December 7, 1941 **2.** 1942 **3.** 1945

What Would You Have Done?

1. Examples: organized a protest outside the lunchroom; written letter to local papers or to NAACP **2. military:** desire to serve the military in a direct way, desire to go overseas; **factory:** not attracted to military service, do not want to go overseas, want to work in factory

Thinking and Writing About History

Possible response: Helping win victory over enemy forces and proving that African Americans could fight side by side with whites might help gain equal rights in United States after war.

Building Skills

1. Perrett: "watershed of the postemancipation struggle for equality"; "relationship to white America had undergone a fundamental change." **Baldwin:** "turning point in the Negro's relation to America." **2. a.** negative **b.** positive **3. Perrett:** African Americans began to effectively fight for their rights during WW II; **Baldwin:** During WW II, African Americans realized they could never trust white society. **4.** should show understanding of text material as well as Perrett's and Baldwin's excerpts **5.** The positions are not mutually exclusive. The fight for equal rights may be facilitated by loss of respect for whites.

Chapter 29 Gains and Losses in the Postwar Years (pp. 314–21)

Overview

In the 1940s and 1950s, widespread use of the mechanical cotton picker set off another mass migration of African Americans out of the South. Most migrants settled in the cities of the Northeast and Midwest. The sudden influx of so many people strained cities' resources. In addition, racist attitudes led to a "white flight" from the cities, depleting their tax base and contributing to their deterioration. The large numbers of African American voters in cities gained the political strength to elect representatives to local, state, and even national governments. During these years, many African American writers, artists, and musicians drew on their urban experiences to create works that won national recognition.

Resources

Chapter 29 Activity Sheet: Charting Data from Maps (pp. 239-240)
Lesson Plan for *The Artist's View* (p. 112)
Chapter 29 Test (p. 279)

Focus Activity

Tell students to read text p. 314 and to study the photo on the same page. They should not go on to p. 315 at this time. Ask them to explain what effect the appearance of the mechanical cotton picker would have on sharecroppers. (*eliminate the need for them*) Ask what they think the response of sharecroppers to this new set of circumstances would be.

Teaching Section 1: A New Wave of Migration (pp. 315–16)

Objective

- To identify relationships through a time chart.

Historical Sidelight

Cotton's Comeback. The boll weevil and competition from synthetic fibers nearly wiped out cotton production in parts of the South by the middle of the 20th century. In the 1980s and 1990s, cotton began to make a comeback as ecologically conscious consumers demanded clothes made of "natural fibers." In 1990, cotton production in the South reached 15.5 million bales. Cotton's return to the South, however, did little to revive the economies of former sharecropping communities. Today, a new group of workers reap the South's cotton with mechanical pickers—crews of Hispanic migrant workers from Texas or Mexico.

Developing the Section

Making Connections. Before students read the section, refer them to the "Snapshot of the Times" on p. 316. Ask how the first two items in the chronology are connected. (*mechanical cotton* *picker took away many jobs in the rural South, increasing migration to the North*) What two items in the list might have been the result of African American migration to the North? (*race riot in Chicago, election of three African Americans to the House*) Ask students to speculate on how the events might be connected. (*rioting resulted, in part, from overcrowding and tensions between whites and African Americans; creation of districts with largely African American populations allowed the election of African Americans to Congress*)

Review and Practice

Assign "Taking Another Look," p. 316.

Answers to Taking Another Look (p. 316)

1. mechanical cotton picker replaced sharecroppers **2.** three African Americans elected to Congress; white politicians sought African American votes; growing numbers of African Americans elected to city posts **3. Critical Thinking 1915:** had to sneak out of South, left by choice; **1940s:** had to leave due to changing labor demands; in both cases, could earn more money in North

Teaching Section 2: The Arts (pp. 317–19)

Objective

- To analyze how leading African American artists of the 1950s and 1960s provided positive images for the African American community.

Developing the Section

Analyzing a Quotation. Before assigning the section, have students read the "Focus On" feature on p. 320. Draw their attention to the opening quotation. Ask them what Johnson said the purpose of *Ebony* was. (*to provide positive Black images*) Ask why Johnson chose such an approach. (*to show that African Americans could do anything if given the chance*) Then assign the section. After students have completed the reading, ask them to describe whether and how they think each of the figures discussed provided a "positive Black image."

Review and Practice

Assign "Taking Another Look," p. 319.

Answers to Taking Another Look (p. 319)

1. dealt with racial tensions, led way for other books of protest **2.** bebop, cool jazz, free form jazz **3. Critical Thinking** The art they produced was excellent and crossed all ethnic boundaries.

Extending the Chapter

Preparing a Musical Retrospective. Divide the class into groups, and have each group find recordings by African American musicians popular in the 1950s and 1960s. Suggest that students check with parents or relatives for albums or tapes. Be sure each group plays selections by different artists. For each recording, students should do research on the chosen performer and music.

Looking Ahead

After students have read "Looking Ahead," p. 319, ask them to speculate on reasons why African Americans in the 1950s might have wanted to begin a new push for civil rights by tackling the issue of segregated schools.

Answers to Close Up (pp. 320–21)

The Who, What, Where of History

1. mechanical cotton picker **2.** one of three African Americans who held seats in House of Representatives in 1954. **3.** jazz saxophonist, developer of bebop **4.** African American novelist who wrote *Native Son* **5.** novel by Ralph Ellison **6.** African American playwright who wrote *A Raisin in the Sun* **7.** form of jazz developed by Parker, Gillespie, and Monk **8.** Cleveland, Ohio **9.** African American painter

Making the Connection

1. mechanical cotton picker forced many African Americans out of jobs in South; migration north to seek work followed **2.** Concentration of African Americans in cities increased their political power. **3.** *Native Son* dealt with tensions between whites and African Americans and led the way for other books of protest by African Americans.

Time Check

1. 1944 **2.** 1950-1960

What Would You Have Done?

yes: discrimination, segregation and limited employment opportunity in South; **no:** had to take low-paying "Negro work" in North, housing expensive and scarce

Thinking and Writing About History

Answers should mention move North, shift away from fieldwork, desegregation, increased political power and artistic expression.

Building Skills

1. taught to fly, but not allowed to fly in combat **2.** that he will be humiliated in front of whites **3.** Racists hold individual actions against an entire ethnic group.

Chapter 30 The Battle for Civil Rights (pp. 322–33)

Overview

In the 1950s, African Americans launched a Civil Rights Movement destined to turn U.S. society upside down. The struggle began in the courts, where NAACP lawyers won the historic case of *Brown* v. *Board of Education* that overturned *Plessy* v. *Ferguson*, which had been the legal basis for segregation. African Americans then set out to gain their full civil rights. They organized campaigns to integrate schools, public facilities, and voting rolls, often meeting bitter resistance at state and local levels. New African American leaders such as Martin Luther King and James Farmer emerged. They urged the federal government to take action to protect African Americans and their rights and, although reluctantly at times, the federal government began to do so. By 1964, a new civil rights law offered African Americans and other minorities greater protections.

Resources

Chapter 30 Activity Sheet: Using a Primary Source (p. 241)
Chapter 30 Test (p. 180)
Outline Map: The United States (p. 308)

Focus Activity

Have students skim the chapter photographs, the "Snapshot of the Times," and the chart on p. 324. Then refer them to the question in "Thinking About the Chapter," p. 322. Ask what tactics their quick skim indicates that civil rights workers used. (*court challenges, organized protests like sit-ins and boycotts*) Ask if what they have seen convinces them that the chapter title is accurate, that it truly was a *battle* for civil rights. (*probably yes*)

Teaching Section 1: Expelling Jim Crow From School (pp. 323–26)

Objective

- To analyze a quotation on the importance of the *Brown* decision as a safeguard to democracy.

Historical Sidelight

Standing Up to Prejudice. In 1943, Army Lt. Jackie Robinson, who would integrate major-league baseball in 1946, boarded a bus at Fort Hood in Texas. The white bus driver ordered him to take a seat in the rear. Robinson, however, knew the rules of the post—no segregation, so he refused and the driver filed charges against Robinson. The commanding officer of the post should have defended an African American officer against complaints by a white civilian. Instead, Robinson, who never had a drink in his life, found himself charged with drunken conduct unbecoming to an officer. Robinson might have been forced out of the army if other African American officers had not appealed to the NAACP. Robinson still had to stand court martial, but under the watchful eye of the NAACP, the court found him not guilty.

Developing the Section

Analyzing a Quotation. After students have read the section, read aloud the following description of the *Brown* decision from the African American newspaper *Chicago Defender:* "[It is] a second emancipation proclamation, . . . more important to our democracy than the atom bomb or the hydrogen bomb." Ask why the reporter might call the decision a second emancipation proclamation. (*because it freed African Americans from Jim Crow*) Remind students of the discussion of the Cold War as discussed on pp. 301–303 of *The Big Picture*. Why might the reporter have considered the atomic bomb a safeguard of democracy? (*protected the nation from the threat of communism*)

Review and Practice

Assign "Taking another Look," p. 326.

Answers to Taking Another Look (p. 326)

1. *McLaurin* v. *Oklahoma State Regents*, *Sweatt* v. *Painter* **2.** produced expert testimony to show that self-esteem of African American children was damaged by segregation in violation of the equal protection clause of 14th Amendment **3. Critical Thinking** Responses should note early psychological damage and continuing economic harm caused by segregation.

Teaching Section 2: Resisting Without Bitterness (pp. 326–27)

Objective

- To analyze the tactics of nonviolent protest.

Developing the Section

Analyzing Tactics. Before students read the section, write the word *nonviolence* on the chalkboard. Head a brainstorming session in which students relate whatever words or phrases they associate with the term. List their responses on the chalkboard. Explain that the concept of nonviolence was the foundation of the nonviolent movement, and that it involved the peaceful refusal to obey unjust laws. Ask students why peaceful resistance to such laws was important. (*might win public sympathy; violent resistance would mark protesters as ordinary lawbreakers, shift the focus of public attention from the unjust laws to violent protest action*). Tell students to keep track of how well protesters met this standard of nonviolence as they read this section and the rest of the material in this chapter and the next dealing with the Civil Rights Movement.

Review and Practice
Assign "Taking Another Look," p. 327.

Answer to Question in Caption (p. 326)
set in motion the modern Civil Rights Movement

Answers to Taking Another Look (p. 327)
1. Rosa Parks's arrest, leaflet **2.** nonviolence, "To resist without bitterness . . . to be beaten and not hit back" **3. Critical Thinking** nonviolent resistance to all forms of injustice

Teaching Section 3: A New Generation (pp. 328–30)

Objectives

- To use photographs to assess some of the tactics and risks involved in nonviolent protest.

Historical Sidelight
Women in the Civil Rights Movement. African American women took visible and often dangerous roles in the Civil Rights Movement. Ella Baker helped direct local branches of the NAACP, served as executive secretary of the SCLC, and helped organize SNCC. Autherine Lucy faced death threats when she became the first African American admitted to the University of Alabama. Lucretia Collins, a Fisk College student, completed the dangerous freedom ride from Nashville to Birmingham. Robin Doris Smith and Diane Nash shared a jail cell after lunch counter sit-ins in South Carolina.

Developing the Section
Analyzing Photographs. Refer students to the photographs on text pp. 328 and 329. Ask what tactics young people used to defeat segregation. (*sat in at lunch counters, organized freedom rides*) From evidence in the photos, what risks were involved in such actions? (*personal abuse and violence*) Ask students to describe the demeanor of the students involved in the sit-in. (*calm, determined*) Have students suggest reasons that photographs such as these served as effective arguments for the Civil Rights Movement.

Review and Practice
Assign "Taking Another Look," p. 330.

Answers to Taking Another Look (p. 330)
1. to test effectiveness of laws barring segregation at lunch counters, buses, and bus terminals **2.** Workers were often assaulted and beaten; some killed. Buses were bombed. **3. Critical Thinking** African Americans still denied almost all basic rights, violence

Teaching Section 4: Marching for Freedom (pp. 330–31)

Objectives

- To understand the historic significance of the year 1963.

Developing the Section
Making Connections. After students have read the section ask them to identify the historic significance of the year 1963. (*centennial of the Emancipation Proclamation*) How did civil rights leaders plan to kick off the year? (*a new round of protests in Birmingham, Alabama*) Why did they pick Birmingham as the site of protests? (*one of the most stubbornly segregated cities in the South*) How were events in Birmingham related to the occurrences in Washington described later in the section? Lead students to see how the violent white backlash in Birmingham contributed to demands for the end of segregation. Political pressure mounted on President Kennedy to call for a civil rights bill and the March on Washington pressured Congress to pass the bill.

Review and Practice
Assign "Taking Another Look," p. 331.

Answers to Taking Another Look (p. 331)
1. to celebrate 100th anniversary of Emancipation Proclamation by marching through one of most segregated cities in South **2.** freedom and equality for all **3. Critical Thinking** People saw the violence suffered by civil rights activists and pressured the government for action.

Extending the Chapter
Recreating History. Divide the class into 12 groups, and assign each group one month in 1963. Direct students to use the magazine collections or microfilm files in their community library to look at one major news publication for their respective month. Choices might include *Ebony*, *Time*,

Newsweek, or *The New York Times*. Tell them to look at the books, records, and people in the news, foreign affairs, and—most of all—happenings in the Civil Rights Movement. Based on this survey, have students prepare a short oral presentation entitled "You Are There–[name of month], 1963" describing some occurence from the month that involved or affected the lives of African Americans.

Looking Ahead

Have students read "Looking Ahead", p. 331. Ask them what direction they would expect the Civil Rights Movement to take after 1963.

Answers to Close Up (pp. 332–33)

The Who, What, Where of History

1. first African American to play baseball in major leagues **2.** first African American to be admitted to University of Oklahoma law school **3.** emphasized psychological effects of segregation **4.** Supreme Court case ruling segregation unconstitutional **5.** Little Rock, Arkansas **6.** refused to give up her bus seat to a white person **7.** Southern Christian Leadership Conference **8.** leader of nonviolent Civil Rights Movement in 1950s and 1960s **9.** Student Non-Violent Coordinating Committee **10.** bus rides into the South, meant to challenge segregation on interstate buses.

Making the Connection

1. laid the basis on which *Plessy* v. *Ferguson* was overturned **2.** Parks's arrest instigated the bus boycott. **3.** Connor's actions caused mounting public pressure on behalf of civil rights. **4.** King adopted Gandhi's philosophy of nonviolence.

Time Check

1. 1954 **2.** 1955–1956

What Would You Have Done?

1. yes: important to advance cause of civil rights; **no:** fear for safety **2.** You know that your actions may be dangerous, but you are working for a cause crucial to nation's future.

Thinking and Writing About History

1. Letters may express horror that troops are preventing enforcement of the law of the land. **2. agree:** morally correct behavior gives opponents no excuse for violence, makes opponents appear to be aggressors, endurance communicates strength; **disagree:** innocent people hurt by refusing to fight back, violence provokes violent response, inaction communicates weakness

Building Skills

1. "That same year", "The following year" **2.** Governor Faubus calls in National Guard; Congress passes Civil Rights Act; Southern Christian Leadership Conference is founded **3.** Thurgood Marshall wins *Sweatt* v. *Painter*; Rosa Parks refuses to give up bus seat; Supreme Court finds that segregation on Alabama buses is illegal **4.** before

Chapter 31 New Directions in the Civil Rights Movement (pp. 334–45)

Overview

In 1964, civil rights workers planned Freedom Summer, a massive voter registration drive in the South, in the face of increasing white violence. Violence, and the limited successes achieved by civil rights workers to this point, led to a revival of interest in black nationalism on the part of many African Americans. Leaders such as Malcolm X and members of the Black Panthers asserted their influence in the African American community. Meanwhile, the eruption of riots in African American neighborhoods of cities across the nation served as a reminder of the poverty that oppressed the lives of many African Americans. African Americans and the Civil Rights Movement had killed Jim Crow, but the problem of poverty and its effects could not be overturned in the courts. President Johnson called for a war on poverty, but that war faltered because of another war the nation was waging—the war in Vietnam.

Resources

Chapter 31 Activity Sheet: Connecting History and Geography (p. 242)
Chapter 31 Test (p. 181)
Unit 9 Writing Workshop: A Position Statement (pp. 294–297)

Focus Activity

Have students compare the "Snapshots of the Times" on pp. 323 and 336. Ask students what tactics African Americans used in the years 1950–1963 to bring about change. (*court cases, boycotts, sit-ins, freedom rides, marches*) How does the "Snapshot" on p. 336 show that both the movement and the responses to it changed over time?

(*mention of riots, assassinations*) Discuss with students the possible reasons for these changes in the Civil Rights Movement.

Teaching Section 1: A Long, Hot Summer (pp. 335–38)

Objective

- To draw connections between Freedom Summer and the 1965 Voting Rights Act.

Developing the Section

Interpreting a Chart. Direct students to the chart on p. 335. Ask them to study the chart and form a generalization about the effect of the Voting Rights Act of 1965. (*It resulted in increased registration of African American voters throughout the South.*) What state had the largest increase? (*Mississippi*) Then ask students to remember where civil rights workers had focused their efforts during Freedom Summer of 1964. (*Mississippi*) Ask students to speculate on how the events of Freedom Summer influenced passage of the Voting Rights Act.

Review and Practice

Assign "Taking Another Look," p. 338.

Answers to Questions in Caption (p. 335)

allowed federal examiners to register African American voters wherever discrimination was practiced; Mississippi and Alabama

Answers to Taking Another Look (p. 338)

1. murder of three civil rights workers in Mississippi, many other instances of attacks in Mississippi **2.** group of American Muslims led by Elijah Muhammad **3. Critical Thinking** Like Garvey, Malcolm advocated unity among people of African descent throughout world; looked to Africa for cultural models.

Teaching Section 2: Year of Rage: 1965 (pp. 338–39)

Objective

- To evaluate effects of events in Selma and Watts on the Civil Rights Movement.

Introducing the Section

Evaluating Events. Before students read the section, refer them to the "Snapshot of the Times" on p. 336. Ask them why 1965 might be called the "year of rage." (*assassination of Malcolm X, rioting*) Then assign the reading. After they finish, write the words *Selma* and *Watts* on the chalkboard. Ask students to suggest how events in each of these places either aided or hindered efforts by African Americans to gain equality.

Review and Practice

Assign "Taking Another Look," p. 339.

Answer to Question in Caption (p. 339)

to encourage voter registration, gain support for a voting rights bill

Answers to Taking Another Look (p. 339)

1. said he would cooperate with other civil rights groups and whites; turned away from separatist policies of Nation of Islam **2.** to register African American voters **3. Critical Thinking** **agree:** Through violence, African Americans demonstrated that they would no longer tolerate prejudice; **disagree:** Watts riots were nothing more than random acts of violence.

Teaching Section 3: Black Power (pp. 340–42)

Objective

- To compare and contrast the positions of Stokely Carmichael and Martin Luther King, Jr.

Historical Sidelight

A Fitting Tribute. Martin Luther King was buried on April 9, 1968, just outside Atlanta, Georgia, where he had started his work with the SCLC. Ralph Abernathy, who took King's place as head of the SCLC, told the crowd: "No coffin can hold his greatness, but we submit his body to the ground." The next day Congress honored King by approving Bill HR 2516—the civil rights bill that had been stalled for two years. On April 11, President Johnson signed the bill, making it a federal crime to interfere with civil rights workers.

Developing the Section

Comparing and Contrasting. Either make copies for the class or have volunteers read aloud the following statements by Stokely Carmichael and Martin Luther King.

> The only way we are going to stop them from whuppin' us is to take over. We've been saying freedom for six years, and we ain't got nothin.' The time for running has come to end. . . . It's time we stand up and take over; move on over [Whitey] or we'll move over you.
>
> —Stokely Carmichael

> Some people are telling us to be like our oppressor, who has a history of using Molotov cocktails [fire bombs], who has a history

of using atomic bombs, who has a history of lynching Negroes. . . . I'm not going to use violence, no matter who says so!

—Dr. Martin Luther King, Jr.

Write *Carmichael* and *King* on the chalkboard. Direct students to review this chapter and Chapter 30, looking for evidence that might support either man's position. For example, a student might suggest the Montgomery bus boycott to support King's views. As students suggest their evidence, be sure they explain how they think it supports the man's position.

Review and Practice

Assign "Taking Another Look," p. 342.

Answers to Questions in Caption (p. 340)

Mississippi, Alabama

Answers to Taking Another Look (p. 342)

1. conflict between King's "Freedom now" and Carmichael's "Black Power" **2. Black Power movement:** opposed assimilation, white membership in groups like SNCC, demanded repayment for years of slavery; **King:** focused on eliminating poverty, which he felt bred violence **3. Critical Thinking** Answers should show an understanding of King's accomplishments and the circumstances of his death.

Teaching Section 4: No Turning Back (pp. 342–43)

Objective

- To draw up a balance sheet evaluating the Civil Rights Movement.

Historical Sidelight

The Civil Rights Memorial. The contributions of those who struggled for civil rights are honored by the Civil Rights Memorial at the Southern Poverty Law Center in Montgomery, Alabama (see text p. 362). The work was designed by Maya Lin, who also created the Vietnam Veterans Memorial (see text p. 352). The memorial has two parts, both made of black granite. One is a 9-foot wall with water spilling over a biblical paraphrase often used by Martin Luther King: " . . . until justice rolls down like waters and righteousness like a mighty stream." Water also ripples over the second part, a pedestal with a nearly 12-foot circular tabletop listing key events and the names of 40 men, women, and children who died in the movement.

Developing the Section

Drawing Up a Balance Sheet. Divide the class into small groups, and have each group draw up a balance sheet of the Civil Rights Movement. One column should list accomplishments of the movement, while the other lists work still to be done. Students should review Chapters 30 and 31 when drawing up their lists. After they have finished, encourage students to write an agenda for change for African Americans during the closing years of the 20th century. In an information-sharing session, assemble a list of proposals in the corner of the chalkboard and refer to it as students work through Unit 10.

Review and Practice

Assign "Taking Another Look," p. 343.

Answers to Taking Another Look (p. 343)

1. deep rooted poverty and widespread unemployment **2.** ended legal segregation, opened education and public facilities to all, gave African Americans political power through Voting Rights Act, exposed flaws within U.S. society, taught people how to effect political and social change **3. Critical Thinking** Students should show an understanding of the accomplishments of the Civil Rights Movement and support their choices with information drawn from the text.

Extending the Chapter

Preparing Oral Histories. Divide the class into four groups, and assign each group one of the four sections in this chapter. Tell students to formulate interview questions to ask people who lived through the events mentioned in their various sections. Review these questions with each group. Then have students locate people in the community who remember the period, conduct interviews with them using their questions. Students should share the results of the interviews with the class in the form of summaries.

Looking Ahead

After students have read "Looking Ahead," p. 343, remind them that African Americans had marched off to war before. Given the events described in the last two chapters, ask students how conditions for African Americans in the armed forces during the Vietnam War might be expected to differ from conditions in earlier wars.

Answers to Close Up (pp. 344–45)

The Who, What, Where of History

1. Council of Federated Organizations **2.** Mississippi Freedom Democratic party **3.** African American woman active in voter registration drives in South, lost her job for registering to vote **4.** African American leader of Nation of Islam who stressed self-help as route to advancement **5.** religious group emphasizing separation of races **6.** leader of SNCC who popularized "Black Power" slogan **7.** Selma, Alabama **8.** Bobby Seale and Huey Newton **9.** group of people with incomes below poverty level **10.** Johnson panel investigating causes of 1960s riots

Making the Connection

1. Johnson hoped to stop further riots by launching the War on Poverty. **2.** Rioting in Selma persuaded Johnson to support a voting rights bill. **3.** Activists focused on improving conditions for the underclass.

Time Check

1. 1968 **2.** 1968 **3.** 1966

What Would You Have Done?

join: party active in attempts to help African American community; **not join:** party's philosophy too radical and militant

Thinking and Writing About History

Responses will differ but should demonstrate knowledge of leaders discussed in chapter and understanding of different philosophies.

Building Skills

1. opinions **2.** sense of humor **3.** opinions **4. Edelman:** "So, he was a new outlet for the anger and the frustration." **Haley:** "There were those who were feeling that Malcolm was having the courage to say aloud, publicly, things which they had felt or which they wished somebody would say." **5.** Edelman and Haley share the opinion that Malcolm X was finally expressing African Americans' previously unstated anger at their position in U.S. society.

Chapter 32 Marching Off to Vietnam (pp. 346–55)

Overview

The Vietnam War deeply divided the nation. Opponents of the war included many members of the Civil Rights Movement. Some African American leaders felt the war siphoned off funds that might be better used to help the poor, and others argued that African Americans accounted for a disproportionate share of the war's casualties. The Vietnam War was the first in the nation's history in which all combat units were integrated. The process of integration had been completed shortly after the Korean War, but it was first tested in battle in Vietnam.

African American troops in Vietnam remained deeply concerned with changes the Civil Rights and Black Power movements were producing back home. The uncertainties of combat and the concurrent turmoil generated by events at home meant that many returning Vietnam veterans faced difficulty in readjusting to civilian life. The difficulties of adjustment were felt by whites as well as African Americans.

Resources

Chapter 32 Activity Sheet: Interpreting a Political Cartoon (p. 244)
Chapter 32 Test (p. 182)
Unit 9 Test (pp. 175–77)

Focus Activity

Write the word *Vietnam* on the chalkboard. Ask students what images the word calls up in their minds. Record responses on the chalkboard. Then assign the chapter-opening story on pp. 346–47. Ask students what event happened just as Wilkins was about to leave for Vietnam. (*assassination of King*) What tour of duty did he almost draw on U.S. soil? (*riot duty in one of the nation's cities*) Remind students that the nation's involvement in the Vietnam War was growing just as the Civil Rights Movement was reaching its peak. Tell them that in this chapter they should be alert for the ways in which these two events influenced each other.

Teaching Section 1: Under Fire (pp. 347–49)

Objective

- To use a chronology to develop empathy for the African American soldiers who served in Vietnam.

Historical Sidelight

Telling the Story of Vietnam. In 1967, a 29-year-old African American reporter named Wallace Terry went to Vietnam to cover the war for *Time* magazine. For seven years, Terry had reported on the Civil Rights Movement in the United States and now he was going to take a look at how African Americans were doing in the first war in which the nation's combat units were fully integrated. Brown's reports from Vietnam appeared in a special issue of *Time* entitled the

"The Negro in Vietnam." In later years, Terry reported on Vietnam from the viewpoint of the African American veterans who fought in Vietnam after 1967. These vets told of continuing racial conflicts and the experience of fighting in a war disapproved of by many Americans. Terry told their stories in frank, often graphic, language in his 1984 best-seller entitled *Bloods.*

Developing the Section

Understanding Time. Refer students to the "Snapshot of the Times" on p. 348. Ask students when the first U.S. combat troops arrived in Vietnam. (*1965*) What events in the "Snapshot" reveal opposition to the war? (*resistance of the draft by Ali, King's antiwar speech, Vietnam Moratorium Day*) Refer students to the "Snapshot" for Chapter 31 (p. 336). What events were taking place in the United States during the first three years of the Vietnam War? (*Freedom Summer, riots, assassinations*) Ask students how news of such events in the United States would have affected African American soldiers in Vietnam.

Review and Practice

Assign "Taking Another Look," p. 349.

Answers to Taking Another Look (p. 349)

1. Vietnam was the first U.S. war in which African Americans were fully integrated into combat units. **2.** War violated his Muslim faith. **3. Critical Thinking** Veteran felt that he was fighting for a people in a foreign country who were better off than his own people in the U.S.

Teaching Section 2: War and Protest (pp. 349–50)

Objectives

- To identify reasons African Americans supported or opposed the Vietnam War.
- To write leaflets explaining African Americans' reasons for fighting in Vietnam.

Developing the Section

1. Analyzing Opposition. Assign students to read the opening paragraph of the section on p. 349. Ask on what grounds Dr. King opposed the war. (*took money away from the Great Society; was contrary to his belief in nonviolence*) Write the words *support* and *oppose* on the chalkboard. Ask students to list in the appropriate columns reasons that African Americans during the 1960s and 1970s might have either backed or opposed the Vietnam War. After students have finished the list, ask if they think African Americans might have had similar reasons for supporting and opposing the Persian Gulf War of 1991. Why or why not?

2. Preparing a Leaflet. Divide students into groups, and have them prepare leaflets in which African American soldiers respond to the Vietcong leaflet cited on text p. 350.

Review and Practice

Assign "Taking Another Look," p. 350.

Answer to Question in Caption (p. 349)

disproportionate number of African Americans fought and died in Vietnam; war drained resources that could have improved conditions in U.S. cities

Answers to Taking Another Look (p. 350)

1. African Americans comprised 20 percent of draftees fighting in Vietnam, but only 10 percent of U.S. population and only 5 percent of commanding officers. In the first 11 months of 1966, African Americans accounted for 22.4 percent of combat deaths. **2.** believed money spent on war would be better spent improving conditions in cities; African Americans active in Civil Rights Movement were often drafted in order to remove them from their communities **3. Critical Thinking** African Americans have always fought for their country.

Teaching Section 3: Coming Home (pp. 350–53)

Objective

- To interpret a chart on African American military service.

Developing the Section

Interpreting a Chart. Refer students to the chart on text p. 353. Ask what generalizations they can form about African American service to the nation. (*Example: African Americans have contributed to the nation's defense ever since the American Revolution.*) Then ask how many African Americans served in World War II. (*1 million*) How many served in Vietnam? (*274,937*) What distinguished the African American experience in Vietnam from the African American experience in World War II? (*fought in integrated units, fought in the midst of a Civil Rights Movement, war lacked the full support of the nation*)

Review and Practice

Assign "Taking Another Look," p. 353.

Answers to Taking Another Look (p. 353)

1. Vietnam Syndrome, felt out of touch with world at home; expected to return home heroes, let down by lack of recognition; battled drug addiction **2.** African American enrollment at all service academies increased; African Americans broke into top ranks of military. **3. Critical Thinking agree:** helped solidify Black Power movement; **disagree:** international conflict irrelevant to domestic issues

Extending the Chapter

Connecting Past to Present. Divide the class into four groups, and assign them to do research and prepare reports on the role of African Americans in one of following branches of the military since the Vietnam War: Army, Navy, Air Force, and Marines. Direct students to look for articles on African Americans in the military in *The Reader's Guide to Periodical Literature.*

Looking Ahead

Assign students "Looking Ahead," p. 353. Then tell them that the next unit brings the African American experience into their own lifetimes. Assign students to start clipping articles from newspapers and magazines that pertain to African Americans today.

Answers to Close Up (pp. 354–55)

The Who, What, Where of History

1. North Vietnamese army **2.** Saigon **3.** North Vietnam **4.** African American boxer who rejected the draft on religious grounds **5.** first African American admiral in U.S. naval history **6.** first African American Chairman of Joint Chiefs of Staff

Making the Connection

1. Money spent on war deprived Great Society programs of needed financial support. **2.** Some protesters regarded Vietnam veterans as wrongdoers and vice versa so both had difficulty readjusting to one another.

Time Check

1. 1950–1953 **2.** 1965 **3.** 1975 **4.** 1982

What Would You Have Done?

1. support: believe soldiers need support, believe in anti-communist action in Vietnam; **protest:** believe war is morally incorrect, unnecessary waste of money and lives **2. would enlist:** believe it will improve my own status, believe in fight against communism; **would not enlist:** do not want to risk life in unnecessary and unjust war, don't believe in fighting for a country which abuses my rights

Thinking and Writing About History

support: Ali should not have to violate personal beliefs to fight in war, takes more courage to defy government than to obey it; **criticize:** Ali should obey the law and should be subject to draft and combat just like everyone else.

Building Skills

1. The North Vietnamese siege of a Marine base at Khensanh ended. **2.** North Vietnamese are the enemy. **3.** no; article presents facts. **4. a.** U.S. command **b.** yes; command wants American public to think war is going well **5.** Responses will vary but should show understanding of material in chapter. **Example:** How is this event going to affect war as a whole?

UNIT 10 Crosscurrents in Today's World (pp. 356–91)

UNIT THEME

Because of the Civil Rights Movement, African Americans are able to bring about major changes in U.S. society.

UNIT CONCEPTS

- In the 1980s and early 1990s, African American leaders set about tearing down the economic barriers that still kept African Americans from equal pay and equal job opportunities.
- The changes brought about by the Civil Rights Movement encouraged some African Americans to return to the South, reversing a nearly century-old trend.
- The economic gap between middle-class and poor African Americans widened, but the tradition of self-help led African Americans to work toward narrowing that gap.
- The extended family and the African American church remained major sources of strength for American Americans.
- Political splits that developed among African Americans during the Civil Rights Movement continued into the present.
- African Americans in the late 20th century left their mark on all walks of life in the United States.
- Other Americans have recognized the vitality of African American culture, thus changing U.S. society as a whole.
- African Americans built new ties with African nations, ensuring that their ancestral heritage will remain strong.

UNIT OVERVIEW

Unit 10 moves from the Civil Rights Movement to the threshold of the 21st century. It looks ahead to a time when there will be no more "firsts" for African Americans because of their full participation in U.S. society. *The Big Picture* and the two chapters in this unit describe: (1) the economic and social conditions of African Americans in today's society, and (2) the ways in which African Americans have helped shape the culture of the United States today while still holding on to their African heritage.

In teaching this unit, you might repeat a statement from the closing chapter by John Johnson, publisher of *Ebony:* "Never before have so many White Americans paid Black Americans that sincerest form of flattery—imitation." Tell students that as the barriers of prejudice come down, African American culture is significantly changing the nation's culture. Ask students to name some of the African Americans who are influencing the thoughts and styles of African Americans and other Americans today.

COOPERATIVE LEARNING ACTIVITY

The following cooperative learning activity can be used for alternative assessment after study of the unit has been completed.

At the end of the unit, remind students that they are the generation who will reach adulthood after the year 2000—in a new century, and a new millennium. Then review the 1991 meeting of civil rights leaders called "A Look Back—A Leap Forward," p. 363. Divide the class into groups, and have them set their own agendas for the future. Tell each group to select at least three areas of U.S. society that they would like to improve or build upon. Under each area, have students list ways they can personally help to achieve these goals, either now or in the years ahead. Call on students to present their plans to the class. In evaluating student presentations, consider the correlation between methods and goals and the clarity of the presentation as a whole.

Unit 10 THE BIG PICTURE (pp. 357–61)

Theme

The Civil Rights Movement won African Americans a larger and more influential place in society, even as the nation's political outlook became more conservative.

Overview

The Big Picture examines the nation after the turmoil of the 1960s. In 1968, voters elected Richard Nixon President. He was the first in a series of Republicans who—except from 1977 to 1981 when Democrat Jimmy Carter served—held the presidency into the 1990s.

Most of these Presidents promised stability and less federal involvement in the affairs of individuals and the states. These Presidents were less willing to press for federal involvement in civil rights matters than Kennedy and Johnson had been. Their appointees to the Supreme Court reflected their more conservative views.

The nation faced new economic concerns in these years. Several recessions shook the economy and revealed the nation's vulnerability to competition from abroad. As in the past, African Americans suffered disproportionately during these recessions.

Still, the advances made by African Americans during the Civil Rights Movement endured. This was most evident in the area of politics where more African Americans took office at local, state, and national levels.

Objectives

- To define African Americans' role in the progress of the United States.
- To use a timeline to analyze some recent changes in U.S. society.
- To draw political cartoons expressing points of view on President Nixon's policies.
- To forecast future job opportunities.
- To analyze the effects of economic policies.
- To speculate on Martin Luther King's reactions to changes since the Civil Rights Movement.

Introducing *The Big Picture*

Request a volunteer read aloud "An African American Speaks" on p. 357. Ask if students agree with the definition of the United States' role contained there. Ask if they agree with what Hope and Moss say is the "special function" African Americans should perform. What ways can students suggest that function might be carried out today?

Using the Timeline

Divide the class into a number of small groups. Assign each group to one of the events from the timeline on pp. 358–59 that took place after 1975. Ask each group to explain how its event illustrates a change in U.S. politics or society since the 1960s.

Teaching *The Big Picture*

1. Designing Political Cartoons. Assign "Changing Attitudes Toward Civil Rights," "The Nixon Years," and "Changes in the Supreme Court," text pp. 357–59. Then have students, working individually or in small groups, design political cartoons expressing reactions to one of the decisions or policies discussed.

2. Forecasting. Refer students to "Economic Downturns" on pp. 359–60. Ask them how the employment situation has changed in recent decades. (*decline in unskilled jobs, increased mechanization, rise in service industries*) Ask what training they think will best equip people to compete in the job market of the future.

3. Analyzing Policies. Write the following headings on the chalkboard: *Cut taxes* and *Cut government spending*. Encourage students to suggest as many effects on U.S. society as they can for these policies. Point out that these policies represented the major promises that Ronald Reagan made when running for President. Then have them read the section "The Reagan Years" on pp. 360–61, comparing their lists with effects cited in the text.

4. Using Historic Imagination. After students have read "I Have a Dream" on text p. 361, tell them to imagine that King has returned to the United States today. Ask how they think he might respond to the changes—or lack of changes—that have taken place since the 1960s.

Review and Practice

Assign "Taking Another Look," p. 361.

Answers to Taking Another Look (p. 361)

1. returned power in many areas to state and local governments, cut back on Great Society programs, criticized war protesters and rioters, tried to shift Supreme Court toward more conservative outlook **2.** recession, caused more competition for decreasing number of jobs **3. a.** people of all colors worked together **b.** Reagan more focused on middle classes; Jackson on improving conditions for all **4. Critical Thinking Examples:** aid to inner cities, aid to improve education, etc.

Chapter 33 Agenda for Change (pp. 362–75)

Overview

The Civil Rights Movement forever changed the United States. In the 1980s, African Americans began, for the first time in almost 100 years, to return to the South—a testimony to the sweeping reforms introduced by the Civil Rights Movement. Throughout the United States, income and educational gaps between African Americans and whites narrowed as the number of middle-class African Americans grew. But problems that had taken centuries to build up would take time to tear down. To resolve these problems, African Americans today, as in the past, are relying on traditions of self-help.

Resources

Chapter 33 Activity Sheet: Analyzing a Map (p. 245)
Outline Map: The United States (p. 308)
Chapter 33 Test (p. 186)

Focus Activity

Assign students the chapter-opening story on pp. 362–63. Ask them what occasion brought John Lewis back to Montgomery. (*30th anniversary of freedom rides*) What change did he notice? (*African Americans and whites boarding buses together*) What was the cost of this change? (*violence and deaths during the Civil Rights Movement*) Encourage students to compile a list of other changes that Lewis might expect to encounter in Montgomery 30 years after the freedom rides.

Teaching Section 1: African Americans Today (pp. 363–66)

Objective

- To use statistics to form generalizations about African Americans in the United States today.

Historical Sidelight

Up from Sharecropping. John Lewis was born in 1940, the son of a sharecropper. During the years of the Civil Rights Movement, he was arrested some 40 times. He still bears the scars of beatings by the police in those years. Lewis first won election to the U.S. Congress as a representative from Atlanta, Georgia, in 1986 and serves on the Democratic Policy and Steering Commitee.

Developing the Section

Interpreting Statistics. Divide the class into small groups. Have them study the tables on pp. 364–65 and then use these figures to write at least four generalizations about African Americans in the United States today.

Review and Practice

Assign "Taking Another Look," p. 366.

Answers to Taking Another Look (p. 366)

1. Over 100,000 more African Americans headed into the South than left it. **2.** more college graduates; fewer drop-outs **3. Critical Thinking** Most make under $24,999 a year; leading business is auto dealership; most live in South.

Teaching Section 2: Overcoming Economic Barriers (pp. 366–70)

Objective

- To organize task forces to identify economic problems and suggest solutions.

Developing the Section

Identifying Problems and Solutions. Divide the class into three groups. Assign one group the section "Pockets of Rural Poverty," the second "the Urban Underclass," and the third "Growing Up in the Towers" and "Making It." Tell students to imagine they are members of a government task force investigating poverty in the rural South, the cities in general, and housing projects in particular. Each group should review its section of the text and prepare a report for the entire class. The reports should discuss problems found in each of the three areas and suggest possible solutions to those problems.

Review and Practice

Assign "Taking Another Look," p. 370.

Answers to Questions in Captions (pp. 367–69)

(p. 367) African American populations larger than 1 million; Idaho has fewer than 100,000 African Americans; Illinois, more than a million (p. 369) More jobs require technical skills.

Answers to Taking Another Look (p. 370)

1. lower wages for African Americans, higher unemployment **2.** loss of middle-class families, loss of tax base, businesses lost income **3. Critical Thinking Examples:** employment counseling; improved housing programs; counseling to avoid teen pregnancy; job retraining programs; improved health care programs

Teaching Section 3: Lending a Helping Hand (pp. 370–72)

Objective

- To gather evidence of the continuing tradition of African American self-help.

Developing the Section

Compiling Evidence. Read aloud the statement by Earl C. Graves on p. 371. Ask students to cite earlier examples of the kind of support Graves is talking about. (*Free African Society, self-help societies of the late 1800s, African American church movement*) As students read the section have them list evidence supporting Graves's remark.

Review and Practice

Assign "Taking Another Look," p. 372.

Answer to Question in Caption (p. 370)

because of her efforts to aid drug-addicted babies

Answers to Taking Another Look (p. 372)

1. Hale House, tutoring and literacy projects, science learning centers **2.** racial solidarity and pride will help African Americans overcome obstacles **3. Critical Thinking** Churches are community gathering place; African American ministers have always played large role in community.

Extending the Chapter

Organizing a Community Action Project. Ask students, working in small groups, to create plans for a community action project to benefit the community. Students should devise ways to implement and fund that project.

Looking Ahead

After students have read "Looking Ahead," p. 372, ask them to define *frontier.* (*new field of learning or endeavor*) Discuss with students what new frontiers the Civil Rights Movement opened for African Americans.

Answers to Close Up (pp. 374–75)

The Who, What, Where of History

1. Nixon supporters who disliked way society was developing but did not want to speak out **2.** Supreme Court case on affirmative action **3.** giving preference in hiring to groups that have suffered from discrimination in the past **4.** increase in prices over period of time **5.** African American who sought Democratic presidential nomination in 1984, 1988 **6.** SCLC president and freedom rider **7.** Montgomery, Alabama **8.** population statistics **9.** difference in access to health care between African Americans and whites **10.** care for drug-addicted babies **11.** festival celebrating kinship among African Americans

Making the Connection

1. Civil Rights Movement won rights for African Americans in the South; many moved to South to enjoy the benefits and escape less desirable circumstances in the North **2.** the unemployed and those earning low wages cannot get same quality health care as others **3.** As many middle-class white families left, cities lost taxes, businesses lost customers, and housing decayed.

Time Check

1. 1984 **2.** 1986 **3.** 1991

What Would You Have Done?

1. Examples: volunteer to help at Hale House; help with the Black Family Reunion; tutor children in a church project **2.** Answers should show a grasp of the purpose of the Reunion.

Thinking and Writing About History

1. Letters should show an understanding of advantages and disadvantages of living in different parts of United States. **2. Examples:** Differences in income between African Americans and whites result in differences in health care, education, and housing. Government might help spur formation of African American owned businesses. **3.** Speeches should show grasp of the value of Hale's work to entire community.

Building Skills

Work should show grasp of similarities and differences between African Americans in North and South in categories listed.

Chapter 34 Crossing New Frontiers (pp. 376–91)

Overview

Building on gains of the Civil Rights Movement, African Americans entered the political scene in growing numbers—as voters and as elected officials at all levels of government. Political differences exist among African Americans, but most agree on the importance of preserving their common African heritage. Efforts to express that heritage have brought new vitality to U.S. culture. As African Americans move forward into the future, they are also looking back to their ancestral home. In the 1990s, a revived Pan-Africanism led to a reaffirmation of ties with the many nations and peoples of Africa.

Resources

Chapter 34 Activity Sheet A: Recognizing Points of View (p. 246)
Chapter 34 Activity Sheet B: Stating and Supporting an Opinion (p. 247)
Outline Map: Africa (p. 306)
Chapter 34 Test (p. 187)
Unit 10 Test (pp. 183–85)

Focus Activity

Divide the class into small groups. Have each group recast the section titles in the form of questions about African Americans today. Encourage the groups to try to formulate answers to those questions. Direct the groups to record both their questions and their answers for reference as they work through the chapter.

Teaching Section 1: A Greater Voice in Politics (pp. 377–81)

Objective

- To make hypotheses about the changing role of African Americans in politics and find evidence relating to those hypotheses.

Historical Sidelight

Into Space. African American scientists and doctors helped the United States win the space race. Former Tuskegee airman Colonel Vance H. Marchbanks monitored the health of the nation's first astronauts and took part in the launch that sent John Glenn into orbit around Earth. When Americans landed on the moon in 1969, they wore spacesuits designed by Marchbanks and rode in a lunar rover with wheels designed by African American astrophysicist Robert E. Sturney. Another African American scientist, George R. Carruthers,was responsible for developing the lunar camera that astronauts set up on the moon.

Developing the Section

Making Hypotheses. Refer students to the "Snapshot of the Times" on p. 378. Ask students how many events listed there involve politics. (*seven*) Tell students that a hypothesis is a temporary conclusion drawn on the basis of available evidence. As more information is gathered, a hypothesis can be proved or disproved. Ask students to form hypotheses about African Americans in politics between 1968 and the present. Then assign the section, telling them to collect any evidence they can find that will prove or disprove their hypotheses.

Review and Practice

Assign "Points of View," p. 381 and "Taking Another Look," p. 381.

Answer to Question in Caption (p. 378)

to back his bid for the presidency

Answers to Points of View (p. 381)

1. problems such as fatherless families have not changed despite progress on racism **2. a.** blaming white people for all African Americans' problems **b.** implies whites have more influence over African Americans than African Americans themselves **3.** will to achieve, national will to provide employment and job training **4. Critical Thinking** More progress needs to be made.

Answers to Taking Another Look (p. 381)

1. more African Americans at all levels of government **2. a.** felt U.S. must create opportunities to advance complete equality **b.** felt affirmative action was part of cycle of dependency **3. Critical Thinking** **agree:** politicians have made huge strides and major changes in American society; **disagree:** politics is not simply a question of race, politicians should be judged on policy, not ethnicity

Teaching Section 2: The Changing Face of the Nation (pp. 382–86)

Objective

- To write a news article summarizing the achievements of African Americans in U.S. culture today.

Developing the Section

Writing a News Article. After students have read the section, assign them, working individually or in small groups, to write news articles entitled: "African Americans—The Pacesetters for the United States." To help students compress information in this section, refer them to "Building Skills," p. 391.

Review and Practice

Assign "Taking Another Look," p. 386.

Answers to Questions in Captions (pp. 383–85)

(p. 383 top) clothing, jewelry (p. 383 bottom) dance that incorporated African American movements and rhythms (p. 384) African American experiences (p. 385) racial tensions, daily experiences of African Americans

Answers to Taking Another Look (p. 386)

1. influence on clothing, names, hairstyles, dance **2.** Many African American artists and styles have become popular in white community. **3. Critical Thinking** greater influence of African American politicians and artists; movement into middle and upper classes

Teaching Section 3: Bridging the Continents (pp. 386–89)

Objective

- To make connections between the experiences of African Americans in the South and those of black South Africans.

Developing the Section

Making Connections. Ask students, based on their reading of this section, to explain why African Americans might identify with black South Africans. (*suffered similar oppression*) How might actions of African Americans during the Civil Rights Movement have influenced black Africans? (*inspiration, examples of political organization*) How might the struggles of black Africans against apartheid influence African Americans? (*renewed awareness and pride in African roots, inspiration to fight for economic equality*)

Review and Practice

Assign "Taking Another Look," p. 389.

Answers to Taking Another Look (p. 389)

1. pressured U.S. government to impose economic sanctions on South Africa **2.** renewed ties between African Americans and black Africans **3. Critical Thinking agree:** point of sanctions was to force South Africa to dismantle apartheid, and South Africa moved to do that; **disagree;** must assure that black South Africans are granted equal rights

Extending the Chapter

Preparing a Festival. Plan an African American festival in which students celebrate their living heritage. Assign a music committee to select records, tapes, or cassettes. Have another group of students design photo montages illustrating present-day African American cultural achievements. Students should choose special foods to bring into class.

Looking Ahead

When students have finished "Looking Ahead," p. 389, remind them that they are among the first generation to grow up in the post-civil rights era. Encourage them to discuss the changes they think their generation will bring to the United States.

Answers to Close Up (pp. 390–91)

The Who, What, Where of History,

1. first African American in space **2.** first African American woman elected to Congress, 1972 Presidential candidate **3.** Jesse Jackson's constituency **4.** first elected African American governor in U.S. **5.** second African American to serve on the Supreme Court **6.** African American choreographer **7.** Alex Haley's book exploring his African heritage **8.** novelist who wrote *The Color Purple* **9.** leader of African National Congress **10.** South African system of strict segregation **11.** limits on foreign trade intended to create political pressure for change

Making the Connection

1. Movement increased number of African American voters and led to a larger role in U.S. politics **2.** U.S. economic sanctions helped pressure South Africa into ending apartheid.

Time Check

1. 1968 **2.**1962—arrested and imprisoned; 1989—freed from prison; 1991—objected to lifting of U.S. sanctions, visited U.S.

What Would You Have Done?

1. King was key figure of century, responsible for sweeping changes in U.S. society, helped win full civil rights for African Americans. **2. stay:** can be symbol of struggle against apartheid; **leave:** free to choose actions opposing apartheid, can speak out openly

Thinking and Writing About History

1. Commercials should mention the candidates' positions on major national issues that could be drawn from the text. **2.** Questions should show knowledge of chosen subject.

Building Skills

A Greater Voice in Politics: Since the Civil Rights Movement, African Americans have gained a far greater role in shaping American politics. **Changing Face of the Nation:** Since the 1970s, African Americans have had a great influence on American culture. **Bridging the Continents:** African Americans have become heavily involved with African policy.

LESSON PLANS FOR *THE ARTIST'S VIEW*

The Artist's View insert, following p. 260 of the student text, contains full-color illustrations of works by African and African American artists and artisans. Additional information about these works and suggested strategies for teaching *The Artist's View* are given below.

AFRICAN ART

Works in this category appear on *The Artist's View*, pp. A1–A4.

OVERVIEW

Africa is a land of more than a thousand different peoples and as many artistic styles. The historic works shown in *The Artist's View* display only a tiny fraction of these styles. African artists most often worked in wood, clay, ivory, and metals such as bronze, silver, and gold. The ways in which artists worked with these materials varied greatly. The artists of West Africa generally followed a realistic style (see the Ife bronze head, p. A2). Artists in the Congo, on the other hand, worked more symbolically (see mask on p. A3). It was the Congolese styles that inspired the European cubists and later modern artists such as Picasso.

Throughout Africa, art and religion went hand in hand. Many societies, such as those in the Congo, believed artists had special contacts with magical forces so they venerated artists as bridges between the physical and spiritual worlds. In areas such as the kingdoms of West Africa, royal families exerted a great deal of influence over artists. In Benin, for example, artists often cast lifelike bronze heads of kings and depicted royal feats in bronze metal reliefs (see p. A4).

In Africa, men and women tended to specialize in the types of art they created. The arts of basketry and pottery-making, for example, belonged to women. So did weaving, with the notable exception of the male weavers who produced the beautiful kente cloth of West Africa (see p. A2). Unlike the women weavers—who worked on large, vertical looms—the men used small, horizontal looms to weave narrow cotton-and-wool strips that they stitched together. Men also produced sculptures of wood, iron, and bronze.

FOCUS ACTIVITY

Tell students that its sculpture has been called one of Africa's greatest gifts to human culture. Ask them to study the artistic works and captions on pp. A1–A4 of *The Artist's View*, and describe the styles and techniques that African sculptors used to create these works.

TEACHING STRATEGY

Divide the class into five groups, and assign each group one of the works of art in *The Artist's View*. Tell students to imagine they are part of a study group sent to Africa to learn about various societies. The first piece of evidence they receive is the work of art they have been assigned. Based on this work, have students prepare two-part reports. The first part of each group's report should describe the work of art itself, while the second part should present any conclusions that students are able to draw about the people who produced it.

COOPERATIVE LEARNING ACTIVITY

Divide students into research teams, and have them investigate various forms of African art. Topics should include: sculpture, architecture, weaving, pottery, jewelry, and so on. Direct each team to attach pictures of representative works to a large poster board. Each poster should have captions similar to those used in *The Artist's View*, explaining what each piece is and its significance. Display the posters on one wall of the classroom for reference throughout the course.

FOLK ART

Works in this category appear on *The Artist's View* pp. A5–A7.

OVERVIEW

Folk art developed in the years before mass-produced machine goods and invention of the camera. It was the product of self-trained artists who wanted either to create artistically pleasing objects for everyday use or to paint portraits as records for future generations. In describing folk art, people commonly use such adjectives as *simple, direct, imaginative, fresh,* and *primitive.*

The vitality of African American folk art can be seen in works such as the quilt, painting, mantle, and face vessel in *The Artist's View*. Many of these works show both the influence of Africa and the ingenuity born of African American slaves. Quilter Harriet Powers (see p. A5), who worked in the late 1800s, depicted Biblical stories and local events of her native town in Georgia. But she used techniques very similar to the stitchery and appliques used in West African fabrics, particularly by the Fon and Dahomean peoples. Both Thomas Day and Joshua Johnson (see p. A6), most of whose works were done in the first half of the 19th century, earned a living by selling their works to whites. Their success attested to a recognition of their talent. Day's woodworking led the citizens of Milton, North Carolina, to exempt him from certain state laws restricting the movements of "people of color." Day also integrated the town's Presbyterian Church by exchanging finely carved church pews for the "right" to sit in them.

As Southerners became increasingly defensive of their "peculiar institution," the names of such talented artists disappeared from the records. It was not until the early 1900s, for example, that researchers found that some 30 widely admired unsigned portraits of white families were the work of an African American artist from Baltimore—Joshua Johnson.

FOCUS ACTIVITY

Ask students to speculate on what they think the term *folk art* might mean. Concentrate on the two parts of the term *folk* (*everyday people*) and *art* (*creative work or skill, object of beauty*). Then ask students to suggest some of the influences that may have shaped the folk art of African Americans.

TEACHING STRATEGY

Tell students that in the 1700s and 1800s, the word *mechanic* meant anyone who worked with his or her hands—including folk artists. Then read aloud the following incomplete review that is taken from the April 16, 1852, issue of the *New York Herald.*

> There is now in Philadelphia an exhibition of colored mechanics . . , and for the first effort it exceeds the most sanguine [hopeful] expectation. . . . On visiting the place I was surprised to see the beautiful specimens of work exhibited there, which would be of credit to any mechanic.

Then direct students to imagine they are reporters at this exhibition. Have them work, in small groups, to complete the news article by describing each of the pieces of folk art on pp. A5–A7 in *The Artist's View*. To develop an historical frame of reference, suggest students review *The Big Picture* for Units 2 and 4.

COOPERATIVE LEARNING ACTIVITY

Assign teams of students to research and write a biographical profile of one of the following African American folk artists: Joshua Johnson, Harriet Powers, Thomas Day, G.W. Hobbs, or Scipio Moorhead. Teams might present their findings in the form of a panel discussion in which students, playing the roles of the artists, describe the times in which they lived.

POST–CIVIL WAR ART

Works in this category appear on *The Artist's View* pp. A7 and A9.

OVERVIEW

During the years following the Civil War, African American artists faced bitterness and often insurmountable barriers of prejudice. Although Reconstruction made it possible for more African Americans to receive formal art training, the market for their work remained limited. Many African American artists in the late 1800s moved to Europe, where they enjoyed freer artistic expression and had a better chance of selling artistic pieces with African or African American themes.

Edmonia Lewis was one of the African American artists who found a home in Rome. Lewis originally studied sculpture at Oberlin College in Ohio. Later, abolitionists sent her to study with sculptors in Italy. But Lewis did not abandon her dual heritage as a Chippewa and an African American. Some of her most famous works include *An Old Indian Arrow Maker and His Daughter, Hiawatha's Marriage,* and *Forever Free* (see p. A9). Another of Lewis' works, *The Death of Cleopatra,* won critical acclaim at the 1876 Philadelphia Centennial Exposition.

The most famous African American artist of the post–Civil War period was Henry Ossawa Tanner. The son of educated, free African American parents, Tanner began his artistic training at age 13. At the Pennsylvania Academy of Fine Arts, he studied painting with Thomas Eakins. Eakins turned Tanner from landscape painting to the study of human figures, as seen in *The Banjo Lesson* (see p. A7). Tanner soon found that the post–Reconstruction United States had no interest in African American subjects painted by an African American artist. So he, too, left for France in 1891. For the rest of his life, Tanner sought to capture intensely spiritual themes from the Bible. His paintings won Tanner awards on both sides of the Atlantic.

FOCUS ACTIVITY

Tell students that Tanner once remarked that race was a "ghetto of isolation and neglect from which [African American artists] must escape if they [are] to gain artistic freedom and recognition." Ask students to explain what they think Tanner's statement means.

TEACHING STRATEGY

Refer students to Unit 7 for information about the conditions African Americans faced in the late 1800s. Then divide them into groups, and assign each group to write letters in which Lewis or Tanner explain his or her reasons for leaving the United States for Europe in the late 1800s. Call on volunteers to read their letters aloud. Then, based on the representative works in *The Artist's View* (pp. A6, A7), ask how these artists helped elevate the dignity of African Americans even though they lived and worked abroad.

COOPERATIVE LEARNING ACTIVITY

Assign students to write poems capturing the themes of *Forever Free* and *The Banjo Lesson*. To help students get started have them brainstorm possible titles for the poems. Suggestions include: "On Memories," "On Liberation."

ART OF THE HARLEM RENAISSANCE AND THE 1930s

`Work in this category appears in *The Artist's View* pp. A7–A10, A12, A14

OVERVIEW

In the 1920s, during the Harlem Renaissance, many African American artists began to experiment with the symbolic styles and geometric designs of their African heritage. The results were such startling works as *Song of the Towers* by Aaron Douglas (see p. A9) and *Les Fetiches* by Lois Mailou Jones (see p. A10).

Intellectual leaders of the New Negro movement (see p. 277) supported the work of African American artists, praising their celebration of **negritude**, or blackness. White Americans poured into Harlem, hoping to catch a glimpse of the outpouring of fresh talent.

The fascination of white intellectuals with African American artists ended with the Great Depression. So did the financial support of white patrons. In the mid-1930s, the federal government stepped in to advance African American creativity in the form of the WPA (see "Focus On," p. 298). Aaron Douglas, Augusta Savage, and Sargent Johnson all received federal funds to continue their search for an African American artistic identity. Johnson's Mask (see p. A13) and Savage's *Gamin* (see p. A14) captured the beauty of African facial features. Other artists, such as Palmer Hayden, took the everyday experiences of African Americans in the cities and turned them to art (see p. A8). Malvin Gray Johnson did the same for African Americans who lived in the Deep South (see p. A10). In 1939, the Baltimore Museum displayed the work of Johnson and others in the first exhibition of African American artists to be shown in the South.

Near the end of the 1930s, the art world "discovered" the work of yet another African American artist—Horace Pippin. Although badly crippled in World War I, Pippin taught himself to paint in a powerful, bold style (see p. A12). His works were part of the original collection of the Museum of Modern Art in New York City. Today, many art critics consider Pippin one of the first African American masters of modernism.

FOCUS ACTIVITY

Refer students to Sargent Johnson's *Mask* on p. A13 and Lois Mailou Jones' *Les Fetiches* on p. A10. Encourage them to compare these works with the Congolese mask on p. A3, noting similarities. Then have students compare *Gamin* by Augusta Savage on p. A14 and *Congolais* by N. Elizabeth Prophet on p. A7 with the Ife head on p. A2. Ask how these works demonstrate what W.E.B. Du Bois called "beauty in black."

TEACHING STRATEGY

Divide students into groups, and assign them one of the following works of art: *Congolais* (p. A7), *The Janitor Who Paints* (p. A8), *Les Fetiches* (p. A10), *Self-Portrait* (p. A10), *John Brown Going to His Hanging* (p. A12), *Mask* (p. A13), and *Gamin* (p. A14). Then direct each group to give a short, dramatic presentation that tells a story about its work of art. For background data, refer students to Unit 8, *The Big Picture*, and Chapters 25–27. After each group has made its presentation, have the class discuss what the art and the dramatization show about the African American experience.

COOPERATIVE LEARNING ACTIVITY

Assign students to find pictures of the African American murals painted for the WPA during the 1930s. African American muralists included: Augusta Savage, Hale Woodruff, Aaron Douglas, and Charles Aston. Have students use an opaque projector to show these murals to the class and discuss what each mural reveals about the African American experience.

ART OF MODERN TIMES

Works in this category appear on *The Artist's View*, pp. A11, A13, and A14–A16.

OVERVIEW

Artists trained in the 1930s moved away from spiritual themes and romantic presentations of African American life toward historical themes and more realistic portrayals of the day-to-day struggles of African Americans. African American artists such as Jacob Lawrence and John Biggers grew out of this tradition. Their murals (see pp. A11, A14), painted in the 1940s and 1950s, explored important events in African American history and depicted themes that served as avenues for African American progress—work, education, the strength of the family, and so on. African Americans, stirred by the activism of the 1960s, expanded upon this tradition. Many saw their art as a vehicle of protest. Faith Ringgold's mixed media art is an example (see p. A15). In explaining her vision of art, Ringgold has said:

> If black art is art at all, it must be expressive of some deep and pervasive truth; and for the black artist in America the most pervasive truth, the one with which he must daily contend, is the unmovable reality that he or she is black in America.

As African American artists move toward more personalized interpretations of the African American experience, they have adopted more abstract styles. Some, such as Romare Bearden (see p. A16), came under the influence of Picasso and other artists who worked in an abstract art style. But ever-present in their art is a consciousness of their African past and the struggle of African Americans to achieve equality.

Contemporary artists draw on their African heritage in creating such works as Xenobia Bailey's *Royal Crown* (see p. A13) or Sultan Rogers' *Walking Stick* (see p. A16). Bailey looks to the Yoruba of West Africa, and Rogers to the African traditions preserved in folk art from the days of slavery.

FOCUS ACTIVITY

Refer students to the design that runs along the top of the pages in *The Artist's View*. Ask students what they think the design symbolizes. (*kente cloth, design from the African American heritage that symbolizes union of Africans and African Americans*)

TEACHING STRATEGY

Read aloud the following description of the role of African American artists in the post–1960s era by Romare Bearden: "You take what you find, for art is that kind of venture. It would seem to me that what the young black painter has that is unique is that he has experiences and a way of looking at them that is unique." Ask students to speculate on the unique experiences that African American artists might draw upon. List these on the chalkboard. Then have students find examples of these influences in the works of Lawrence, Bailey, Biggers, Ringgold, Bearden, and Rogers.

COOPERATIVE LEARNING ACTIVITY

Tell students that murals have been an important vehicle of African American expression since the 1930s. If you have murals painted by African Americans in your community, send student photographers to take pictures of them. As an alternative approach, assign students to use tempera paints and poster board to design a series of panels for display in the classroom. A topic might be key events in the Civil Rights Movement.

BRINGING ART INTO THE CLASSROOM

The following cooperative learning activities can be used for alternative assessment in conjunction with *The Artist's View*, either in its entirety or throughout the course at appropriate times.

Designing a Book. Divide the class into groups. Assign each group one of the unit-opening pages from *The African American Experience.* Direct them to research and design a new opening montage for their unit using works by African or African American artists. Tell them that their pages should reflect the content and themes of the unit. Allow them to use photographs of sites or people mentioned in the unit if works by African Americans pertinent to the period are not available. In evaluating the designs, consider the correspondence of the chosen art to subject matter and artistic quality of the design.

Selecting Representative Art. Divide the class into groups, and assign each group one of the units in the book. Direct them to research the art created by Africans or African Americans during the period covered by their unit. They are to select, as a group, one piece of art that seems most representative of their period. Groups should obtain illustrations showing the art they have selected and present oral reports to the class in which they describe the work, its creator (or if the individual artist is unknown, the society in which it was created), and why it was selected. In evaluating the reports, consider thoroughness of research, organization of presentation, and appropriateness of selection.

Illustrating a Time Period. Divide the class into five groups, one for each of the periods discussed in the Lesson Plans for *The Artist's View*. Assign each group to do further research into its period, and then to create jointly an art work that is appropriate to the period. Each group should also prepare an oral report on how its work demonstrates characteristics of its period. In evaluating the project, consider the appropriateness of the work chosen to its time period and the understanding of the period as demonstrated in the oral report.

DIRECTORY OF BOOKS, AUDIOVISUAL MATERIALS, AND COMMUNITY RESOURCES

BOOKS

KEY
IS — Intermediate school students
HS — High school students
TR — Teachers

GENERAL REFERENCE

Adoff, Arnold, ed. *The Poetry of Black America: Anthology of the 20th Century*. HarperCollins Children's Books, 1973. IS/HS

Aptheker, Herbert. *A Documentary History of the Negro People in the United States*. Vol. 1: *From Colonial Times Through the Civil War*. Vol. 2: *From the Reconstruction Years to the Founding of the National Association for the Advancement of Colored People, 1910*. Carol Publishing Group (Citadel Press), 1989. HS/TR

———. *Essays in the History of the American Negro*. International Publishers, 1969. These historical essays cover African American involvement in key events of U.S. history. HS/TR

Asante, Molefi K., and Mattson, Mark T. *Historical and Cultural Atlas of African Americans*. Macmillan, 1991. HS/TR

Bearden, Romare, and Henderson, Harry. *A History of African American Artists*. Pantheon, 1990. IS/HS

Bennett, Lerone, Jr. *Before the Mayflower: A History of Black America*. Rev. ed. Viking Penguin Books, 1984. Begins with the West African empires and concludes with the civil rights struggles of the 20th century. HS/TR

Bingham, Marjorie Wall, and Gross, Susan Hill. *Women in Africa of the Sub-Sahara*. Vol. 1: *Ancient Times to the 20th Century*. Glenhurst Publications, 1982. TR

Bontemps, Arna, and Conroy, Jack. *Anyplace But Here*. Hill & Wang, 1966. Collection of migration stories, including those of Frederick Douglass, Marcus Garvey, and Jelly Roll Morton. HS/TR

Clarke, John Henrick, ed. *American Negro Short Stories*. Hill & Wang, 1966. Authors represented include Ernest J. Gaines, Paule Marshall, Richard Wright, and John O. Killens. Fiction. HS/TR

Du Bois, W.E.B. *The Negro*. Oxford University Press, 1970. African and African American contributions to world history. HS/TR

Foner, Philip S. *History of Black Americans: From Africa to the Emergence of the Cotton Kingdom*. Greenwood Press, 1975. TR

Franklin, John Hope, and Meier, August, eds. *Black Leaders of the 20th Century*. University of Illinois Press, 1982. Such 20th-century African American leaders as Adam Clayton Powell, Jr., Mary McLeod Bethune, Malcolm X, and Martin Luther King, Jr. HS

Franklin, John Hope, and Moss, Alfred A., Jr. *From Slavery to Freedom: A History of Negro Americans*. Alfred A. Knopf, 1987. Covers the African American experience from the great civilizations of Ghana, Mali, and Songhai to life in the United States in the 1980s. HS/TR

Gates, Henry Louis, Jr., ed. *The Schomburg Library of 19th-Century Black Women Writers*. 30 vols. Oxford University Press, 1988. Rare works of fiction, poetry, biography, autobiography, essays, and journalism. HS/TR

Giddings, Paula. *When and Where I Enter: The Impact of Black Women on Race and Sex in America*. Morrow, 1984. Roles of African American women from the 1890s to the late 1960s and on the fight to transcend double discrimination. HS/TR

Honour, Hugh. *The Image of the Black in Western Art*. Vol. 4: *From the American Revolution to World War I*. Pt. 1: *Slaves and Liberators*. Pt. 2: *Black Models and White Myths*. Harvard University Press, 1989. HS/TR

Hornsby, Alton, ed. *The Black Almanac*. Barron's Educational Series, 1977. Collection of scholarly articles on the history of African Americans. TR

Katz, William Loren. *Eyewitness: The Negro in American History*. David S. Lake Publishers, 1974. Evocative excerpts of letters and other documents. IS/HS/TR

King, Woodie, and Milner, Ronald, ed. *Black Drama Anthology*. NAL-Dutton, 1986. Collection of works by modern African American playwrights. HS/TR

Litwack, Leon F., and Meier, August, eds. *Black Leaders of the 19th Century*. University of Illinois Press, 1988. Essays about 16 African American leaders, including Alexander Crummell, Harriet Tubman, and Richard Allen. HS/TR

Lomax, Louis. *The Negro Revolt*. New American Library, 1963. An account of the freedom struggle of African Americans from the 17th to the 20th century. HS/TR

Meltzer, Milton. *The Black Americans: A History in Their Own Words, 1619-1983*. Rev. ed. HarperCollins Children's Books, 1987. Excerpts from letters, diaries, journals, autobiographies, testimonies in court. IS/HS/TR

Porter, James A. *Modern Negro Art*. Ayer, 1969. Mid-18th century to World War II. HS/TR

Ragsdale, Bruce A., and Treese, Joel D. *Black*

Americans in Congress, 1870 to 1989. U.S. Government Printing Office, 1990. HS/TR

Shaw, Arnold. *Black Popular Music in America: From the Spirituals, Minstrels, and Ragtime to Soul, Disco, and Hip-Hop*. Schirmer Books, 1986.

Smythe, Mabel. *The Black American Reference Book*. Prentice Hall, 1976. Each Chapter covers a different theme in African American history. TR

Sterling, Dorothy. *We Are Your Sisters: Black Women in the 19th Century*. Norton, 1985. A chronicle of the lives of African American women through their letters, diaries, and memoirs. HS/TR

Washington, Booker T. *Story of the Negro*. Negro University Press, 1969. A look at the history of the African American people. HS/TR

Williams, Chancellor. *The Destruction of Black Civilization*. Rev. ed. Third World Press, 1987. A historical perspective of African civilization (emphasis on Egypt). HS/TR

Woodson, Carter G. *The Negro in Our History*. 1922. A scholarly look into African American history. TR

UNIT 1

Bernal, Martin. *Black Athena: The Afroasiatic Roots of Classical Civilization*. Vol. 1: *The Fabrication of Ancient Greece 1785-1985*. Vol. 2: *The Archaeological and Documentary Evidence*. Rutgers University Press, 1987 and 1991. One scholar's theory of how the diffusion of Afroasiatic culture helped shape ancient Greek civilization. TR

Chu, Daniel, and Skinner, Elliott. *A Glorious Age in Africa: The Story of Three Great African Empires*. African World, 1990. IS/HS

Davidson, Basil. *Africa in History*. Rev. ed. Macmillan, 1991. TR

———. *African Kingdoms*. Time/Life Books, 1966. A study of life in the villages of ancient Africa and in its centralized states. IS/HS

———. *The Lost Cities of Africa*. Rev. ed. Little, Brown, 1988. An account of African civilizations south of the Sahara 1,500 years prior to the introduction of colonialism. HS/TR

Diop, Chiekh Anta. *Civilization or Barbarism: An Authentic Anthropology*. Translated by Yaa-Lengi Meema Ngemi. Chicago Review Press (Lawrence Hill Books), 1991. Assembled studies demonstrating Africa's central role in the evolution of civilization. TR

Murphy, E. Jefferson. *History of African Civilization*. Dell, 1974. HS/TR

Oliver, Roland, and Oliver, Caroline, eds. *Africa in the Days of Exploration*. Prentice Hall, 1965. Descriptions of Africa, from the Muslim travelers and geographers of the 10th century through the European explorers of the 19th century (includes some oral tradition). HS

UNIT 2

Blassingame, John W. *The Slave Community: Plantation Life in the Ante-Bellum South*. 2nd rev. enl. ed. Oxford University Press, 1979. Exploration of the life experiences of African American slaves, set forth in the context of their heritage, culture, and religion. HS/TR

Thomas, Thomas, ed. *Black Voyage: Eyewitness Accounts of the Atlantic Slave Trade*. Little, Brown, 1971. Powerful primary source material. HS/TR

Van Sertima, Ivan. *They Came Before Columbus*. McKay (Fodor), 1989. A history of Africans in ancient America. HS/TR

Wood, Peter H. *Black Majority: Negroes in Colonial South Carolina from 1670 Through the Stono Rebellion*. Norton, 1975. HS/TR

UNIT 3

Davis, Burke. *Black Heroes of the American Revolution*. Harcourt Brace Jovanovich, 1991. IS

Durham, Philip, and Jones, Everett L. *The Negro Cowboys*. University of Nebraska Press, 1983. History of the thousands of African American cowboys, drawn from personal memoirs. HS/TR

Katz, William Loren. *The Black West*. Rev. ed. Open Hand, 1987. An account of the African American role in the settling of the lands west of the Mississippi. HS

Miller, Robert. *Buffalo Soldiers*. Silver Burdett Press, 1991. Story of the African American cavalry and infantry in the lands west of the Mississippi. Fiction. IS

———. *Cowboys*. Silver Burdett Press, 1991. Tall tale about an African American cowboy in Colorado. Fiction. IS

Quarles, Benjamin. *The Negro in the American Revolution*. Norton, 1973. Study of African American soldiers and the changes in their status after the war. HS

UNIT 4

Cable, Mary. *Black Odyssey: The Case of the Slave Ship Amistad*. Penguin, 1977. HS

Haley, Alex. *Roots*. Dell, 1980. This story of an African American family unfolds in the author's search for his roots in West Africa. HS/TR

Hurmence, Belinda, ed. *Before Freedom: 48 Oral Histories of Former North and South Carolina Slaves*. NAL-Dutton, 1990. IS/HS

Lester, Julius. *Long Journey Home*. Scholastic, 1988. Six short stories, based on fact, written by this award-winning author. Historical fiction. IS/HS

———. *To Be a Slave*. Scholastic, 1986. The story of slaves recorded through personal accounts (Newbery Honor Award). IS/HS

Mellon, James, ed. *Bullwhip Days: The Slaves Remember*. Avon, 1990. Oral history compiled from interviews of former African American slaves during the Great Depression. HS/TR

Richmond, Merle. *Phillis Wheatley*. Chelsea House, 1989. Biography of "the mother of Black literature in America." IS/HS

Walker, Margaret. *Jubilee*. Bantam, 1984. The story of a woman's life from slavery to emancipation. Fiction. HS/TR

Williams, Sherley Anne. *Dessa Rose*. Berkley Publishing Group, 1987. The story of an African American woman, leader of a slave rebellion. Fiction. TR

UNIT 5

Blockson, Charles L. *The Underground Railroad: First-Person Narratives of Escapes to Freedom in the North*. Prentice Hall, 1987. HS/TR

Douglass, Frederick. *Narrative of the Life of Frederick Douglass, an American Slave*. Edited by Houston A. Baker, Jr. Viking Penguin, 1982. HS/TR

Douty, Esther M. *Forten the Sailmaker, Pioneer Champion of Negro Rights*. Rand McNally, 1968. Biography of a free African American man, an abolitionist and an entrepreneur. IS/HS

Filler, Louis. *The Crusade Against Slavery: Friends, Foes, and Reforms 1820-1860*. 2nd rev. ed. Reference Publications, 1986. A historian's look into the abolitionist cause. TR

Lester, Julius. *This Strange New Feeling*. Scholastic, 1985. A story of three couples, who, even in the face of slavery, come to care for each other. Historical fiction. IS/HS

Litwack, Leon F. *North of Slavery: The Negro in the Free States, 1790-1860*. University of Chicago Press, 1965. Examination of racial discrimination in the pre-Civil War North. TR

McFeely, William S. *Frederick Douglass*. Norton, 1990. HS/TR

Meltzer, Milton. *Underground Man*. Harcourt Brace Jovanovich, 1990. A novel about a young white man's experiences on the Underground Railroad (based on real events). IS/HS/TR

Morrison, Toni. *Beloved*. NAL-Dutton, 1988. Pulitzer Prize-winning story of a runaway African American slave and her family. Fiction. HS/TR

Quarles, Benjamin. *Black Abolitionists*. Da Capo Press, 1991. Study of the role of African Americans in the crusade against slavery. HS

Still, William. *Underground Railroad*. Ayer, 1968. Reprint of an 1872 memoir written by a free African American who aided those escaping on the Underground Railroad. HS/TR

Wilson, Harriet E. *Our Nig: Sketches from the Life of a Free Black*. Random House (Vintage), 1983. This fictional account of a free African American woman's life in New England in the 1800s was the first novel published by an African American in the United States. HS/TR

UNIT 6

Douty, Esther M. *Charlotte Forten: Free Black Teacher*. Garrard, 1971. Instructive account of the African American woman who taught ex-slaves on an island off the coast of South Carolina. IS/HS

Foner, Eric. *Reconstruction: America's Unfinished Revolution, 1863-1877*. HarperCollins, 1988. Chronicle of responses to changes set in motion by the Civil War and the end of slavery. TR

Gaines, Ernest J. *The Autobiography of Miss Jane Pittman*. Bantam, 1982. Born into slavery, this African American woman lived to see emancipation and the growth of the country through the civil rights era. HS/TR

Long, Richard A., ed. *Black Writers and the American Civil War*. Book Sales, Inc., 1989. HS/TR

McPherson, James. *Battle Cry of Freedom: The Era of the Civil War*. Ballantine, 1989. Authoritative history of the Civil War. HS/TR

——— *The Negro's Civil War: How American Blacks Felt and Acted During the War for the Union*. Ballantine, 1991. Narrative compiled of newspaper and manuscript excerpts documenting African Americans' roles in the Civil War. HS/TR

Morris, Robert C. *Reading, 'Riting, and Reconstruction: The Education of Freedmen in the South, 1861-1870*. University of Chicago Press, 1981. HS/TR

Sobel, Mechal. *The World They Made Together: Black and White Values in 18th-Century Virginia*. Princeton University Press, 1989. TR

Sterling, Dorothy. *The Making of an Afro-American: Martin Robison Delany 1812-1885*. Doubleday, 1971. HS/TR

UNIT 7

Gray, James Marion. *George Washington Carver*. Silver Burdett Press, 1990. Biography. IS

Halasa, Malu. *Mary McLeod Bethune*. Chelsea House, 1989. Biography of an outstanding educator, civil rights activist, and adviser to U.S. presidents. IS/HS

Hayden, Robert C. *Seven Black American Scientists*. Addison-Wesley, 1970. Includes Ernest E. Just, Charles Henry Turner, and Charles Drew. IS/HS

Sammons, Vivian Ovelton. *Blacks in Science and Medicine*. Hemisphere, 1989. Unique resource that includes listings of more than 1,500 African Americans who contributed to these disciplines. HS/TR

Washington, Booker T. *Future of the American Negro*. Metro Books, 1969. HS/TR

———. *Up From Slavery*. Carol Publishing Group (University Books), 1989. Classic self-portrait of the African American educator who was founder of Tuskegee Institute. HS/TR

Woodward, C. Vann. *The Strange Career of Jim Crow*. 3rd rev. ed. Oxford University Press, 1974. HS/TR

UNIT 8

Bontemps, Arna. *The Harlem Renaissance Remembered.* Dodd, Mead, 1972. Profiles of Harlem Renaissance artists and writers. HS/TR

Brown, Gene. *Duke Ellington.* Silver Burdett Press, 1990. Profile of the great jazz pianist, composer, and bandleader. IS

Cronon, E. David. *Black Moses: The Story of Marcus Garvey and the Universal Negro Improvement Association.* 2nd ed. University of Wisconsin Press, 1960. HS/TR

Duberman, Martin B. *Paul Robeson.* Ballantine, 1990. A biography of the great singer and activist. HS/TR

Du Bois, W.E.B. *The Autobiography of W.E. Burghardt Du Bois.* Edited by Herbert Aptheker. International Publishers, 1973. HS/TR

———. *The Souls of Black Folk.* Random House (Vintage), 1990. Essays by the famed African American professor and civil rights leader. HS/TR

Hurston, Zora Neale. *Dust Tracks on a Road: An Autobiography.* HarperCollins, 1991. Self-portrait of the author and anthropologist. HS/TR

Johnson, James Weldon. *The Autobiography of an Ex-Colored Man.* Viking Penguin, 1990. An enduring novel, the tale of an African American man who chooses to pass for white. HS/TR

Lemann, Nicholas. *The Promised Land: The Great Black Migration and How It Changed America.* Alfred A. Knopf, 1991. The great migration from rural society to the cities, between the early 1940s and the 1960s. HS/TR

Lincoln, C. Eric. *The Avenue, Clayton City.* Morrow, 1988. The gripping story of an African American community in the South between the two world wars. HS/TR

Lyons, Mary E. *Sorrow's Kitchen: The Life and Folklore of Zora Neale Hurston.* Macmillan, 1990. Biography of this prolific writer and important figure of the Harlem Renaissance. HS

Meltzer, Milton. *Langston Hughes: A Biography.* HarperCollins Children's Books, 1988. IS/HS

———. *Mary McLeod Bethune: Voice of Black Hope.* Viking Kestrel, 1987. IS/HS

Moses, Wilson Jeremiah. *The Golden Age of Black Nationalism, 1850-1925.* Oxford University Press, 1988. In-depth coverage, including ideology of its leaders. TR

Taylor, Mildred D. *Let the Circle Be Unbroken.* Bantam, 1981. This sequel to *Roll of Thunder, Hear My Cry* (See next entry) concerns itself with a friend of the Logan family who is charged with murder and tried by an all-white jury. Fiction. IS/HS

———. *Roll of Thunder, Hear My Cry.* Bantam, 1984. 1977 Newbery Honor Book tells of the Logan family of Mississippi and their survival during the Depression. Fiction. IS/HS

UNIT 9

Albert, Peter J., and Hoffman, Ronald, ed. *We Shall Overcome: Martin Luther King, Jr., and the Black Freedom Struggle.* Pantheon Books, U.S. Capitol Historical Society, 1990. Collection of reflections by leading activists and scholars of the civil rights era. HS/TR

Baldwin, James. *Notes of a Native Son.* Beacon Press, 1990. Baldwin's search for himself as an African American man, a writer, and an American. HS/TR

Bates, Daisy. *The Long Shadow of Little Rock.* University of Arkansas Press, 1987. A first-person account. HS/TR

Branch, Taylor. *Parting the Waters: America in the King Years, 1954-63.* Simon & Schuster, 1989. HS

Bush, Martin H. *The Photographs of Gordon Parks.* Wichita State University, 1983. Forty-year retrospective of Parks's work. IS/HS/TR

Cagin, Seth, and Dray, Philip. *We are Not Afraid: The Story of Goodman, Schwerner, and Chaney and The Civil Rights Campaign for Mississippi.* Bantam, 1991. HS/TR

Clark, Kenneth B. *Dark Ghetto: Dilemmas of Social Power.* 2nd ed. University Press of New England (Wesleyan University Press), 1989. An exploration of the urban ghetto and its problems, including crime, drugs, and infant mortality. TR

Cleaver, Eldridge. *Soul on Ice.* Delta, 1968. Essays by this member of the Black Panthers. HS/TR

Davies, Mark. *Malcolm X: Another Side of the Movement.* Silver Burdett Press, 1990. IS

Davis, Benjamin O., Jr. *Benjamin O. Davis, Jr., American: An Autobiography.* Smithsonian, 1991. HS/TR

Elder, Lonne, III. *Ceremonies in Dark Old Men.* Farrar, Straus & Giroux, 1969. A play about a man and his sons and their struggle to avoid eviction. HS/TR

Ellison, Ralph. *Invisible Man.* Random House (Vintage), 1989. Profound interpretation of the African American experience in American society. Fiction. HS/TR

Friese, Kai Jabir. *Rosa Parks: The Movement Organizes.* Silver Burdett Press, 1990. Biography of the civil rights activist. IS

Hansberry, Lorraine. *A Raisin in the Sun.* NAL-Dutton, 1989. Play about the projected move of an African American working class family from Chicago to a white suburb. HS/TR

Hardin, Vincent. *Hope and History: Why We Must Share the Story of the Movement.* Orbis Books, 1990. Essays for teachers concerning the post-World War II movement for African American freedom. TR

Hess, Debra. *Thurgood Marshall: The Fight for Equal Justice.* Silver Burdett Press, 1990.

Biography of the first African American Supreme Court justice. IS

Jackson, Jesse. *Straight From the Heart*. Rev. ed. Augsburg Fortress Press, 1987. The author looks at his own life and his many roles: human rights advocate, preacher, political leader, diplomat. HS/TR

Johnson, Jacqueline. *Stokely Carmichael: The Story of Black Power*. Silver Burdett Press, 1990. IS

Jones, LeRoi. *Home (Social Essays)*. Morrow, 1966. Impressions of and opinions on some of the major events of the 1960s, including the assassination of Malcolm X and the Birmingham bombings. HS/TR

Killens, John O. *Youngblood*. University of Georgia Press, 1982. A stirring tale of the courage of the Youngblood family of Crossroads, Georgia, a factory town. HS/TR

King, Martin Luther, Jr. *A Testament of Hope*. Edited by James M. Washington. HarperCollins, 1986. HS/TR

Lukas, J. Anthony. *Common Ground: A Turbulent Decade in the Lives of Three American Families.* Alfred A. Knopf, 1985. Examination of racial conflict in the 1960s and 1970s through the study of three Boston families (one African American, two white). HS/TR

Malcolm X, with Haley, Alex. *The Autobiography of Malcolm X*. Ballantine, 1987. Compelling self-portrait of the late activist and Muslim leader. HS/TR

Meredith, James. *Three Years in Mississippi*. Indiana University Press, 1966. A first-person account of "integration" of the University of Mississippi. HS/TR

Parks, Gordon. *Born Black*. Lippincott, 1971. Photo essays commissioned by *Life* magazine on the turbulent 1960s and those who influenced the times (e.g., Malcolm X, the Black Panthers, Stokely Carmichael). HS/TR

Peck, James. *Freedom Ride*. Grove Press, 1962. First-person account by a white participant. HS/TR

Raines, Howell. *My Soul Is Rested: Movement Days in the Deep South Remembered*. Viking Penguin, 1983. This oral history of the Civil Rights Movement includes accounts by Rosa Parks, Bayard Rustin, James Farmer, and Julian Bond. HS/TR

Robeson, Paul. *Here I Stand*. Beacon Press, 1988. Autobiography of this great singer, including his political views and his arraignment before the House Un-American Activities Committee. HS/TR

Robinson, Jo Ann. *The Montgomery Bus Boycott and the Women Who Started It: The Memoir of Jo Ann Gibson Robinson*. Edited by David J. Garrow. University of Tennessee Press, 1987. Story of Robinson and the Women's Political Council, the real leaders of the boycott that roused the nation. HS/TR

Rowland, Della. *Martin Luther King, Jr.: The Dream of a Peaceful Revolution*. Silver Burdett Press, 1990. Recounting of Dr. King's life during the Civil Rights Movement of the 1950s and 1960s. IS

Rubel, David. *Fannie Lou Hamer: From Sharecropping to Politics*. Silver Burdett Press, 1990. IS

Scheader, Catherine. *Shirley Chisholm: Teacher and Congresswoman*. Enslow Publications, 1990. Biography of the teacher, congresswoman, and first African American woman to run for President of the United States. HS/TR

Shange, Ntozake. *Betsey Brown*. St. Martin's Press, 1985. Integration, racism, and class conflict as seen through the eyes of an African American 13-year-old in St. Louis in 1959. IS/HS

Sowell, Thomas. *Civil Rights: Rhetoric or Reality?* Morrow, 1985. An attempt to measure how much the legislative and judicial promises of equal rights have been fulfilled. TR

Terry, Wallace. *Bloods: An Oral History of the Vietnam War by Black Veterans*. Ballantine, 1985. HS/TR

Wilkinson, Brenda. *Jesse Jackson: Still Fighting for the Dream*. Silver Burdett Press, 1990. Biography of Reverend Jackson's life and work, including Operation Breadbasket, Operation PUSH, and the Rainbow Coalition, up to the 1988 presidential campaign. IS

UNIT 10

Bingham, Marjorie Wall, and Gross, Susan Hill. *Women in Africa of the Sub-Sahara*. Vol. 2: *The 20th Century*. Glenhurst Publications, 1982. Study of the diversity of women's lives across history in more than 1,000 African societies. TR

Chase, Judith Wragg. *Afro-American Art and Craft*. Van Nostrand Reinhold, 1971. A look at the influences of African culture and traditions in the works of African American artists. HS/TR

Evans, Mari, ed. *Black Women Writers 1950-1980: A Critical Evaluation*. Doubleday (Anchor Press), 1984. Analysis of works includes those of Toni Morrison, Maya Angelou, and Audre Lorde. HS/TR

Gates, Henry Louis, Jr., ed. *Bearing Witness*. W.W. Norton, 1991. Selections from the autobiographies of 20th-century African Americans. HS/TR

———. *Black Literature and Literary Theory*. Routledge, Chapman & Hall, 1984. TR

———. *Figures in Black: Words, Signs, and the "Racial" Self*. Oxford University Press, 1987. Redefining of Eurocentric literary criticism to a more pluralistic view. TR

Herskovitz, Melville J. *The Myth of the Negro Past*. Beacon Press, 1990. Anthropological classic on the preservation of African heritage in the Americas in the face of oppression. TR

Landry, Bart. *The New Black Middle Class.* University of California Press, 1987. Author presents the argument that racism thrives in economic oppression. TR

Mathabane, Mark. *Kaffir Boy: The True Story of a Black Youth's Coming of Age in Apartheid South Africa.* NAL-Dutton (Plume), 1987. HS/TR

Paton, Alan. *Cry, the Beloved Country.* Macmillan, 1987. The racial problems of South Africa as explored by a white opponent to apartheid. Fiction. HS/TR

Redford, Dorothy S., with D'Orso, Michael. *Somerset Homecoming: Recovering a Lost Heritage.* Doubleday, 1988. One woman's search for her African ancestors who were captured into slavery, the study of the plantation they worked and its community. IS/HS

Shuker, Nancy. *Maya Angelou.* Silver Burdett Press, 1990. Biography. IS/HS

AUDIOVISUAL MATERIALS

UNIT 1

Egypt: Quest for Eternity. This National Geographic Society production visits the great temples and tombs of Luxor, Karnak, and the Land of the Dead. 60 minutes. No. VES1076. Distributor: KU (video, purchase).

Life on Earth. Episode 13. *The Compulsive Communicators.* A BBC-TV exploration of the origins of the human race 3 million years ago in Africa, with author and anthropologist David Attenborough. 58 minutes. Distributor: FI, 1981.

Negro Kingdoms of Africa's Golden Age. Coverage includes trans-Saharan transport, the growth of Islam, the emergence of the mighty empires, initiation of the slave trade. 17 minutes. Distributor: ATLAP, 1968.

UNIT 2

In Search of the American Dream Series. Origins. Begins with the arrival of 20 Africans brought to Jamestown, Virginia, in 1619, and examines the impact of slavery on African Americans. Shows how the African cultural heritage—music, dance, art, blues, storytelling—manifests itself in American life. 52 minutes; color. No. QF-2988. Distributor: FHS (rental/purchase).

Roots. Emmy-winning production of Alex Haley's novel—the saga of an African American family—with LeVar Burton and Cicely Tyson. 720 minutes; color. No. WA11117. 6 vols. Distributor: FI, 1977 (film/video, purchase).

Trading in Africans: The Dutch Outposts in West Africa. Looks at the European view of Africans in the mid-17th century, at the nature of the slave trade. 50 minutes; color. No. QF-2643. Distributor: FHS (video, rental/purchase).

UNIT 3

Benjamin Banneker: The Man Who Loved the Stars. A look at this African American scientist and symbol of the abolitionist movement, with Ossie Davis. 58 minutes. Distributor: BFA.

The Black Cowboy. Stories of African American cowboys, including interviews with today's generation on the range and the rodeo circuit. 25 minutes. Distributor: ADL (film)

Equally Free. Re-creation of the Virginia Convention at Williamsburg, May 1776, calling for declaration of human rights and individual freedoms. 21 minutes. Distributor: NGS, 1975 (film/video).

UNIT 4

Slavery and Slave Resistance. Traces slavery's origins, racial stereotyping, and active and passive resistance to slavery. 26 minutes. Distributor: C/MTI, 1969 (film/video).

Solomon Northup's Odyssey. This "American Playhouse" production follows the true story of a free African American of the North who was drugged, kidnapped, and sold into slavery by bounty hunters. Starring Avery Brooks. 118 minutes. Distributor: SHV (video, rental).

UNIT 5

The Abolitionists. The origins, development, and importance of the crusade against slavery. 15 minutes. Distributor: AITECH (video).

Harriet Beecher Stowe: Uncle Tom's Cabin. The George Aiken dramatization, here presented abridged, became the most frequently performed play of all time throughout the world. 45 minutes; color. No. QF-933. Distributor: FHS (rental/purchase).

Harriet Tubman and the Underground Railroad. Description of the first 19 trips this conductor made from 1850 to 1860. 2 parts; 25 minutes each. Distributor: CRM (film/video).

The Sellin' of Jamie Thomas. Eleven-year-old Jamie, his mother, and father are sold to different owners. The family escapes to the North where they have to raise enough money to buy their freedom. 2 parts; 24 minutes each; color. Nos. QF-1394, QF-1395. Distributor: FHS (purchase).

A Woman Called Moses. NBC-TV looks at the life of Harriet Tubman. Starring Cicely Tyson. 196 minutes. Distributor: SF (film, purchase).

UNIT 6

The Civil War. A portrait of the United States in

1860: a nation of 33 states with a population of 30 million and vast political, philosophical, and economic gulfs separating North and South. 42 minutes; color. No. QF-2465. Distributor: FHS (rental/purchase).

1861-1877: Civil War and Reconstruction. Covers the Emancipation Proclamation and the 13th and 15th Amendments to the U.S. Constitution. 20 minutes. Distributor: CRM (film/video).

Freedom Road. NBC-TV production, based on a Howard Fast novel about a former African American slave who won a seat in the South Carolina state legislature during Reconstruction. Starring Muhammad Ali. Recommended by the NEA. 186 minutes. Distributor: WHV, 1979 (video, rental/purchase).

On My Own: The Traditions of Daisy Turner. Remembrances of a 102-year-old African American, 1 of 13 children who grew up in the hills of Grafton, Vermont. 28 minutes. Distributor: FL, 1986 (video, rental/purchase).

Women in American Life. Program 1. *1861-1880: Civil War, Recovery and Westward Expansion.* Includes early leaders of women's rights movement. 15 minutes. No. 8985. Distributor: NWHP, 1988 (video, rental/purchase).

UNIT 7

Art in America: Black Artists of the U.S.A. Studies the work of African Americans from the 18th and 19th centuries through the 1970s. 25 minutes. Distributor: SU (film/video, rental).

The Autobiography of Miss Jane Pittman. Portrait of the African American woman, born a slave, who lived to see the Civil Rights Movement; based on the Ernest J. Gaines novel. Starring Cicely Tyson. 110 minutes; color. No. PS9507. Distributor: KU (video, purchase).

Booker T. Washington: The Life and Legacy. The famed educator and founder of Tuskegee Institute. 30 minutes. Distributor: TBFF, 1982 (film, rental/purchase).

Discovering Jazz. Traces the history of jazz from roots in 19th-century African America to the 1960s. 22 minutes. Distributor: BF (film/video).

George Washington Carver. Traces the life of the scholar and researcher whose work revolutionized agriculture in the post-Civil War South. 11 minutes; color. No. QF-1759. Distributor: FHS (purchase).

Men of Bronze. The 369th regiment who served in France as part of the French Army in World War I. 60 minutes. Distributor: FI, 1977 (film); PAV (video).

Two Dollars and a Dream. Biography of turn-of-the-century entrepreneur Madame C. J. Walker. 55 minutes. Distributor: FL, 1987 (film/video, rental/purchase).

UNIT 8

Almos' A Man. Richard Wright's story of a young African American man searching for manhood. Starring LeVar Burton. 39 minutes. Distributor: C/MTI (video, rental).

Bessie Smith. Examines the life of the woman whose rich and powerful contralto led her from grinding rural poverty to her undisputed title as Empress of the Blues. 15 minutes; color. No. QF-1846. Distributor: FHS (video, purchase).

From These Roots. Winner of 22 international film awards, this William Greaves documentary for the Schomburg Center for Research and Black Culture takes a look at the cultural and social developments of the Harlem Renaissance. 28 minutes. Distributor: TBFF (film, rental).

I Know Why the Caged Bird Sings. Maya Angelou's story of a young African American girl growing up in Arkansas during the Great Depression. 96 minutes; color. No. US261. Distributor: KU, 1979 (video, purchase).

I Remember Harlem. Four segments: *The Early Years: 1600-1930*; *The Depression Years*; *Toward Freedom: 1940-1965*; *Toward a New Day: 1965-1980.* 3 hours, 52 minutes; color. No. QF-170. Distributor: FHS (film/video, purchase).

The Jesse Owens Story. A docudrama about the famous track star. 175 minutes; color. Distributor: KU, 1984 (video, purchase).

Marcus Garvey: Toward Black Nationhood. Documentary examines the career of the pioneer black nationalist; shows how his legacy inspired the Civil Rights Movement, and liberation movements throughout the Third World. 42 minutes; color. No. QF-752. Distributor: FHS (video, rental/purchase).

Mildred D. Taylor: Roll of Thunder, Hear My Cry. Taylor talks about the origins of her novel, which chronicles a black child's progression from innocence to disillusionment. 26 minutes; color. No. QF-2800. Distributor: FHS (rental/purchase).

Uncommon Images, James Van Der Zee. A celebration of the acclaimed photographer and his life's work—capturing the history of Harlem in photographs from the beginning of the 20th century to the 1960s. 22 minutes. Distributor: FL, 1977 (film/video, rental/purchase).

Women in American Life. Program 3. *1917-1942: Cultural Image and Economic Reality.* Covers employment opportunities created by World War I; lynching, as it became an issue for women's organizations; the Harlem Renaissance; the Great Depression. 17 minutes. No. 8987. Distributor: NWHP, 1988 (video, rental/purchase).

UNIT 9

Adam Clayton Powell. Documentary film on the life of the Harlem preacher, who served 26 years in Congress. 58 minutes. Distributor: BFA, 1977 (film/video, rental/purchase).

Daughters of the Black Revolution. Yolanda King, daughter of Martin Luther King, Jr., Reena Evers-Everette, daughter of Medgar Evers, and Attallah Shabazz, daughter of Malcolm X, talk with Phil Donahue about their fathers' lives and work. 28 minutes; color. No. QF-1556. Distributor: FHS (video, rental/purchase).

Eyes on the Prize: America's Civil Rights Years Series. An award-winning look at the civil rights era, from 1954 to 1965, through archival film footage and contemporary interviews. 6 parts; 60 minutes each. Distributor: PBS, 1986 (video, rental). Series includes:

Part 1. *Awakenings (1954-1956).* The Montgomery bus boycott, the Emmett Till trial, the birth of the SCLC.

Part 2. *Fighting Back (1957-1962). Brown* v. *Board of Education,* the integration of the Little Rock school system, James Meredith's enrollment at the University of Mississippi.

Part 3. *Ain't Scared of Your Jails (1960-1961).* The formation of SNCC, the freedom rides of 1961.

Part 4. *No Easy Walk (1962-1966).* The Civil Rights Movement as a mass movement, jailing of schoolchildren in Birmingham, the March on Washington.

Part 5. *Mississippi: Is This America? (1962-1964).* Coverage of the voting rights campaign in Mississippi, including Medgar Evers, James Chaney, Fannie Lou Hamer.

Part 6. *Bridge to Freedom (1965).* Images of the freedom march in Selma and review of gains made by the movement.

Eyes on the Prize II: 1965-. This continuation of the series examines community power in the school system, Black Power in the streets, and confrontations in government, in prisons, and in neighborhoods across the country. 8 parts; 60 minutes each. Distributor: PBS (video).

The Fateful Decade: From Little Rock to the Civil Rights Bill. Covers desegregation of Little Rock's Central High School; the acceleration of the Civil Rights Movement, clashes with police and jailing of demonstrators, the murder of Medgar Evers, the bombing of the Baptist church in Birmingham, sit-ins and protests, the Montgomery march; Martin Luther King, Jr.'s, famous "I Have a Dream" speech, his funeral; President Johnson's signing of the civil rights bill of 1968. 27 minutes; color. No. QF-2609. Distributor: FHS (video, rental/purchase).

From the Ku Klux Klan to the Black Panthers. Includes the prison uprising at Attica in 1967; a Klan rally and cross burning; Little Rock; the black nationalist movement, the Black Muslims; Montgomery, Birmingham, and the Civil Rights Movement; Malcolm X; the Newark riots; Eldridge Cleaver, Huey Newton and the Black Panthers. 14 minutes. No. QF-2559. Distributor: FHS (video, purchase).

Malcolm X. A Biography of Malcolm X. 15 minutes; color. No. QF-1751. Distributor: FHS (video, purchase).

Martin Luther King, Jr. Examines the life of the ordained minister and galvanizing orator. 27 minutes; color. No. QF-1745. Distributor: FHS (video, rental/purchase).

Martin Luther King, Jr.: Portrait of an American. Biography. 28 minutes; color. No. QF-1690. Distributor: FHS (video, rental/purchase).

Martin Luther King, Jr., Day: The Making of a Holiday. This is the story of how celebrating Martin Luther King, Jr.'s, birthday became law. 28 minutes; color. No. QF-1691. Distributor: FHS (video, rental/purchase).

Mississippi Summer. An Emmy-winning documentary showing events leading up to the historic summer of 1964—the 1954 Supreme Court ruling on the integration of public schools; the Civil Rights Act of 1957; the effort to keep James Meredith out of the University of Mississippi; the assassination of Medgar Evers; the Civil Rights Act of 1964. 58 minutes; color. No. QF-1266. Distributor: FHS (rental/purchase).

Never Turn Back: The Life of Fannie Lou Hamer. Chronicle of the Civil Rights Movement. 60 minutes. Distributor: REPRO (film).

To Be Young, Gifted and Black. The life and works of dramatist Lorraine Hansberry in an award-winning film. 90 minutes. Distributor: IU, 1972 (film/video, rental/purchase).

UNIT 10

Alex Haley: The Search for Roots. Haley explains the power of his dream to write *Roots,* and the obstacles that stood in the way of its fulfillment. 18 minutes; color. No. QF-141. Distributor: FHS (film/video, purchase).

Biko: Breaking the Silence. A documentary exploring the life of the martyred South African activist. 55 minutes. Distributor: FL, 1987 (video, rental/purchase).

Black in White America. A look at life as experienced by contemporary African Americans, including the pre-civil rights generation, the middle class, and city dwellers. 60 minutes. Distributor: Res (video, purchase).

Chuck Davis, Dancing Through West Africa. Portrait of African dance and life, with focus on three ethnic groups in West Africa. 28 minutes. Distributor: FL, 1986 (film/video, rental/purchase).

The Constitution: That Delicate Balance. Episode 12. *Affirmative Action Versus Reverse Discrimination.* Explores affirmative action statutes, the issues and controversies; with former U.S. attorney general Griffin Bell, 60 minutes. Distributor: FI, 1984 (video, rental).

Cry Freedom. Film by Richard Attenborough about the late South African activist Stephen Biko and journalist Donald Woods. Starring Denzel Washington. 157 minutes; color. No. MCA80763. Distributor: KU, 1987 (video, purchase).

The Dance Theater of Harlem. Established to provide Harlem youngsters with the opportunity to perform ballet professionally, this world-class artistic troupe is explored in "60 Minutes" segment. 14 minutes; color. No. QF-1995. Distributor: FHS (video, purchase).

Dance Theatre of Harlem. This "Great Performances" video charts the company from its early days in a Harlem garage to international stature. 60 minutes. Distributor: IU, 1977 (film/video, rental/purchase).

Dr. Billy Taylor. An interview, at the piano, with the man who has done as much as any living musician to advance the acceptance of jazz as an indigenous American art form. 26 minutes; color. No. QF-2934. Distributor: FHS (rental/purchase).

Great Black Women. Women who succeeded despite the odds. Features Coretta Scott King, Lena Horne, Shirley Chisholm, Tina Turner, Oprah Winfrey, Marva Collins, Whoopie Goldberg, Patti LaBelle, and "Mother Hale." 52 minutes; color. No. QF-2308. Distributor: FHS (rental/purchase).

General Colin Powell: What I've Learned. Relates the story of Powell, who was born in Harlem and grew up in the South Bronx, and went on become Chairman of the Joint Chiefs of Staff. 28 minutes; color. No. QF-2797. Distributor: FHS (purchase).

Lorraine Hansberry: The Black Experience in the Creation of Drama. The life and work of the leading African American woman playwright, showing how she used the obstacles that confronted her to focus her artistic vision. 35 minutes; color. No. QF-128. Distributor: FHS (film/video, purchase).

Negro Ensemble Company. A look at the nationally acclaimed company established to create a "theater of excellence concentrating primarily on themes of black life." 58 minutes; color. Distributor: FHS, 1987 (video, purchase).

Nelson Mandela: The History of a Struggle. Covers Mandela's life and activities up to imprisonment, the background against which they occurred, and the events in the struggle against apartheid that ultimately led to his release. 30 minutes; color. No. QF-2592. Distributor: FHS (video, rental/purchase).

South Africa: A Nation on the Brink. Covers the arrival of Europeans, independence, and apartheid. One filmstrip, 1 cassette, 1 illustrated guide. No. 5150. Distributor: KU, 1988 (film, purchase).

The Story of English. Episode 5. *Black on White.* An exploration of African American English, from its roots in West Africa to the Caribbean patois and today's "rap." 60 minutes. Distributor: FI, 1986 (video, rental).

Key to the Film Distribution Companies

ADL: Anti-Defamation League of B'nai Brith
Media Marketing Department
823 United Nations Plaza
New York, NY 10017
212-490-2525

AITECH: Agency for Instructional Technology
Box A
Bloomington, IN 47402-0120
812-339-2203
800-457-4509

ATLAP: Atlantis Productions
1252 La Granada Drive
Thousand Oaks, CA 91362
805-495-2790

BF: Barr Films
3490 East Foothill Boulevard
P.O. Box 5667
Pasadena, CA 91107
818-338-7878

BFA: BFA Educational Media
468 Park Avenue South
New York, NY 10016
212-684-5910

C/MTI: Coronet/MTI Film & Video
108 Wilmot Road
Deerfield, IL 60015
708-940-1260

CRM: CRM
2215 Faraday Avenue
Carlsbad, CA 92008
619-431-9800
800-421-0833

FHS: Films for the Humanities and Sciences
P.O. Box 2053
Princeton, NJ 08543-2053
609-452-1128
800-257-5126

FI: Films Inc.
5547 N. Ravenswood Avenue
Chicago, IL 60640-1199
312-878-2600

FL: Filmakers Library
124 East 40th Street
New York, NY 10016
212-808-4980

IU: Indiana University Film Rental Order
Audiovisual Center
Bloomington, IN 47405-5901
812-335-2103

KS: Killiam Shows, Inc.
6 East 39th Street
New York, NY 10016
212-679-8230

KU: Knowledge Unlimited
P.O. Box 52
Madison, WI 53701-0052
608-836-6660
800-356-2303

NGS: National Geographic Society
Educational Services
Washington, DC 20036
301-921-1330

NWHP: National Women's History Project
7738 Bell Road
Windsor, CA 95492
707-838-6000

PAV: Pacific Arts Video
50 N. La Cienega Boulevard, Suite 210
Beverly Hills, CA 90211
213-657-2233
800-538-5856

PBS: PBS Video
1320 Braddock Place
Alexandria, VA 22314
800-424-7963

REPRO: Rediscovery Productions
2 Halfmile Common
Westport, CT 06880
203-226-4489

Res: Resolution
1 Mill Street
Burlington, VT 05401
800-843-0048

SF: Spectacor Films
7920 Sunset Boulevard, 4th Floor
Los Angeles, CA 90046
213-464-4100

SHV: Sony Home Video
(Check your local Sony video distributor.)

SU: Syracuse University Film Rental Center
1455 E. Colvin Street
Syracuse, NY 13244-5150
315-443-2452

TBFF: The Black Filmmaker Foundation
80 Eighth Avenue, Suite 1704
New York, NY 10011
212-924-1198

WHV: Worldvision Home Video, Inc.
660 Madison Avenue
New York, NY 10021
212-832-3838

COMMUNITY RESOURCES

African-American Institute
833 United Nations Plaza
New York, NY 10017
212-949-5666

Afro-American Historical and Cultural Museum
7th and Arch Streets
Philadelphia, PA 19106
215-574-0380

Afro-American Resource Center
P.O. Box 746
Howard University
Washington, DC 20059
202-636-7242

Anacostia Museum
1901 Fort Place SE
Washington, DC 20560
202-357-2700

Association for the Study of Afro-American Life and History
1401 14th Street NW
Washington, DC 20005
202-667-2822

Civil Rights Monument
400 Washington Avenue
Montgomery, AL 36106
205-264-0286

Connecticut Afro-American Historical Society
444 Orchard Street
New Haven, CT 06511
203-776-4907

Du Sable Museum of African American History
740 East 56th Place
Chicago, IL 60637
312-947-0600

Ethnic Cultural Center
3931 Brooklyn Avenue NE
Seattle, WA 98105
206-543-4635

George Washington Carver Museum
Tuskegee Institute
Tuskegee, AL 36088
205-727-3200

Inner City Arts Council
642 West North Avenue
Milwaukee, WI 53212
414-265-5050

Museum of African-American Culture
1403 Richland Street
Columbia, SC 29201
803-252-1450 or 803-252-3964

Museum of African-American History
301 Frederick Douglass Avenue
Detroit, MI 48202
313-833-9800

Museum of African-American Life and Culture
1111 First Avenue
Dallas, TX 75315-0153
214-565-9026

Museum of Afro-American History
46 Joy Street
Boston, MA 02114
617-742-1854

National Afro-American Museum and Cultural Center Project
The Ohio Historical Society
1982 Velma Avenue
Columbus, OH 43211
614-297-2300

Nat'l Ass'n for the Advancement of Colored People
260 Fifth Avenue
New York, NY 10001
212-481-4100

National Museum of African Art
Smithsonian Institution
950 Independence Avenue SW
Washington, DC 20560
202-357-4600

The Rhode Island Black Heritage Society
1 Hilton Street
Providence, RI 02905
401-751-3490

Schomburg Center for Research in Black Culture
New York Public Library
515 Lenox Avenue
New York, NY 10037
212-862-4000

Name ______________________________ Date______________

UNIT 1 TEST: The African Homeland

I. MATCHING Decide which definition from the right column best explains a term in the left column. Then write the letter of that definition in the space next to the term.

_____	**1.** plateau	**a.**	Egyptian ruler
_____	**2.** domesticate	**b.**	thick plant growth in hot, wet climates
_____	**3.** escarpment	**c.**	tame for human use
_____	**4.** dynasty	**d.**	elevated piece of level land
_____	**5.** pharaoh	**e.**	rapids
_____	**6.** savanna	**f.**	ruling family
_____	**7.** cataract	**g.**	flat grassland with few trees
_____	**8.** rain forest	**h.**	steep cliff

II. UNDERSTANDING TIME Read the following list of events. Then number the events from 1 to 10 in the order in which they happened.

_____ New Kingdom ends.

_____ Almoravids conquer Ghana.

_____ Moroccans invade Songhai.

_____ Empire of Mali is established.

_____ Kush conquers Egypt.

_____ Farming begins along the Nile.

_____ Islamic rule begins in North Africa.

_____ Hyksos invade Egypt.

_____ Axum conquers Kush.

_____ Menes unites Upper and Lower Egypt.

III. MULTIPLE CHOICE Choose the answer that best completes the sentence or answers the question. Then write the letter of your choice in the space at the left.

_____ **9.** Among the continents, Africa is the:
a. largest. **b.** second largest. **c.** smallest. **d.** second smallest.

_____ **10.** The largest part of the African continent is often referred to as:
a. South Africa. **b.** West Africa. **c.** Egypt. **d.** sub-Saharan Africa.

_____ **11.** The prominent feature of the African landscape that extends from the Red Sea to Mozambique is the:
a. Kalahari Desert. **b.** Sahara. **c.** Tanzanian rain forest. **d.** Great Rift Valley.

_____ **12.** Human remains nearly two million years old have been found in the:
a. Olduvai Gorge. **b.** Kalahari Desert. **c.** Nile Valley. **d.** Sahara.

_____ **13.** The invention of farming took place during the:
a. Old Stone Age. **b.** New Stone Age. **c.** Old Kingdom. **d.** New Kingdom.

_____ **14.** Recognizing its important contribution to the region, the historian Herodotus called Egypt "the gift of the:
a. Mediterranean." **b.** Nile." **c.** Red Sea." **d.** Sahara."

_____ **15.** The period that has been called Egypt's Golden Age came during the:
a. Old Kingdom. **b.** Middle Kingdom. **c.** New Kingdom. **d.** rule of the Kushite pharaohs.

_____ **16.** The city of Meroë owed its importance to:
a. the slave trade. **b.** its excellent Red Sea port. **c.** iron making. **d.** the salt trade.

_____ **17.** The West African empires of Ghana, Mali, and Songhai all owed a great part of their wealth to the trade in:
a. iron. **b.** gold. **c.** slaves. **d.** rice.

_____ **18.** After A.D. 1000, the dominant religion in the West African kingdoms was:
a. Islam. **b.** Christianity. **c.** Judaism. **d.** ancestor worship.

_____ **19.** Which of the following *best* describes the practice of slavery in the kingdoms of West Africa before the 1500s?
a. Slavery was unknown. **b.** Most slaves were harshly treated. **c.** Most slaves were captured Europeans or Indians. **d.** Most slaves could buy or earn their freedom after a period of time.

_____ **20.** Marriage customs of most West African societies permitted:
a. a man to have only one wife. **b.** a man to have more than one wife. **c.** a woman to have more than one husband. **d.** a form of divorce.

IV. COMPLETING THE IDEA Choose the name from the list below that best completes each of the following sentences. Then write it in the space provided.

Kashta	Mary Leakey	Askia Muhammad
Ezana	Akhenaton	Abu Bakr
Muhammad	Mansa Musa	Hatshepsut
Sundiata		

21. During the New Kingdom, _______________ became the first woman to rule over Egypt.

22. According to legend, the kingdom of Mali was founded by _______________.

23. _______________ introduced into Egypt a form of religion that centered on the belief in one god rather than in many gods and goddesses.

24. In 1959, _______________ was one of the anthropologists who discovered human remains nearly two million years old in Africa.

25. Under the rule of _______________, the Songhai empire reached the height of its power.

26. An Arabian merchant named ________________________ founded the religion of Islam in A.D. 622.

27. The efforts of ________________________ helped establish the city of Timbuktu as an important center of African learning and culture.

28. The Almoravid leader ________________________ launched a jihad against the people of Ghana and won control of that nation.

29. The ruler ________________________ defeated the Kushite empire and proclaimed Christianity the official religion of Axum.

30. After a successful invasion, ________________________ became the first of a line of Kushites who ruled Egypt for 80 years.

V. **ESSAY Choose one of the following topics. Then write your answer in paragraph form on a separate sheet of paper.**

A. Explain why you agree or disagree with the following statement: "Human civilization might be called a gift of Africa." Cite evidence from the text to support your position.

B. How did geographical factors help shape civilizations in Africa? Discuss at least two different societies in your answer.

Name ______________________________ Date ______________

CHAPTER 1 TEST: Egypt, Kush, and Axum

I. MATCHING Decide which description from the right column best applies to a person or place in the left column. Then write the letter of that description in the space next to the term.

_____	**1.** Axum	**a.** trading port on the Red Sea
_____	**2.** Adulis	**b.** region to the south of Egypt
_____	**3.** Nubia	**c.** first African center of iron manufacture
_____	**4.** Meroë	**d.** nation that conquered Egypt in 750 B.C.
_____	**5.** Kashta	**e.** leader of forces that conquered Egypt in 750 B.C.
_____	**6.** Kush	**f.** kingdom from which Ethiopians trace their origins

II. MULTIPLE CHOICE Choose the answer that best completes the sentence or answers the question. Then write the letter of your choice in the space to the left.

_____ **7.** The first recorded Egyptian expedition to southern lands was led by: **a.** Kashta. **b.** Ezana. **c.** Herkhuf. **d.** Merenra.

_____ **8.** One explanation for the population make-up of ancient Egypt was its: **a.** isolation. **b.** extensive contacts with neighboring countries. **c.** laws concerning immigration. **d.** lack of ports.

_____ **9.** Much of the wealth of ancient Nubia came from: **a.** copper. **b.** wheat. **c.** silver. **d.** gold.

_____ **10.** From about 750 to 663 B.C., the rulers of Egypt were: **a.** Kushites. **b.** Mesopotamians. **c.** Greeks. **d.** Libyans.

_____ **11.** One factor that contributed to the defeat of Egypt in 663 B.C. was: **a.** famine. **b.** Egypt's failure to use gunpowder. **c.** the treachery of the Hyksos. **d.** the superiority of the invaders' iron weapons.

_____ **12.** Which of the following factors *did not* contribute to the growth of Meroë? **a.** It was close to Egypt. **b.** It was near rich iron deposits. **c.** It had good farmland around it. **d.** It was convenient to trade routes.

_____ **13.** Which of the following statements *best* describes how trade in Meroë changed over time? **a.** Trade with Egypt grew increasingly important. **b.** Trade with Rome was cut off. **c.** Trade with Greece flourished. **d.** Trade with African regions to the south grew increasingly important.

_____ **14.** The economic base of Axum's empire was: **a.** gold mining. **b.** iron making. **c.** trade. **d.** cotton production.

_____ **15.** After the A.D. 600s, what distinguished Axum from neighboring North African nations? **a.** its early conversion to Islam **b.** its refusal to give up Christianity **c.** its cotton trade **d.** its reliance on bronze weapons

III. ESSAY Choose one of the following topics. Then write your answer in paragraph form on a separate sheet of paper.

A. How did ancient Egypt affect the development of kingdoms to its south?

B. Which was more important to the development of civilizations in northeastern Africa, trade or warfare? Explain.

Name ________________________________ Date ______________

CHAPTER 2 TEST: Great Empires of West Africa

I. MATCHING Decide which definition from the right column best explains each term in the left column. Then write the letter of that definition in the space next to the term.

______	**1.** griot	**a.**	an early type of gun that enabled a Moroccan army to defeat Songhai in 1591
______	**2.** hajj	**b.**	the process by which gold and salt changed hands in Ghana
______	**3.** silent trade	**c.**	holy war for the spread of Islam
______	**4.** jihad	**d.**	storytellers who memorize and pass down through word of mouth the history of a people
______	**5.** harquebus	**e.**	pilgrimage to the holy city of Mecca, required of devout Muslims

II. MULTIPLE CHOICE Choose the answer that best completes the sentence or answers the question. Then write the letter of your choice in the space to the left.

______ **6.** The wealth of Ghana was based on: **a.** rice and the slave trade. **b.** gold and salt. **c.** cotton and bronze. **d.** wheat and silver.

______ **7.** An important factor that helped the Soninke people people to defeat their neighbors was: **a.** iron weapons. **b.** guns. **c.** a strong navy. **d.** the cross bow.

______ **8.** According to legend, Mali was founded by: **a.** Sumangura. **b.** Abu Bakr. **c.** Sundiata. **d.** Mansa Musa.

______ **9.** The West African city that became a center of Muslim learning and culture was: **a.** Kumbi. **b.** Gao. **c.** Timbuktu. **d.** Sankore.

______ **10.** Before the coming of the Europeans, slaves in Africa were usually: **a.** Africans captured in war. **b.** Egyptians. **c.** Indians purchased in Red Sea ports. **d.** Indians captured in wars.

______ **11.** One reason salt was an important trade good was its use in: **a.** fertilizing crops. **b.** making medicines. **c.** manufacturing iron. **d.** preserving foods.

______ **12.** The chief trade goods of the Songhai empire were: **a.** gold and salt. **b.** gold and slaves. **c.** gold and ivory. **d.** gold and bronze.

______ **13.** Unlike earlier African empires, Songhai included in its trade network: **a.** India. **b.** East Africa. **c.** North Africa. **d.** Europe and Southwest Asia.

______ **14.** The king who persuaded some of Islam's finest scholars and architects to come to Mali was: **a.** Mansa Musa. **b.** Sunni Ali. **c.** Abu Bakr. **d.** Sundiata.

______ **15.** Sunni Ali angered some Muslim religious leaders because he: **a.** refused to give them financial support. **b.** converted to Christianity. **c.** allowed conquered peoples to retain their old religious beliefs. **d.** expanded the Songhai empire.

III. ESSAY Choose one of the following topics. Then write your answer in paragraph form on a separate sheet of paper.

A. Do you think the spread of Islam aided or held back the growth of West African kingdoms? Explain.

B. What common factor can you identify in the rise of the kingdom of Ghana and the fall of the Songhai empire? Explain.

Name ______________________________ Date ______________

CHAPTER 3 TEST: The West African Heritage

I. MATCHING Decide which definition in the right column best explains each term in the left column. Then write the letter of that definition in the space next to the term.

______	**1.** bridewealth	**a.**	belief one's dead relatives can be reached through prayer
______	**2.** elder	**b.**	having more than one wife at a time
______	**3.** extended family	**c.**	common form in West African music
______	**4.** ancestor worship	**d.**	top rank in West African society
______	**5.** polygyny	**e.**	parents, children, and other relatives living in one household
______	**6.** subsistence farming	**f.**	payment made by groom's family to bride's family
______	**7.** call-and-response	**g.**	raising just enough for one's own needs

II. MULTIPLE CHOICE Choose the answer that best completes the sentence or answers the question. Then write the letter of your choice in the space to the left.

______ **8.** Most Africans who were brought to the Americas originally came from: **a.** North Africa. **b.** South Africa. **c.** East Africa. **d.** West Africa.

______ **9.** Among many West African peoples, marriages were: **a.** arranged by families when children were young. **b.** decisions left up to the couples involved. **c.** not permitted until both the man and woman were 21. **d.** permitted during only two months of the year.

______ **10.** Having several wives in West African society was a sign that a man was: **a.** disregarding social customs. **b.** not a Muslim. **c.** wealthy. **d.** very poor.

______ **11.** Outside the great West African trading centers, most people made their livings as: **a.** sheepherders. **b.** hunters. **c.** farmers. **d.** metal workers.

______ **12.** In West African kingdoms, land for farming usually belonged to: **a.** individual farmers. **b.** the community. **c.** the king. **d.** village priests.

______ **13.** Which of the following was *not* part of the religious beliefs of most West African peoples? The belief that: **a.** a person's soul survived after death. **b.** there was only one god. **c.** spirits lived in all things. **d.** there were many gods and goddesses.

______ **14.** Many West African peoples believed that they could get help against evil spirits by: **a.** praying to deceased ancestors. **b.** meditating. **c.** taking a new husband or wife. **d.** moving to a new village.

______ **15.** A North American musical instrument that is derived from the African mbanza is the: **a.** melodeon. **b.** xylophone. **c.** harmonica. **d.** banjo.

III. ESSAY Choose one of the following topics. Then write your answer in paragraph form on a separate sheet of paper.

A. What advantages and disadvantages might an extended family provide for an individual? Explain one example of each.

B. Do you think the original religious beliefs of the West Africans made those people more or less willing to accept the arrival of Islam and Christianity? Explain.

Name ______________________________ Date______________

UNIT 2 TEST: Africans in the Americas

I. MATCHING Decide which definition in the right column best explains a term in the left column. Then write the letter of that definition in the space provided next to the term.

______	**1.** conquistador	**a.** West African slave-trading center
______	**2.** silent trade	**b.** one who exchanged work for passage to America
______	**3.** factory	**c.** method of exchanging enslaved Africans for products
______	**4.** triangular trade	**d.** Spaniard sent to establish outposts in the Americas
______	**5.** indentured servant	**e.** route followed in the sugar–slave trade

II. UNDERSTANDING TIME Each letter on the time line indicates when one of the events from the list below took place. Write the letter indicating when an event happened in the space provided next to the description of the event.

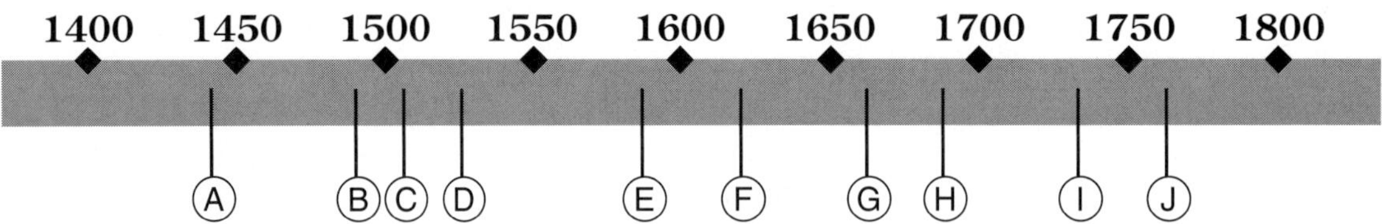

______ **6.** The Atlantic slave trade begins.

______ **7.** The first Africans arrive at Jamestown.

______ **8.** The Spanish Armada is defeated.

______ **9.** Pennsylvania Quakers bar slave traders from membership.

______ **10.** The first Africans are sold as slaves in Europe.

______ **11.** Virginia passes its first laws recognizing slavery.

______ **12.** The British grant independence to Africans escaped from slavery in Jamaica.

______ **13.** Columbus first reaches the Americas.

______ **14.** Enslaved Africans overthrow a Spanish colony in South Carolina.

______ **15.** The first antislavery protest in North America is issued.

III. MULTIPLE CHOICE Choose the answer that best completes the sentence or answers the question. Then write the letter of your choice in the space provided.

______ **16.** European exploration of Africa had its roots in the:
a. conquest of Mexico. **b.** fall of the Roman empire. **c.** Crusades. **d.** defeat of the Spanish Armada.

______ **17.** The raiders who rounded up captives for sale to Europeans at slave factories along the West African coast were generally:
a. Arabs. **b.** Africans. **c.** Egyptians. **d.** Indians.

_____ **18.** The trans-Atlantic trade in African slaves grew because of the death of thousands of enslaved:
a. Vikings. **b.** Native Americans. **c.** Muslims. **d.** Irish.

_____ **19.** Because of the short growing season and rocky soil, a relatively small number of enslaved Africans were brought to:
a. the New England Colonies. **b.** the Middle Colonies. **c.** the Southern Colonies. **d.** the West Indian colonies.

_____ **20.** Which of the following *best* describes the attitude of most North American colonists toward slavery?
a. They believed it was an evil that must be ended. **b.** They thought it was wrong, but necessary. **c.** They believed it should be expanded because the Bible approved of slavery. **d.** They did not give much thought to the question of whether one person should own another.

_____ **21.** To justify the mass enslavement of Africans, Europeans:
a. practiced racism. **b.** promised an eventual end to the slave trade. **c.** sought the approval of the pope. **d.** established free schools for enslaved Africans.

_____ **22.** Enslaved Africans reached the Americas after a trip known as the:
a. seasoning. **b.** colonizing. **c.** Great Circle. **d.** Middle Passage.

_____ **23.** One result of the slave trade was the:
a. growth of cotton-cloth factories in East Africa. **b.** failure of West Africans to develop other commerce and manufacturing. **c.** development of strong nation-states in West Africa. **d.** weakening of European control of the sugar trade.

_____ **24.** In the mid-1700s, the West Indies began to send increasing numbers of Africans to:
a. Britain's North American colonies. **b.** Spain's South Atlantic colonies. **c.** Mexico. **d.** the Mediterranean islands.

_____ **25.** Plantation owners came to prefer the use of enslaved Africans rather than indentured servants. Which of the following was *not* a reason for this choice?
a. Enslaved Africans worked for life rather than for a set term. **b.** Indentured servants could not be taught proper farming methods. **c.** The skin color of enslaved Africans made escape difficult for them. **d.** Indentured servants could appeal to the home country if mistreated.

IV. COMPLETING THE IDEA Choose the item from the list below that best completes each of the following sentences. Then write it in the space provided.

Nzinga	John Locke	the West Indies
Bartolomé de Las Casas	Portugal	Maryland
Mathias De Sousa	Pennsylvania	Balboa
Great Britain		

26. In 1663, ________________________ passed a law enslaving Africans and their children *durante vita,* or for life.

27. The most severe instances of racism toward Africans took place in the colonies of

________________________.

28. Although he believed that governments existed to protect the life, liberty, and property of people, ________________________ gave no rights to enslaved persons when he drew up a plan of government for the Carolinas.

29. For nearly 30 years, ________________________ waged a war that greatly disrupted the inland slave trade in West Africa.

30. At least 30 Africans accompanied ________________________ during the 1513 expedition in which he sighted the Pacific Ocean.

31. Africans in ________________________ gradually managed to win more rights than Africans in other colonies.

32. The attempts of ________________________ to protect Native Americans contributed to the increased enslavement of Africans.

33. Explorers and traders from ________________________ became active in the West African slave trade in the mid-1400s.

34. ________________________ was an African indentured servant who won election to the Maryland General Assembly.

35. For over 200 years, many nations struggled for control of ________________________ and its rich sugar trade.

V. ESSAY Choose one of the following topics. Then write your answer in paragraph form on a separate sheet of paper.

A. In 1526, Affonso, king of the Kongo in West Africa, wrote to the king of Portugal protesting the slave trade. Write a brief version of what you think Affonso might have said.

B. Do you think a victory by the Spanish Armada in 1588 would have stopped the growth of slavery on the North American mainland? Explain.

Name ______________________________ Date ______________

CHAPTER 4 TEST: The Atlantic Slave Trade

I. MATCHING Decide which definition in the right column best explains a term in the left column. Then write the letter of that definition in the space provided next to the term.

_____ **1.** slavery

_____ **2.** Middle Passage

_____ **3.** slave factory

_____ **4.** silent trade

_____ **5.** dancing of the slaves

a. method of exchanging goods used by African and white slave traders

b. place where African slave traders brought slaves to sell them to European slave traders

c. owning human beings as property

d. exercise forced on enslaved Africans

e. enslaved Africans' trip across the Atlantic Ocean

II. MULTIPLE CHOICE Choose the answer that best completes the sentence or answers the question. Then write the letter of your choice in the space provided.

_____ **6.** The European who struggled to end the enslavement of Native Americans was: **a.** Christopher Columbus. **b.** Queen Isabella. **c.** Vasco da Gama. **d.** Bartolomé de Las Casas.

_____ **7.** Cheap goods brought to Africa by Europeans in the slave trade: **a.** brought new prosperity to Africa. **b.** were thrown away by Africans. **c.** held back the development of manufacturing and commerce in Africa. **d.** made some African slave traders unwilling to trade.

_____ **8.** The European nations that first controlled the African slave trade were: **a.** England and France. **b.** Portugal and Spain. **c.** Portugal and England. **d.** the Netherlands and Spain.

_____ **9.** During the 1600s, Africans forced into slavery were: **a.** mainly from the Yoruba and Asante peoples. **b.** from a people whose name has been lost. **c.** from a large number of West African peoples. **d.** mostly Dahomeans.

_____ **10.** Which of the following statements *best* describes the relationship between African and European slave traders shortly after 1500? **a.** They each tried to gain exclusive control of the trade. **b.** They cooperated. **c.** They ignored each other. **d.** They often went to war.

_____ **11.** For every African who died in the slave trade, how many reached the coastal trading centers alive? **a.** 1 **b.** 2 **c.** 5 **d.** 10

_____ **12.** Crews of slave ships lived in constant fear of: **a.** slave uprisings. **b.** shortages of water. **c.** storms. **d.** sharks.

_____ **13.** A West African ruler who battled the Portuguese and their slave traders was: **a.** Angola. **b.** Matamba. **c.** Nzinga. **d.** Hausa.

_____ **14.** Estimates of the total number of Africans lost to the slave trade range from: **a.** 2 to 7 million. **b.** 9 to 21 million. **c.** 25 to 50 million. **d.** 61 to 72 million.

_____ **15.** Which of the following statements *best* describes Africans taken in the slave trade? **a.** They were exclusively farmers. **b.** They included few artisans. **c.** They included all but the nobles. **d.** They came from all ranks and skills.

III. ESSAY Choose one of the following topics. Then write your answer in paragraph form on a separate sheet of paper.

A. Why were some Africans willing to work with the Europeans in enslaving other Africans? List and explain at least two reasons.

B. Some slave ships lost up to half their human cargo during the Middle Passage. Explain why ship captains did not treat their African passengers better.

Name ______________________________ Date ______________

CHAPTER 5 TEST: The West Indies: First Stop for Africans

I. MATCHING Decide which definition in the right column best explains a term in the left column. Then write the letter of that definition in the space provided next to the term.

_____	**1.** triangular trade	**a.**	something raised for sale, not personal use
_____	**2.** racism	**b.**	escaped enslaved African of Jamaica
_____	**3.** plantation	**c.**	false belief that one race is superior to another
_____	**4.** Maroon	**d.**	huge farm
_____	**5.** cash crop	**e.**	pattern that emerged from the trade in sugar and enslaved Africans

II. MULTIPLE CHOICE Choose the answer that best completes the sentence or answers the question. Then write the letter of your choice in the space provided.

_____ **6.** In 1739, the British signed a peace treaty that granted independence to Africans who had escaped from slavery in: **a.** Haiti. **b.** St. Kitts. **c.** Bermuda. **d.** Jamaica.

_____ **7.** The European nation that first took possession of the West Indies in the early 1500s was: **a.** England. **b.** France. **c.** the Netherlands. **d.** Spain.

_____ **8.** Dyewoods, cotton, and spices are all examples of West Indian: **a.** imports. **b.** manufactures. **c.** tariffs. **d.** cash crops.

_____ **9.** To raise sugar in the West Indies, England for a time used the labor of the: **a.** Swedish. **b.** Danish. **c.** Irish. **d.** Dutch.

_____ **10.** One reason Europeans generally did not use the forced labor of other Europeans was: **a.** the existence of treaties barring such practices. **b.** the great expense. **c.** opposition to enslaving Christians. **d.** slave rebellions in Europe.

_____ **11.** In the 1600s, traders bought enslaved Africans in Africa for about $25 and sold them in the West Indies for about: **a.** $50. **b.** $75. **c.** $100. **d.** $150.

_____ **12.** Three of the most valuable products of the West Indies were: **a.** sugar, molasses, and rum. **b.** sugar, corn, and rice. **c.** rum, chocolate, and oranges. **d.** sugar, bananas, and tea.

_____ **13.** The sugar–slave trade involved routes that connected West Africa, the West Indies, and: **a.** Mexico. **b.** Brazil. **c.** French colonies in Canada. **d.** English colonies in North America.

_____ **14.** Racism was *most severe* in the West Indian colonies of which nation? **a.** Great Britain **b.** France **c.** Spain **d.** Portugal

_____ **15.** One reason that Europeans in the West Indies used Africans rather than Native Americans as slaves was that Native Americans: **a.** were too expensive. **b.** died because of lack of resistance to European diseases. **c.** resisted too fiercely. **d.** made treaties with the Europeans.

III. ESSAY Choose one of the following topics. Then write your answer in paragraph form on a separate sheet of paper.

A. Explain why the actions of the Maroons in Jamaica might have led slave owners to take harsher measures toward enslaved Africans elsewhere in the West Indies.

B. "The mere existence of slavery was a guarantee that slaves would be ill-treated." Explain why you agree or disagree with this statement, using evidence from the text.

Name ______________________________ Date ______________

CHAPTER 6 TEST: Africans in the Thirteen Colonies

I. MATCHING Decide which description from the right column best identifies a person in the left column. Then write the letter of the description in the space provided.

_____ **1.** James Oglethorpe

_____ **2.** William Penn

_____ **3.** Mathias De Sousa

_____ **4.** Estevanico

_____ **5.** Luis Vasquez de Ayllon

a. founded a colony as a religious haven for Quakers but allowed slavery there

b. African who journeyed with Spaniards through much of present-day southwestern U. S.

c. led founders of Georgia and, at first, insisted on slavery ban there

d. led a group, including 100 Africans, that tried to establish a colony in what is now South Carolina

e. former indentured servant who was elected to the Maryland General Assembly in 1641

II. MULTIPLE CHOICE Choose the answer that best completes the sentence or answers the question. Then write the letter of your choice in the space provided.

_____ **6.** In 1619, the first Africans to live in England's North American colonies arrived in: **a.** Philadelphia. **b.** Baltimore. **c.** Plymouth. **d.** Jamestown.

_____ **7.** The first Africans to arrive in England's North American colonies were treated as: **a.** slaves. **b.** indentured servants. **c.** ambassadors. **d.** criminals.

_____ **8.** A 1660 Virginia law recognized that Africans were: **a.** indentured servants. **b.** slaves for life. **c.** slaves who would be free after 20 years. **d.** entitled to all rights except voting.

_____ **9.** In 1691, the Virginia House of Burgesses banned: **a.** importation of enslaved Africans. **b.** marriage between Europeans and Africans. **c.** reading education for Africans. **d.** African attendance at church.

_____ **10.** England formed the Royal African Company to: **a.** build colonies in Africa. **b.** prevent colonists from buying Africans from rival nations. **c.** build tobacco plantations in Africa. **d.** import sugar from Africa.

_____ **11.** The founders of Carolina gave land to settlers who: **a.** imported Africans as indentured servants. **b.** imported Africans as slaves. **c.** freed enslaved Africans. **d.** baptized enslaved Africans.

_____ **12.** The founders of Georgia wanted all settlers there to: **a.** import enslaved Africans. **b.** import indentured servants. **c.** contribute to a general fund to buy enslaved Africans. **d.** start on an equal economic footing without slavery.

_____ **13.** The *main* reason that New York and New Jersey had fewer enslaved Africans than Southern colonies was: **a.** climate. **b.** politics. **c.** religion. **d.** racism.

_____ **14.** The group that issued the first antislavery protest in North America was made up of: **a.** Dutch Separatists. **b.** Irish Catholics. **c.** Spanish Jews. **d.** German Quakers.

_____ **15.** Which of the following *best* describes the part colonial New Englanders played in the slave trade? **a.** They owned many of the ships involved in it. **b.** They protested against it. **c.** They used enslaved Africans in the fishing industry. **d.** They passed laws limiting it.

III. ESSAY. Choose one of the following topics. Then write your answer in paragraph form on a separate sheet of paper.

A. How do you think the development of the Southern Colonies would have been affected if they had chosen to bar slavery early in the 1700s?

B. What do you think was more effective in limiting the growth of slavery in Massachusetts, the climate or the 1641 code of laws drafted by the Puritans? Explain your answer.

Name ______________________________ Date ______________

UNIT 3 TEST: African Americans and a New Nation

I. MATCHING Decide which definition from the right column best fits a term in the left column. Then write the letter of the definition in the space next to the term.

_____	**1.** levy		**a.** refuse to buy goods as a protest
_____	**2.** Parliament		**b.** written plan of government
_____	**3.** compromise		**c.** British lawmaking body
_____	**4.** amendment		**d.** impose a tax
_____	**5.** nation		**e.** end of slavery
_____	**6.** boycott		**f.** settlement of a dispute in which each side gives up something
_____	**7.** constitution		**g.** a country independent of the control of another
_____	**8.** abolition		**h.** a change in a constitution or other legal document

II. UNDERSTANDING TIME. Choose the time period in which each of the events listed below took place. Then write the letter of the period in the space provided. (A letter may be used more than once).

1760 (A) 1770 (B) 1780 (C) 1790 (D) 1800 (E) 1810 (F) 1820

_____ **9.** African Americans are recruited to serve in the Continental Army.

_____ **10.** The United States buys Louisiana from France.

_____ **11.** The United States goes to war with Britain over violations of rights at sea.

_____ **12.** Britain wins the French and Indian War.

_____ **13.** The Declaration of Independence is signed.

_____ **14.** Slavery is barred in the Northwest Territory.

III. MULTIPLE CHOICE Choose the answer that best completes the sentence or answers the question. Then write the letter of your choice in the space provided.

_____ **15.** One result of the British victory in the French and Indian War was:
a. freedom for enslaved African Americans who fought for the British. **b.** an alliance with France. **c.** increased territory for the British. **d.** independence for Canada.

_____ **16.** To help pay for its empire, Great Britain:
a. legalized the slave trade. **b.** imposed a series of taxes on its North American colonies. **c.** sold some of its possessions to Spain. **d.** declared restrictions on the slave trade.

_____ **17.** In the 1770s, most colonists considered the idea of the abolition of slavery:
a. too mild. **b.** too radical. **c.** a useful compromise. **d.** an urgent need.

_____ **18.** Why did colonial laws generally forbid African Americans from owning guns?
a. There was a severe shortage of guns. **b.** Lawmakers feared that African Americans lacked proper training in gun use. **c.** British regulations barred such ownership. **d.** Slave owners feared that armed African Americans might stage rebellions.

_____ **19.** Which of the following best sums up the attitudes of colonists toward Britain's tax policies?
a. "No taxation without representation!" **b.** "All men are created equal." **c.** "Liberty and Property!" **d.** "Government of the people shall not perish from the earth."

_____ **20.** To protest Britain's economic policies, colonists:
a. increased their purchases of tea. **b.** refused to buy goods from the home country. **c.** joined abolition groups. **d.** elected new representatives to Parliament.

_____ **21.** Before the Revolution, some free African Americans trained with colonists to be ready to fight the British at a moment's notice. These fighters were known as the:
a. Yankees. **b.** Redcoats. **c.** Minutemen. **d.** Mountain Men.

_____ **22.** The document that inspired African Americans to support the Patriot cause during the Revolution was the:
a. Bill of Rights. **b.** Constitution. **c.** Declaration of Independence. **d.** Northwest Ordinance.

_____ **23.** Which statement *best* describes the experiences of African Americans in the Continental Army?
a. They usually fought sided by side with white Americans. **b.** They were not allowed to enlist. **c.** They usually fought in separate units. **d.** They refused to join the Continental Army as a protest over slavery.

_____ **24.** In the Revolutionary War, the British tried to undercut African American support of the Patriots by:
a. freeing enslaved Africans in its Jamaican colony. **b.** cutting off the slave trade to North America. **c.** announcing a new policy of abolition in the 13 colonies. **d.** offering freedom to African American slaves who fought in the British army.

_____ **25.** As originally written, the Declaration of Independence contained:
a. an attack on slavery. **b.** a promise of freedom for African Americans. **c.** a proposal to tax the slave trade. **d.** a timetable for abolition.

_____ **26.** Which of the following statements *best* describes slavery in the United States in 1804?
a. Only four states still permitted it. **b.** Only four states had abolished it. **c.** All Northern states had abolished it. **d.** The number of states permitting it had not changed since the Revolution.

_____ **27.** In 1787, a dispute over slavery threatened the work of the:
a. Free African Society. **b.** Confederation Congress. **c.** Continental Congress. **d.** Constitutional Convention.

_____ **28.** The Constitution was adopted following a compromise that did nothing to abolish slavery itself but:
a. allowed the slave trade to continue, permitting Congress to end it after 1808. **b.** prohibited cruel treatment of enslaved persons. **c.** allowed escaped slaves their freedom. **d.** granted citizenship to African Americans.

_____ **29.** A measure passed by Congress in 1787 barred slavery in the region:
a. west of the Mississippi and south of the Missouri River. **b.** west of the Mississippi and north of the Missouri River **c.** north of the Potomac and east of the Ohio River. **d.** north of the Ohio River and east of the Mississippi.

_____ **30.** The expansion of the nation through the purchase of Louisiana and Florida:
a. increased debate over slavery. **b.** ended debate over slavery. **c.** had no effect on slavery. **d.** was part of the compromise that ended slavery.

IV. COMPLETING THE IDEA. Choose the item from the list that best completes each of the following sentences. Then write it in the space provided.

Lord Dunmore	Free African Society	Thomas Jefferson
Northwest Ordinance	Constitution	Phillis Wheatley
Louisiana Purchase	Absalom Jones	Continental Army
Toussaint L'Ouverture		

31. When first writing the Declaration of Independence, ______________________ condemned Britain for permitting slavery.

32. ______________________, royal governor of Virginia, encouraged African Americans to fight for Britain during the Revolution.

33. The ______________________ extended United States lands far west of the Mississippi.

34. Some 5,000 African Americans served in the ______________________ during the Revolution.

35. ______________________ was one of the founders of an early self-help organization for African Americans.

36. In 1799, members of the ______________________ sent a petition to Congress calling for an end to slavery.

37. ______________________ was a well-known African American poet.

38. The ______________________ was an early step by the national government to restrict slavery.

39. ______________________ called himself the "Black Napoleon" of Haiti.

40. As the result of a compromise, the ______________________ stated that each enslaved person would be counted as three fifths of a person when determining representation.

V. ESSAY. Choose one of the following topics. Then write your answer in paragraph form on a separate sheet of paper.

A. How did the promises and protections of the Declaration of Independence and the Constitution apply to the lives of African Americans in the nation's early years? Explain.

B. Did the expansion of the United States speed up the end of slavery, or did it delay it? Give evidence to support your opinion.

Name ______________________________ Date ______________

CHAPTER 7 TEST: The American Revolution: Liberty for All?

I. MATCHING Decide which definition from the right column best explains a term in the left column. Then write the letter of the definition in the space next to the term.

_____ **1.** Redcoats
_____ **2.** Vermont
_____ **3.** Boston Massacre
_____ **4.** Minutemen
_____ **5.** Boston Tea Party

a. action taken by colonists to protest new British tax
b. colonists who fought British at Concord
c. first state to end slavery
d. violent conflict with the British that led to the deaths of five colonists in 1770
e. name given by Patriots to British troops

II. MULTIPLE CHOICE Choose the answer that best completes the sentence or answers the question. Then write the letter of your choice in the space to the left.

_____ **6.** The African American opponent of British rule killed in the Boston Massacre was: **a.** William Whipple. **b.** Crispus Attucks. **c.** John Wheatley. **d.** Cuffe Whitemore.

_____ **7.** The first African American writer to have a book published was: **a.** Pomp Blackman. **b.** Anne Bradstreet. **c.** Phillis Wheatley. **d.** Susanah Wheatley.

_____ **8.** To punish Boston for actions taken by Patriots, the British government passed: **a.** a new tea tax. **b.** the Treaty of Paris. **c.** the Virginia Resolutions. **d.** the Intolerable Acts.

_____ **9.** Prince Estabrook was one of the Minutemen in the first battle of the Revolution at: **a.** Lexington. **b.** Concord. **c.** Trenton. **d.** Yorktown.

_____ **10.** Washington asked Congress to approve the enlistment of African Americans in the Continental Army because: **a.** Southern landowners urged him to do so. **b.** the British had promised freedom to African Americans who joined their army. **c.** Northern politicians demanded the move. **d.** his troops had asked him to.

_____ **11.** Approximately how many African Americans served in the Continental Army during the Revolution? **a.** 1,000 **b.** 5,000 **c.** 10,000 **d.** 20,000

_____ **12.** After the Revolution, some 20,000 African Americans who had sided with the British were: **a.** executed. **b.** sent to Africa. **c.** granted their freedom and settled in other British colonies. **d.** sentenced to prison.

_____ **13.** One result of the American Revolution was: **a.** the spread of slavery to Northern states. **b.** the end of slavery in Southern states. **c.** the end of slavery in Northern states. **d.** the end of slavery in Britain.

_____ **14.** The major reason more slave owners did not free enslaved African Americans after the Revolution was: **a.** economic. **b.** religious. **c.** the terms of the Treaty of Paris. **d.** new laws passed by Congress.

_____ **15.** By 1800 approximately how many African Americans were enslaved? **a.** 100,000 **b.** 200,000. **c.** 500,000 **d.** 700,000.

III. ESSAY Choose one of the following topics. Then write your answer in paragraph form on a separate sheet of paper.

A. How beneficial to African American liberty was the Revolution? Support your opinion with facts.

B. If you had been an African American at the time of the Revolution, on which side would you have chosen to fight? Give your reasons.

Name ______________________________ Date ______________

CHAPTER 8 TEST: Forging a New Constitution

I. MATCHING Decide which definition from the right column best describes a term in the left column. Then write the letter of that definition in the space next to the term.

_____	**1.** almanac	**a.**	plan of government drawn up during the Revolution
_____	**2.** Articles of Confederation	**b.**	organization founded to improve the situation of African Americans in Philadelphia
_____	**3.** federal system	**c.**	book of weather forecasts and astronomical facts
_____	**4.** Free African Society	**d.**	system in which each branch of government has some control over the other branches
_____	**5.** checks and balances	**e.**	plan under which the power to govern is divided between national and state governments

II. MULTIPLE CHOICE Choose the answer that best completes the sentence or answers the question. Then write the letter of your choice in the space provided.

_____ **6.** The African American who helped survey the city of Washington was: **a.** Richard Allen. **b.** Absalom Jones. **c.** Benjamin Banneker. **d.** Cuffe Whitemore.

_____ **7.** After the Revolution, approximately what portion of the nation's free African Americans lived in the North? **a.** an eighth **b.** a quarter **c.** a third **d.** half

_____ **8.** The Northern state with the largest African American population was: **a.** Connecticut. **b.** New York. **c.** Pennsylvania. **d.** New Jersey.

_____ **9.** African Americans in Philadelphia won some white support for their calls for liberty by their actions during: **a.** the Constitutional Convention. **b.** a yellow-fever epidemic. **c.** a flood. **d.** the Confederation Congress.

_____ **10.** Many Philadelphia churches showed prejudice toward African Americans by: **a.** charging a head tax. **b.** asking them to sit in separate "African" pews. **c.** requiring them to attend special schools. **d.** forcing them to worship on Saturdays.

_____ **11.** The original purpose of the 1787 convention at Philadelphia was to: **a.** declare independence. **b.** revise the Articles of Confederation. **c.** work out a plan of abolition. **d.** sign a peace treaty with Britain.

_____ **12.** All of the delegates to the Constitutional Convention were: **a.** lawyers. **b.** slave owners. **c.** rich. **d.** white men.

_____ **13.** An early law barring slavery in some parts of the nation was the: **a.** Northwest Ordinance. **b.** Articles of Confederation. **c.** Louisiana Purchase. **d.** Census Act.

_____ **14.** Which of the following statements *best* describes the Constitution's original position on slavery? **a.** It protected slavery. **b.** It completely ignored slavery. **c.** It set a date for the abolishing of slavery. **d.** It made slavery expensive.

_____ **15.** The Constitution's position on slavery was the result of: **a.** pressure by abolition groups. **b.** the wish to damage Britain's slave trade. **c.** pressure from Northern manufacturers. **d.** efforts to win support from Southern slave owners and slave traders in the North and South.

III. ESSAY Choose one of the following topics. Then write your answer in paragraph form on a separate sheet of paper.

A. How do you think African Americans living in 1787 felt about the compromises about slavery made at the Constitutional Convention? Explain.

B. How did African Americans in the North attempt to improve their lives in the years just after the Revolution? How effective were these efforts?

Name ______________________________ Date ______________

CHAPTER 9 TEST: Expanding the Nation

I. MATCHING Decide which description in the right column best identifies a person in the left column. Write the letter of that description in the space provided.

_____	**1.** James Beckwourth	**a.** drummer at the Battle of New Orleans
_____	**2.** Richard Allen	**b.** leader of a revolt by enslaved Africans
_____	**3.** Jordan Noble	**c.** founder of Chicago
_____	**4.** Toussaint L'Ouverture	**d.** Native American who aided Lewis and Clark
_____	**5.** York	**e.** Mountain Man
_____	**6.** Jean Baptiste Point Du Sable	**f.** organizer of African American efforts to fortify Philadelphia during the War of 1812
_____	**7.** John Davis	**g.** African American member of group that surveyed Louisiana
_____	**8.** Sacajawea	**h.** African American sailor in War of 1812

II. MULTIPLE CHOICE Choose the answer that best completes the sentence or answers the question. Then write the letter of your choice in the space provided.

_____ **9.** The city of Chicago was founded as: **a.** a mining camp. **b.** a fishing village. **c.** a fur-trading post. **d.** a factory town.

_____ **10.** In 1791, a revolt broke out among enslaved Africans in: **a.** Haiti. **b.** Spain. **c.** Georgia. **d.** Florida.

_____ **11.** One result of the 1791 revolt, identified in Question 10, was: **a.** the United States takeover of Florida. **b.** war with Britain. **c.** Napoleon's decision to sell the entire Louisiana Territory to the United States. **d.** independence for California.

_____ **12.** The goal of the Lewis and Clark expedition was to: **a.** defeat the Spanish in Florida. **b.** explore the Louisiana Purchase. **c.** acquire Haiti. **d.** start fur trade with California.

_____ **13.** During the War of 1812, African Americans made up approximately what portion of U.S. naval forces? **a.** one tenth **b.** one sixth **c.** one third **d.** one half

_____ **14.** Two African American units helped defeat the British in the battle of: **a.** Canada. **b.** Lake Erie. **c.** New Orleans. **d.** Florida.

_____ **15.** Escaped African American slaves from South Carolina were often aided by the Seminoles of: **a.** Florida. **b.** Georgia. **c.** Louisiana. **d.** Canada.

_____ **16.** A word that describes a government's taking over a new territory is: **a.** amend. **b.** appeal. **c.** annul. **d.** annex.

_____ **17.** In 1819, to avoid a war with Spain, the United States: **a.** bought Florida. **b.** gave up its claims to Cuba. **c.** went to war with Britain instead. **d.** agreed to set up a reservation for Seminoles.

_____ **18.** The fur trappers who helped open the Far West were known as: **a.** Black Seminoles. **b.** Mountain Men. **c.** Native Americans. **d.** Jackson's Men.

_____ **19.** An important early route into California, named for a famous fur trapper, was: **a.** the Rose River. **b.** the Erie Canal. **c.** Cut-Nose Canyon. **d.** Beckwourth Pass.

_____ **20.** By the 1840s, some Mountain Men were earning a living by: **a.** cattle ranching. **b.** cotton growing. **c.** commercial fishing. **d.** guiding settlers.

III. ESSAY Choose one of the following topics. Then write your answer in paragraph form on a separate sheet of paper.

A. In what ways did the efforts of free African Americans aid the nation's growth in the early 1800s?

B. How did slavery play a part in the nation's acquisition of Florida?

Name ______________________________ Date______________

UNIT 4 TEST: Free and Enslaved

I. MATCHING Decide which definition from the right column best fits a term in the left column. Then write the letter of the definition in the space provided.

_____	**1.** discrimination	**a.**	settler who moves into a country
_____	**2.** abolitionist	**b.**	device to separate seeds from cotton fibers
_____	**3.** immigrant	**c.**	religious song
_____	**4.** cotton gin	**d.**	one who seeks an end to slavery
_____	**5.** spiritual	**e.**	unjust treatment based on such characteristics as skin color

II. UNDERSTANDING TIME Decide in which period each of the events listed below took place. Then write the letter of the period in the space provided. (A letter may be used more than once.)

1600 — (A) — 1700 — (B) — 1780 — (C) — 1800 — (D) — 1820 — (E) — 1840

_____ **6.** The Atlantic slave trade officially ends in the United States.

_____ **7.** The cotton gin is invented.

_____ **8.** The Stono uprising occurs.

_____ **9.** The first U.S. factory opens in Rhode Island.

_____ **10.** David Walker's *Appeal* is published.

_____ **11.** A slave uprising takes place in Hartford, Connecticut.

_____ **12.** The British guarantee the independence of Jamaican Maroons.

_____ **13.** The American Colonization Society is founded.

_____ **14.** Nat Turner's rebellion occurs.

_____ **15.** A slave revolt breaks out in New York City.

III. MULTIPLE CHOICE Choose the answer that best completes the sentence or answers the question. Then write the letter of your choice in the space provided.

_____ **16.** Of the 8 million whites who lived in the South in 1860, about how many owned slaves? **a.** 80,000 **b.** 385,000 **c.** 1,250,000 **d.** 3,350,000

_____ **17.** In the 1840s and 1850s, large numbers of settlers came to the United States from: **a.** Spain and Portugal. **b.** Italy and Greece. **c.** Poland and Sweden. **d.** Ireland and Germany.

_____ **18.** Slavery was banned in the Midwestern states east of the Mississippi Rivers by the: **a.** Treaty of Paris. **b.** Northwest Ordinance. **c.** Constitution. **d.** Bill of Rights.

_____ 19. By the 1820s, fewer enslaved Africans were needed in the states of the Upper South because:
a. a mechanical tobacco picker had been invented. **b.** large numbers of German immigrants had settled there. **c.** tobacco production had worn out the soil. **d.** textile factories had become the region's chief businesses.

_____ 20. The growing slave trade between regions during of the early 1800s increased the importance of which of the following for African Americans? **a.** slave codes **b.** the extended family **c.** personal liberty laws **d.** work-for-hire contracts

_____ 21. Because slave owners bought Africans to earn profits, they tended to: **a.** spend as little as possible on their upkeep. **b.** demand guarantees of health from slave sellers. **c.** feed and clothe slaves well to protect their investment. **d.** limit the hours slaves worked to ensure they would not break down.

_____ 22. One of the results of the Vesey conspiracy was that South Carolina: **a.** passed laws limiting the rights of free African Americans. **b.** exiled all free African Americans. **c.** began to ship free African Americans to Haiti. **d.** founded the first branch of the American Colonization Society.

_____ 23. Most states tried to reduce the possibility of slave rebellions by:
a. encouraging African Americans to convert to Christianity. **b.** creating special African American militias. **c.** passing laws that gave African Americans the right to buy their freedom. **d.** passing tough slave codes.

_____ 24. By 1860, nearly half of all free African Americans in the United States lived in: **a.** Maryland. **b.** the South. **c.** the Midwest. **d.** Philadelphia.

_____ 25. Which of the following would have been *most likely* to support a colony in Liberia? **a.** Frederick Douglass **b.** David Walker **c.** Paul Cuffe **d.** William Lloyd Garrison

IV. COMPLETING THE IDEA Choose the item from the list that best completes each of the following sentences. Then write it in the space provided.

Cotton Belt	James Forten	Massachusetts
the Midwest	James Monroe	New England
Peter Poyas	Virginia	David Walker
Eli Whitney		

26. ______________________ was the site of the most of the factories built in the United States in the early 1800s.

27. ______________________ played an important role in negotiating the establishment of Liberia.

28. The contributions of ______________________ helped start *The Liberator,* the newspaper run by William Lloyd Garrison.

29. The ______________________ included the states that stretched west from Georgia to Texas.

30. An invention by ______________________ helped make cotton the South's major cash crop.

31. In ______________________ African Americans were permitted to serve on juries.

32. Nat Turner's rebellion took place in ______________________.

33. In his 1829 booklet, ______________________ urged African Americans to rebel against slavery.

34. Denmark Vesey was aided in his plan to attack Charleston by ______________________.

35. Family-run farms in ______________________, which raised cash crops like corn and wheat, were aided by improvements in transportation.

V. **ESSAY Choose one of the following topics. Then write your answer in paragraph form on a separate piece of paper.**

A. How do you think Paul Cuffe would have responded to David Walker's *Appeal*? Explain your opinion.

B. Of the people discussed in this unit, which made the most important contribution toward bringing about the end of slavery? Explain your choice.

Name ______________________________ Date ______________

CHAPTER 10 TEST: The Tyranny of Slavery

I. MATCHING Decide which definition from the right column best explains a term in the left column. Then write the letter of the definition in the space next to the term.

______	**1.** dialect		**a.** person who assisted a plantation overseer
______	**2.** spiritual		**b.** device that separated seeds from cotton fibers
______	**3.** immigrant		**c.** religious song
______	**4.** slave driver		**d.** form of a language
______	**5.** cotton gin		**e.** person who moves into a new country to settle

II. MULTIPLE CHOICE Choose the answer that best completes the sentence or answers the question. Then write the letter of your choice in the space to the left.

______ **6.** By 1860, approximately what percentage of African American slaves worked in cotton fields? **a.** 15 **b.** 40 **c.** 75 **d.** 90

______ **7.** On a typical cotton plantation, enslaved Africans worked: **a.** an eight-hour day. **b.** from sunrise to sunset. **c.** only during morning hours. **d.** half the time for the owner and half the time for themselves.

______ **8.** Cotton became the main crop of the South following the 1793 invention of the: **a.** cotton baler. **b.** cotton picker. **c.** cotton reaper. **d.** cotton gin.

______ **9.** In the United States, the worst conditions for African Americans were found in the: **a.** tobacco fields of Virginia. **b.** small farms of Appalachia. **c.** rice paddies of the Carolinas. **d.** cotton fields of the Deep South.

______ **10.** The free African American who stirred up antislavery feeling by writing a book about being kidnapped and sold as a slave was: **a.** Uncle Silas. **b.** Solomon Northup. **c.** Henry Brown. **d.** Harriet Jacobs.

______ **11.** The Atlantic slave trade to the United States officially ended in: **a.** 1796. **b.** 1808. **c.** 1820. **d.** 1833.

______ **12.** Enslaved Africans saw similarities between their situation and the Bible's account of the: **a.** Ghanaians in Mali. **b.** Israelites in Egypt. **c.** early Christians in Rome. **d.** Romans in Israel.

______ **13.** Which of the following pairs of words is African in origin? **a.** canoe, moccasin **b.** chili, screen **c.** succotash, lamp **d.** tote, okra

______ **14.** The strongest defense against the cruelties of slavery available to Africans in the United States was the: **a.** family. **b.** courts. **c.** Constitution. **d.** free market.

______ **15.** One result of the invention of the cotton gin was the: **a.** growing popularity of Christianity among African Americans. **b.** end of slavery in New England. **c.** drop in the price of slaves. **d.** increased breakup of African American families.

III. ESSAY Choose one of the following topics. Then write your answer in paragraph form on a separate sheet of paper.

A. How might folktales like the Brer Rabbit stories have helped enslaved Africans survive the cruelties of slavery?

B. Explain why enslaved Africans might have chosen to call one another "aunt," "uncle," "brother," or "sister," even when they had no actual family relationship.

Name ________________________________ Date______________

CHAPTER 11 TEST: Armed Resistance to Slavery

I. MATCHING Decide which description from the right column best identifies a person in the left column. Then write the letter of the description in the space provided.

_____ **1.** Charles Deslondes
_____ **2.** Jemmy
_____ **3.** Gabriel Prosser
_____ **4.** Nat Turner
_____ **5.** Denmark Vesey
_____ **6.** David Walker

a. leader of an unsuccessful attack on New Orleans in 1811
b. African American from Virginia known as the Prophet
c. publisher of an 1829 booklet urging African Americans to rebel against slavery
d. leader of a 1739 uprising in which an arsenal was looted and plantations were burned
e. freed African American who organized a plan to take over Charleston, South Carolina
f. planner of attack on Richmond, Virginia in 1800 which failed when two African Americans informed white authorities

II. MULTIPLE CHOICE Choose the answer that best completes the sentence or answers the question. Then write the letter of your choice in the space provided.

_____ **7.** After a rebellion of enslaved Africans was put down, colonial officials usually passed: **a.** laws limiting the import of enslaved Africans. **b.** laws abolishing slavery. **c.** new taxes on slave owners. **d.** tough slave codes.

_____ **8.** Some Africans resisted slavery by becoming fugitives or: **a.** overseers. **b.** runaways. **c.** immigrants. **d.** soldiers.

_____ **9.** Slave codes were meant to limit the: **a.** import of enslaved Africans. **b.** personal movements of slaves. **c.** prices paid for slaves. **d.** cruel practices of slave owners.

_____ **10.** Which of the following tried to weaken Great Britain by encouraging enslaved Africans to escape from South Carolina and Georgia? **a.** the Spanish **b.** the Dutch **c.** the French **d.** the Mexicans

_____ **11.** One of Gabriel Prosser's goals was to create: **a.** an African American house in Congress. **b.** a new system of agriculture in the South. **c.** a free trade agreement with Haiti. **d.** an African American state in Virginia.

_____ **12.** The bloodiest uprising of enslaved Africans was the: **a.** Stono uprising. **b.** Prosser conspiracy. **c.** Nat Turner rebellion. **d.** Vesey conspiracy.

_____ **13.** Several revolts of enslaved Africans were inspired by reports of the successful uprising of other Africans enslaved in: **a.** Haiti. **b.** Canada. **c.** Florida. **d.** Bermuda.

_____ **14.** Revolts shocked white people who believed: **a.** slavery was dying out. **b.** African Americans were satisfied with their lives. **c.** new laws would soon abolish slavery. **d.** Christian African Americans would not take up arms against other Christians.

_____ **15.** One of the earliest slave revolts in the colonies took place in 1658 in: **a.** Philadelphia, Pennsylvania. **b.** Richmond, Virginia. **c.** Baltimore, Maryland. **d.** Hartford, Connecticut.

III. ESSAY Choose one of the following topics. Then write your answer in paragraph form on a separate sheet of paper.

A. Do you think that any of the uprisings of enslaved Africans discussed in this chapter might have succeeded? Explain your answer.

B. Explain the following statement by a historian: "The slaves of the Old South should not have to answer for their failure to mount more frequent and effective revolts; they should be honored for having tried at all under the most discouraging circumstances."

Name ______________________________ Date______________

CHAPTER 12 TEST: Free African Americans in the North and South

I. MATCHING Decide which description in the right column best identifies a person in the left column. Then write the letter of the description in the space provided.

_____ **1.** Paul Cuffe

_____ **2.** Prudence Crandall

_____ **3.** James Forten

_____ **4.** Pierre Chastang

_____ **5.** Nancy Gardiner Prince

a. entrepreneur who built a sail-making factory

b. African American who opened a dressmaking business in Russia

c. Quaker principal who accepted African American students in a Connecticut boarding school

d. entrepreneur who built a fishing fleet and transported numbers of African Americans to Africa

e. African American freed in Mobile, Alabama, for service during the War of 1812 and an 1819 epidemic

II. MULTIPLE CHOICE Choose the answer that best completes the sentence or answers the question. Then write the letter of your choice in the space provided.

_____ **6.** The term describing a person who worked to end slavery is: **a.** abolitionist. **b.** colonizationist. **c.** factor. **d.** entrepreneur.

_____ **7.** The term describing a person who risks money to earn a profit is: **a.** abolitionist. **b.** colonizationist. **c.** factor. **d.** entrepreneur.

_____ **8.** The unjust treatment of a person or persons based on a characteristic such as religion or skin color is: **a.** servitude. **b.** abolition. **c.** migration. **d.** discrimination.

_____ **9.** By 1860, approximately what percentage of African Americans were free? **a.** 6 **b.** 11 **c.** 22 **d.** 34

_____ **10.** In 1860, the state with the largest population of free African Americans was: **a.** Rhode Island. **b.** Pennsylvania. **c.** Maryland. **d.** Georgia.

_____ **11.** The colony founded in Africa for African Americans was: **a.** Chad. **b.** Liberia. **c.** Mali. **d.** Nigeria.

_____ **12.** To provide help to families in case of sickness or death, free African Americans in the Northeast founded: **a.** resettlement groups. **b.** mutual-aid societies. **c.** craft unions. **d.** colonization clubs.

_____ **13.** Beginning in the 1830s, free African American laborers and servants had a more difficult time earning a living because of: **a.** increased competition from immigrants. **b.** new taxes on freed African Americans. **c.** personal liberty laws. **d.** new Constitutional amendments.

_____ **14.** In 1840, only Maine, Massachusetts, New Hampshire, and Vermont had laws that: **a.** barred African Americans from voting. **b.** required African Americans to own $250 worth of property to vote. **c.** forced African Americans to pass special tests before voting. **d.** granted equal voting rights to African American men.

_____ **15.** Which of the following statements *best* describes conditions for free African Americans in the South in the early 1800s? **a.** In general, they were not as well off as free African Americans in the North. **b.** In general, they were no worse off than free African Americans in the North. **c.** They enjoyed greater freedoms than African Americans in the North. **d.** They experienced little or no discrimination.

III. ESSAY Choose one of the following topics. Then write your answer in paragraph form on a separate sheet of paper.

A. If you had been a free African American in the 1830s, would you have preferred to live in the North or the South? Explain your answer.

B. Why did white Southerners play the most active parts in the founding of the American Colonization Society?

Name ______________________________ Date ______________

UNIT 5 TEST: Challenges to Slavery

I. MATCHING Decide which definition from the right column best fits a term in the left column. Then write the letter of the definition in the space provided.

_____ **1.** militant
_____ **2.** Underground Railroad
_____ **3.** denomination
_____ **4.** congregation
_____ **5.** public opinion

a. religious group
b. collective beliefs of the people
c. system for aiding escaped slaves
d. aggressively active
e. local group that meets for worship

II. UNDERSTANDING TIME For each pair of events below, decide which event took place first. Then write its letter in the space provided.

_____ **6. a.** passage of Northwest Ordinance **b.** end of the Atlantic slave trade
_____ **7. a.** founding of American Anti-Slavery Society **b.** founding of American Colonization Society
_____ **8. a.** first publication of *The Liberator* **b.** burning of abolitionist homes in New York City
_____ **9. a.** formal organization of the African Methodist Episcopal church **b.** founding of Mother Bethel Church
_____ **10. a.** first women's rights convention **b.** founding of the Female Anti-Slavery Society
_____ **11. a.** publication of *Uncle Tom's Cabin* **b.** passage of the Fugitive Slave Act of 1850
_____ **12. a.** murder of Elijah P. Lovejoy **b.** publication of Walker's *Appeal*
_____ **13. a.** Harriet Tubman acting as a conductor on Underground Railroad **b.** Quakers begin to shelter escaped slaves

III. MULTIPLE CHOICE Choose the answer that best completes the sentence or answers the question. Then write the letter of your choice in the space provided.

_____ **14.** A major strategy that abolitionists used in their struggle against slavery was:
a. taxing it out of existence. **b.** annexation. **c.** publicizing its evils. **d.** annulment.

_____ **15.** In their early years, leading abolitionist organizations excluded from their membership which of the following?
a. Southerners **b.** free African Americans **c.** immigrants **d.** women

_____ **16.** Those who wanted to do away with slavery in a slow, orderly way were known as:
a. radicals. **b.** liberators. **c.** temporizers. **d.** gradualists.

_____ **17.** One outgrowth of the abolitionist movement was the development of:
a. the women's rights movement. **b.** the temperance movement. **c.** free public high schools. **d.** asylums for the mentally ill.

_____ **18.** One of the factors that spurred abolitionists to greater action in the 1830s was the:
a. passage of a new fugitive slave bill. **b.** growth of slavery in the Cotton Belt. **c.** overturning of the Northwest Ordinance. **d.** publication of *Uncle Tom's Cabin.*

_____ **19.** Which of the following was *not* one of the methods used by abolitionists?
a. newspapers **b.** public lectures **c.** poll taxes **d.** committees to aid runaway slaves

_____ **20.** In 1793, Southern slave owners convinced Congress to pass the first:
a. federal fugitive slave law. **b.** tax on abolitionist organizations. **c.** law exiling runaway slaves. **d.** federal fund to repay owners of escaped slaves.

_____ **21.** Which of the following organizations would have been *most* useful to a slave fleeing a Mississippi plantation?
a. American Colonization Society **b.** American Anti-Slavery Society **c.** Underground Railroad **d.** Liberty party

_____ **22.** The independent African American church movement grew because of:
a. a split in the abolition movement. **b.** discrimination by white churches. **c.** disagreement over the temperance movement. **d.** the desire to end colonization.

_____ **23.** African American churches often became highly active in the:
a. temperance movement. **b.** movement for free public high schools. **c.** abolition movement. **d.** prison reform movement.

IV. COMPLETING THE IDEA Choose the item from the list that best completes each of the following sentences. Then write it in the space provided.

Dorothea Dix	Free-Soil party	Richard Allen
Seneca Falls Declaration	Frederick Douglass	William Lloyd Garrison
Declaration of Sentiments	Horace Mann	Harriet Beecher Stowe
New York Vigilance Committee	American Colonization Society	American Society for the Promotion of Temperance

24. In Massachusetts, _______________ introduced reforms in education that soon spread to other states.

25. The _______________ was a statement of rights that women did not have but were entitled to.

26. A novel by _______________ was responsible for turning large numbers of Americans against slavery.

27. The _______________ played a major role in the establishment of Liberia.

28. A protest by Absalom Jones and _______________ started the independent African American church movement.

29. Thanks to the efforts of _______________, the treatment of the mentally ill improved in the United States.

30. The _______________ was a statement calling for liberation of more than 2 million African Americans living in slavery.

31. Former slave ________________________ became a leading abolitionist and founded the antislavery newspaper *North Star.*

32. The fiery abolitionist editor ________________________ demanded an immediate end to slavery in his newspaper, *The Liberator.*

33. The ________________________ was part of one of the earliest attempts to reform U.S. society.

34. Under David Ruggles, the ________________________ worked to aid runaway slaves.

35. The ________________________ aimed at preventing the spread of slavery to new territories rather than abolishing it entirely.

V. ESSAY Choose one of the following topics. Then write your answer in paragraph form on a separate sheet of paper.

A. Decide which of the following most effectively advanced the cause of freedom for African Americans: Richard Allen, Harriet Tubman, Frederick Douglass. Explain your choice.

B. "African Americans could have made churches more powerful agents in the struggle to end slavery if they had chosen to remain members of and work within white churches." Explain why you agree or disagree with this statement.

Name ______________________________ Date ______________

CHAPTER 13 TEST: Abolitionists

I. MATCHING Decide which description from the right column best identifies a person in the left column. Then write the letter of the description in the space provided.

_____ 1. Frances Ellen Watkins

_____ 2. Henry Highland Garnet

_____ 3. Elijah Lovejoy

_____ 4. Sojourner Truth

_____ 5. William Wells Brown

_____ 6. John Mercer Langston

a. antislavery newspaper publisher killed by Alton, Illinois, mob in 1832

b. abolitionist orator who became women's rights champion after the Civil War

c. author of antislavery pamphlets and histories of African Americans

d. born free in Maryland, became one of the most popular African American poets

e. abolitionist lawyer who argued African Americans should be given voting rights

f. pastor of Presbyterian church in New York later appointed U. S. minister to Liberia

II. MULTIPLE CHOICE Choose the answer that best completes the sentence or answers the question. Then write the letter of your choice in the space provided.

_____ 7. Some early abolitionists feared they would lose public support if their approach was too aggressively active, or: **a.** sedate. **b.** equivocal. **c.** militant. **d.** liberated.

_____ 8. A major abolitionist organization founded in 1833 was the: **a.** Free-Soil party. **b.** American Anti-Slavery Society. **c.** American Colonization Society. **d.** American Society for the Promotion of Temperance.

_____ 9. Sarah Douglass and the daughters of James Forten were among the founders of the: **a.** Liberty party. **b.** American Colonization Society. **c.** Female Anti-Slavery Society of Philadelphia. **d.** Free-Soil party.

_____ 10. The first religious group in the 13 colonies to oppose slavery was the: **a.** Mormons. **b.** Quakers. **c.** Presbyterians. **d.** Baptists.

_____ 11. In 1834, mobs burned the homes of 20 abolitionists in: **a.** Baltimore. **b.** Philadelphia. **c.** Boston. **d.** New York City.

_____ 12. William Lloyd Garrison believed that the American Anti-Slavery Society should become more: **a.** conservative. **b.** radical. **c.** discriminating. **d.** tolerant.

_____ 13. The antislavery newspaper published by Frederick Douglass was the: **a.** *North Star.* **b.** *Liberator.* **c.** *Defender.* **d.** *Truth.*

_____ 14. By the mid-1800s, how many African American communities had antislavery newspapers? **a.** 3 **b.** 8 **c.** 17 **d.** 35

_____ 15. One step that African American mutual-aid societies took in the antislavery struggle was the formation of: **a.** colonies. **b.** legal-aid societies. **c.** conventions. **d.** asylums.

III. ESSAY Choose one of the following topics. Then write your answer in paragraph form on a separate sheet of paper.

A. Why do you think abolitionists often drew hostile responses in the North, where the states had ended slavery?

B. Do you believe Garrison's call for more radical action helped or hurt the antislavery cause? Explain.

Name ______________________________ Date ______________

CHAPTER 14 TEST: Escaping from Slavery

I. MATCHING Decide which description in the right column best identifies a person in the left column. Write the letter of the description in the space provided.

_____ **1.** Levi Coffin

_____ **2.** Mary Ann Shadd

_____ **3.** David Ruggles

_____ **4.** Harriet Tubman

_____ **5.** Henry Brown

_____ **6.** Ellen Craft

_____ **7.** William Still

a. arranged to be shipped to freedom in a box

b. African American woman who posed as a white male planter while escaping from slavery

c. head of the New York Vigilance Committee

d. "president" of the Underground Railroad

e. founder of the *Provincial Freeman*

f. led more than 300 slaves to freedom in 19 trips on the Underground Railroad

g. one of the Quaker founders of the Underground Railroad

II. MULTIPLE CHOICE Choose the answer that best completes the sentence or answers the question. Then write the letter of your choice in the space provided.

_____ **8.** From 1830 to 1860, approximately how many African American slaves took the Underground Railroad to freedom each year? **a.** 1,200 **b.** 2,500 **c.** 5,500 **d.** 11,000

_____ **9.** On the Underground Railroad, the homes that provided escaped slaves with food and shelter were known as: **a.** depots. **b.** stations. **c.** switching yards. **d.** terminals.

_____ **10.** The African American and white abolitionists who helped guide escaped slaves to freedom on the Underground Railroad were known as: **a.** engineers. **b.** porters. **c.** redcaps. **d.** conductors.

_____ **11.** To guide themselves to the North, escaped slaves searched the night sky for the "Drinking Gourd," or the: **a.** full moon. **b.** Little Dipper. **c.** Milky Way. **d.** Big Dipper.

_____ **12.** After passage of the Fugitive Slave Law of 1850, more than 15,000 African Americans relocated to: **a.** Canada. **b.** Mexico. **c.** Haiti. **d.** Jamaica.

_____ **13.** Among the first people in the North to help shelter escaped African American slaves were the: **a.** Congregationalists. **b.** Methodists. **c.** Episcopalians. **d.** Quakers.

_____ **14.** To tell slaves about the Underground Railroad, antislavery societies: **a.** held lectures in Southern churches. **b.** took ads in Southern newspapers. **c.** hung posters in local stores. **d.** sent agents into the South.

_____ **15.** White abolitionists who helped escaped African American slaves in the South faced the danger of: **a.** prison. **b.** lawsuits by slave owners. **c.** expulsion to the North. **d.** execution.

III. ESSAY Choose one of the following topics. Then write your answer in paragraph form on a separate sheet of paper.

A. Suppose you were a fugitive African American slave. Would you have chosen to settle in a Northern state and fight slavery, or would you move to Canada, where you might have greater freedom? Explain.

B. If you had worked for the Underground Railroad, what arguments would you have used to persuade a couple to let their home be used as a shelter for escaped slaves?

Name ______________________________ Date ______________

CHAPTER 15 TEST: African American Churches

I. MATCHING Decide which description in the right column best identifies a person in the left column. Then write the letter of the description in the space provided.

_____ **1.** William Whipper

_____ **2.** Samuel Ringgold Ward

_____ **3.** Frederick Douglass

_____ **4.** Richard Allen

_____ **5.** Thomas James

_____ **6.** Thomas Paul

_____ **7.** Absalom Jones

a. African American former slave who founded African Methodist Episcopal Zion churches in New York State

b. founder of St. Thomas Free African Church

c. opened a free-labor grocery in Philadelphia

d. opposed the organization of separate African American churches

e. founded Mother Bethel Church

f. organized African American Baptist churches in New York City and Boston

g. African American minister and abolitionist who fled the country after passage of the Fugitive Slave Act of 1850

II. MULTIPLE CHOICE Choose the answer that best completes the sentence or answers the question. Then write the letter of your choice in the space provided.

_____ **8.** Another name for a religious group is: **a.** factor. **b.** denomination. **c.** tenet. **d.** valuation.

_____ **9.** In the 1800s, some African Americans protested separate church services by forming their own groups for worship, or: **a.** conventions. **b.** delegations. **c.** congregations. **d.** invocations.

_____ **10.** The first independent African American church in the United States was: **a.** St. George Methodist. **b.** St. James African Methodist Episcopal Zion. **c.** Mother Bethel African Methodist Episcopal. **d.** St. Thomas Free African.

_____ **11.** The first African American denomination in the United States was formally organized in: **a.** 1776. **b.** 1790. **c.** 1816. **d.** 1821.

_____ **12.** Most African American abolitionists believed that independent African American churches: **a.** were not important to the antislavery struggle. **b.** gave them greater freedom to organize antislavery protests. **c.** could not succeed. **d.** harmed the antislavery struggle.

_____ **13.** Southern opposition to independent African American churches strengthened because of: **a.** fear of slave rebellions. **b.** loss of income for white churches. **c.** loss of Sunday School members. **d.** the arrival of new immigrants.

_____ **14.** African American churches in Pennsylvania and New York led drives to boycott products made: **a.** by immigrant labor. **b.** in the South. **c.** by whites. **d.** by slave labor.

_____ **15.** African American churches received their funds from: **a.** white churches. **b.** their members. **c.** city taxes. **d.** the federal government.

III. ESSAY Choose one of the following topics. Then write your answer in paragraph form on a separate sheet of paper.

A. If you had been a member of an independent African American church in the years before the Civil War, what antislavery activities would you have recommended your church support?

B. Why did white Southerners oppose or attempt to limit independent African American churches?

Name ______________________________ Date ______________

UNIT 6 TEST: Hope for a New Way of Life

I. MATCHING Decide which definition from the right column best explains a term in the left column. Then write the letter of the definition in the space next to the term.

_____ **1.** popular sovereignty
_____ **2.** Black Codes
_____ **3.** lynch
_____ **4.** Reconstruction
_____ **5.** secede

a. withdraw from an organization
b. rebuilding of the Union
c. idea that people of a territory should decide whether they want slavery
d. murder by mob action
e. limits on the rights of African Americans

II. UNDERSTANDING TIME Read the following list of events. Then number the events from 1 to 10 in the order in which they happened.

_____ Civil War ends.
_____ Kansas – Nebraska Act is passed.
_____ Reconstruction begins.
_____ Mexican War begins.
_____ Lincoln is elected President.
_____ California becomes a state.
_____ Southern states secede.
_____ Reconstruction ends.
_____ Missouri Compromise is reached.
_____ Emancipation Proclamation is signed.

III. MULTIPLE CHOICE Choose the answer that best completes the sentence. Then write the letter of your choice in the space provided.

_____ **6.** As a result of the Missouri Compromise, the number of slave states in the Union: **a.** was greater than the number of free states. **b.** was less than the number of free states. **c.** remained equal to the number of free states. **d.** could never be greater than the number of free states.

_____ **7.** As part of the Compromise of 1850, Congress passed the: **a.** Black Codes. **b.** Fugitive Slave Act. **c.** 13th Amendment. **d.** Kansas – Nebraska Act.

_____ **8.** One effect of the Kansas – Nebraska Act was the: **a.** acquisition of Louisiana. **b.** formation of the Freedmen's Bureau. **c.** secession of South Carolina. **d.** formation of a new political party.

_____ **9.** In 1860, the Republicans chose as their candidate for President: **a.** Ulysses S. Grant. **b.** Abraham Lincoln. **c.** Jefferson Davis. **d.** Andrew Johnson.

_____ **10.** The Civil War began when Confederate forces fired on: **a.** Washington, D.C. **b.** Montgomery, Alabama. **c.** Fort Sumter. **d.** Appomattox.

_____ **11.** When the Civil War began, the North had a population of 22 million, while the South had a population of:
a. 9 million. **b.** 13 million. **c.** 17 million. **d.** 23 million.

_____ **12.** Lincoln believed that the North would gain a strong moral reason for fighting the war from the:
a. Freedmen's Bureau. **b.** Radical Republicans. **c.** Black Codes. **d.** Emancipation Proclamation.

_____ **13.** Most African American units in the Union army were commanded by:
a. African American officers elected by the soldiers. **b.** African American officers assigned by the army. **c.** a combination of African American and white officers. **d.** white officers.

_____ **14.** Radical Republicans attacked Johnson's plan for rebuilding the Union as:
a. too generous. **b.** too harsh. **c.** too costly. **d.** incomplete.

_____ **15.** Equal protection of the laws was guaranteed to all citizens by the:
a. 13th Amendment. **b.** 14th Amendment. **c.** 15th Amendment. **d.** Civil Rights Act.

_____ **16.** States could not deny African Americans the right to vote under the:
a. 13th Amendment. **b.** 14th Amendment. **c.** 15th Amendment. **d.** Black Codes.

_____ **17.** Slavery was forbidden by the:
a. 13th Amendment. **b.** 14th Amendment. **c.** 15th Amendment. **d.** Civil Rights Act.

_____ **18.** After 1867, the South was divided into:
a. ten states. **b.** six territories. **c.** five military districts. **d.** four reservations.

_____ **19.** One of the factors that contributed to the end of Reconstruction was:
a. the nation's economic problems. **b.** war with Mexico. **c.** the discovery of gold in Colorado. **d.** the re-election of Andrew Johnson.

_____ **20.** Efforts to drive Native Americans from western lands were undertaken by the:
a. U.S. Army. **b.** Radical Republicans. **c.** Freedmen's Bureau. **d.** Bureau of Indian Affairs.

IV. COMPLETING THE IDEA Choose the item from the list that best completes each of the following sentences. Then write it in the space provided.

Compromise of 1850	Confederate States of America
Dred Scott	Emancipation Proclamation
Freedmen's Bureau	Kansas – Nebraska Act
Ku Klux Klan	Mexican War
Missouri Compromise	Radical Republicans

21. California was admitted to the Union as part of the _________________________.

22. The _________________________ had a harsh plan for rebuilding the nation after the Civil War.

23. The Missouri Compromise was repealed by the _________________________.

24. In the _________________________ decision, the Supreme Court ruled that Congress could not prohibit slavery in the territories.

25. Maine was admitted to the Union as part of the ________________________.

26. By signing the ________________________, Lincoln declared free all African Americans in those parts of the South that were still in rebellion.

27. The ________________________ aimed at terrorizing African Americans and preventing them from voting.

28. The United States acquired California, Nevada, Utah, and most of New Mexico, Arizona, and Colorado as a result of the ________________________.

29. In 1861, delegates at Montgomery, Alabama, formed the ________________________.

30. The ________________________ helped provide African Americans with food, medicine, books, and schools.

V. ESSAY Choose one of the following topics. Then write your answer in paragraph form on a separate piece of paper.

A. Did the division of the United States into slave and free states make a civil war inevitable? Explain your answer.

B. Compare the lives of African Americans on the Great Plains with the lives of African Americans in the South in the years after the Civil War. What different kinds of hardship did each face? How were their lives alike?

Name ______________________________ Date ______________

CHAPTER 16 TEST: The Road to the Civil War

I. MATCHING Decide which description in the right column best identifies a person in the left column. Then write the letter of the description in the space provided.

_____ **1.** Anthony Burns

_____ **2.** Roger Taney

_____ **3.** John Brown

_____ **4.** Martin Robinson Delaney

_____ **5.** Dred Scott

a. African American who became the subject of an important Supreme Court case

b. Chief Justice of the Supreme Court

c. African American runaway slave whose arrest set off protest demonstrations in Boston

d. abolitionist who tried to start a slave uprising

e. African American physician and abolitionist

II. MULTIPLE CHOICE Choose the answer that best completes the sentence or answers the question. Then write the letter of your choice in the space provided.

_____ **6.** Stiff penalties for people who refused to help slave catchers were called for by the: **a.** Constitution. **b.** Fugitive Slave Act. **c.** Supreme Court. **d.** Republican party.

_____ **7.** In the 1850s, many free African Americans increasingly sought safety in: **a.** Bermuda. **b.** Jamaica. **c.** Haiti. **d.** Canada.

_____ **8.** After the arrest of a fugitive slave in Boston in 1854, the federal government: **a.** used soldiers and a navy ship to ensure his return to slavery. **b.** ordered his release. **c.** appealed his case to the Supreme Court. **d.** refused to become involved in the case.

_____ **9.** Some Northern states tried to aid escaped slaves by passing: **a.** fugitive slave laws. **b.** personal liberty laws. **c.** *ex post facto* laws. **d.** Black Codes.

_____ **10.** Dred Scott claimed his freedom on the grounds that he: **a.** had purchased it. **b.** had lived in free territory. **c.** was born free. **d.** had served in the army.

_____ **11.** The idea that African Americans could not be citizens was part of the: **a.** Fugitive Slave Act. **b.** Constitution. **c.** Missouri Compromise. **d.** Dred Scott decision.

_____ **12.** In 1857, the Supreme Court ruled which of the following to be unconstitutional? **a.** the Missouri Compromise **b.** the Fugitive Slave Act **c.** the Compromise of 1850 **d.** the Northwest Ordinance

_____ **13.** One effect of the Dred Scott decision was to: **a.** bar slavery west of the Mississippi. **b.** overturn the Fugitive Slave Act. **c.** permit slavery in Northern states. **d.** open all federal territories to slavery.

_____ **14.** John Brown believed that slavery would be abolished by: **a.** a revolt by African Americans. **b.** court action. **c.** new federal laws. **d.** massive public protests.

_____ **15.** John Brown met with African American former slaves in Canada in order to: **a.** petition Congress to end slavery. **b.** aid the Underground Railroad. **c.** defy the Fugitive Slave Act. **d.** draw up a constitution for a nation of Freed African Americans.

III. ESSAY Choose one of the following topics. Then write your answer in paragraph form on a separate sheet of paper.

A. Which of the three issues decided by the Supreme Court in the Dred Scott case do you think was most important to African Americans at the time? Explain.

B. Do you believe John Brown's raid aided or harmed the antislavery cause? Explain.

Name ______________________________ Date ______________

CHAPTER 17 TEST: The Civil War and the End of Slavery

I. MATCHING Decide which definition in the right column best explains each term in the left column. Then write the letter of the definition in the space next to the term.

_____ **1.** border states
_____ **2.** contrabands
_____ **3.** discrimination
_____ **4.** emancipation

a. liberation of slaves in accordance with Lincoln's plan
b. unjust treatment experienced by African American soldiers
c. one Union army source of information about Confederate troop movements
d. group whose power slowed Lincoln in movement toward freeing African American slaves

II. MULTIPLE CHOICE Choose the answer that best completes the sentence or answers the question. Then write the letter of your choice in the space provided.

_____ **5.** Because of a severe labor shortage by 1862, Southern fortifications were often built by: **a.** women. **b.** children. **c.** slaves. **d.** immigrants.

_____ **6.** Lincoln's main goal in fighting the Civil War was to: **a.** destroy slavery. **b.** save the border states. **c.** save the Union. **d.** remove the threat of abolition.

_____ **7.** Lincoln believed that African Americans and whites: **a.** should work out a plan to end slavery. **b.** could not live together peacefully in the United States. **c.** were complete equals. **d.** could not legally protest emancipation.

_____ **8.** By freeing the slaves, Lincoln hoped to: **a.** weaken Southern war efforts. **b.** win support from border states. **c.** force Great Britain to enter the war. **d.** end the problem of contrabands.

_____ **9.** Lincoln announced the Emancipation Proclamation after the Union victory at Antietam because: **a.** he had not thought of it earlier. **b.** many African Americans had been killed in the battle. **c.** the battle had been fought in a border state. **d.** he did not want the Proclamation to be seen as a sign of weakness.

_____ **10.** The Emancipation Proclamation freed all enslaved African Americans in the: **a.** North and South. **b.** border states. **c.** areas held by Union troops. **d.** areas held by Confederate armies.

_____ **11.** Demanding wages for work, giving information to Union troops, and destroying owners' property were different forms of African American: **a.** impressment. **b.** resistance. **c.** emancipation. **d.** discrimination.

_____ **12.** In 1865, the Confederate government decided that African American slaves could: **a.** buy their freedom. **b.** become citizens. **c.** own land. **d.** serve in the army.

_____ **13.** The Union changed its policy about enlisting African Americans because of: **a.** early Union defeats on the battlefield. **b.** a Supreme Court decision. **c.** pressure from white troops. **d.** petitions from African Americans.

_____ **14.** Before 1864, African American soldiers in the Union army: **a.** did not wear the same uniform as white soldiers. **b.** served in mixed units with white soldiers. **c.** were not permitted in border states. **d.** were paid less than white soldiers.

_____ **15.** African Americans made up approximately what percentage of the Union's armed forces during the Civil War? **a.** 1 **b.** 10 **c.** 20 **d.** 30

III. ESSAY Choose one of the following topics. Then write your answer in paragraph form on a separate sheet of paper.

A. Do you think the Emancipation Proclamation helped or hindered the Union cause during the Civil War? Give reasons for your answer.

B. If you had been an African American at the time of the Civil War, would you have been willing to fight in the Union army? Give reasons for your position.

Name ______________________________ Date ______________

CHAPTER 18 TEST: The Promise and Failure of Reconstruction

I. MATCHING Decide which definition in the right column best explains each term in the left column. Then write the letter of the definition in the space next to the term.

_____	**1.** Reconstruction	**a.**	purchase of equipment and supplies by delayed payment
_____	**2.** surname	**b.**	organization aimed at limiting African Americans' freedoms
_____	**3.** Freedmen's Bureau	**c.**	family name
_____	**4.** credit	**d.**	organization that set up 4,500 schools
_____	**5.** Ku Klux Klan	**e.**	system of farm labor
_____	**6.** sharecropping	**f.**	time when former Confederate states again became part of the Union

II. MULTIPLE CHOICE Choose the answer that best completes the sentence or answers the question. Then write the letter of your choice in the space provided.

_____ **7.** During Reconstruction, an aim of many African Americans was to: **a.** end marriages that had been forced by slave owners. **b.** become active members of white churches. **c.** elect Democratic governments in Southern states. **d.** reunite families separated under slavery.

_____ **8.** At the end of the Civil War, newly freed African Americans hoped for federal action to enable them to: **a.** become independent farmers. **b.** attend college. **c.** emigrate to Africa. **d.** emigrate to Canada.

_____ **9.** Which of the following phrases *best* describes sharecropping? **a.** "40 acres and a mule" **b.** "the richest man in the world" **c.** "popular sovereignty" **d.** "a cycle of poverty and debt"

_____ **10.** The first African American to serve in the U.S. Senate was: **a.** John Solomon Lewis. **b.** Hiram Revels. **c.** P. B. S. Pinchback. **d.** Blanche K. Bruce.

_____ **11.** Approximately how many African Americans served in Southern state legislatures from 1865 to 1877? **a.** 50 **b.** 150 **c.** 300 **d.** 600

_____ **12.** The first African American governor in U.S. history was: **a.** John Solomon Lewis. **b.** Hiram Revels. **c.** P. B. S. Pinchback. **d.** Blanche K. Bruce.

_____ **13.** The major aim of white secret societies that grew up after the Civil War was: **a.** raising funds for the colonization of African Americans in Africa. **b.** repeal of the 14th Amendment. **c.** ensuring the election of Republican governments. **d.** the destruction of Reconstruction governments.

_____ **14.** The end of Reconstruction came in 1877 with: **a.** the resignation of P. B. S. Pinchback. **b.** the removal of the last U.S. troops from the South. **c.** ratification of the 15th Amendment. **d.** the dissolving of the Freedmen's Bureau.

_____ **15.** After Reconstruction, political power in the South was held by: **a.** white Democrats. **b.** African American Democrats. **c.** white Republicans. **d.** African American Republicans.

III. ESSAY Choose one of the following topics. Then write your answer in paragraph form on a separate sheet of paper.

A. Which of the changes that took place during Reconstruction do you think was the most important for African Americans? Explain.

B. The period of Reconstruction has been called the "tragic era." Use evidence from your reading to explain why this title is or is not appropriate.

Name ______________________________ Date ______________

CHAPTER 19 TEST: Miners, Farmers, and Cowhands

I. COMPLETING THE IDEA Choose the name from the list that best completes each of the following sentences. Then write it in the space provided.

Clara Brown Nat Love Henry Adams William Leidesdorff Benjamin Singleton

1. ______________________ believed in a God-given mission to lead African Americans from the South to Kansas.

2. A former slave who saved and invested money earned by washing miners' clothing, ______________________ became one of Colorado's richest citizens.

3. One of the organizers of the Committee of 500 was ______________________.

4. ______________________ was a ship captain who became a merchant and one of San Francisco's civic leaders.

5. Also known as Deadwood Dick, ______________________ was perhaps the most famous African American cowhand.

II. MULTIPLE CHOICE Choose the answer that best completes the sentence or answers the question. Then write the letter of your choice in the space provided.

_____ **6.** In 1857, news of the discovery of gold set off a rush of people to: **a.** Colorado. **b.** Kansas. **c.** California. **d.** Oklahoma.

_____ **7.** Most African Americans in California made their living as: **a.** gold miners. **b.** sharecroppers. **c.** Mountain Men. **d.** merchants, barbers, and craftspeople.

_____ **8.** African Americans who fled the South for Kansas and other western areas in 1879 and 1880 were known as: **a.** Seventy-niners. **b.** Exodusters. **c.** Fugitives. **d.** Committees.

_____ **9.** Henry Adams and Benjamin Singleton believed that the best economic opportunities for African Americans would come from setting up: **a.** African American colleges. **b.** African American trade schools. **c.** secret societies. **d.** separate African American communities.

_____ **10.** The Committee of 500 was founded for the purpose of: **a.** reporting on conditions among newly freed African Americans. **b.** defending African Americans from attacks by the Ku Klux Klan. **c.** enrolling African American voters. **d.** improving conditions for African Americans in California.

_____ **11.** Settlers who farmed the Great Plains were known as: **a.** sharecroppers. **b.** newcomers. **c.** sodbusters. **d.** drivers.

_____ **12.** Schools in rural areas of the western states and territories were generally: **a.** segregated. **b.** not segregated. **c.** closed to African Americans. **d.** too expensive for African Americans.

_____ **13.** In cattle drives, cattle were driven from Texas to railroads in: **a.** Missouri. **b.** Kansas. **c.** Illinois **d.** California.

_____ **14.** A typical cattle drive trail crew contained how many African Americans? **a.** 2 **b.** 4 **c.** 8 **d.** 10

_____ **15.** African American cowhands' wages were usually: **a.** a fourth of those received by white cowhands. **b.** half of those received by white cowhands. **c.** equal to those received by white cowhands. **d.** slightly more than those paid to Mexican cowhands.

III. ESSAY Choose one of the following topics. Then write your answer in paragraph form on a separate sheet of paper.

A. If you had been an African American living in the South in 1879, would you have joined the Exodusters? Explain.

B. Why do you think African Americans experienced less prejudice in the western states and territories than they did in the South in the years after the Civil War? Give reasons.

Name ______________________________ Date ______________

UNIT 7 TEST: Freedom Without Equality

I. MATCHING Decide which definition in the right column best explains a term in the left column. Then write the letter of the definition in the space provided.

_____	**1.** civil rights	**a.**	system of laws segregating African Americans
_____	**2.** convict-lease system	**b.**	to deny rights of citizenship
_____	**3.** ragtime	**c.**	total value of all goods and services produced in a country
_____	**4.** monopoly	**d.**	control of an industry
_____	**5.** Jim Crow	**e.**	musical form based on offbeat rhythms
_____	**6.** blues	**f.**	hiring out of imprisoned African Americans as laborers
_____	**7.** gross national product	**g.**	musical form that grew out of African American work songs
_____	**8.** disfranchise	**h.**	those rights given to U.S. citizens by the Constitution and its amendments

II. UNDERSTANDING TIME Choose the time period in which each of the events below took place. Then write the letter of the period in the space provided. (A letter may be used more than once.)

1875 (A) 1880 (B) 1885 (C) 1890 (D) 1895 (E) 1900

_____ **9.** Congress passes a civil rights bill.

_____ **10.** Tuskegee Institute is founded.

_____ **11.** The Supreme Court gives its decision in *Plessy* v. *Ferguson*.

_____ **12.** Ida B. Wells begins her antilynching crusade.

_____ **13.** The Supreme Court declares a federal civil rights bill unconstitutional.

_____ **14.** Booker T. Washington gives his Atlanta Compromise speech.

_____ **15.** The first African American bank is founded.

_____ **16.** The Populist party seats 90 African American delegates at its convention.

_____ **17.** Booker T. Washington takes a job at Hampton Institute.

_____ **18.** The "Maple Leaf Rag" is published.

_____ **19.** An African American doctor performs the first successful heart surgery.

III. MULTIPLE CHOICE Choose the answer that best completes the sentence or answers the question. Then write the letter of your choice in the space provided.

_____ **20.** During Reconstruction, many Southerners recognized that, to develop and prosper, their region would have to:
a. increase cotton output. **b.** persuade immigrants to settle there. **c.** industrialize. **d.** force African Americans to move out.

_____ **21.** One of the few labor groups to accept African Americans as members in the late 1800s was the:
a. American Federation of Labor. **b.** Knights of Labor. **c.** True Reformers. **d.** Harvester's Union.

_____ 22. Poll taxes, literacy tests, and grandfather clauses were all means of:
a. attracting immigrant workers to the South. **b.** keeping African Americans from voting. **c.** overturning Jim Crow laws. **d.** encouraging labor union growth.

_____ 23. The two major sources of laborers for the nation's growing industries in the late 1800s were U.S.-born farm workers and immigrants from:
a. eastern and southern Europe. **b.** Asia. **c.** northern Europe. **d.** Latin America.

_____ 24. In its ruling in the case of *Plessy* v. *Ferguson*, the Supreme Court established the:
a. idea of "one man – one vote." **b.** right of workers to form labor unions. **c.** principle of states' rights. **d.** separate but equal principle.

_____ 25. One result of the Supreme Court's overturning of a federal civil rights law was the:
a. strengthening of civil rights laws in 15 Northern states. **b.** increase in the number of immigrants moving to the South. **c.** movement of African Americans from large cities to farms and small towns. **d.** destruction of the sharecropping system in 8 Southern states.

_____ 26. Which of the following would Booker T. Washington have considered *most* important for African Americans?
a. being able to vote **b.** buying a home in a white neighborhood **c.** eating in an unsegregated restaurant **d.** having a job that paid a decent wage

_____ 27. In order to promote the growth of African American-owned businesses, Booker T. Washington launched the:
a. National Negro Business League. **b.** NAACP. **c.** Populist party. **d.** Knights of Labor.

_____ 28. In the late 1800s, most African American colleges emphasized:
a. industrial arts training. **b.** training men for the ministry. **c.** the same education as the leading white colleges. **d.** training doctors and nurses.

_____ 29. African Americans believed that laws requiring segregation violated the:
a. 4th Amendment. **b.** 11th Amendment. **c.** 14th Amendment. **d.** 19th Amendment.

_____ 30. Between 1892 and 1900, over 3,000 people — mostly African Americans — lost their lives as a result of:
a. sharecropping accidents. **b.** the convict-lease system. **c.** lynchings. **d.** strikes by labor unions.

IV. COMPLETING THE IDEA Choose the name from the list that best completes each of the following sentences. Then write it in the space provided.

Ida B. Wells	Matthew Henson	Fisk Jubilee Singers
George Washington Carver	W. C. Handy	Booker T. Washington
Scott Joplin	Madame C. J. Walker	Henry Grady
Daniel Hale Williams		

31. "Memphis Blues" and "St. Louis Blues" by _________________________ introduced the blues to the general public.

32. Author of *The Red Record,* _________________________ fought for freedom and equality for African Americans and was one of the founders of the NAACP.

33. African American _________________________ was a member of the Peary expedition in 1909 and one of the first people to reach the North Pole.

34. The editor of the *Atlanta Constitution,* ______________________ called for change and the creation of a "New South."

35. Although best-known for short ragtime pieces, ______________________ also wrote ballets and the opera *Treemonisha.*

36. ______________________ raised funds to finance a leading African American university.

37. ______________________ founded Chicago's Provident Hospital as a place to train African American medical personnel and performed the first successful heart operation in history there.

38. By 1910, the cosmetics company founded by ______________________ had sales of $1,000 a day and employed 5,000 salespeople around the world.

39. National fame came to scientist ______________________ as the result of experiments and discoveries made at Tuskegee Institute.

40. The programs of ______________________ were based on the ideas that African Americans should accommodate to segregation and advance through industrial education, self-help, and business ownership.

V. **ESSAY Choose one of the following topics. Then write your answer in paragraph form on a separate sheet of paper.**

A. Do you think Ida B. Wells supported the ideas that Booker T. Washington set out in the Atlanta Compromise? Explain.

B. Why do you think so many influential white politicians and business people supported Booker T. Washington?

Name ______________________________ Date ______________

CHAPTER 20 TEST: African Americans in the New South

I. MATCHING Decide which definition in the right column best explains a term in the left column. Then write the letter of the definition in the space provided.

_____ **1.** Jim Crow
_____ **2.** convict-lease system
_____ **3.** civil rights
_____ **4.** disfranchise

a. to deny rights of citizenship
b. those things guaranteed to U.S. citizens by the Constitution
c. system of laws requiring segregation of African Americans in the South
d. hiring out of imprisoned African Americans as laborers

II. MULTIPLE CHOICE Choose the answer that best completes the sentence. Then write the letter of your choice in the space provided.

_____ **5.** After Reconstruction, African Americans in the South faced segregation: **a.** less often than during Reconstruction. **b.** only in employment. **c.** in few aspects of their daily lives. **d.** in many aspects of their daily lives.

_____ **6.** In the post-Reconstruction period, African American sharecroppers discovered that: **a.** they could quickly get rich under that system. **b.** they could usually buy their own farms in a few years. **c.** they were constantly in debt to and often cheated by landowners. **d.** sharecropping paid better than working in factories.

_____ **7.** In a typical Southern town, the monthly pay of an African American woman worker after Reconstruction was about: **a.** \$5 to \$6. **b.** \$15 to \$20. **c.** \$25 to \$32. **d.** \$35 to \$45.

_____ **8.** One of the few labor unions that accepted African Americans as members was the: **a.** Knights of Labor. **b.** United Mine Workers. **c.** American Federation of Labor. **d.** International Harvesters' Union.

_____ **9.** Ill will between white and African American workers increased when African Americans were hired as: **a.** managers. **b.** strikebreakers. **c.** security guards. **d.** janitors.

_____ **10.** A fee paid in order to vote is a: **a.** property test. **b.** poll tax. **c.** grandfather tax. **d.** literacy test.

_____ **11.** African Americans believed that laws requiring segregation violated the "equal protection" clause of the: **a.** 5th Amendment. **b.** 10th Amendment. **c.** 14th Amendment. **d.** 16th Amendment.

_____ **12.** The Supreme Court ruled that "separate but equal" facilities for African Americans and whites were acceptable in the case of: **a.** *Plessy* v. *Ferguson.* **b.** *Dred Scott* v. *Sanford.* **c.** *Marbury* v. *Madison.* **d.** *McCulloch* v. *Maryland.*

_____ **13.** In more than 20 cities, African Americans protested segregation by: **a.** protest marches. **b.** protest songs. **c.** boycotting streetcar companies that segregated their cars. **d.** writing letters to members of Congress.

_____ **14.** In the South after Reconstruction, literacy and property tests for white male voters were often waived because of the: **a.** 14th Amendment. **b.** poll tax. **c.** civil rights laws. **d.** grandfather clause.

_____ **15.** The African American who became known for a campaign against lynching was: **a.** Ida B. Wells. **b.** Ferdinand Barnett. **c.** Clara Brown. **d.** George H. White.

III. ESSAY Choose one of the following topics. Then write your answer in paragraph form on a separate sheet of paper.

A. Imagine you are an unemployed African American in the post-Reconstruction South. The all-white local factory union goes on strike. The factory-owner, who has never hired African Americans, offers you a job as a strikebreaker. Would you accept? Explain.

B. Do you agree or disagree with the decision in *Plessy* v. *Ferguson*? Explain.

Name ______________________________ Date ______________

CHAPTER 21 TEST: Living in the Jim Crow World

I. MATCHING Decide which description from the right column best identifies a person in the left column. Then write the letter of the description space provided.

_____ **1.** Madame C. J. Walker

_____ **2.** Booker T. Washington

_____ **3.** C. C. Spaulding

_____ **4.** Samuel Chapman Armstrong

a. designed cosmetics for African Americans

b. leader of North American Mutual Life Insurance Company, the largest U.S. business owned and operated by African Americans

c. founder of Hampton Institute, an African American college

d. leading U.S. spokesman for African Americans by late 1800s and early 1900s.

II. MULTIPLE CHOICE Choose the answer that best completes the sentence or answers the question. Then write the letter of your choice in the space provided.

_____ **5.** Booker T. Washington was educated, and later taught, at: **a.** Oberlin College. **b.** Tuskegee Institute. **c.** Hampton Institute. **d.** Grambling State College.

_____ **6.** The 1895 speech that brought Booker T. Washington national fame was known as the: **a.** Atlanta Compromise. **b.** Red Record. **c.** New York Proposal. **d.** Tuskegee Plan.

_____ **7.** Under Washington Tuskegee Institute offered African Americans excellent: **a.** fine arts education. **b.** graduate education. **c.** classical education. **d.** industrial education.

_____ **8.** By 1906, enrollment at Tuskegee Institute had reached: **a.** 750 students. **b.** 1,125 students. **c.** 1,500 students. **d.** 3,300 students.

_____ **9.** Which of the following did Washington believe was *most* important for African American advancement in the U. S.? **a.** education and job skills **b.** political protest **c.** election to political office **d.** repeal of Jim Crow laws

_____ **10.** Washington assured white audiences that economic integration did *not* mean: **a.** economic superiority. **b.** political majority. **c.** structural equality. **d.** social integration.

_____ **11.** In 1900, Washington founded an organization to promote commercial achievement that was called the: **a.** Self-Help Council. **b.** Mutual Aid Association. **c.** National Negro Business League. **d.** Atlanta Institute.

_____ **12.** Because white companies refused African Americans' business or charged very high rates, many African American self-help societies set up their own: **a.** streetcar companies. **b.** railroad companies. **c.** grain storage companies. **d.** insurance companies.

_____ **13.** Banks provided two important services to African American communities — a place to deposit savings and a source of: **a.** credit. **b.** information. **c.** entrepreneurship. **d.** political power.

_____ **14.** Most African American-owned businesses were located in: **a.** rural areas. **b.** suburbs. **c.** segregated neighborhoods of cities and towns. **d.** central business districts of large cities.

_____ **15.** African American-owned businesses were the means by which a significant number of African Americans: **a.** launched themselves into the middle class. **b.** left the South. **c.** returned to sharecropping. **d.** overturned laws on segregation.

III. ESSAY Choose one of the following topics. Then write your answer in paragraph form on a separate sheet of paper.

A. Do you agree or disagree with Washington's idea that African Americans and whites "in all things . . . purely social . . . can be as separate as the fingers, yet one as the hand in all things essential to mutual progress"? Explain.

B. Do you think Washington was right to secretly fund challenges to discriminatory voting laws and segregation, or should he have opposed such practices openly? Explain.

Name ______________________________ Date ______________

CHAPTER 22 TEST: Advances in Education, Arts, and Science

I. MATCHING Decide which description in the right column best identifies a person in the left column. Write the letter of the description in the space provided.

______	**1.** Scott Joplin	**a.** invented more than 300 uses for the peanut
______	**2.** Edmonia Lewis	**b.** invented the shoe-lasting machine
______	**3.** W. C. Handy	**c.** performed first successful heart surgery
______	**4.** Lewis Latimer	**d.** was leading ragtime composer
______	**5.** George Washington Carver	**e.** worked with Thomas Edison to improve electric lighting
______	**6.** Jan Matzeliger	**f.** called "Father of the Blues"
______	**7.** Daniel Hale Williams	**g.** sculpted *Forever Free,* showing a newly freed African American mother and child

II. MULTIPLE CHOICE Choose the answer that best completes the sentence or answers the question. Then write the letter of your choice in the space provided.

______ **8.** About half of the nation's African American doctors and dentists graduated from: **a.** Howard University. **b.** Hampton Institute. **c.** Fisk University. **d.** Tuskegee Institute.

______ **9.** Some African American artists of the late 1800s responded to racial prejudice in the United States by: **a.** moving to Europe to work. **b.** refusing to take literacy tests. **c.** refusing to emigrate. **d.** returning federal grants they had received.

______ **10.** One of the first medical schools for African Americans was located at: **a.** Shaw University. **b.** Hampton Institute. **c.** Grambling State College. **d.** Tuskegee Institute.

______ **11.** Which of the following was developed by George Washington Carver? **a.** condensed milk **b.** 100 uses for the sweet potato **c.** method for operating on the heart **d.** automatic air brake

______ **12.** By 1910, approximately what percentage of the nation's African American population was literate? **a.** 30 **b.** 50 **c.** 70 **d.** 90

______ **13.** The musical form that grew out of African American work songs and uses the call-and-response pattern of African music is: **a.** spirituals. **b.** the blues. **c.** jazz. **d.** ragtime.

______ **14.** Henry Ossawa Tanner was a noted African American: **a.** musician. **b.** surgeon. **c.** inventor **d.** painter.

______ **15.** The high stepping promenade begun by African American slaves as a way to poke fun at plantation owners was: **a.** ragtime. **b.** the blues. **c.** jazz. **d.** the cakewalk.

III. ESSAY Choose one of the following topics. Then write your answer in paragraph form on a separate sheet of paper.

A. Which of the artists or inventors described in this chapter do you consider most important? Explain.

B. Imagine that you are living in the late 1800s and can donate a large sum of money for the education of African Americans. Would you prefer to have your money go to a university like Howard, to a school that specialized in industrial education like Tuskegee, or to a combined elementary and high school? Explain.

Name ______________________________ Date ______________

UNIT 8 TEST: Protest and Hope in a New Century

I. MATCHING Decide which definition from the right column best explains a term in the left column. Then write the letter of the definition in the space provided.

_____ **1.** Great Migration
_____ **2.** Harlem Renaissance
_____ **3.** New Deal
_____ **4.** Talented Tenth
_____ **5.** Niagara Movement
_____ **6.** Pan-Africanism
_____ **7.** Progressivism
_____ **8.** Red Summer
_____ **9.** Great Depression
_____ **10.** Black Cabinet

a. early 20th century reform movement
b. period of race riots after World War I
c. African American advisers to Roosevelt
d. creative outpouring by African American artists during the 1920s
e. severe economic slump of the 1920s and 1930s
f. Roosevelt's program for national recovery
g. movement of African Americans out of the South between 1915 and 1930
h. belief that people of African descent had common interests and should join in a common struggle for freedom
i. well-educated African Americans who would lead all African Americans, according to Du Bois
j. group that insisted on an end to racial discrimination and full equality for African Americans

II. UNDERSTANDING TIME Read the following list of events. Then choose the year that an event happened from the list below and write it in the space provided. (Each year should be used only once.)

1908	1910	1914	1916	1919
1925	1929	1932	1935	1941

_____ **11.** Red Summer
_____ **12.** beginning of World War I
_____ **13.** Springfield Massacre
_____ **14.** height of Harlem Renaissance
_____ **15.** Franklin Roosevelt elected to first term as President
_____ **16.** founding of the NAACP
_____ **17.** A. Philip Randolph plans march on Washington
_____ **18.** founding of the CIO
_____ **19.** stock market crash
_____ **20.** arrival of Marcus Garvey in the United States

III. MULTIPLE CHOICE Choose the answer that best completes the sentence or answers the question. Then write the letter of your choice in the space provided.

_____ **21.** The programs of which of the following were *most* likely to appeal to ordinary African Americans?
a. the Niagara Movement **b.** the NAACP **c.** the UNIA **d.** the AFL

_____ **22.** The poor, overcrowded, and rundown areas of cities are called:
a. monopolies. **b.** tenements. **c.** rurals. **d.** slums.

_____ **23.** Unlike Booker T. Washington, W. E. B. Du Bois believed that the best way for African Americans to gain equality was through:
a. peaceful resistance. **b.** industrial education. **c.** temporary acceptance of segregation. **d.** collective bargaining.

_____ **24.** People who move from one place to settle in another are often called:
a. occupants. **b.** vagrants. **c.** tenants. **d.** migrants.

_____ **25.** After the election of 1932, the large majority of African American voters shifted their loyalty to the:
a. Socialist party. **b.** Republican party. **c.** Black Workers party. **d.** Democratic party.

_____ **26.** A section of a city where many members of one ethnic group are forced to live because of discrimination is called a:
a. veto. **b.** ghetto. **c.** soddy. **d.** slum.

_____ **27.** Which of the following helped bring about the Great Migration?
a. Progressivism and the founding of the CIO **b.** crop failures in the South and World War I **c.** the Great Depression and bans on discrimination in the North **d.** the Red Summer and the Niagara Movement

_____ **28.** The National Labor Relations Act guaranteed workers the right to negotiate with employees through unions, a process known as:
a. collective bargaining. **b.** strikebreaking. **c.** industrial organizing. **d.** disfranchising.

_____ **29.** To oversee an order barring discrimination in defense industries, government agencies, and work-training programs, President Roosevelt set up the:
a. CIO. **b.** FSA. **c.** UNIA. **d.** FEPC.

_____ **30.** The ideas that African Americans should take pride in their ethnicity, study and identify with the history and culture of Africa, and rely on themselves rather than on white people to get ahead are all parts of:
a. racial discrimination. **b.** collective compromise. **c.** black nationalism. **d.** cultural accommodation.

IV. COMPLETING THE IDEA Choose the name from the list that best completes each of the following sentences. Then write it in the space provided.

Walter White	Bessie Smith	A. Philip Randolph
Eleanor Roosevelt	W. E. B. Du Bois	Mary Church Terrell
Langston Hughes	Robert S. Abbott	Mary McLeod Bethune
Marcus Garvey		

31. ________________________ served as the first president of the National Association of Colored Women and worked for voting rights and health and education programs for African American women.

32. In the pages of the *Chicago Defender,* ________________________ attacked discrimination, segregation, and lynching and urged African Americans to leave the South.

33. After ten years of undercover work gathering information about lynching and race riots, ________________________ became executive secretary of the NAACP in 1930.

34. Known as a "staunch ally" of African Americans, ______________________ pushed President Franklin Roosevelt and other federal officials into appointing more African Americans to government positions.

35. A scholar, writer, and editor, ______________________ opposed many of Booker T. Washington's ideas and demanded full civil rights for African Americans.

36. Considered by many to be the "glue" that held Roosevelt's Black Cabinet together, ______________________ oversaw National Youth Administration programs aimed at providing educational opportunities for African American high school and college students.

37. Jamaican-born ______________________ started the first extensive black nationalist movement that appealed to the great mass of African Americans.

38. Known as one of the leading African American writers of the 1920s and 1930s, ______________________ often tried to work the rhythms of jazz and the blues into poetry.

39. Plans by ______________________ for a massive march on Washington led President Roosevelt to issue Executive Order 8802.

40. The blues style of ______________________, whose recording of "Down Hearted Blues" sold 2 million copies in 1923, continues to influence popular vocalists to this day.

V. **ESSAY Choose one of the following topics. Then write your answer in paragraph form on a separate sheet of paper.**

A. Do you think Marcus Garvey would have approved of the way A. Philip Randolph attempted to secure better economic opportunities for African Americans? Explain.

B. Which of the African Americans discussed in this unit did the most, in your opinion, to improve conditions for all African Americans? Explain.

Name ______________________________ Date ______________

CHAPTER 23 TEST: The Civil Rights Struggle

I. MATCHING Decide which description from the right column best identifies a person in the left column. Then write the letter of the decription in the space provided.

_____ **1.** T. Thomas Fortune

_____ **2.** Walter White

_____ **3.** Mary Church Terrell

_____ **4.** William Monroe Trotter

_____ **5.** W. E. B. Du Bois

a. author of *The Souls of Black Folk* who attacked Booker T. Washington's strategies

b. executive secretary of the NAACP in 1930

c. founder of a national group of clubs which worked for voting rights and health and education programs for African American women

d. publisher of the *Guardian* who opposed the idea that African Americans should temporarily accommodate themselves to segregation

e. moving force behind the Afro-American League, which promoted citizen's rights and economic equality for African Americans

II. MULTIPLE CHOICE Choose the answer that best completes the sentence. Then write the letter of your choice in the space provided.

_____ **6.** According to Du Bois, "the Negro race . . . is going to be saved by its exceptional men," a group he called the: **a.** Niagara Movement. **b.** Progressives. **c.** Talented Tenth. **d.** Guardians.

_____ **7.** The Committee of Forty met in 1910 and founded the: **a.** National Mutual-Aid Society. **b.** NAACP. **c.** Afro-American League. **d.** National Negro Business League.

_____ **8.** The group founded in 1905 that insisted on full civil rights for African Americans was the: **a.** Niagara Movement. **b.** Progressives. **c.** Talented Tenth. **d.** Guardians.

_____ **9.** The first African American to receive a doctoral degree from Harvard University was: **a.** Walter White. **b.** W.E.B. Du Bois. **c.** Mary Church Terrell. **d.** T. Thomas Fortune.

_____ **10.** The NAACP magazine was the: **a.** *Liberator.* **b.** *Defender.* **c.** *Guardian.* **d.** *Crisis.*

_____ **11.** Du Bois thought African Americans could gain civil rights and economic progress by: **a.** peaceful resistance. **b.** accommodation. **c.** reverse discrimination. **d.** disfranchisement.

_____ **12.** The 1908 event that sparked the call for the First National Negro Conference was the: **a.** Atlanta Compromise. **b.** Springfield Massacre. **c.** Tuskegee Incident. **d.** Boston Riot.

_____ **13.** According to the NAACP, "the main force upon which [to rely] for the victory of justice" was: **a.** private funding. **b.** the Supreme Court. **c.** public schools. **d.** public opinion.

_____ **14.** Although an NAACP-sponsored bill passed the House in the 1920s, the opposition of Southern Senators prevented passage of a law that would have made a federal crime of: **a.** job discrimination. **b.** lynching. **c.** school segregation. **d.** poll taxes.

_____ **15.** A major part of the NAACP's long-term strategy against laws that discriminated against African Americans was to: **a.** use boycotts in states and cities with such laws. **b.** elect enough African American politicians to overturn such laws. **c.** attack such laws in court. **d.** counsel African Americans to disobey such laws.

III. ESSAY Choose one of the following topics. Then write your answer in paragraph form on a separate sheet of paper.

A. Do you think the NAACP was correct to focus on issues of political and social discrimination, or should it have tried to deal with the bread-and-butter economic concerns of most African Americans? Explain.

B. Write a brief editorial that might have appeared in the first issue of the *Crisis* stating the goals of the magazine and its founding organization.

Name ______________________________ Date ______________

CHAPTER 24 TEST: The Great Migration

I. MATCHING Decide which definition in the right column best explains a term in the left column. Then write the letter of the definition in the space provided.

_____	**1.** jazz	**a.** insect that attacks cotton plants
_____	**2.** ghetto	**b.** one who moves from one place to settle in another
_____	**3.** migrant	**c.** combination of spirituals, blues, and other elements
_____	**4.** boll weevil	**d.** area where people of an ethnic group are forced to live because of discrimination

II. MULTIPLE CHOICE Choose the answer that best completes the sentence or answers the question. Then write the letter of your choice in the space provided.

_____ **5.** Between 1915 and 1930, over a million African Americans left the South as part of what was called the: **a.** Niagara Movement. **b.** Black Exodus. **c.** Great Migration. **d.** Progressive Movement.

_____ **6.** In 1917, the NAACP organized a silent parade in New York City to protest: **a.** an outbreak of race riots. **b.** the drafting of African Americans into the armed forces. **c.** unequal pay for African American factory workers. **d.** segregation in public schools.

_____ **7.** By 1922, more the 85 percent of the South's cotton fields had been ruined by: **a.** boll weevils. **b.** overplanting. **c.** erosion. **d.** floods.

_____ **8.** The most influential African American newspaper between 1915 and 1930 was the: **a.** *Cleveland Gazette.* **b.** *Chicago Defender.* **c.** *Pittsburgh Courier.* **d.** *Washington Bee.*

_____ **9.** Under Georgia law, before leaving farms sharecroppers had to: **a.** pay a poll tax. **b.** plant a final crop. **c.** arrange for replacement workers. **d.** pay off their debts.

_____ **10.** Even before the United States entered World War I, the war's effects were felt in the form of the: **a.** cutoff of cheap immigrant labor. **b.** increase in the number of immigrants. **c.** increased demand for cotton. **d.** decreased demand for cotton.

_____ **11.** Of the 370,000 African Americans trained for combat in the U.S. armed forces, approximately how many actually fought? **a.** 100,000 **b.** 160,000 **c.** 220,000 **d.** 280,000

_____ **12.** One effect of the entry of 4 million white workers into the U.S. armed forces after 1917 was the: **a.** importation of Chinese laborers. **b.** closing of many factories. **c.** recruitment of African American workers. **d.** public outcry that African Americans be drafted into the armed forces as well.

_____ **13.** One religious group that attracted followers among African American newcomers to cities was the: **a.** Nation of Islam. **b.** Mother Bethel Church. **c.** African Methodist Episcopal Zion Church. **d.** Baptist Church.

_____ **14.** The organization founded in 1910 that aimed to help African Americans who had left the South in search of jobs was the: **a.** National Negro Business League. **b.** Afro-American League. **c.** National Association of Colored Women. **d.** National Urban League.

_____ **15.** During World War I, African American combat troops served in: **a.** African American regiments commanded by African American officers. **b.** African American regiments commanded by white officers. **c.** integrated regiments commanded by white officers. **d.** integrated regiments commanded by white or African American officers.

III. ESSAY Choose one of the following topics. Then write your answer in paragraph form on a separate sheet of paper.

A. Considering the conditions African Americans faced in 1917, would you have agreed or disagreed with Du Bois's statement "If this is our country, then this is our war"? Explain.

B. Why do you think many white Southerners would have been opposed to the movement of African Americans to the North and Midwest between 1915 and 1930?

Name ______________________________ Date ______________

CHAPTER 25 TEST: Black Nationalism

I. COMPLETING THE IDEA Choose the name from the list that best completes each of the following sentences. Then write it in the space provided.

Kwame Nkrumah   Paul Cuffe   Marcus Garvey   Claude McKay

1. One of the earliest supporters in the United States of the ideas that came to be called Pan-Africanism was ______________.
2. In his work Jamaican-born poet ______________ urged African Americans to resist discrimination and violence.
3. ______________ became the leading spokesman of black nationalism in the early 1920s.
4. Inspired by the ideas of Pan-Africanism, ______________ became the first president of Ghana.

II. MULTIPLE CHOICE Choose the answer that best completes the sentence. Then write the letter of your choice in the space provided.

_____ **5.** Many African Americans who had found jobs in U.S. factories during World War I lost them after the war to: **a.** women who would work for lower pay. **b.** immigrants from Europe. **c.** returning white veterans. **d.** immigrants from Asia.

_____ **6.** African Americans, as well as Catholics and Jews, were threatened after World War I by the: **a.** Knights of Labor. **b.** Niagara Movement. **c.** Jim Crow system. **d.** Ku Klux Klan.

_____ **7.** A series of riots broke out in U.S. cities in 1919 during the period known as: **a.** Red Summer. **b.** Great War. **c.** Springfield Massacre. **d.** Exodus.

_____ **8.** The belief that people of African descent have common interests and should join in a common struggle for freedom is known as: **a.** Pan-Africanism. **b.** Progressivism. **c.** colonization. **d.** desegregation.

_____ **9.** The belief that African Americans should take pride in their ethnicity and rely on themselves rather than on white people to get ahead is part of: **a.** accommodation. **b.** emancipation. **c.** social integration. **d.** black nationalism.

_____ **10.** Marcus Garvey was born in: **a.** Ghana. **b.** Jamaica. **c.** Liberia. **d.** Trinidad.

_____ **11.** To help African Americans win equality through economic, political, and cultural independence, Garvey founded the: **a.** Universal Negro Improvement Association. **b.** Negro Business League. **c.** African Colonization Society. **d.** Afro-American Society.

_____ **12.** To demonstrate his belief that businesses owned and managed by African Americans offered a path to economic independence, Garvey founded the: **a.** True Reformers Bank. **b.** Harlem Hotel. **c.** New York Mutual Life Insurance Company. **d.** Black Star Line.

_____ **13.** Stories about African Americans that were usually left out of white publications were published by Garvey in the: **a.** *Crisis.* **b.** *Negro Homeland.* **c.** *Defender.* **d.** *Negro World.*

_____ **14.** Garvey's movement collapsed in the mid-1920s as a result of his: **a.** public backing of the ideas of Booker T. Washington. **b.** conviction for mail fraud. **c.** public argument with W. E. B. Du Bois. **d.** insulting of President Coolidge.

_____ **15.** Believing that prejudice would deny African Americans in the U. S. justice and equality, Garvey proposed: **a.** creating an independent nation for African Americans in the Southwest. **b.** drawing up a new Constitution for the U. S. **c.** creating and settling a powerful nation in Africa. **d.** moving African Americans to Haiti and Jamaica.

III. ESSAY Choose one of the following topics. Then write your answer in paragraph form on a separate sheet of paper.

A. Which element of Garvey's program do you think best enabled him to "capture the imagination of the masses"? Explain.

B. Do you think that leaders of the NAACP would have backed Garvey's programs? Explain.

Name ______________________________ Date ______________

CHAPTER 26 TEST: The Harlem Renaissance

I. MATCHING Decide which description from the right column best identifies a person in the left column. Then write the letter of the description in the space provided.

_____ **1.** Bessie Smith
_____ **2.** Aaron Douglas
_____ **3.** Louis Armstrong
_____ **4.** Jean Toomer
_____ **5.** Augusta Savage
_____ **6.** Arthur Schomburg
_____ **7.** Zora Neale Hurston
_____ **8.** Duke Ellington

a. composer of "Sophisticated Lady" and "Mood Indigo"
b. Empress of the Blues
c. anthropologist and novelist, author of *Their Eyes Were Watching God*
d. sculptor who directed the Harlem Community Art Center
e. author of a single novel, *Cane,* that combined fiction, poetry, and drama
f. popular and influential musician known as "Satchmo"
g. illustrator of books by African American writers and creator of murals depicting African American history
h. collector of material on African American history and culture

II. MULTIPLE CHOICE Choose the answer that best completes the sentence. Then write the letter of your choice in the space provided.

_____ **9.** The burst of creativity among African American writers, musicians, and artists during the 1920s is known as the: **a.** Great Migration. **b.** New Deal. **c.** Harlem Renaissance. **d.** Progressive Movement.

_____ **10.** The charitable organization that offered prizes to African American artists and writers and arranged traveling exhibits of work by African American painters and sculptors was the: **a.** Harmon Foundation. **b.** Catagonia Club. **c.** National Negro Business League. **d.** New Negro Alliance.

_____ **11.** The elegant homes of New York City's successful African American professionals stood in an area known as: **a.** Tin Pan Alley. **b.** Charleston. **c.** Black Bottom. **d.** Striver's Row.

_____ **12.** One reason that African American artists and writers were attracted to New York City was that it: **a.** offered financial aid to artists. **b.** was the center of the nation's book, magazine, and music publishing industries. **c.** was cheaper to live there than in other cities. **d.** had outlawed all forms of racial discrimination.

_____ **13.** *Shuffle Along and Hot Chocolates* are examples of: **a.** books published by African American writers. **b.** popular dances of the 1920s. **c.** Harlem nightclubs that did not admit African Americans. **d.** Broadway shows by African Americans.

_____ **14.** Early in the 1900s, the musical form known as jazz originated in: **a.** New Orleans. **b.** Cleveland. **c.** Detroit. **d.** Harlem.

_____ **15.** The event that brought an end to the U.S. economic boom of the 1920s was the: **a.** revolution in Russia. **b.** stock market crash. **c.** beginning of another world war. **d.** election of President Calvin Coolidge.

III. ESSAY Choose one of the following topics. Then write your answer in paragraph form on a separate sheet of paper.

A. What do you think a writer for an African American newspaper meant by the statement, "The NEW NEGRO, unlike the old time negro, does not fear the face of the day"?

B. Which artist of the Harlem Renaissance would you most like to learn more about? Explain.

Name ______________________________ Date ______________

CHAPTER 27 TEST: The Great Depression and the New Deal

I. MATCHING Deside which description from the right column best identifies an item in the left column. Then write the letter of your choice in the space provided.

_____ **1.** Eleanor Roosevelt

_____ **2.** New Negro Alliance

_____ **3.** Mary McLeod Bethune

_____ **4.** Black Cabinet

_____ **5.** New Deal

_____ **6.** Robert C. Weaver

_____ **7.** Congress of Industrial Organizations

_____ **8.** A. Philip Randolph

a. started "Buy Where You Work" campaigns to win jobs for African Americans

b. named to President's Cabinet in 1966 after several federal goverment jobs

c. director of the Division of Negro Affairs of the National Youth Administration under President Roosevelt

d. prominent African Americans named to serve in Roosevelt's government

e. organization whose charter was hailed as "a Bill of Rights for Negro labor."

f. founder of the Brotherhood of Sleeping Car Porters

g. invited African American leaders to the White House, and pushed President Roosevelt to improve conditions for African Americans

h. proposals by Roosevelt to combat the Great Depression

II. MULTIPLE CHOICE Choose the answer that best completes the sentence or answers the question. Then write the letter of your choice in the space provided.

_____ **9.** During the early years of the Great Depression, jobs usually held by African Americans were taken by: **a.** whites. **b.** immigrants from Latin America. **c.** immigrants from China. **d.** immigrants from Japan.

_____ **10.** Many African Americans were reluctant to vote for Franklin D. Roosevelt in 1932 because he was a: **a.** Republican. **b.** Democrat. **c.** New Yorker. **d.** Socialist.

_____ **11.** The Social Security Act of 1935 proved indirectly unfair to African Americans because it did not cover: **a.** people who had not paid poll taxes. **b.** miners and mechanics. **c.** people who failed literacy tests. **d.** farmers and domestic workers.

_____ **12.** One of the largest employers of African Americans among New Deal agencies was the: **a.** FEPC. **b.** UNIA. **c.** WPA. **d.** NRA.

_____ **13.** The number of African American employees in the federal government went from 50,000 in 1933 to which of the following numbers in 1941? **a.** 20,000 **b.** 45,000 **c.** 95,000 **d.** 150,000

_____ **14.** President Roosevelt barred discrimination in defense industries, government agencies, and work training programs through: **a.** the AFL. **b.** the CCC. **c.** Executive Order 8802. **d.** the National Labor Relations Act.

_____ **15.** To pressure President Roosevelt to end discrimination against African American workers, A. Philip Randolph announced a: **a.** boycott of white-owned stores. **b.** march on Washington. **c.** strike by African American workers. **d.** campaign to form a new labor organization.

III. ESSAY Choose one of the following topics. Then write your answer in paragraph form on a separate sheet of paper.

A. Which New Deal program do you think helped African Americans the most? Explain.

B. **a.** What did Frederick Douglass mean by his statement, "The Republicans are the ship. All else is the sea"? **b.** How did this idea affect African Americans voting in the 1932 election?

Name ______________________________ Date______________

UNIT 9 TEST: The Civil Rights Revolution

I. MATCHING Decide which definition from the right column best fits a term in the left column. Then write the letter of the definition in the space provided.

_____ **1.** Cold War
_____ **2.** sit-in
_____ **3.** Black Muslims
_____ **4.** de facto segregation
_____ **5.** Black Eagles
_____ **6.** nonviolence
_____ **7.** Vietnam Syndrome
_____ **8.** black power
_____ **9.** Silent Majority
_____ **10.** underclass

a. movement emphasizing control by African Americans of their own communities
b. 99th Pursuit Squadron
c. peaceful refusal to obey unjust laws
d. form of protest begun by students in Greensboro, North Carolina, in 1960
e. period of international conflict that stopped short of war
f. members of the Nation of Islam
g. feelings of anger and confusion experienced by military veterans
h. people with incomes below poverty level
i. situation in which African Americans are set apart by social and economic forces rather than by laws
j. people angered and upset by the turmoil of the 1960s

II. UNDERSTANDING TIME Choose the time period in which each of the events below took place. Then write the letter of the period in the space provided. (A letter may be used more than once.)

1940 (A) 1945 (B) 1950 (C) 1955 (D) 1960 (E) 1965 (F) 1970 (G) 1975

_____ **11.** U.S. troops fight in Korea.
_____ **12.** Martin Luther King is assassinated.
_____ **13.** African Americans are admitted to Officer Candidate School.
_____ **14.** Black Panther party is formed.
_____ **15.** Federal troops are sent to integrate schools in Little Rock, Arkansas.
_____ **16.** U.S. troops leave Vietnam.
_____ **17.** Jackie Robinson integrates major league baseball.
_____ **18.** Freedom rides take place in the South.
_____ **19.** The Supreme Court decides *Brown* v. *Board of Education of Topeka.*
_____ **20.** Campaign begins to desegregate Birmingham, Alabama.

III. MULTIPLE CHOICE Choose the answer that best completes the sentence or answers the question. Then write the letter of your choice in the space provided.

_____ **21.** Which of the following was a major cause of the movement of many African Americans out of the South from 1945 to 1960?
a. the boll weevil **b.** the mechanical cotton picker **c.** the shoe-lasting machine **d.** the CIO

_____ **22.** During World War II, African American troops served:
a. in fully integrated units. **b.** only as support troops. **c.** mainly in segregated units. **d.** exclusively in the United States.

_____ **23.** During World War II, large numbers of African Americans for the first time got high-paying, skilled jobs in defense industries due, in part, to the efforts of the:
a. COFO. **b.** MFDP **c.** SCLC. **d.** FEPC.

_____ **24.** The Supreme Court ruled that "separate educational facilities are inherently unequal" in the case of:
a. *Sweatt* v. *Painter*. **b.** *McLaurin* v. *Oklahoma State Regents*. **c.** *Plessy* v. *Ferguson*. **d.** *Brown* v. *Board of Education of Topeka*.

_____ **25.** Partly as a result of the freedom rides, the federal government:
a. got a court order directing CORE to dissolve. **b.** jailed James Farmer and Martin Luther King. **c.** issued tougher regulations barring segregation in interstate travel. **d.** sent federal troops to Greensboro, North Carolina.

_____ **26.** President Johnson blocked the seating of Mississippi Freedom Democratic Party delegates at the 1964 Democratic National Convention because he:
a. didn't want to anger white Southern voters and politicians. **b.** believed them to be Communists. **c.** felt they did not truly represent African Americans of the South. **d.** wanted to gain the support of African American voters.

_____ **27.** The aim of the COFO drive in 1964 and the Selma campaign in 1965 was to:
a. close segregated schools. **b.** wipe out illiteracy among African Americans. **c.** integrate public transportation. **d.** register African American voters.

_____ **28.** By 1967, Martin Luther King had come to believe that efforts to build a "Great Society" through programs to aid the poor had been crippled by the:
a. Black Panther party. **b.** Dixiecrats. **c.** movement of African Americans out of the South. **d.** war in Vietnam.

_____ **29.** According to the Kerner Commission, the main cause of riots that ripped through U.S. cities in the 1960s was:
a. drug abuse. **b.** prejudice. **c.** unemployment. **d.** assimilation.

_____ **30.** During a protest over the Vietnam War, two African American students were killed by police at:
a. North Carolina A.&T. College. **b.** Jackson State University. **c.** Tuskegee Institute. **d.** the University of Mississippi.

IV. COMPLETING THE IDEA Choose the name from the list that best completes each of the following sentences and write it in the space provided.

Malcolm X	Colin Powell	Lorraine Hansberry
James Meredith	Thurgood Marshall	Fannie Lou Hamer
Stokely Carmichael	A. Philip Randolph	Martin Luther King
James Farmer		

31. Riots exploded in 1962 when ________________________ attempted to integrate the University of Mississippi.

32. As a representative of the Mississippi Freedom Democratic Party, ______________ ________________________ brought word of the African American struggle for voting rights to a nationwide audience in 1964.

33. The Chairman of the Joint Chiefs of Staff, who coordinated the efforts of the nation's armed forces during the war in Iraq in 1991, was ________________________.

34. Although a march on Washington planned for 1941 never took place, the one __________ ________________________ organized in 1963 drew some 250,000 demonstrators.

35. In 1964, ________________________ won the Nobel Peace Prize for nonviolent efforts to win equality for African Americans.

36. After winning a number of major cases as the NAACP's chief lawyer, ______________ ________________________ became the first African American appointed to the Supreme Court.

37. ________________________ helped build CORE into a national civil rights organization, one that staged the freedom rides through the South.

38. Inspired by the ideas of Marcus Garvey, ________________________ attracted many followers in the 1950s and 1960s with his calls for black nationalism.

39. ________________________ called for Black Power and urged SNCC to stop recruiting whites into its ranks.

40. In 1959, ________________________ scored a Broadway hit with the play *A Raisin in the Sun*.

V. ESSAY Choose one of the following topics. Then write your answer in paragraph form on a separate sheet of paper.

A. Which of the civil rights campaigns discussed in this unit had the greatest impact on the lives of African Americans? Explain.

B. In 1969, the Kerner Commission report said, "Our nation is moving toward two societies, one black, one white–separate and unequal." Do you think the commission's prediction was correct? Explain.

Name ____________________ Date ____________

CHAPTER 28 TEST: World War II and African Americans

I. MATCHING Decide which description from the right column best identifies a person or group in the left column. Then write the letter of your choice in the space provided.

_____ **1.** WAVES

_____ **2.** Benjamin O. Davis, Jr.

_____ **3.** FEPC

_____ **4.** Dorie Miller

_____ **5.** Black Eagles

_____ **6.** A. Philip Randolph

a. recipient of Navy Cross for heroism during the attack on Pearl Harbor

b. women's branch of the U.S. Navy

c. planner of a protest march on Washington

d. group organized to end discrimination in defense industries

e. commander of 99th Fighter Squadron and 332nd Fighter Group

f. African American 99th Pursuit Squadron

II. MULTIPLE CHOICE Choose the answer that best completes the sentence or answers the question. Then write the letter of your choice in the space provided.

_____ **7.** The "Double-V" campaign that African Americans waged during World War II was for victory: **a.** on the land and on the sea. **b.** over Germany and over Japan. **c.** over discrimination at home and over the enemy overseas. **d.** over segregation in the South and lack of employment in defense industries.

_____ **8.** A major training base for African American fliers during World War II was: **a.** Tuskegee Institute. **b.** Hampton Institute. **c.** Howard University. **d.** Oberlin College.

_____ **9.** Approximately how many African Americans were officers in the U.S. armed forces at the beginning of World War II? **a.** 12 **b.** 120 **c.** 650 **d.** 1,600

_____ **10.** At the beginning of World War II, African Americans were not permitted to serve in the: **a.** navy. **b.** army and Marines. **c.** army. **d.** Marines and Army Air Corps.

_____ **11.** African American and white soldiers fought in temporarily integrated units during the battle of: **a.** Japan. **b.** Sicily. **c.** the Bulge. **d.** Normandy.

_____ **12.** The most serious race riot during World War II took place in 1943 in: **a.** Detroit, Michigan. **b.** Tuskegee, Alabama. **c.** Salina, Kansas. **d.** Washington, D.C.

_____ **13.** During World War II, many African Americans left Southern farms in order to: **a.** escape the effects of severe flooding. **b.** take jobs in defense industries. **c.** avoid new Jim Crow laws. **d.** become migrant farm workers.

_____ **14.** Compared to what they had earned before, the wages earned by African American women during World War II were: **a.** lower. **b.** about the same. **c.** slightly higher. **d.** the highest they had ever been.

_____ **15.** In 1940, Walter White, A. Philip Randolph, and T. Arnold Hill urged President Roosevelt to: **a.** declare war on Germany. **b.** keep the United States out of war at all costs. **c.** develop a nuclear bomb. **d.** end the segregationist policies of the military.

III. ESSAY Choose one of the following topics. Then write your answer in paragraph form on a separate sheet of paper.

A. If you had been a 21-year-old African American and wanted to enter the armed forces, shortly after Pearl Harbor, in which branch would you have wanted to serve? Explain.

B. In general, do you think that conditions for African Americans improved or worsened during the period from 1941 to 1945? Explain.

Name ______________________________ Date ______________

CHAPTER 29 TEST: Gains and Losses in the Postwar Years

I. COMPLETING THE IDEA Choose the name from the list that best completes each of the following sentences and write it in the space provided.

Ruth Brown	Ralph Ellison	Lorraine Hansberry
Jacob Lawrence	Richard Wright	Mahalia Jackson
Charlie Parker	Gwendolyn Brooks	

1. Saxophonist ______________ was one of the developers of bebop and is ranked with Louis Armstrong as one of the geniuses of jazz.
2. *Invisible Man,* by ______________ is a novel dealing with the way white people refused to accept African Americans as part of U.S. society.
3. The rich singing voice of ______________ helped bring African American gospel music to a larger audience that included many white people.
4. The series of painted panels depicting the lives of Frederick Douglass and Harriet Tubman was among the best-known works of ______________.
5. *Native Son* by ______________ became the first national bestseller by an African American writer.
6. One of the important early rock 'n' roll performers was ______________.
7. *A Raisin in the Sun,* by ______________, became a hit Broadway play in 1959.
8. The poems of ______________ deal with African Americans in the ghetto.

II. MULTIPLE CHOICE Choose the answer that best completes the sentence or answers the question. Then write the letter of your choice in the space provided.

_____ 9. By 1960, almost all sharecroppers in the South had been replaced by: **a.** migrant workers from Haiti. **b.** mechanical cotton pickers. **c.** migrant workers from Mexico. **d.** mechanical planter-plows.

_____ 10. After the 1950s, public housing projects in cities were occupied mainly by: **a.** Native Americans. **b.** white people. **c.** white people and African Americans. **d.** African Americans.

_____ 11. Between 1950 and 1960, approximately how many African Americans left the South for the nation's largest non-Southern cities? **a.** 500,000 **b.** 1 million **c.** 2 million **d.** 4 million

_____ 12. When segregation exists, even though it is not required by law, it is known as: **a.** de facto segregation. **b.** de jure segregation. **c.** virtual segregation. **d.** common segregation.

_____ 13. In 1954, William Dawson, Adam Clayton Powell, and Charles C. Diggs all: **a.** were elected to seats in the House of Representatives. **b.** were elected U.S. Senators. **c.** were named to the federal courts. **d.** became advisers to the President.

_____ 14. An Oscar award for best actor of 1963 was awarded to: **a.** Sidney Poitier. **b.** Harry Belafonte. **c.** Chuck Berry. **d.** Bill Cosby.

_____ 15. In 1952, some 18,000 fans in Cleveland, Ohio, attended the first concert to feature: **a.** bebop. **b.** cool jazz. **c.** free form jazz. **d.** rock 'n' roll.

III. ESSAY Choose one of the following topics. Then write your answer in paragraph form on a separate sheet of paper.

A. Which of the artists or performers discussed in this chapter do you think has had the greatest impact on popular culture? Explain.

B. If you had been an African American representative from a large Northern city in the mid-1950s, what would have been the most important thing you could have accomplished for your district? Explain.

Name ______________________________ Date ______________

CHAPTER 30 TEST: The Battle for Civil Rights

I. MATCHING Decide which description from the right column best identifies a person in the left column. Then write the letter of your choice in the space provided.

_____	**1.** James Farmer	**a.** refused to obey Montgomery, Alabama, Jim Crow law
_____	**2.** Jo Ann Robinson	**b.** head of CORE
_____	**3.** Thurgood Marshall	**c.** broke color barrier in major league baseball
_____	**4.** Rosa Parks	**d.** planned the Montgomery bus boycott
_____	**5.** Jackie Robinson	**e.** director of the NAACP's Legal Defense and Education Fund

II. MULTIPLE CHOICE Choose the answer that best completes the sentence or answers the question. Then write the letter of your choice in the space provided.

_____ **6.** Protesting unjust laws by refusing to obey them is known as: **a.** reverse discrimination. **b.** accommodation. **c.** citizen's enforcement. **d.** nonviolence.

_____ **7.** The CORE plan to test the effectiveness of court orders barring segregation in interstate bus transportation was the: **a.** sit-in. **b.** bus boycott. **c.** freedom ride. **d.** protest march.

_____ **8.** The form of protest in which African Americans refused to leave white restaurants and lunch counters until they were served was the: **a.** sit-in. **b.** freedom strike. **c.** meal boycott. **d.** food strike.

_____ **9.** The Supreme Court declared segregation of public schools unconstitutional in the 1954 case of: **a.** *Sweatt* v. *Painter.* **b.** *Plessy* v. *Ferguson.* **c.** *McLaurin* v. *Oklahoma State Regents.* **d.** *Brown* v. *Board of Education of Topeka.*

_____ **10.** President Eisenhower ordered federal troops to enforce integration of the public high school in: **a.** Topeka, Kansas. **b.** Little Rock, Arkansas. **c.** Birmingham, Alabama. **d.** Montgomery, Alabama.

_____ **11.** The founder of the SCLC and the most visible and eloquent spokesman for the Civil Rights Movement was: **a.** E.D. Nixon. **b.** Thurgood Marshall. **c.** James Farmer. **d.** Martin Luther King.

_____ **12.** Which of the following would have been the *least* likely to support the programs of the SCLC? **a.** Orval Faubus **b.** Diane Nash **c.** Ezell Blair **d.** Ralph Abernathy

_____ **13.** Thousands of school-age children joined demonstrations and were arrested in the campaign to desegregate: **a.** Topeka, Kansas. **b.** Little Rock, Arkansas. **c.** Birmingham, Alabama. **d.** Montgomery, Alabama.

_____ **14.** In order to pressure Congress into passing a civil rights bill, A. Philip Randolph, Bayard Rustin, and other African American leaders organized a 1963: **a.** freedom ride. **b.** march on Washington. **c.** transportation boycott. **d.** sit-down strike.

_____ **15.** The civil rights group organized by young people in 1960 based, in part, on Martin Luther King's ideas was: **a.** SNCC. **b.** the Urban League. **c.** CORE. **d.** the MIA.

III. ESSAY Choose one of the following topics. Then write your answer in paragraph form on a separate sheet of paper.

A. Early in the 1960s, one civil rights leader said, "We've got to have a crisis to bargain with." What you think he meant by this statement? Explain.

B. One historian has called Greensboro the turning point in the Civil Rights Movement, saying "Montgomery was a reaction; Greensboro was an act." What you think he meant by this statement? Explain.

Name ______________________________ Date ______________

CHAPTER 31 TEST: New Directions in the Civil Rights Movement

I. COMPLETING THE IDEA Choose the name from the list that best completes each of the following sentences and write it in the space provided.

Fannie Lou Hamer Stokely Carmichael Malcolm X James Meredith Bobby Seale

1. The most forceful spokesman for the Nation of Islam, ______________, later split from that group to form his own movement to gain political power for African Americans.

2. ______________ was the leader of SNCC who popularized the slogan "Black Power."

3. After joining SNCC, ______________ became involved in Freedom Summer and later spoke for the Mississippi Freedom Democratic Party at the Democratic National Convention in 1964.

4. On the second day of a march from Tennessee to Mississippi to encourage voter registration, ______________ was shot by a white man armed with a shotgun.

5. Together with Huey Newton, ______________ formed the militant political party known as the Black Panthers.

II. MULTIPLE CHOICE Choose the answer that best completes the sentence or answers the question. Then write the letter of your choice in the space provided.

_____ **6.** Riots broke out in 125 cities across the United States following the 1968 assassination of: **a.** Robert Kennedy. **b.** Malcolm X. **c.** Martin Luther King, Jr. **d.** James Meredith.

_____ **7.** The black nationalism preached by Malcolm X was inspired in part by the example of: **a.** Booker T. Washington. **b.** Marcus Garvey. **c.** Frederick Douglass. **d.** Elijah McCoy.

_____ **8.** In 1964, COFO organized a campaign called Freedom Summer that had as its goal: **a.** voter registration. **b.** ending illiteracy among African Americans. **c.** repealing the poll tax. **d.** organizing city workers in Memphis, Tennessee.

_____ **9.** Members of the Nation of Islam are also known as: **a.** Black Panthers. **b.** Black Muslims. **c.** Black Advocates. **d.** Black Shriners.

_____ **10.** In 1965, Martin Luther King and the SCLC joined SNCC in a campaign to register African American voters in: **a.** Memphis, Tennessee. **b.** Los Angeles, California. **c.** Rochester, New York. **d.** Selma, Alabama.

_____ **11.** Those who argued for Black Power said that African Americans did not want to be: **a.** exiled from white society. **b.** merged into white society. **c.** segregated from white society. **d.** equated with white society.

_____ **12.** The group of people with incomes below the poverty level make up the nation's: **a.** radicals. **b.** migrants. **c.** underclass. **d.** majority.

_____ **13.** According to the Kerner Commission, what has shaped the nation's history and threatens its future? **a.** assimilation **b.** prejudice **c.** the underclass **d.** integration

_____ **14.** Partly as a result of events in Selma, President Johnson announced his support for: **a.** a federal voting rights act. **b.** a law to protect civil rights protesters. **c.** an amendment to the Constitution. **d.** a new march on Washington.

_____ **15.** By 1967, Martin Luther King had come to believe that the nation's main enemy was: **a.** Congress. **b.** illiteracy. **c.** the Black Power movement. **d.** economic injustice.

III. ESSAY Choose one of the following topics. Then write your answer in paragraph form on a separate sheet of paper.

A. Why do you think civil rights leaders organized so many campaigns around the issue of voter registration?

B. Do you think Martin Luther King agreed or disagreed with the ideas of Malcolm X? Explain.

Name ______________________________ Date______________

CHAPTER 32 TEST: Marching Off to Vietnam

I. MATCHING Decide which description from the right column best identifies a place in the left column. Then write the letter of the description in the space provided.

_____	**1.** Hanoi	**a.** where the United States was involved in a war from 1950 to 1953
_____	**2.** Saigon	**b.** site of "Soulsville"
_____	**3.** Korea	**c.** country with a Communist government
_____	**4.** North Vietnam	**d.** Communist capital city
_____	**5.** South Vietnam	**e.** country to which the United States began sending military advisers in the early 1960s

II. MULTIPLE CHOICE Choose the answer that best completes the sentence or answers the question. Then write the letter of your choice in the space provided.

_____ **6.** African Americans made up about 10 percent of the nation's population in the late 1960s, but they accounted for approximately what percentage of men fighting in Vietnam? **a.** 3 **b.** 7 **c.** 14 **d.** 20

_____ **7.** The process of integrating U.S. armed forces was sped by a conflict in: **a.** Korea. **b.** Cuba. **c.** Europe. **d.** Japan.

_____ **8.** The United States began to send combat troops to Vietnam in: **a.** 1953. **b.** 1965. **c.** 1967. **d.** 1973.

_____ **9.** By the time of the war in Vietnam, U.S. fighting units were: **a.** 30 percent integrated. **b.** 55 percent integrated. **c.** 83 percent integrated. **d.** 100 percent integrated.

_____ **10.** The difficulty that many Vietnam veterans faced in readjusting to civilian life after the war was called: **a.** Vietnam Moratorium. **b.** Vietcong. **c.** Vietnam Syndrome. **d.** Vietnam Wall.

_____ **11.** By 1968, approximately what percentage of African Americans in the United States opposed the war in Vietnam? **a.** 25 **b.** 45 **c.** 60 **d.** 70

_____ **12.** The African American whose refusal to serve in the U.S. armed forces sparked a storm of controversy was: **a.** Milton Olive. **b.** Muhammad Ali. **c.** Colin Powell. **d.** Samuel Gravely, Jr.

_____ **13.** Many African American leaders opposed the war in Vietnam because they felt that the funds spent on it: **a.** should be spent on reforming the electoral process. **b.** were not enough to ensure victory. **c.** were raised mostly from African Americans. **d.** could be used to improve conditions in the cities.

_____ **14.** One reason that many veterans felt uncomfortable upon returning to the United States after fighting in Vietnam was the: **a.** low pay they had received for their military service. **b.** extensive public protest against the war. **c.** attack by the President on the quality of U.S. troops. **d.** requirement that they sign up again for the draft.

_____ **15.** The African American who was Chairman of the U.S. Joint Chiefs of Staff at the time of the 1991 war with Iraq was: **a.** Colin Powell. **b.** John Wilkins. **c.** James T. Boddie. **d.** Samuel Gravely, Jr.

III. ESSAY Choose one of the following topics. Then write your answer in paragraph form on a separate sheet of paper.

A. If you were an African American who had fought in Vietnam, how would you feel about protests against the war after you returned to the United States? Explain.

B. Do you approve or disapprove of the decision Muhammad Ali made in 1967? Explain.

Name ______________________________ Date ______________

UNIT 10 TEST: Cross-Currents in Today's World

I. MATCHING Decide which definition from the right column best explains a term in the left column. Then write the letter of the definition in the space provided.

_____ **1.** inflation
_____ **2.** Silent Majority
_____ **3.** affirmative action
_____ **4.** African/African American Summit
_____ **5.** apartheid
_____ **6.** Rainbow Coalition
_____ **7.** economic sanctions
_____ **8.** African National Congress
_____ **9.** demographics
_____ **10.** Black Family Reunion

a. supporters of Jesse Jackson
b. celebration of "African tradition . . . of sharing"
c. limits on trade with a country
d. group to whom President Nixon appealed
e. policy that gives preference to those who have suffered from discrimination
f. meeting that continued tradition of Pan-Africanism
g. Nelson Mandela's political party
h. population statistics
i. rigid government-imposed separation of blacks and whites
j. general increase in prices

II. UNDERSTANDING TIME Read the following list of events. Then choose the year an event happened from the list below and write it in the space provided. (Each year should be used only once.)

1962	1974	1976	1978	1981
1984	1986	1987	1990	1991

_____ **11.** Nelson Mandela is released from prison.
_____ **12.** Jesse Jackson first runs for President.
_____ **13.** Alex Haley's *Roots* is published.
_____ **14.** The UN expels South Africa.
_____ **15.** The Supreme Court decides *Bakke* v. *University of California.*
_____ **16.** Congress votes to limit trade with South Africa.
_____ **17.** General Colin Powell leads troops in Persian Gulf War.
_____ **18.** Nelson Mandela is arrested in South Africa.
_____ **19.** The first Black Family Reunion is held.
_____ **20.** Ronald Reagan becomes President.

III. MULTIPLE CHOICE Choose the answer that best completes the sentence or answers the question. Then write the letter of your choice in the space provided.

_____ **21.** The case of *Bakke* v. *University of California* involved a complaint about:

a. civil rights demonstrations. **b.** the voting rights of African Americans. **c.** African American access to public housing. **d.** an affirmative action program.

_____ **22.** Under President Reagan, the federal government cut spending for:

a. military programs. **b.** social programs. **c.** political programs. **d.** military and social programs.

_____ **23.** The 1990 census revealed that African Americans were returning in increasing numbers to:

a. the Northeast. **b.** farms. **c.** the South. **d.** small towns.

_____ **24.** What is a major factor affecting access to health care, medication, and preventive services for African Americans?

a. economics **b.** Jim Crow laws **c.** poll taxes **d.** literacy tests

_____ **25.** In 1991, over the objections of Nelson Mandela and African American civil rights leaders, President Bush:

a. imposed economic sanctions on South Africa. **b.** signed a defense treaty with South Africa. **c.** ended economic sanctions on South Africa. **d.** visited South Africa.

_____ **26.** Approximately what percentage of African Americans who enter high school today graduate?

a. 57 **b.** 71 **c.** 86 **d.** 93

_____ **27.** Today almost two-thirds of all African American elected officials are found in the:

a. Northeast. **b.** South. **c.** Midwest. **d.** West.

IV. COMPLETING THE IDEA Choose the name from the list that best completes each of the following sentences. Then write it in the space provided.

Leon Sullivan	Mae C. Jamison	David Dinkins
Vincent Lane	Toni Morrison	L. Douglas Wilder
Spike Lee	Jesse Jackson	

28. A physician, chemist, and expert in African American studies, ____________________

____________________ was a NASA astronaut who first flew into space in 1991.

29. A former aide to Martin Luther King, ____________________ gained national attention by organizing Operation Breadbasket and PUSH.

30. ____________________ won a Pulitzer Prize for the best-selling novel *Beloved.*

31. ____________________ organized a meeting of African and African American educators, politicians, and business people to discuss African and African American issues.

32. In 1990, ____________________ of Virginia was the first African American to be elected governor of a state.

33. The films of ____________________ have aroused controversy in both white and African American communities.

34. ________________________ set aside a multi-million-dollar real estate career to become head of the Chicago Housing Authority.

35. The 1990 election of ________________________ as mayor of New York City meant that for the first time an African American headed the nation's largest city.

V. ESSAY Choose one of the following topics. Then write your answer in paragraph form on a separate sheet of paper.

A. What do you consider the most important contribution African Americans have made to U.S. culture in the past 20 years? Explain.

B. What do you consider the single most important thing that could be done to improve conditions for African Americans in U.S. society today? Explain.

Name ______________________________ Date ______________

CHAPTER 33 TEST: Agenda for Change

I. MATCHING Decide which description in the right column best identifies a person in the left column. Then write the letter of the description in the space provided.

_____	**1.** Dorothy Height	**a.** head of Chicago Housing Authority
_____	**2.** John Lewis	**b.** organizer of the Black Family Reunion
_____	**3.** Clara McBride Hale	**c.** U.S. Representative and former freedom rider
_____	**4.** Vincent Lane	**d.** creator of program to care for drug-addicted infants
_____	**5.** Earl G. Graves	**e.** publisher of *Black Enterprise*

II. MULTIPLE CHOICE Choose the answer that best completes the sentence or answers the question. Then write the letter of your choice in the space provided.

_____ **6.** The 1990 census revealed that for the first time in this century increasing numbers of African Americans were moving to the: **a.** Northeast. **b.** South. **c.** Midwest. **d.** West.

_____ **7.** In 1990, about 13 percent of white households earned less than $10,000 a year, while for African American households the figure was about: **a.** 10 percent. **b.** 14 percent. **c.** 22 percent. **d.** 33 percent.

_____ **8.** Experts predict trends and changes in how people live through the study of population statistics or: **a.** inputs. **b.** demographics. **c.** registrations. **d.** datums.

_____ **9.** Many of the nation's cities have been left impoverished by the: **a.** creation of public housing. **b.** effects of the Great Migration. **c.** changing nature of the middle class. **d.** flight of white families to the suburbs.

_____ **10.** The income of college-educated African Americans is approximately what percentage of the income of college-educated whites? **a.** 55 **b.** 65 **c.** 85 **d.** 95

_____ **11.** "Permanently entrapped population . . . without sufficient income to secure a decent quality of life" is a description of the: **a.** underclass. **b.** urban core. **c.** migrants. **d.** rural dwellers.

_____ **12.** A desire to promote the "African tradition . . . of sharing" and stimulate the sense that African Americans are one people lay behind the organization of the: **a.** Chicago Housing Authority. **b.** Civil Rights Memorial. **c.** SNCC. **d.** Black Family Reunion.

_____ **13.** Recognizing a long tradition among African Americans, one expert has said, "If you want to deal effectively with the black community, you have to deal with the: **a.** churches." **b.** middle class." **c.** politicians." **d.** schools."

_____ **14.** According to one government report, what group may "feel little in common with poor blacks, because their experiences will have been so dramatically different in so many ways"? **a.** members of the underclass **b.** middle-class African Americans **c.** social workers **d.** whites on welfare

_____ **15.** A white child born in 1989 can expect to live 79.9 years, while an African American child born at the same time can expect to live: **a.** 65.6 years. **b.** 69.9 years. **c.** 75.4 years. **d.** 81.3 years.

III. ESSAY Choose one of the following topics. Then write your answer in paragraph form on a separate sheet of paper.

A. If you were an African American living in an inner city in the Northeast who had the chance to move to the South, would you do so? Explain.

B. What kinds of programs to do think would be most helpful to the African American underclass?

Name ______________________________ Date ______________

CHAPTER 34 TEST: Crossing New Frontiers

I. COMPLETING THE IDEA Choose the name from the list that best completes each of the following sentences and write it in the space provided.

Katherine Dunham	Mae C. Jamison	L. Douglas Wilder	Shirley Chisholm
Nelson Mandela	Alice Walker	Guion S. Bluford, Jr.	Jesse Jackson

1. In 1990, ______________ became the nation's first elected African American governor.
2. *The Color Purple* by ______________ became a best-seller, won a Pulitzer Prize, and was made into a hit movie.
3. ______________ spent 26 years in prison for attempting to change government policies toward blacks.
4. A graduate of NASA's astronaut training program, ______________ became the first African American in space.
5. After election to Congress in 1968, ______________ ran for the Democratic nomination for President in 1972.
6. Alvin Ailey and Arthur Mitchell built on the work of such African American pioneers of modern dance as ______________.
7. The first African American woman astronaut was ______________.
8. ______________ put together the Rainbow Coalition while campaigning for the Democratic presidential nomination in 1984 and 1988.

II. MULTIPLE CHOICE Choose the answer that best completes the sentence. Then write the letter of your choice in the space provided.

_____ 9. Louise Mailou Jones, Elizabeth Catlett-Mora, and Romare Bearden are all African American: **a.** actors. **b.** dancers. **c.** singers. **d.** artists.

_____ 10. During the 1980s, many African Americans urged President Bush to declare: **a.** a national war against drugs. **b.** an unemployment emergency. **c.** huge budget cuts. **d.** an economic aid package for South Africa.

_____ 11. The system under which the South African government rigidly separated its black and white people was known as: **a.** griot. **b.** kente. **c.** dashiki. **d.** apartheid.

_____ 12. In 1983, President Reagan signed a bill making a national holiday of: **a.** the anniversary of the Emancipation Proclamation. **b.** Martin Luther King, Jr.'s birthday. **c.** Black History Day. **d.** Booker T. Washington's birthday.

_____ 13. To pressure the government of South Africa to change its policies toward its black citizens, some nations imposed limits on trade that were known as economic: **a.** sanctions. **b.** accommodations. **c.** affirmations. **d.** settlements.

_____ 14. The first African/African American Summit continued the tradition of: **a.** apartheid. **b.** economic sanctions. **c.** disfranchisement. **d.** Pan-Africanism.

_____ 15. To pressure South Africa to change its policies, the UN voted in 1974 to: **a.** send troops to South Africa. **b.** recognize a black government for South Africa. **c.** close international air routes to South Africa. **d.** expel South Africa from the UN.

III ESSAY Choose one of the following topics. Then write your answer in paragraph form on a separate sheet of paper.

A. Do you think an African American will be elected President during your lifetime? Explain.

B. In what ways do you think African Americans might increase their ties to their African homeland?

ANSWER KEY FOR UNIT AND CHAPTER TESTS

UNIT 1 TEST: The African Homeland

MATCHING **1.** d **2.** c **3.** h **4.** f **5.** a **6.** g **7.** e **8.** b

UNDERSTANDING TIME *correct order:* 4, 8, 10, 9, 5, 1, 7, 3, 6, 2.

MULTIPLE CHOICE **9.** b **10.** d **11.** d **12.** a **13.** b **14.** b **15.** a **16.** c **17.** b **18.** a **19.** d **20.** b

COMPLETING THE IDEA **21.** Hatshepsut **22.** Sundiata **23.** Akhenaton **24.** Mary Leakey **25.** Askia Muhammad **26.** Muhammad **27.** Mansa Musa **28.** Abu Bakr **29.** Ezana **30.** Kashta

ESSAY **A.** Reasons for agreement include that the earliest human remains were found in Africa; farming was practiced there in very ancient times; Egypt produced one of the first great civilizations. Reasons for disagreement include that early farming was not exclusive to Africa; civilizations sprang up in other places that had no contact with Africa. **B.** Possible geographic factors are, in Egypt, desert climate, seasonal flooding of the Nile; in Meroë, iron deposits, fertile soil, and access to the Red Sea; in Ghana, access to both gold deposits and salt deposits, desert climate.

Chapter 1: Egypt, Kush, and Axum

MATCHING **1.** f **2.** a **3.** b **4.** c **5.** e **6.** d

MULTIPLE CHOICE **7.** c **8.** b **9.** d **10.** a **11.** d **12.** a **13.** d **14.** b **15.** b

ESSAY **A.** The following might be included: Egypt sometimes invaded neighboring lands, those lands sometimes invaded Egypt, technology and culture spread through trading contacts, neighbors sometimes adopted Egyptian forms of rule. **B.** Responses will differ. Warfare spread military technology and allowed one nation to impose its will on another; however, trade probably produced more interchanges of different types of goods and ideas to more receptive people.

Chapter 2: Great Empires of West Africa

MATCHING **1.** d **2.** e **3.** b **4.** c **5.** a

MULTIPLE CHOICE **6.** b **7.** a **8.** c **9.** c **10.** a **11.** d **12.** c **13.** d **14.** a **15.** c

ESSAY **A.** Responses will differ. The arrival of Islam brought new technologies. Increased contacts meant expanded trade and greater wealth. On the negative side, Islamic leaders imposed their own rule, changing the nature of African development. **B.** Both were affected by advances in military technology. Ghana used iron weapons to defeat its neighbors, whereas the Songhai fell to a smaller Moroccan army equipped with guns.

Chapter 3: The West African Heritage

MATCHING **1.** f **2.** d **3.** e **4.** a **5.** b **6.** g **7.** c

MULTIPLE CHOICE **8.** d **9.** a **10.** c **11.** c **12.** b **13.** b **14.** a **15.** d

ESSAY **A.** Possible advantages: sharing of burdens in hard times, availability of helping hands, security in sickness or old age. Possible disadvantages: lack of privacy, stifling of initiative, hostility to ideas from outside. **B.** West Africans believed in a Creator and an afterlife, elements common to Islam and Christianity. However, African beliefs in many gods and in spirits living in all things would conflict with both Christianity and Islam.

UNIT 2 TEST: Africans in the Americas

MATCHING **1.** d **2.** c **3.** a **4.** e **5.** b

UNDERSTANDING TIME **6.** C **7.** F **8.** E **9.** J **10.** A **11.** G **12.** I **13.** B **14.** D **15.** H

MULTIPLE CHOICE **16.** c **17.** b **18.** b **19.** a **20.** d **21.** a **22.** d **23.** b **24.** a **25.** b

COMPLETING THE IDEA **26.** Maryland **27.** Great Britain **28.** John Locke **29.** Nzinga **30.** Balboa **31.** Pennsylvania **32.** Bartolomé de Las Casas **33.** Portugal **34.** Mathias De Sousa **35.** the West Indies

ESSAY **A.** Students' letters should reflect that the slave trade led Africans to kidnap other Africans as slaves, and that the country was depopulated as a result. **B.** Student responses should note that the Spanish had brought enslaved Africans to the Americas well before the English did. If the English had been defeated, there is no reason to believe that the Spanish would not have tried to expand their territory or would not have used African slaves.

Chapter 4: The Atlantic Slave Trade

MATCHING **1.** c **2.** e **3.** b **4.** a **5.** d

MULTIPLE CHOICE **6.** d **7.** c **8.** b **9.** c **10.** b **11.** a **12.** a **13.** c **14.** c **15.** d

ESSAY **A.** Possible responses: desire for wealth, desire to gain political advantage over neighboring peoples, coercion by Europeans, the fact that slavery was already an accepted practice among Africans. **B.** Possible reasons: greater expense in treating enslaved Africans better, higher profits to be made from carrying more Africans, treating Africans like animals might have made the practice of slavery more acceptable to captains and crews.

Chapter 5: The West Indies: First Stop for Africans

MATCHING **1.** e **2.** c **3.** d **4.** b **5.** a

MULTIPLE CHOICE **6.** d **7.** d **8.** d **9.** c **10.** c **11.** d **12.** a **13.** d **14.** a **15.** b

ESSAY **A.** Possible response: The fact that some escaped slaves could win freedom might inspire other enslaved Africans to do the same. Slave owners would crack down harshly to keep slaves from plotting escape or rebellion.
B. Students who agree: any arbitrary violation of a person's rights is ill treatment; slave owners might treat enslaved persons as less than human. Students who disagree: under the Spanish or African treatment of enslaved Africans, they became an integral part of society, might be well treated, and could win or buy their freedom.

Chapter 6: Africans in the Thirteen Colonies

MATCHING **1.** c **2.** a **3.** e **4.** b **5.** d

MULTIPLE CHOICE **6.** d **7.** b **8.** b **9.** b **10.** b **11.** b **12.** d **13.** a **14.** d **15.** a

ESSAY **A.** Possible response: A different type of economy might have developed without a steady supply of cheap labor: more subsistence farming, rather than plantations raising cash crops.
B. Responses will differ. The New England climate, with its shorter growing season, would have been more effective at keeping people from investing in enslaved Africans than the 1641 law, which would have barred few slaves.

UNIT 3 TEST: African Americans and a New Nation

MATCHING **1.** d **2.** c **3.** f **4.** h **5.** g **6.** a **7.** b **8.** e

UNDERSTANDING TIME **9.** C **10.** E **11.** F **12.** A **13.** B **14.** C

MULTIPLE CHOICE **15.** c **16.** b **17.** b **18.** d **19.** a **20.** b **21.** c **22.** c **23.** a **24.** d **25.** a **26.** c **27.** d **28.** a **29.** d **30.** a

COMPLETING THE IDEA **31.** Thomas Jefferson **32.** Lord Dunmore **33.** Louisiana Purchase **34.** Continental Army **35.** Absalom Jones **36.** Free African Society **37.** Phillis Wheatley **38.** Northwest Ordinance **39.** Toussaint L'Ouverture **40.** Constitution

ESSAY **A.** Responses will differ. These promises and protections were denied to the majority of African Americans. Although by 1804 all northern states had passed laws to end slavery, prejudice and discrimination remained strong. In the South, slavery became more firmly entrenched as cotton growing spread. **B.** By opening new lands where the institution could be established, the expansion made slavery stronger. On the other hand, opening new lands hastened the end of slavery by increasing debate over the subject.

Chapter 7: The American Revolution: Liberty for All?

MATCHING **1.** b **2.** c **3.** d **4.** a **5.** b

MULTIPLE CHOICE **6.** b **7.** c **8.** d **9.** a **10.** b **11.** b **12.** c **13.** d **14.** a **15.** d

ESSAY **A.** Responses will differ. Some 20,000 African Americans won freedom by siding with the British. For those who supported the Patriots, results were mixed. Some individual owners granted freedom. By 1804, all Northern states passed laws to end slavery. For most African Americans, however, slavery remained.
B. Varied responses are expected. Some 20,000 African Americans responded to British promises of freedom. On the Patriot side, some served as slaves; others hoped to gain freedom; still others believed that the new nation would fulfill the promise of the words "all men are created equal."

Chapter 8: Forging a New Constitution

MATCHING **1.** c **2.** a **3.** e **4.** b **5.** d

MULTIPLE CHOICE **6.** c **7.** c **8.** c **9.** b

10. b **11.** b **12.** d **13.** a **14.** a **15.** d

ESSAY A. The following points should be included: slavery would not be abolished; the slave trade could continue until 1808, at which time Congress could abolish it; a tax could be imposed on imported slaves; each enslaved person would count as three fifths of a person when representation in Congress was determined; states had to return escaped slaves to their owners. **B.** Students might point out the role of African American self-help groups like the Free African Society whose actions helped spur the growth of the abolition movement.

Chapter 9: Expanding the Nation

MATCHING **1.** e **2.** f **3.** a **4.** b **5.** g **6.** c **7.** h **8.** d

MULTIPLE CHOICE **9.** c **10.** a **11.** c **12.** b **13.** b **14.** c **15.** a **16.** d **17.** a **18.** b **19.** d **20.** d

ESSAY A. Most will point out that African American contributions were important. African American labor aided economic growth. Some helped explore new territories and build fur trade. Others fought in the War of 1812. **B.** Responses will differ. Escaped African Americans found shelter with the Seminole Indians of Spanish Florida. Southern slave owners pushed the federal government to annex Florida and destroy this haven for escaped African Americans. This pressure led to military action and the purchase of Florida.

UNIT 4 TEST: Free and Enslaved

MATCHING **1.** e **2.** d **3.** a **4.** b **5.** c

UNDERSTANDING TIME **6.** D **7.** C **8.** B **9.** C **10.** E **11.** A **12.** B **13.** D **14.** E **15.** B

MULTIPLE CHOICE **16.** b **17.** d **18.** b **19.** c **20.** b **21.** a **22.** a **23.** d **24.** b **25.** c

COMPLETING THE IDEA **26.** New England **27.** James Monroe **28.** James Forten **29.** Cotton Belt **30.** Eli Whitney **31.** Massachusetts **32.** Virginia **33.** David Walker **34.** Peter Poyas **35.** the Midwest

ESSAY A. Responses should acknowledge that Cuffe was a backer of colonization and thus might have disapproved of Walker's call for resistance. **B.** Choices should be supported by examples drawn from the text.

Chapter 10: The Tyranny of Slavery

MATCHING **1.** d **2.** c **3.** e **4.** a **5.** b

MULTIPLE CHOICE **6.** c **7.** b **8.** d **9.** d **10.** b **11.** b **12.** b **13.** d **14.** a **15.** d

ESSAY A. Students should indicate an awareness that the tales helped preserve African culture and also conveyed a message that the weak could eventually triumph over the strong. **B.** Students might respond that the use of such names by African Americans showed their awareness that slavery, by breaking up standard family patterns, had created the need for a new, extended family.

Chapter 11: Armed Resistance to Slavery

MATCHING **1.** a **2.** d **3.** f **4.** b **5.** e **6.** c

MULTIPLE CHOICE **7.** d **8.** b **9.** b **10.** a **11.** d **12.** c **13.** a **14.** b **15.** d

ESSAY A. Students should indicate an awareness that the odds against a successful revolt were very great, since African Americans usually lacked firearms and were in a minority in most parts of the South. **B.** Basically the historian is saying that the effort to gain freedom against overwhelming odds was a noble one and that the African Americans who did rebel were not responsible for the fact that the odds were against them.

Chapter 12: Free African Americans in the North and South

MATCHING **1.** d **2.** c **3.** a **4.** e **5.** b

MULTIPLE CHOICE **6.** a **7.** d **8.** d **9.** b **10.** c **11.** b **12.** b **13.** a **14.** d **15.** b

ESSAY A. Some students may feel that free African Americans had a better chance of making a living in the South, while others may argue that there were fewer laws limiting freedoms for African Americans in the North and therefore that was the better place to live. **B.** Students should recognize that many white Southerners considered free African Americans a threat to the system of slavery and wanted them out of the country.

UNIT 5 TEST: Challenges to Slavery

MATCHING **1.** d **2.** c **3.** a **4.** e **5.** b

UNDERSTANDING TIME **6.** a **7.** b **8.** a **9.** b **10.** b **11.** b **12.** b **13.** b

MULTIPLE CHOICE **14.** c **15.** d **16.** d **17.** a **18.** b **19.** c **20.** a **21.** c **22.** b **23.** c

COMPLETING THE IDEA **24.** Horace Mann **25.** Seneca Falls Declaration **26.** Harriet Beecher Stowe **27.** American Colonization Society **28.** Richard Allen **29.** Dorothea Dix **30.** Declaration of Sentiments **31.** Frederick Douglass **32.** William Lloyd Garrison **33.** American Society for the Promotion of Temperance **34.** New York Vigilance Committee **35.** Free-Soil party

ESSAY **A.** Choices will differ. Be sure that each choice is supported by facts drawn from the text. **B.** Students who agree will probably argue that African Americans could have forced white churches to play a more active role in the struggle against slavery. Those who disagree may argue that separate churches provided African Americans more freedom to organize and to direct their own campaigns against slavery.

Chapter 13: Abolitionists

MATCHING **1.** d **2.** f **3.** a **4.** b **5.** c **6.** e

MULTIPLE CHOICE **7.** c **8.** b **9.** c **10.** b **11.** d **12.** b **13.** a **14.** c **15.** b

ESSAY **A.** Student responses might acknowledge the existence of racism in the North or the fear that free African Americans might take jobs from white workers. **B.** Those who side with Garrison might indicate a belief that slavery was an evil so great that drastic action was needed to end it. Others might feel that a more moderate approach could have ended slavery without violence.

Chapter 14: Escaping from Slavery

MATCHING **1.** g **2.** e **3.** c **4.** f **5.** a **6.** b **7.** d

MULTIPLE CHOICE **8.** b **9.** b **10.** d **11.** d **12.** a **13.** d **14.** d **15.** a

ESSAY **A.** Some students might feel that they could have done more to end slavery by staying in the United States; others may have wanted to build new lives in a land that did not permit slavery. **B.** Most answers will probably stress the evil of slavery and the effects it had on the African Americans trapped in the system.

Chapter 15: African American Churches

MATCHING **1.** c **2.** g **3.** d **4.** e **5.** a **6.** f **7.** b

MULTIPLE CHOICE **8.** b **9.** c **10.** c **11.** c **12.** b **13.** a **14.** d **15.** b

ESSAY **A.** Boycotts of products made by slave labor, the holding of abolition meetings, and use of church buildings as stations on the Underground Railroad are among the possibilities. **B.** Students should recognize that whites feared that African Americans meeting freely, without white oversight or supervision, would plot rebellions or otherwise work to end slavery.

UNIT 6 TEST: Hope for a New Way of Life

MATCHING **1.** c **2.** e **3.** d **4.** b **5.** a

UNDERSTANDING TIME *correct order:* 8, 4, 9, 2, 5, 3, 6, 10, 1, 7

MULTIPLE CHOICE **6.** c **7.** b **8.** d **9.** b **10.** c **11.** a **12.** d **13.** d **14.** d **15.** b **16.** c **17.** a **18.** c **19.** a **20.** a

COMPLETING THE IDEA **21.** Compromise of 1850 **22.** Radical Republicans **23.** Kansas-Nebraska Act **24.** Dred Scott **25.** Missouri Compromise **26.** Emancipation Proclamation **27.** Ku Klux Klan **28.** Mexican War **29.** Confederate States of America **30.** Freedmen's Bureau

ESSAY **A.** Students should show an awareness that repeated efforts at compromise failed, and that sectional tensions continued to increase. They might also note that any peaceful solution would almost certainly have entailed the continuation of slavery in some form.
B. Responses will differ. The physical challenge of life on the Great Plains typically was greater. However, African Americans in the South faced more difficult social conditions in their struggle against whites intent on regaining control over Southern life.

Chapter 16: The Road to the Civil War

MATCHING **1.** c **2.** b **3.** d **4.** e **5.** a

MULTIPLE CHOICE **6.** b **7.** d **8.** a **9.** b **10.** b **11.** d **12.** a **13.** d **14.** a **15.** d

ESSAY A. Expect varied responses. The decisions that the Missouri Compromise was unconstitutional and that slaves were property that Congress could not legally take from their owners, were damaging to African Americans. However, the ruling that neither the Declaration of Independence nor the Constitution applied to African Americans effectively cut them off from hope of participating in American society. **B.** Some students may say that the raid was harmful because it reduced the chances for a peaceful solution to the slavery questions. Others may feel that by helping to bring on the war, the raid helped bring about the end of slavery.

Chapter 17: The Civil War and the End of Slavery

MATCHING **1.** d **2.** c **3.** b **4.** a

MULTIPLE CHOICE **5.** c **6.** c **7.** b **8.** a **9.** d **10.** d **11.** b **12.** d **13.** a **14.** d **15.** b

ESSAY A. Some students may argue that the Emancipation Proclamation led Southerners to resist more fiercely. Others might note that it gave the North an important additional issue to fight for and that it encouraged the enlistment of African Americans in the Union army . **B.** Some students may say they would be unwilling to fight in segregated units and for lower pay than white soldiers received. Others may say that the chance to end slavery by defeating the South would have convinced them to fight.

Chapter 18: The Promise and Failure of Reconstruction

MATCHING **1.** f **2.** c **3.** d **4.** a **5.** b **6.** e

MULTIPLE CHOICE **7.** d **8.** a **9.** d **10.** b **11.** d **12.** c **13.** d **14.** b **15.** a

ESSAY A. Some students may cite the Constitutional amendments that guaranteed rights to African Americans and the beginning of African American participation in politics. Others may focus on more personal matters, such as the opportunities to marry legally, to raise a family free from fear of its being broken up by slave sales, and to work for oneself. Students should explain the reasons for their choices.

B. Arguments supporting the label "tragic" should mention the failure of many reforms to outlast the Reconstruction era. Arguments against the label would be that the lasting reforms, however limited, represented a great advance over slavery. Students should cite specific policies or reforms.

Chapter 19: Miners, Farmers, and Cowhands

COMPLETING THE IDEA **1.** Benjamin Singleton **2.** Clara Brown **3.** Henry Adams **4.** William Leidesdorff **5.** Nat Love

MULTIPLE CHOICE **6.** a **7.** d **8.** b **9.** d **10.** a **11.** c **12.** b **13.** b **14.** a **15.** c

ESSAY A. Some students might welcome the challenge of a new place and a new way of life. Other might feel that conditions would be too hard, while still others might be unwilling to leave family, friends, and a familiar way of life. **B.** Students might note that slavery was never an integral part of the economic and social system of the West. In addition, conditions often were so difficult that the struggle for daily survival helped break down social barriers.

UNIT 7 TEST: Freedom Without Equality

MATCHING **1.** h **2.** f **3.** e **4.** d **5.** a **6.** g **7.** c **8.** b

UNDERSTANDING TIME **9.** A **10.** B **11.** E **12.** D **13.** B **14.** D **15.** C **16.** D **17.** A **18.** E **19.** D

MULTIPLE CHOICE **20.** c **21.** b **22.** b **23.** a **24.** d **25.** a **26.** d **27.** a **28.** c **29.** b **30.** c

COMPLETING THE IDEA **31.** W. C. Handy **32.** Ida B. Wells **33.** Matthew Henson **34.** Henry Grady **35.** Scott Joplin **36.** Fisk Jubilee Singers **37.** Daniel Hale Williams **38.** Madame C. J. Walker **39.** George Washington Carver **40.** Booker T. Washington

ESSAY A. Responses may differ. Students will probably conclude that she would not. Her active campaign against lynching did not fit with Washington's ideas of accommodating to segregation. **B.** Students might note that whites felt little threat from Washington. He seemed to indicate that African Americans would accept segregation and low paying jobs and not demand civil rights or the vote.

Chapter 20: African Americans in the New South

MATCHING **1.** c **2.** d **3.** b **4.** a

MULTIPLE CHOICE **5.** d **6.** c **7.** a **8.** a **9.** b **10.** b **11.** c **12.** a **13.** c **14.** d **15.** a

ESSAY **A.** Responses will differ. Students who would accept a job might feel they needed the money and owed little to all-white unions. Students who would refuse might resent being the tool of white employers who had never hired them before and might fire them after the strike. **B.** Agreement with the decision would probably be based on the idea that if the equality in "separate but equal" had been enforced, the decision might have been considered fair. Disagreement would be based on the assertion, which proved to be the case in the carrying out of the decision, that "separate" is almost by definition not "equal."

Chapter 21: Living in the Jim Crow World

MATCHING **1.** a **2.** d **3.** b **4.** c

MULTIPLE CHOICE **5.** c **6.** a **7.** d **8.** c **9.** a **10.** d **11.** c **12.** d **13.** a **14.** c **15.** a

ESSAY **A.** Some students might argue that such separation is hard to maintain in an open society and would lead to dangerous tensions. Others might agree that, as long as there are no legal limitations on citizens' rights, voluntary social separation is possible. **B.** Some students may note that Washington's approach had positive effects, letting him build Tuskegee and advance African American interests without strong opposition from whites. Others might suggest that since he was the most prominent African American his public protests would have been more effective than secret actions.

Chapter 22: Advances in Education, the Arts, and Science

MATCHING **1.** d **2.** g **3.** f **4.** e **5.** a **6.** b **7.** c

MULTIPLE CHOICE **8.** a **9.** a **10.** a **11.** b **12.** c **13.** b **14.** d **15.** d

ESSAY A. Responses will differ. They should be supported by information about the artist or inventor drawn from the text. **B.** Students who support a school like Howard might reason that African Americans needed access to the same types of education available to whites. Students who support Tuskegee might cite Washington's programs. Students who would support the elementary/high school might argue that education is most important in the early years and that African American schools suffered under the Jim Crow system.

➤ UNIT 8 TEST: Protest and Hope in a New Century

MATCHING **1.** g **2.** d **3.** f **4.** i **5.** j **6.** h **7.** a **8.** b **9.** e **10.** c

UNDERSTANDING TIME **11.** 1919 **12.** 1914 **13.** 1908 **14.** 1925 **15.** 1932 **16.** 1910 **17.** 1941 **18.** 1935 **19.** 1929 **20.** 1916

MULTIPLE CHOICE **21.** c **22.** d **23.** a **24.** d **25.** d **26.** b **27.** b **28.** a **29.** d **30.** c

COMPLETING THE IDEA **31.** Mary Church Terrell **32.** Robert S. Abbott **33.** Walter White **34.** Eleanor Roosevelt **35.** W. E. B. Du Bois **36.** Mary McLeod Bethune **37.** Marcus Garvey **38.** Langston Hughes **39.** A. Philip Randolph **40.** Bessie Smith

ESSAY **A.** Those who believe Garvey would have approved might say that the demands of Randolph and the direct action of the march seemed Garvey-like. Others might argue that Garvey would have wanted African Americans to build their own economic structures and not get involved with whites.
B. Responses will differ. They should be supported with information drawn from the text.

Chapter 23: The Civil Rights Struggle

MATCHING **1.** e **2.** b **3.** c **4.** d **5.** a

MULTIPLE CHOICE **6.** c **7.** b **8.** a **9.** b **10.** d **11.** a **12.** b **13.** d **14.** b **15.** c

ESSAY **A.** Some may feel that the NAACP empowered African Americans and gave the means to gain decent jobs. Others will believe that being able to pay the rent and put food on the table are always the more important issues. **B.** Student editorials might stress the need to make a broader public aware of discrimination, the need to fight discrimination in the courts, and the need for federal action to end lynching.

Chapter 24: The Great Migration

MATCHING **1.** c **2.** d **3.** b **4.** a

MULTIPLE CHOICE **5.** c **6.** a **7.** a **8.** b **9.** d **10.** a **11.** a **12.** c **13.** a **14.** d **15.** b

ESSAY A. Some may argue that the exclusion of African Americans from full participation in U.S. society justified a refusal to support the war. Others might agree with Du Bois that African American citizens should support the government in time of crisis. **B.** Responses will differ. Some students may point out that African Americans provided a plentiful source of cheap labor in the South. If many of them left, competition to find workers would drive wages up, cutting into profits for the owners of farms and factories.

Chapter 25: Black Nationalism

COMPLETING THE IDEA **1.** Paul Cuffe **2.** Claude McKay **3.** Marcus Garvey **4.** Kwame Nkrumah

MULTIPLE CHOICE **5.** c **6.** d **7.** a **8.** a **9.** d **10.** b **11.** a **12.** d **13.** d **14.** b **15.** c

ESSAY **A.** Some students may note that African American owned corporations offered the greatest chance of empowering African Americans. Others may argue that the UNIA newspaper would bring news of Garvey's ideas to the greatest number of people. Whatever choices they make, be sure students explain them.
B. Responses will differ. Students should indicate that the NAACP would probably disapprove. It was primarily interested in winning rights for African Americans within U.S. society. Garvey was more interested in getting African Americans to create an independent, viable society of their own.

Chapter 26: The Harlem Renaissance

MATCHING **1.** b **2.** g **3.** f **4.** e **5.** d **6.** h **7.** c **8.** a

MULTIPLE CHOICE **9.** c **10.** a **11.** d **12.** b **13.** d **14.** a **15.** b

ESSAY **A.** Students should note a new willingness on the part of African Americans to confront discrimination and prejudice and demand their rights. **B.** Responses will differ. Make sure that students explain their choices.

Chapter 27: The Great Depression and the New Deal

MATCHING **1.** g **2.** a **3.** c **4.** d **5.** h **6.** b **7.** e **8.** f

MULTIPLE CHOICE **9.** a **10.** b **11.** d **12.** c **13.** d **14.** c **15.** b

ESSAY **A.** Choices will differ. Leading candidates include the PWA, the FSA, the NYA, and the WPA. Students might note that the WPA became one of the largest employers of African Americans, while the NYA's programs provided educational opportunities to thousands of African American youths. **B. a.** By his statement, Douglass meant that the only political party offering hope to African Americans in the late 1800s was the Republican party, since the Democratic party was seen as the party of slavery and, later, post-Reconstruction repression. **b.** In 1932, even though African Americans suffered terribly in the Great Depression, most still supported Republican Herbert Hoover because of their distrust of the Democratic party.

UNIT 9 TEST: The Civil Rights Revolution

MATCHING **1.** e **2.** d **3.** f **4.** i **5.** b **6.** c **7.** g **8.** a **9.** j **10.** h

UNDERSTANDING TIME **11.** C **12.** F **13.** A **14.** F **15.** D **16.** G **17.** B **18.** E **19.** C **20.** E

MULTIPLE CHOICE **21.** b **22.** c **23.** d **24.** d **25.** c **26.** a **27.** d **28.** d **29.** b **30.** b

COMPLETING THE IDEA **31.** James Meredith **32.** Fannie Lou Hamer **33.** Colin Powell **34.** A. Philip Randolph **35.** Martin Luther King **36.** Thurgood Marshall **37.** James Farmer **38.** Malcolm X **39.** Stokely Carmichael **40.** Lorraine Hansberry

ESSAY **A.** Cases can be made for a number of campaigns, including the NAACP's legal campaign that culminated in the *Brown* decision, the Montgomery bus boycott, the Greensboro sit-ins, the Birmingham campaign, Freedom Rides, and the Selma campaign. Students should cite specific elements of the chosen campaign.
B. Students are free to agree or disagree with the quotation, but they should support their opinions with examples.

Chapter 28: World War II and African Americans

MATCHING **1.** b **2.** e **3.** d **4.** a **5.** f **6.** c

MULTIPLE CHOICE **7.** c **8.** a **9.** a **10.** d **11.** c **12.** a **13.** b **14.** d **15.** d

ESSAY **A.** Answers should show students' understanding that African Americans could not serve in the Marines or the Army Air Corps at this time, and that their roles in the navy were limited. **B.** Responses will differ. As evidence, students should cite developments both in the military services and on the home fronts.

Chapter 29: Gains and Losses in the Postwar Years

COMPLETING THE IDEA: **1.** Charlie Parker **2.** Ralph Ellison **3.** Mahalia Jackson **4.** Jacob Lawrence **5.** Richard Wright **6.** Ruth Brown **7.** Lorraine Hansberry **8.** Gwendolyn Brooks

MULTIPLE CHOICE **9.** b **10.** d **11.** c **12.** a **13.** a **14.** a **15.** d

ESSAY **A.** Choices will vary. Specific connections should be drawn between the performer from the chapter and current popular performers. **B.** Responses will differ. Possibilities include influencing legislation, bringing federal money to the people of the district, and acting as a spokesperson for African Americans in general.

Chapter 30: The Battle for Civil Rights

MATCHING **1.** b **2.** d **3.** e **4.** a **5.** c

MULTIPLE CHOICE **6.** d **7.** c **8.** a **9.** d **10.** b **11.** d **12.** a **13.** c **14.** b **15.** a

ESSAY **A.** Interpretations will differ but should recognize the general idea, held by many African Americans, that they could gain the attention of white people only by fostering a crisis of some kind. **B.** The key is that the Greensboro sit-ins were an African American initiative. Earlier campaigns, such as the Montgomery bus boycott, had been responses to earlier white actions.

Chapter 31: New Directions in the Civil Rights Movement

COMPLETING THE IDEA **1.** Malcolm X **2.** Stokely Carmichael **3.** Fannie Lou Hamer **4.** James Meredith **5.** Bobby Seale

MULTIPLE CHOICE **6.** c **7.** b **8.** a **9.** b **10.** d **11.** b **12.** c **13.** b **14.** a **15.** d

ESSAY **A.** Students should show a general awareness that political power is important in the gaining and holding of civil rights. **B.** Students should demonstrate an awareness of the ideas of each leader, including a recognition that Malcolm X's ideas changed at the end of his life.

Chapter 32: Marching Off to Vietnam

MATCHING **1.** d **2.** b **3.** a **4.** c **5.** e

MULTIPLE CHOICE **6.** d **7.** a **8.** b **9.** d **10.** c **11.** d **12.** b **13.** d **14.** b **15.** a

ESSAY **A.** Students should recognize that the protests were not directed against the soldiers themselves. On the other hand, the protests rejected the value of what the soldiers had risked their lives for. **B.** Students should demonstrate awareness of both points of view on the question, that is, the opposition to a war that one does not approve of, as opposed to the legal and moral obligation to perform military service.

➤ UNIT 10 TEST: Cross-Currents in Today's World

MATCHING **1.** j **2.** d **3.** e **4.** f **5.** i **6.** a **7.** c **8.** g **9.** h **10.** b

UNDERSTANDING TIME **11.** 1990 **12.** 1984 **13.** 1976 **14.** 1974 **15.** 1978 **16.** 1987 **17.** 1991 **18.** 1962 **19.** 1986 **20.** 1981

MULTIPLE CHOICE **21.** d **22.** b **23.** c **24.** a **25.** c **26.** c **27.** b

COMPLETING THE IDEA **28.** Mae C. Jamison **29.** Jesse Jackson **30.** Toni Morrison **31.** Leon Sullivan **32.** L. Douglas Wilder **33.** Spike Lee **34.** Vincent Lane **35.** David Dinkins

ESSAY **A.** Choices will differ. Students should demonstrate familiarity with the contributions they choose and should give concrete reasons for their preferences. **B.** Responses will differ. Students should demonstrate an awareness of current issues, drawn from the text and from their own observations.

Chapter 33: Agenda for Change

MATCHING **1.** b **2.** c **3.** d **4.** a **5.** e

MULTIPLE CHOICE **6.** b **7.** d **8.** b **9.** d **10.** c **11.** a **12.** d **13.** a **14.** b **15.** b

ESSAY **A.** Responses will vary. Students should show an awareness of the differing conditions and the changes that are taking place in each region. **B.** Students should demonstrate an awareness of the problems that are faced and should give reasons to support their suggested solutions.

Chapter 34: Crossing New Frontiers

COMPLETING THE IDEA **1.** L. Douglas Wilder **2.** Alice Walker **3.** Nelson Mandela **4.** Guion S. Bluford, Jr. **5.** Shirley Chisholm **6.** Katherine Dunham **7.** Mae C. Jamison **8.** Jesse Jackson

MULTIPLE CHOICE **9.** d **10.** a **11.** d **12.** a **13.** a **14.** d **15.** d

ESSAY **A.** Responses will differ. Students should demonstrate understanding both of the progress that has been made to date and of the obstacles that remain. **B.** Students should show their understanding of what has already been undertaken. They should also spell out one or more new ideas and indicate what they would accomplish.

Name ______________________________ Date ______________

CHAPTER 1 Activity Sheet: Using a Timeline: Ancient African Civilizations

A timeline is a useful tool for understanding how events are related in time. A timeline shows when a historical event took place in relation to other events. A timeline also indicates the course of events over long periods of time. Study the timeline below, which contains information about ancient civilizations in Africa. Then answer the questions that follow.

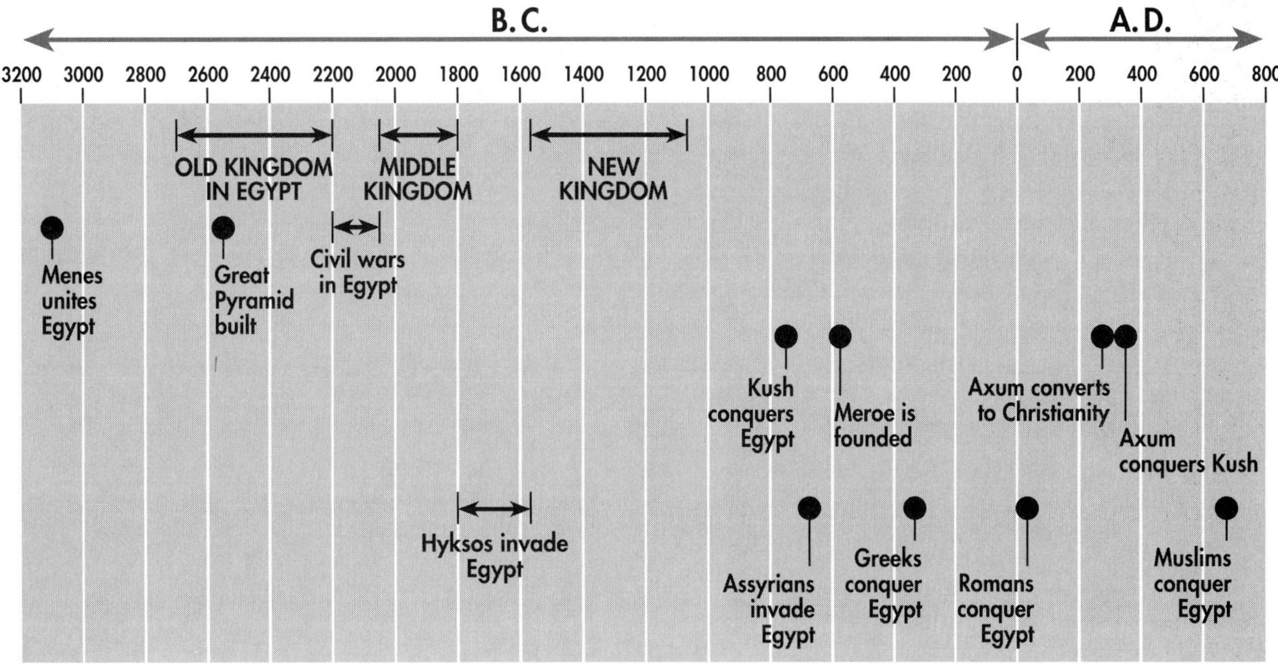

1. What is the earliest date shown on the timeline? ______________
2. What is the latest date shown on the timeline? ______________
3. What is the total number of years covered by this timeline? ______________
4. How many years are there in each equal section? ______________
5. For approximately how many years did the New Kingdom last? ______________
6. Which of Egypt's three kingdoms lasted for the shortest period of time?

____
7. What event took place during the time of the Old Kingdom? ______________
8. What event took place in 591 B.C.? ______________
9. Approximately when did Menes unite Egypt? ______________
10. Who was first to invade or conquer Egypt? ______________
11. During the period shown on the timeline, how many different groups invaded or conquered Egypt?

____

Name ______________________________ Date ______________

CHAPTER 2 Activity Sheet: Reading a Map: West African Trade Routes and Empires

Maps are useful tools for historians as well as geographers. Using maps, historians are able to summarize movements, economic conditions, political changes, and other historic events in any given period of time. Maps are also useful tools for students. To gather information from a historical map, look at all the map's parts. First, look at the *title.* It usually indicates the purpose, content, and time period of the map. Second, look for the *compass rose,* or directional arrow, which shows where north is on the map. Third, find the *map scale,* which shows the actual distance on the earth that a given distance on the map represents. Finally, study the *map key,* which explains the special symbols used on the map.

The map below summarizes the role of trade in aiding the growth of empires in West Africa. Read the map carefully by studying all its parts. Then answer the questions that follow.

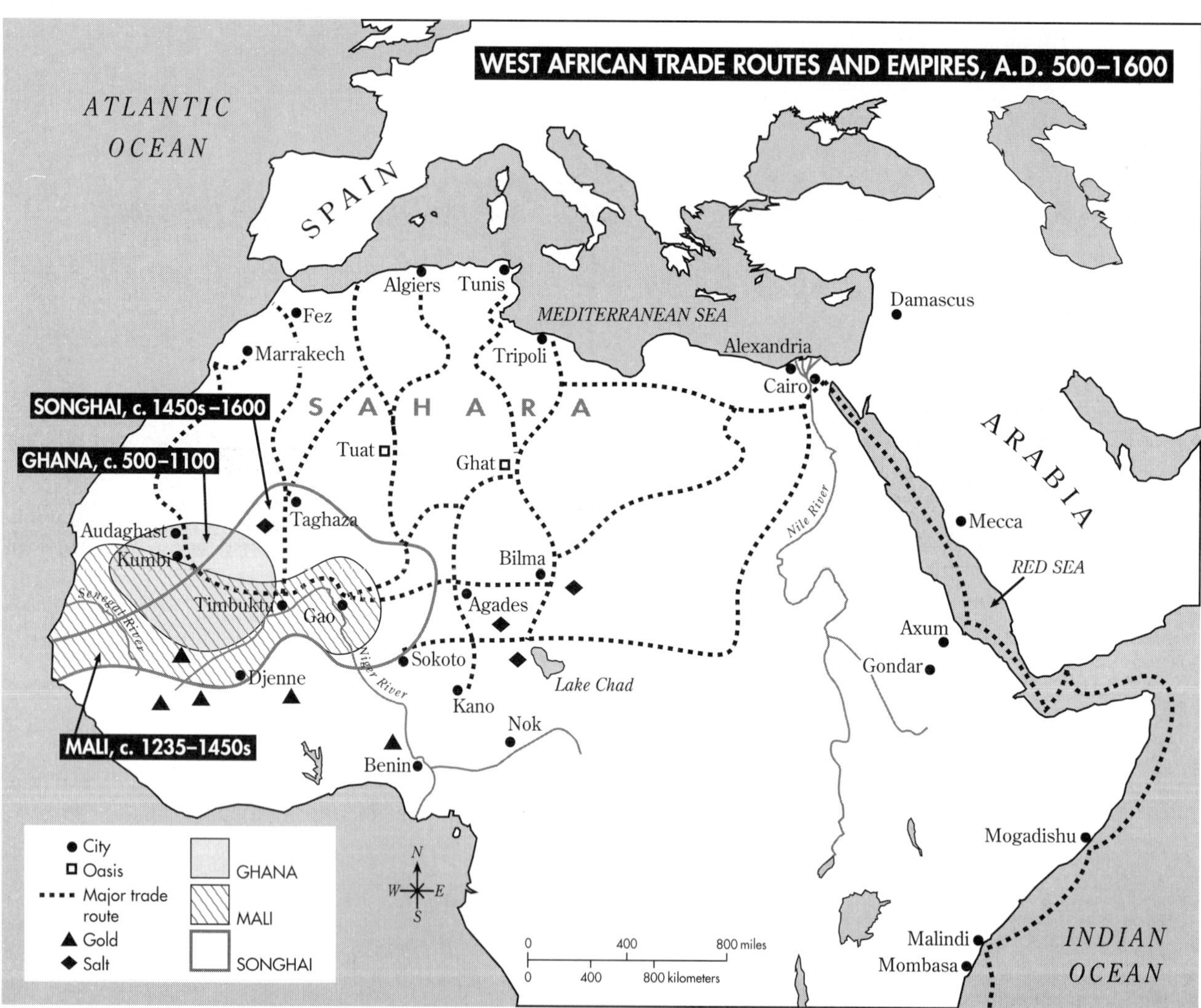

1. What is the purpose of this map?

____

____

2. What body of water lies to the south of Bilma?

____

Name ______________________ Date ______________

CHAPTER 2 Activity Sheet (continued)

3. Name two of the cities that are shown on the Niger River.

____

4. What city lies directly east of Timbuktu?

____

5. In what direction is a trader traveling from Djenne to Timbuktu?

____

____

6. What physical feature shown on the map occupies much of North Africa?

____

7. Approximately how many miles would a caravan have to travel from Fez to Timbuktu?

____

____

8. What source of salt is the nearest to Kano?

____

9. What was probably the major product exported from Djenne?

____

10. Which West African Empire covered territory that was once part of other West African empires?

____

11. Along what river would goods going from Gao to Benin travel?

____

12. Why would Ghat have been an important stopping place for travelers going from Cairo to Gao?

____

____

13. How might gold from Djenne have reached Mombasa on the coast of the Indian Ocean? List the places a caravan would have traveled through.

____

____

Name ______________________________ Date ______________

CHAPTER 3 Activity Sheet: Interpreting a Primary Source: A Traveler in Mali

A *primary source,* an original document or account from a period of history, is a valuable historical tool. Primary sources include letters, diaries, legal documents, eye-witness accounts, and business records. Textbooks are *secondary sources,* accounts based on primary sources and other types of information. Although primary sources offer eyewitness information, their authors may not always have had access to all the facts when writing. They may also have been influenced by prejudice or bias.

The account below is a primary source. It was written by Ibn Battuta, a Muslim born in North Africa in 1304, who traveled throughout the Muslim world. In 1352 he visited the West African empire of Mali, spending several months there. The document below is part of his account of this trip and lists the qualities of the people of Mali that he admires. Read the list and answer the questions that follow.

1. The small number of acts of injustice that one finds there; for the Negroes are, of all peoples, those who most abhor [hate] injustice. The sultan [ruler] pardons no one who is guilty of it.
2. The complete and general safety one enjoys throughout the land. The traveler has no more reason than the man who stays at home to fear brigands [outlaws], thieves, or ravishers.
3. The blacks do not confiscate [steal] the goods of white men [that is, of North Africans] who die in their country, not even when these consist of big treasures. They deposit them, on the contrary, with a man of confidence among the whites until those who have a right to the goods present themselves and take possession.
4. They make their prayers punctually; . . . On Fridays, anyone who is late at the mosque will find nowhere to pray, the crowd is so great. . . .
5. . . . If by chance a man has no more than one shirt or a soiled tunic, at least he washes it before putting it on to go to public prayer.
6. They zealously learn the Koran by heart. Those children who are neglectful in this are put in chains until they have memorized the Koran.

Source: *The African Past* © 1964 by Basil Davidson

1. a. What religion do the people of Mali practice?

____

b. Explain how you know. ______________________________

____

2. What evidence can you find in the primary source that Mali had trading contacts with other nations?

____

____

3. Did Ibn Battuta approve or disapprove of the treatment of children described in item 6? Explain.

____

____

4. Is Ibn Battuta's opinion of the people of Mali favorable or unfavorable? Explain.

____

____

5. Do you think Ibn Battuta's account of Mali is or is not reliable? Explain.

____

____

Name ______________________ Date ______________

CHAPTER 4 Activity Sheet: Explaining Illustrations: The Slave Ship *Brookes*

The illustrations below are diagrams of an actual slave ship, the *Brookes*. The original views were prepared in 1788, by a committee making a report on the African slave trade. The ship was built to accommodate 451 enslaved persons. On one of its voyages, however, the *Brookes* carried as many as 609 enslaved Africans. Study the three crosswise drawings (Views A, B, & C) and the view looking down at the platforms and the lower deck (View D). Note the labels. Then answer the questions that follow.

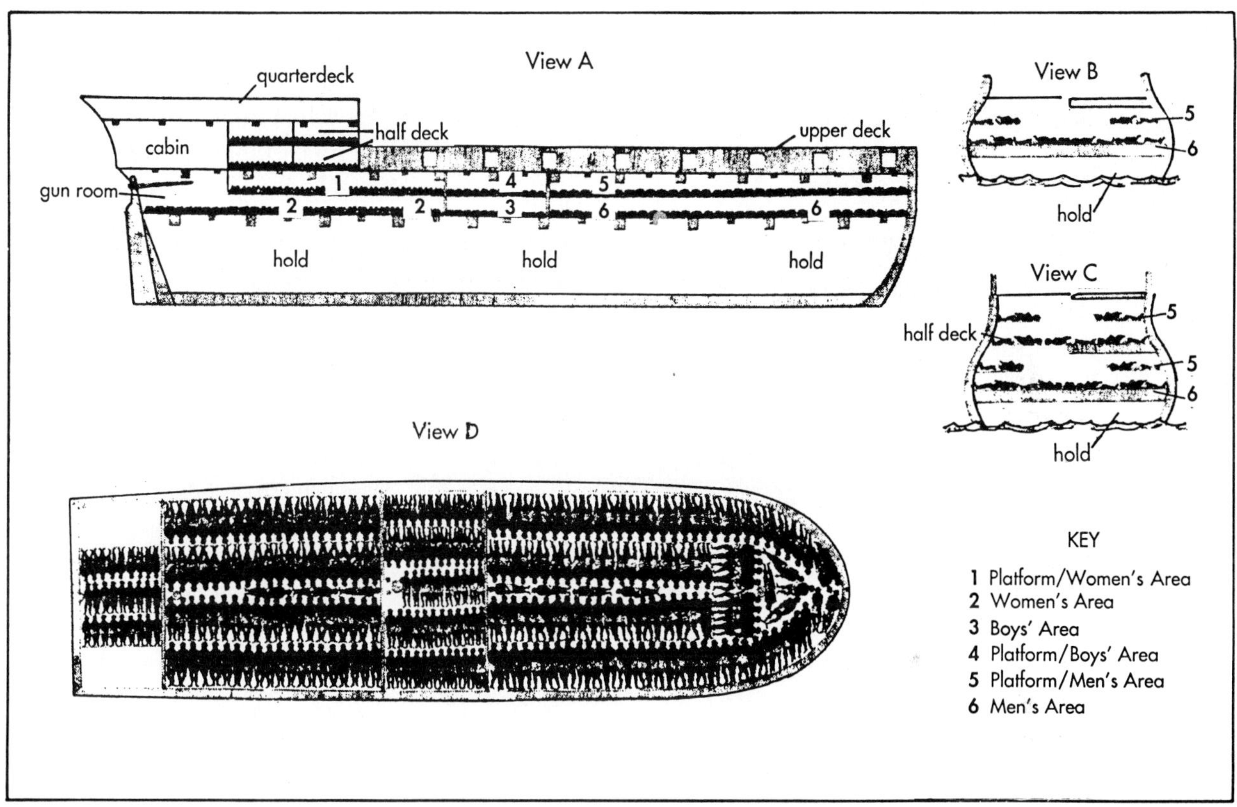

1. What do all the views show?

____

2. What does View A represent?

____

3. What does the number 4 indicate?

____

4. What do views B and C show?

____

5. What does View D show?

____

6. Based on these views, how would you describe the conditions for Africans on such a ship?

____

____

Name ______________________________ Date ______________

CHAPTER 5 Activity Sheet: Interpreting a Circle Graph: Where Africans Were Taken in the Americas

Statistics are numerical facts about a subject that are systematically collected, classified, and plotted in tables, charts, and graphs. Statistics are often shown in the form of line graphs, bar graphs, and circle graphs. These graphs can make it easier to see relationships among numerical facts. For example, statistics plotted on a circle graph, or pie graph as it is sometimes called, help show the relationship of parts to the whole.

The circle graph in this activity shows an aspect of the Atlantic slave trade. European nations with colonies in the Americas played the largest part in this trade. To discover the nations involved and the trade they carried on, read the title of the graph and the key carefully, then study the graph itself. Finally, answer the questions that follow. Note that figures on a graph like this are often rounded, or written as the closest whole number. In other words, the figure of 6 percent on a graph might actually be 5.8 or 6.2 percent.

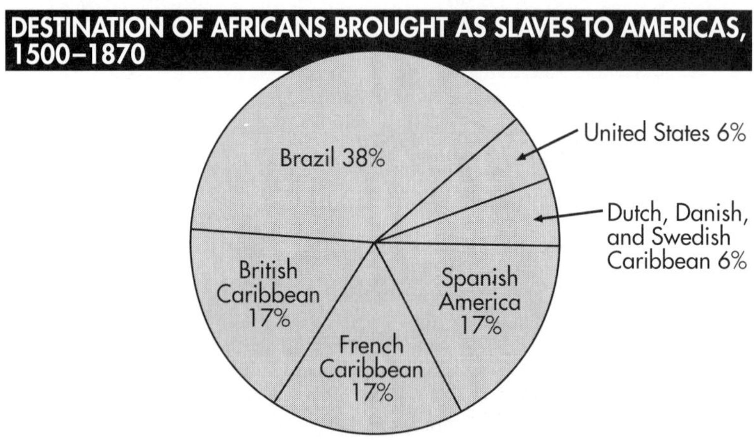

Source: Robert Fogel and Stanley Engerman, *Time on the Cross: The Economics of American Negro Slavery* (Boston: Little, Brown and Company, 1974), p. 14

1. Briefly explain what this graph shows.

____

____

2. What region imported the lowest percentage of Africans as slaves from 1500 to 1870?

____

3. What does the "17 percent" in the area of the graph that shows the British Caribbean mean?

____

4. What percentage of enslaved Africans went to territory in the Caribbean controlled by the French?

____

5. Add up all up percentages given on the graph.

a. What is the total? ______________________________

b. What does this figure represent? ______________________________

c. Have the figures on this graph been rounded? ______________________________

d. How do you know? ______________________________

____

Name ______________________ Date ______________

CHAPTER 6 Activity Sheet: Drawing Conclusions from a Map and a Table: The Colonial Economy

A conclusion is a decision or judgment reached by reasoning from the available evidence. Evidence can take many forms, including documents, photographs, statistics, and maps. To reach, or draw, a sound conclusion, the evidence should be studied carefully to see that it really supports the conclusion. Often, more than one form of evidence is needed in order to reach a conclusion about an issue.

Evidence about the colonial economy can be discovered in the following map and table. Examine them carefully to determine the relationship between the economic activities of Britain's North American colonies and the size of the colonies' African populations. Then answer the questions.

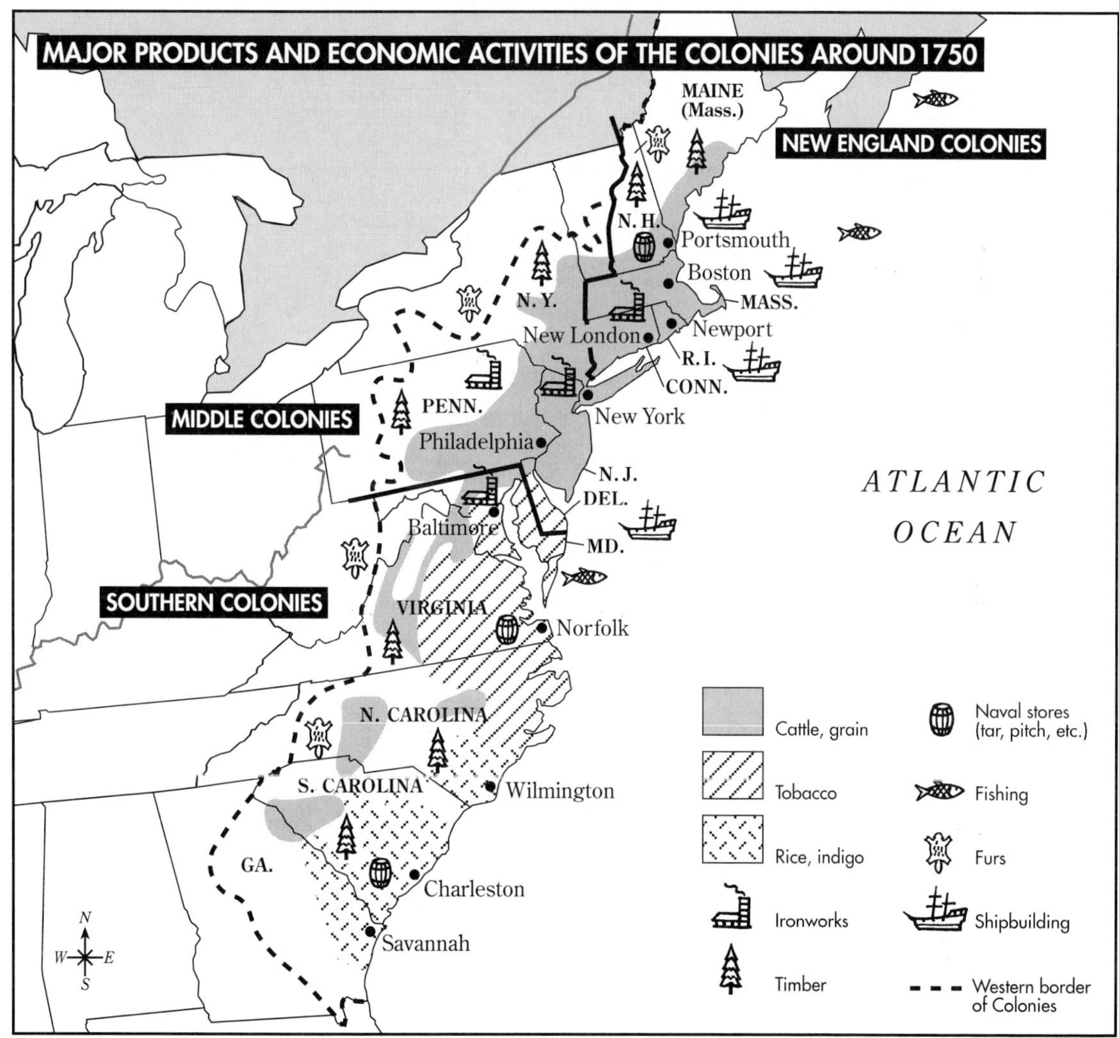

1. What does the map illustrate?

____

2. What colonies made up the group known as the Middle Colonies?

____

3. What were the most important products and economic activities in New Hampshire?

____

Name ______________________ Date ______________

CHAPTER 6 Activity Sheet (continued)

4. In which colonies was iron produced?

____

5. What was the most common product or economic activity in the colonies?

____

6. Was any product or economic activity found in only one group of colonies?

____

Now study the following table.

POPULATION IN THE COLONIES, 1750			
Colony	**Total Pop.**	**European Pop.**	**African Pop.**
New Hampshire	27,505	26,955	550
Massachusetts	188,000	183,925	4,075
Rhode Island	33,226	29,879	3,347
Connecticut	111,280	108,270	3,010
New York	76,696	65,682	11,014
New Jersey	71,393	66,039	5,354
Pennsylvania	119,666	116,794	2,872
Delaware	28,704	27,208	1,496
Maryland	141,073	97,623	43,450
Virginia	231,033	129,581	101,452
North Carolina	72,984	53,184	19,800
South Carolina	64,000	25,000	39,000
Georgia	5,200	4,200	1,000

Source: *Historical Statistics of the United States*

7. Of the New England Colonies which had the largest African population?

____

8. In which colony was the African population greater than the European population?

____

9. Which group of colonies — the New England, Middle, or Southern — had the largest African population?

____

10. Based on the map and the table, what conclusion can you draw about the relationship between economic activities or products and the size of the African population in the colonies?

____

____

____

Name ______________________________ Date ______________

CHAPTER 7 Activity Sheet: Interpreting a Primary Source: Slavery and Independence

As part of the record of the Revolutionary period, the Declaration of Independence is a primary source, an original document that comes from an actual time period. It was written and approved by Americans in 1776. The passage below is from an early draft of the Declaration of Independence.

Thomas Jefferson included this passage when he first wrote the document, but the passage was unacceptable to the Southern delegates at the Continental Congress and they voted to remove it. Read the passage carefully. Decide where Jefferson was placing the blame for slavery in the colonies. Then consider whether Jefferson's passage accurately reflected why African American slavery existed in the colonies. Finally, answer the questions that follow the passage.

> He [King George III] has waged cruel war against human nature itself, violating its most sacred rights of life and liberty in the persons of a distant people who never offended him, captivating and carrying them into slavery in another hemisphere, or to incur miserable death in their transportation thither. This piratical warfare, the opprobrium [shameful behavior] of *infidel* [non-Christian] powers, is the warfare of the Christian king of Great Britain. Determined to keep open a market where MEN [people] should be bought and sold, he has prostituted [misused for financial gain] his negative [veto power] for suppressing every legislative attempt to prohibit or to restrain this execrable [hateful] commerce [trade]; . . . he is now exciting these very people to rise in arms among us, and to purchase that liberty of which he deprived them, by murdering the people upon whom *he* also obtruded [forced] them; thus paying off former crimes committed against the *liberties* of one people, with crimes which he urges them to commit against the *lives* of another.

1. Who are the "persons of a distant people" referred to in the passage?

   ____

2. What accusation does Jefferson make against the King?

   ____

3. According to Jefferson, how does the King propose that these people win their liberty?

   ____

   ____

4. Based on this passage, what role did colonial merchants, shipowners, and plantation owners play in the trade described?

   ____

   ____

   ____

5. Do you think this passage is a fair and accurate picture of the situation described? Explain.

   ____

   ____

6. Why do you think that Southern representatives at the Continental Congress removed this passage before adopting the Declaration of Independence?

   ____

   ____

Name ______________________________ Date ______________

CHAPTER 8 Activity Sheet: Interpreting a Chart: African American Population, 1740–1790

A chart is an organized way of recording statistics and other data according to categories. When statistics are recorded by categories, comparisons can be made to discover patterns and trends. In the chart below, the percentage of African Americans in the population is organized into two categories: year and geographic location. The chart covers ten year periods from 1740 to 1790. Population percentages are shown for five geographic locations: the nation as a whole; the South—the region made up of the present-day states of Maryland, Virginia, North Carolina, South Carolina, Georgia, Kentucky, and Tennessee; and three of the states within the South. Study the chart carefully. Then write **true** or **false** for each of the statements following the table.

AFRICAN AMERICANS AS A PERCENTAGE OF THE TOTAL POPULATION

Year	United States	The South	Virginia	Maryland	South Carolina
1740	16.6	25.2	33.2	20.7	66.7
1750	20.2	39.4	43.9	30.8	60.9
1760	20.4	39.6	41.4	30.1	60.9
1770	21.4	41.6	42.0	31.5	60.5
1780	20.7	38.6	41.0	32.8	53.9
1790	19.3	35.2	40.9	33.7	43.7

Source: *Historical Statistics of the United States*

_____ **1.** One pattern shown by the chart is an increase in the percentage of African Americans in the total population of the United States for each year listed.

_____ **2.** The percentage of African Americans in the total population of the United States was greatest in 1770.

_____ **3.** The percentage of African Americans in the total population of the South was greatest in 1750.

_____ **4.** In 1780, the percentage of African Americans in the total population of the United States was 20.7. This means that, on average, 21 out of every 100 people in the United States were African Americans.

_____ **5.** Between 1740 and 1790, the percentage African Americans in the South increased every ten years.

_____ **6.** Between 1740 and 1790, Maryland had a greater percentage of African Americans in its population than South Carolina.

_____ **7.** Between 1740 and 1790, the percentage of African Americans in Maryland's population increased 13 percent.

_____ **8.** Between 1740 and 1790, the increase in Virginia's percentage of African Americans was less than the increase in Maryland's percentage.

_____ **9.** In South Carolina, African Americans were in the majority for every year shown.

_____ **10.** In 1780, the percentages of the African American population decreased in every geographic location except for Maryland.

Name ______________________________ Date ______________

CHAPTER 9 Activity Sheet: Explaining a Map: The United States and the War of 1812

The careful reading of maps and their map keys opens up their valuable treasures. To make full use of a map, always be sure to read its key carefully. The map below shows the United States during the War of 1812. Study this map and its key to increase your understanding of the war and of the conditions African Americans faced at that time.

A. COMPLETION Read the map above, and then, in the space provided, write the word or phrase that completes each of the following statements.

1. The nation of ______________________ controlled land immediately to the south of the United States.

2. The nation of ______________________ controlled land immediately to the north of the United States.

3. At the time of the war, ______________________ were the U.S. territories that permitted slavery.

4. U.S. victory at the battle of ______________________ stopped a British advance from Canada south through Lake Champlain.

Name ______________________________ Date ______________

CHAPTER 9 Activity Sheet (continued)

5. The battle of ______________________ was actually fought after the war's end because the news that a peace agreement had been reached in December 1814 was slow in reaching the United States.

B. MATCHING Match the descriptions in the right-hand column with the names in the left-hand column. Write the letter of the description in the space provided.

_____ **1.** Ohio River — **a.** state that barred slavery *after* entering the Union

_____ **2.** Vermont — **b.** first state to bar slavery

_____ **3.** Maryland — **c.** state where battle of Fort McHenry took place

_____ **4.** St. Lawrence River — **d.** route to the Great Lakes

_____ **5.** New York — **e.** route to the Mississippi River

_____ **6.** Ohio — **f.** state where the battle of Lake Erie took place

C. TRUE OR FALSE Use the information on the map to decide whether the following statements are true or false. In the space next to each statement, write either **true** or **false**.

_____ **1.** All states north of the Ohio River permitted slavery.

_____ **2.** The battle of Fort McHenry resulted in a U.S. victory.

_____ **3.** Louisiana was the newest state to enter the Union.

_____ **4.** The first battle of the war took place in New Orleans.

_____ **5.** New Jersey was the last of the Northern states to abolish slavery.

_____ **6.** No Southern states had barred slavery.

D. CRITICAL THINKING Use the information that you gained in reading the text to help you answer the following questions about features shown on the map.

1. What effect did the Northwest Ordinance have on slavery in the territories?

____

____

____

2. What areas shown on the map were acquired as a result of the Louisiana Purchase?

____

____

____

3. What effect did the addition of Florida to U.S. territory have on African Americans?

____

____

____

Name ______________________ Date ______________

CHAPTER 10 Activity Sheet: Interpreting a Map: The Cotton Kingdom

Maps present a variety of information about a place or a region. The map title and the map key provide information about the purpose of a map. The text surrounding the map also provides information about the map. Adding the text information to the map's visual picture gives a fuller picture of the topic being studied and leads to a better understanding of the facts and ideas involved.

The map below shows an area of the South. By the early 1800s, cotton had become the major crop of the South. The labor of enslaved Africans and the invention of the cotton gin made cotton growing a profitable business. But why was the South better suited to cotton growing than other parts of the United States? To answer this question, study the map. Read the information about cotton growing. Then answer the questions that follow.

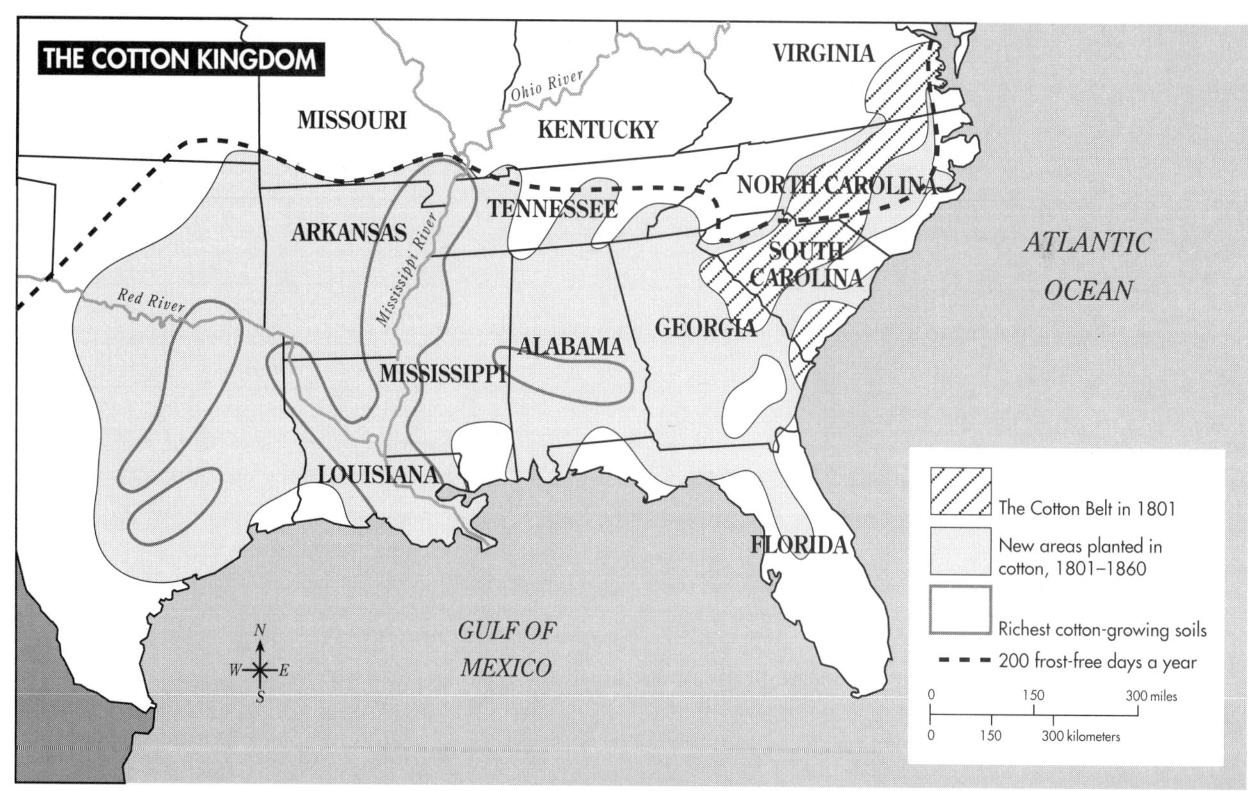

COTTON GROWING

Cotton plants need a long growing season. The plants do best in areas that have at least 200 days free from frost. This requirement limits large-scale cotton growing to areas where there is no frost for at least seven months a year.

Cotton also needs plenty of water while growing and a dry fall season for the cotton bolls, or pods, to ripen. Growing cotton where rainfall totals less than 25 inches (38 centimeters) a year is risky unless crops can be irrigated. More than 25 inches (38 centimeters) of rain falls each year across almost all parts of the South. Most of the rain falls in summer when the cotton plants need it most. Also, the fall season is usually dry in the South so that cotton ripens properly. Only areas along the Gulf of Mexico, where hurricanes are common in the fall, get too much rain for cotton to ripen.

Cotton growing, however, takes nutrients [foods] from the soil without giving anything back. As a result, soil in the South wore out. As it wore out, cotton growers cleared new lands. In the process, they moved farther and farther west. The spread of cotton fields across the Southwest gave unity to the region called the Cotton Kingdom.

Name ______________________________ Date ______________

CHAPTER 10 Activity Sheet (continued)

1. What is the purpose of this map?

____

____

2. Which of the states named on the map have less than half of their land in the Cotton Kingdom?

____

____

3. In which states named on the map is cotton grown north of the 200-day-frost-free line?

____

____

4. What states shown on the map had the main cotton-growing areas in 1801?

____

____

5. To what states had cotton growing spread between 1801 and 1806?

____

____

6. Based on information in the text and on the map, what reasons can you suggest for the fact that the cotton-growing area of Florida was not larger?

____

____

7. In what states is the best cotton-growing soil found?

____

____

8. Based on information in the text, why did cotton-growing never spread any farther west in Texas or Oklahoma than the area shown on the map?

____

____

9. Based on the information in the text and on the map, what reasons can you suggest for the spread of cotton westward?

____

____

____

____

____

Name ______________________________ Date ______________

CHAPTER 11 Activity Sheet: Recognizing Cause and Effect: A Former Slave Speaks

What happened to African Americans in the South as a result of armed resistance to slavery? When you ask a question like this, you are interested in causes and effects. A *cause* is a person, thing, or event that makes something happen. An *effect* is the thing that is made to happen by the person, thing, or event. As you read about history, look for cause-and-effect relationships. Sometimes certain words can give you clues. Such words and phrases as *because, due to,* and *reason that* often signal causes. Such words and phrases as *brought about, as a result of, therefore, thus,* and *if . . . then* often signal effects. When causes and effects are not directly stated, stop and ask yourself, "What was the effect of this event?" or "What caused this to happen?"

The reading below is taken from an interview with Charity Bowery, a former enslaved African American. The interview appeared in 1848 in *The Liberator,* William Lloyd Garrison's abolitionist newspaper. After reviewing Chapter 11 in your textbook, read the interview and answer the questions that follow.

> In the course of my conversation with this interesting woman [Charity Bowery], she told me much about the patrols, who, armed with arbitrary [unlimited] power, and frequently intoxicated, break into the houses of the colored people, and subject them to all manner of outrages. But nothing seemed to have excited her imagination as much as the insurrection of Nat Turner. . . .
>
> "On Sundays," said she, " I have seen the negroes up in the country going way under large oaks, and in secret places, sitting in the woods with spelling books. The brightest and best men were killed in Nat's time. Such ones are always suspected. All the colored folks were afraid to pray in the time of the old prophet Nat. There was no law about it; but the whites reported it round among themselves, that if a note was heard, we should have some dreadful punishment; and after that, the low [poor] whites would fall upon any slaves they heard praying or singing a hymn, and often killed them before their master or mistress could get to them."

1. What was the cause of Charity Bowery's excited imagination?

____

2. According to Charity Bowery, what were three effects of Nat Turner's insurrection?

a. ______________________________

____

b. ______________________________

____

c. ______________________________

____

3. Why do you think whites reacted so violently to the slaves praying or singing hymns?

____

____

____

Name ______________________________ Date ______________

CHAPTER 12 Activity Sheet: Making Inferences: Free African Americans

An inference is a conclusion or judgment reached by reasoning from evidence at hand — facts that have been gathered and analyzed as to their meaning. These facts may come from many places — textbooks, magazine articles, newspapers, photographs, and public documents of all kinds. In making an inference, carefully consider how all the specific facts or pieces of evidence point to an unstated, but implied, idea. Making an inference means stating this implied idea in your own words. In everyday language, it is often called "reading between the lines."

See what inference you can draw about the status of free African Americans in the United States before 1865 by studying the excerpt and public document below. The excerpt is taken from a recent history of African Americans. The public document is a photographic reproduction of the kind of document that Simon Hackett and other free African Americans were often required to carry, even in northern states which had abolished slavery by 1804. First read the excerpt, answering the questions that follow. Then study the reproduction of the public document, answering the questions that follow it.

> Wherever free Negroes settled, they lived somewhat precariously [insecurely] upon the sufferance [consent] of the whites. Their legal status was fairly high during the colonial period and was strengthened somewhat during the Revolutionary period. After that time, however, their status deteriorated [lessened] until, toward the end of the slave period, the distinction between slaves and free Negroes had diminished to a point where in some instances it was hardly discernible. Free Negroes found it especially difficult to maintain their freedom. A white person could claim, however fraudulently [falsely], that a Negro was a slave, and there was very little the Negro could do about it. There was, moreover, the danger of the Negro's being kidnapped, as often happened. The chances of being reduced to servitude or slavery by the courts were also great. A large majority of free Negroes lived in daily fear of losing what freedom they had. One slip or ignorance of the law would send them back into slavery. Several states, such as Virginia, Tennessee, Georgia, and Mississippi, required registration. Florida, Georgia, and several other states compelled Negroes to have white guardians. All Southern states required them to have passes; and if one was caught without a certificate of freedom, he was presumed to be a slave.

Source: *From Slavery to Freedom* © 1988 by McGraw-Hill, Inc.

1. What happened to the status of free African Americans after the Revolutionary period?

____

____

____

2. What dangers did a free African American face during this time?

____

____

____

Name ______________________________ Date ______________

CHAPTER 12 Activity Sheet (continued)

City and County of New-York, ss. Joseph Harmon

of the tenth Ward, of the said city, being duly sworn saith that he has for four years last past, been well acquainted with Simon Hackett a black man, that the said Simon resides in the said city, that he is about the age of thirty four years, and was born at Boston in the State of Massachusetts as this deponent is informed and verily believes, that during all the said time whilst this deponent has been acquainted with the said Simon as aforesaid, the said Simon hath been reputed and considered to be free, and hath continually acted as a freeman during the said time, and that the said Simon was born free ~~in or before~~

as this deponent is also informed and believes. And further this deponent saith not.

SWORN the twenty fourth *day of April, 1811. Before me*

Joseph Harmon

[illegible] Alderman

Source: *The Crusade Against Slavery*, Harper & Row, © 1960.

3. Where and when was the document above issued?

____

4. a. Where was Simon Hackett born? ______________________________

b. Where did he live? ______________________________

c. What was his status when he was born? ______________________________

5. According to the author of the excerpt, does *will, deed, receipt,* or *certificate of freedom* best describe the document shown above?

____

6. According to the author of the excerpt, what could possibly happen to Simon Hackett, and other free African Americans if they traveled into a Southern state, even with a legal document in hand stating they were free?

____

____

____

7. Do you think a free African American was safer in the North than in the South? Explain.

____

____

____

Name ______________________________ Date ______________

CHAPTER 13 Activity Sheet: Comparing and Contrasting Primary Sources: Arguments over Abolition

By the mid-1800s, arguments over abolition were growing more heated. Primary sources provide a clearer understanding of this issue. Two readings below take opposing viewpoints. **Reading A** is taken from instructions that the American Anti-Slavery Society gave to one of its agents in 1834. **Reading B** is from a book by an anonymous author published in 1836. Study both readings carefully. Note places in the readings where the authors deal with similar issues, but take opposing viewpoints. Finally, answer the questions that follow.

Reading A

You will inculcate [impress] every where, the great fundamental principle of IMMEDIATE ABOLITION, as the duty of all masters, on the ground that slavery is both unjust and unprofitable. Insist principally on the SIN OF SLAVERY, because our main hope is in the consciences of men, and it requires little logic to prove that it is always safe to do right. . . .

We reprobate [condemn] the idea of compensation [payment] to slave holders, because it implies the right of slavery. It is also unnecessary, because the abolition of slavery will be an advantage, as free labor is found to be more profitable than the labor of slaves. We also reprobate all plans of expatriation [resettlement outside the U.S.], . . . as a remedy for slavery, for they all proceed from prejudice against color; and we hold that the duty of the whites in regard to this cruel prejudice is not to indulge it, but to repent and overcome it.

The people of color ought at once to be emancipated and recognized as citizens, and their rights secured as citizens, and their rights secured as such, equal in all respects to others, according to the cardinal [chief] principle laid down in the American Declaration of Independence. Of course we have nothing to do with any *equal* laws which the states may make, to prevent or punish vagrancy [wandering around without means to make a living], idleness, and crime, either in whites or blacks.

Reading B

The object of those who have espoused [backed] the cause of the slave is averred [claimed] to be emancipation. They pronounce his bondage a sin against heaven and claim the freedom of every negro in the country. . . .

This emancipation is claimed *immediately.* They will not submit to any gradual measures for the attainment of their wishes....When asked, what will be the consequences of so mad and precipitate [hasty] a movement, they inform us that consequences do not enter into their calculations—slavery is a sin, of which the slave-holder should repent, not gradually, but at once. . . .

The immediate emancipation, thus claimed for the blacks is required to be unconditional. They admit no restraint upon the negro. He is to be turned loose at once. No barrier, no bond, no check—nothing to guard the negros from their own improvidence [lack of planning], . . . nothing to protect the master or his wife and daughters from the . . . revenge and cruelty of the brutal and unchained slave . . . .

The emancipation, thus urged, is expected to be attained without compensation to the master. . . . The abolitionists, in advocating [urging] emancipation without compensation, . . . do not regard, the fact, that the slaves have fallen into the hands of their present owners as *property,* that the laws . . . regard them and respect them, *as property.* These facts are wholly immaterial to the abolitionists.

Name ______________________ Date ______________

CHAPTER 13 Activity Sheet: (continued)

1. What is the major argument against slavery made in Reading A?

____

____

2. What stand on expatriation does the American Anti-Slavery Society take in Reading A?

____

____

3. What does Reading A say was the main goal of abolitionists?

____

____

4. What does Reading B say was the main goal of abolitionists?

____

____

5. What are three arguments made in Reading B against the immediate abolition of slavery?

   a. ______________________

   ____

   b. ______________________

   ____

   c. ______________________

   ____

6. Explain how the author of Reading A might have responded to each of these arguments.

   a. ______________________

   ____

   b. ______________________

   ____

   c. ______________________

   ____

Name ______________________________ Date ______________

CHAPTER 14 Activity Sheet: Recognizing a Point of View: An African American's Letter

A point of view is the position from which a person looks at something. A point of view is also reflected in a person's opinions, attitudes, or judgments. A point of view stems from a person's experiences and understandings. Because people's experiences and understandings differ, their points of view also differ. When reading primary source material, be aware of the writer's point of view. Information contained in the primary source can help you understand a point of view.

The reading below is taken from a letter written in 1844 by Henry Bibb, an African American. Read it carefully, looking for clues to Bibb's experiences, understandings, and point of view. Then, answer the questions that follow.

> You may perhaps think hard of us for running away from slavery, but as to myself, I have but one apology to make for it, which is this: I have only to regret that I did not start at an earlier period. I might have been free long before I was. But you had it in your power to have kept me there much longer than you did. I think it is very probable that I should have been a toiling slave on your property to-day, if you had treated me differently.
>
> To be compelled to stand by and see you whip and slash my wife without mercy, when I could afford her no protection, not even by offering myself to suffer the lash in her place, was more than I felt it to be the duty of a slave husband to endure, while the way was open to Canada. My infant child was also frequently flogged by Mrs. Gatewood, for crying, until its skin was bruised literally purple. This kind of treatment was what drove me from home and family, to seek a better home for them. But I am willing to forget the past. I should be pleased to hear from you again, on the reception of this, and should also be very happy to correspond with you often, if it should be agreeable to yourself. I subscribe [sign] myself a friend to the oppressed, and Liberty forever.

1. What might a slave owner call Henry Bibb?

____

____

2. To whom is Bibb writing his letter?

____

____

3. From what place is he probably writing this letter?

____

____

4. What is Bibb's purpose in writing the letter?

____

____

5. What forced Bibb to flee?

____

____

6. What is Bibb's attitude toward the person to whom he is writing the letter?

____

____

Name ______________________________ Date ______________

CHAPTER 15 Activity Sheet: Using a Map and Time Chart: The African Methodist Episcopal Church

Examining two different sources of information gives a more complete picture of a topic. The chronology and map below both give information about the organization and early history of the African Methodist Episcopal (AME) church. The chronology details the growth of membership while the map provides information on the time period in which congregations were established in various states across the nation. Study both carefully and answer the questions that follow.

Chronology

1787 Richard Allen and Absalom Jones withdraw from St. George Methodist Episcopal Church in Philadelphia because of discrimination against African Americans.

1794 Richard Allen founds Mother Bethel African Methodist Episcopal church in Philadelphia.

1816 The African Methodist Episcopal (AME) church is officially organized with five member churches and about 1,000 members.

1822 Angry white reaction to the Denmark Vesey conspiracy leads an AME congregation to move from Charleston, South Carolina, to the North.

1856 The AME church establishes Wilberforce University in Ohio, the first institution of higher learning founded by African Americans in the United States.

1861 The AME church has about 20,000 members.

1881 The *AME Review*, the oldest journal in the world owned and published by African American people, is founded.

1884 The AME church has over 400,000 members.

1896 The AME church has over 450,000 members.

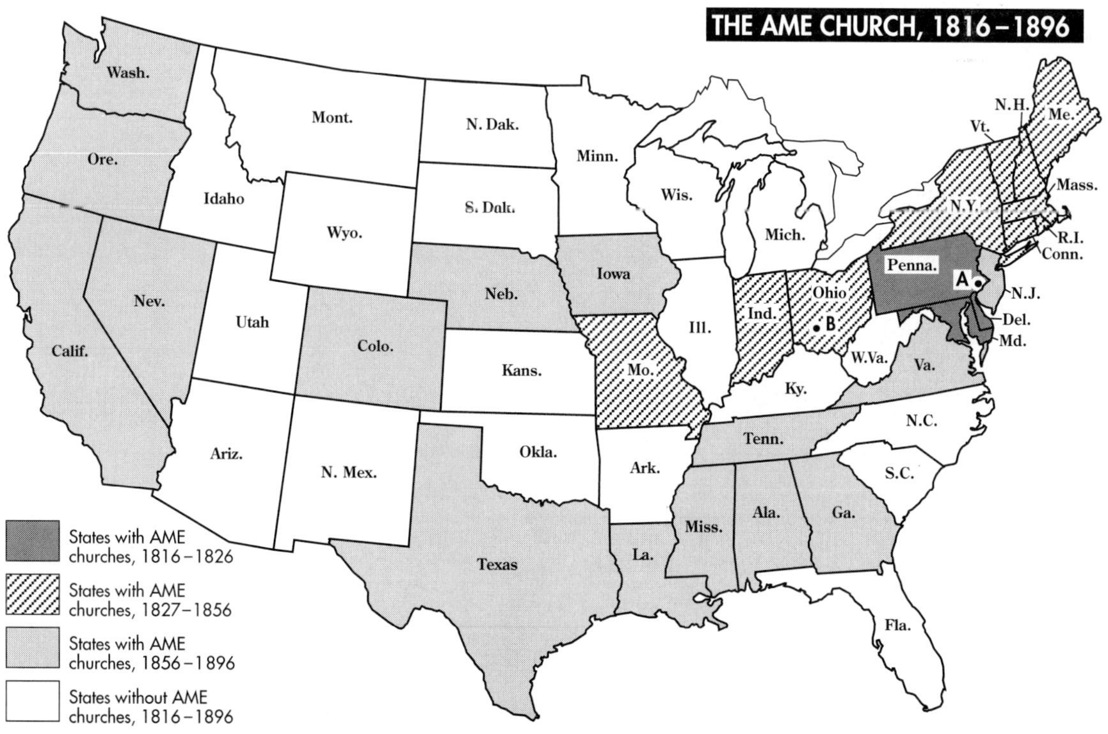

Name ______________________________ Date ______________

CHAPTER 15 Activity Sheet: (continued)

1. a. Who founded the African Methodist Episcopal church?

____

b. Why did they found the AME church?

____

____

2. a. Between what two years listed in the chronology did the AME membership increase by 380,000?

____

b. What was the increase in membership from 1816 to 1896?

____

3. a. In which period shown on the map were congregations established in the most states?

____

b. In which period shown on the map were congregations established in the fewest states?

____

4. a. What event in the history of the AME occurred at the place marked on the map by the letter A?

____

____

b. What event took place at letter B?

____

____

5. What fact helps explain why no AME churches were founded in South Carolina during the periods covered by the map?

____

____

6. a. According to the map, when did the AME church expand into the Southern states?

____

____

b. Using your knowledge of the history of this period, why do you think the AME church expanded into the South at this time?

____

____

____

Name ______________________________ Date ______________

CHAPTER 16 Activity Sheet: Summarizing a Primary Source: An African American Opinion

To summarize material means to restate it in shorter, more general terms. Summarizing a primary source reading can help you to better understand and remember a reading's key points. When summarizing a passage, it is helpful to underline the main ideas or make notes about them. Then restate, or paraphrase, those major ideas in your own words. The reading below is taken from an 1860 speech by H. Ford Douglass, a free African American from Illinois. Note the key points as you read the speech. Then answer the questions that follow.

> We have four parties in this country that have marshalled [set] themselves on the highway of American politics, asking for the votes of the American people. . . . We have what is called the Union party, led by Mr. Bell of Tennessee; we have what is called the Democratic party, led by Stephen A. Douglas, of Illinois; we have the party called the Seceders, or the Slave-Code Democrats, led by John C. Breckinridge, of Kentucky, and then we have the Republican party, led by Abraham Lincoln, of Illinois. . . . So far as the principles of freedom and the hopes of the black man are concerned, all these parties are barren and unfruitful; neither of them seeks to lift the negro out of his fetters [chains] and rescue this day from odium [shame] and disgrace.
>
> . . .
>
> [W]hile the Republicans are willing to steal our thunder, they are unwilling to submit to the conditions imposed upon the party that assumes to be anti-slavery. They say that they cannot go as fast as you anti-slavery men go in this matter; they cannot afford to be uncompromisingly honest . . .; that they want to take time; that they want to do the work gradually.
>
> . . .
>
> I do not believe in the anti-slavery of Abraham Lincoln. . . . What does he propose to do? Simply to let the people and the Territories regulate their domestic institutions in their own way. . . . In regard to the repeal of the Fugitive Slave Law, . . . What did he say at Freeport? Why, that the South was entitled to a Fugitive Slave Law; and although he thought the law could be modified a little, yet, he said, if he was in Congress, he would have it done in such a way as *not to lessen its efficiency!*
>
> . . .
>
> No party, it seems to me is entitled to the sympathy of anti-slavery men, unless that party is willing to extend to the black man all the rights of a citizen. . . . In the State of Illinois . . . [m]en of my complexion are not allowed to testify in a court of justice, where a white man is a party. If a white man happens to owe me anything, unless I can prove it by the testimony of a white man, I cannot collect the debt. Now, two years ago, I went through the State of Illinois for the purpose of getting signers to a petition, asking the Legislature to repeal the "Testimony Law," so as to permit colored men to testify against white men. I went to prominent Republicans, and among others, to Abraham Lincoln and Lyman Trumbull [senator from Illinois] . . . and neither of them dared to sign that petition, to give me the right to testify in a court of justice! . . . In the State of Illinois, they tax the colored people for every conceivable purpose. They tax the negro's property to support schools for the education of the white man's children, but the colored people are not permitted to enjoy any of the benefits resulting from the taxation. We are compelled to impose upon ourselves additional taxes, in order to educate our children. . . .[I]f we sent our children to school, Abraham Lincoln would kick them out, in the name of Republicanism and anti-slavery!

Name ______________________ Date ______________

CHAPTER 16 Activity Sheet (continued)

1. Name each of the four political parties and their presidential candidates in the election of 1860.
   - a. ______________________
   - b. ______________________
   - c. ______________________
   - d. ______________________
2. Why does H. Ford Douglass favor none of these parties and candidates in the election of 1860?

____

3. Why does Douglass say the Republicans are not really antislavery?

____

____

4. Why does Douglass not believe in the antislavery of Abraham Lincoln?

____

____

5. According to Douglass, what is Abraham Lincoln's position on the Fugitive Slave Law?

____

____

6. What does Douglass say about African Americans, political parties, and citizens' rights?

____

____

7. What is the Illinois "Testimony Law"?

____

____

8. Briefly paraphrase Douglass's complaints about taxation of African Americans in Illinois.

____

____

9. Briefly summarize Douglass's three major arguments against supporting the Republicans.

____

____

____

____

____

____

Name ______________________________ Date ______________

CHAPTER 17 Activity Sheet: Understanding Points of View: A Civil War Song

As a primary source, a song can indicate people's points of view about a historic event or period. The song below was sung by the African American soldiers of the 54th Massachusetts Infantry. Keep the chapter in mind as you read these selected verses and the chorus of the song. Then answer the questions that follow.

Frémont he told them when the war it first begun,
How to save the union and the way it should be done.
But Kentucky swore so hard and Old Abe he had his fears,
Till ev'ry hope was lost but the colored volunteers.

Chorus:
Oh, give us a flag all free without a slave;
We'll fight to defend it as our fathers did so brave;
The gallant Comp'ny "A" will make the Rebels dance,
And we'll stand by the Union if we only have a chance.

Old Jeff says he'll hang us if we dare to meet him armed,
A very big thing, but we are not at all alarmed;
For he first had to catch us before their way is clear,
And that is "what's the matter" with the colored volunteer. [Chorus]

So rally, boys, rally, let us never mind the past;
We had a hard road to travel, but our day is coming fast;
For God is for the right and we have no need to fear,
The Union must be saved by the colored volunteer. [Chorus]

1. The person mentioned in the first line of the song's first verse was General John C. Frémont. In 1860, Lincoln placed Frémont in command of federal troops in Missouri. When Frémont ordered the takeover of rebel properties and emancipated all African American slaves in the state, Lincoln removed him from command. Based on this song, what did the volunteers of the 54th Infantry think about Frémont's actions?

____

____

2. Who was "Old Abe" and what fears would he have had about Kentucky?

____

____

3. Who was "Old Jeff" and what threats did he aim at the African American volunteers?

____

____

4. Were the soldiers of the 54th eager or reluctant to serve in the army? Explain.

____

____

Name ______________________________ Date ______________

CHAPTER 18 Activity Sheet: Comparing and Contrasting Maps: Changes on a Southern Plantation

Maps of the same area in different time periods often provide evidence of social changes. The maps below show the same Southern plantation. The first map shows the plantation in the 1860s, before the start of the Civil War. The second map shows the same plantation in the 1880s, after Reconstruction. To understand the changes that took place in the intervening years, read the passage below, study the two maps carefully, and answer the questions that follow.

> [After the Civil War] freedmen were averse [opposed] to signing labor contracts because . . . so many white landowners expected to continue to treat them like slaves. Especially repugnant [disagreeable] was the idea of being again herded together in the plantation slave quarters, with their communal [group] facilities for cooking and washing and infant care, and their lack of privacy. Emancipation did much to strengthen the black family. Families divided by slave sales could now be reunited. Marital [marriage] arrangements between blacks, which had no legal validity [standing] during slavery, could be regularized. . . . The precious new security of family life was not something blacks were willing to jeopardize [endanger] by returning to slave quarters.

Source: *Reconstruction* © 1986 by Eric Foner

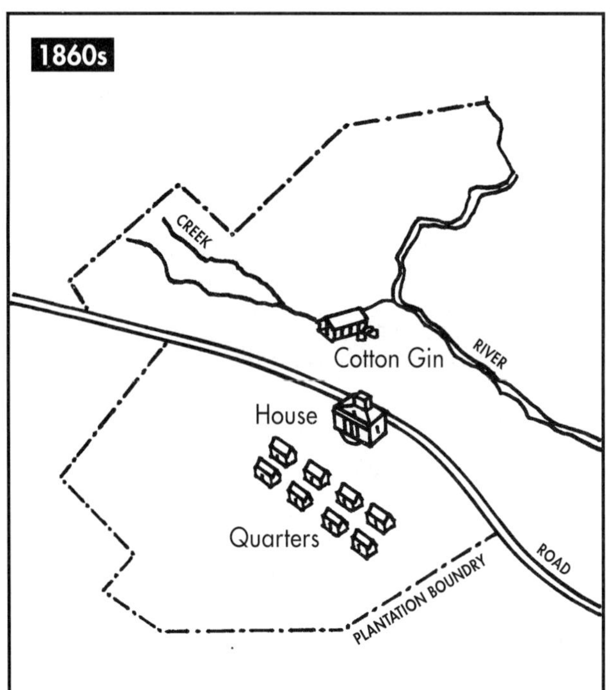

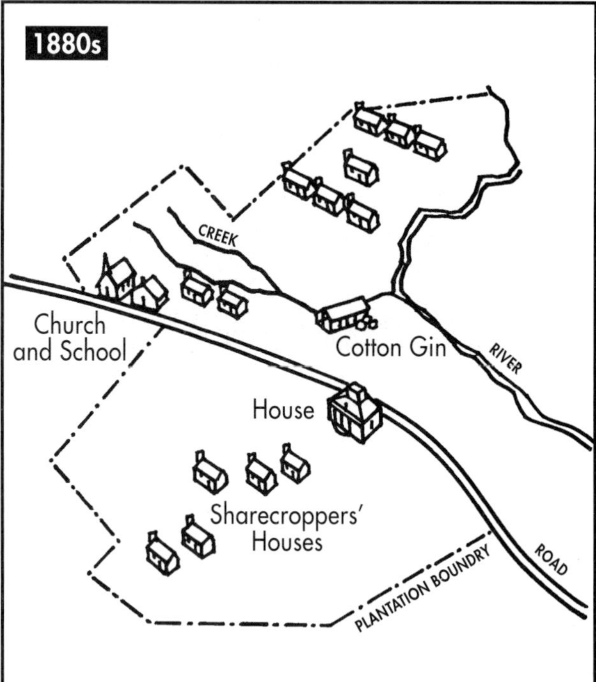

1. What do you think was the major crop grown on this plantation in the 1860s?

____

2. What evidence can you find to support your conclusion?

____

____

CHAPTER 18 Activity Sheet (continued)

3. Do you think this was still the major crop in the 1880s? Why?

____

____

4. Who do you think lived in the building labeled “House”?

____

5. Who probably lived in the buildings labeled “Quarters”?

____

6. Suggest at least three reasons why a plantation owner in the 1860s might have wanted the “Quarters” plantation buildings arranged in rows near his House?

a. ______________________________

____

b. ______________________________

____

c. ______________________________

____

7. Suggest three ways the plantation of the 1880s differs from that of the 1860s.

a. ______________________________

____

b. ______________________________

____

c. ______________________________

____

8. Why might plantation workers have favored the arrangement of buildings shown on the 1880s map? Suggest three reasons.

a. ______________________________

____

b. ______________________________

____

c. ______________________________

____

Name ______________________ Date ______________

CHAPTER 19 Activity Sheet: Drawing Conclusions: African Americans Move West

In the late 1870s, as Democrats regained control of Southern governments, some African Americans began moving out of the South rather than live in states with governments hostile to them and their concerns. They were attracted to new places by advertisements in newspapers, circulars, and posters, like the one below. Study its contents and answer the questions that follow.

To the Colored Citizens of the United States.

NICODEMUS, GRAHAM CO., KAN., July 2d. 1877.

We, the Nicodemus Town Company of Graham County, Kan., are now in possession of our lands and the Town Site of Nicodemus, which is beautifully located on the N.W. quarter of Section 1, Town 8, Range 21, in Graham Co., Kansas, in the great Solomon Valley, 240 miles west of Topeka, and we are proud to say it is the finest country we ever saw. The soil is of a rich, black, sandy loam. The country is rather rolling, and looks most pleasing to the human eye. The south fork of the Solomon river flows through Graham County, nearly directly east and west and has an abundance of excellent water, while there are numerous springs of living water abounding throughout the Valley. There is an abundance of fine Magnesian stone for building purposes, which is much easier handled than the rough sand or hard stone. Ther is also some timber; plenty for fire use, while we have no fear but what we will find plenty of coal.

Now is your time to secure your home on Goverment Land in the Great Solomon Valley of Western Kansas.

1. When did the poster appear?

____

2. Where is Nicodemus?

____

3. What is the purpose of the poster?

____

4. What makes Nicodemus attractive to new settlers?

____

____

____

5. Who currently owns the land in Nicodemus?

____

6. If you were an African American of the 1870s, considering a move west, what else would you want to know about Nicodemus? List at least three questions.

   a. ______________________

   b. ______________________

   c. ______________________

Name ______________________________ Date ______________

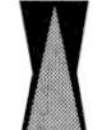

CHAPTER 20 Activity Sheet: Comparing Supreme Court Opinions: *Plessy* v. *Ferguson*

In 1896 the Supreme Court rendered a landmark decision in *Plessy* v. *Ferguson,* a case that upheld the constitutionality of a Louisiana law. This law provided for "equal but separate accommodations for white and colored races" on passenger trains within the state. The lawyers for Plessy argued that the law violated the 13th Amendment, which abolished slavery or involuntary servitude. They also argued that it violated the 14th Amendment's guarantees of "equal protection of the laws" to American citizens.

When the Supreme Court renders a verdict, the justices explain their votes in majority and minority opinions. The chart below presents notes that could be derived from reading the majority and minority opinions of *Plessy* v. *Ferguson*. Comparing these opinions provides insight into the controversial issues of the case. Read the passages carefully and compare their main ideas. Then answer the questions that follow.

ISSUES	MAJORITY OPINION NOTES	MINORITY OPINION NOTES
13th Amendment	No violation because "a legal distinction between the white and colored races "does not" reestablish a state of involuntary servitude."	A violation because racial distinctions have no bearing on "those entitled to be protected in the enjoyment" of their civil rights.
14th Amendment	**1.** Amendment not meant "to abolish distinctions based upon color, or to enforce social, as distinguished from political, equality." **2.** Similar laws upholding separation of the races in education "have been held to be a valid exercise of legislative power."	**1.** The Louisiana law detracts from the "dignity and glory of American citizenship, and contributes to the security of personal liberty, promised by the 14th Amendment. **2.** The 14th Amendment was intended to protect African Americans from "unfriendly legislation," which the Louisiana law clearly is.
The Louisiana Law	**1.** The Louisiana law is in accordance with "established usages, customs, and traditions of the people." **2.** It preserves "the public peace and good order." **3.** It is no worse "than the acts of Congress requiring separate schools for colored children in the District of Columbia." **4.** It will not lead to more restrictive laws because "every exercise of the police power must be reasonable."	**1.** The law does not enact a "rule applicable alike to white and colored citizens." **2.** The law favors whites over African Americans. **3.** The law interferes with "the personal liberty" of citizens in public places. **4.** Will lead to more restrictive laws because states can then require other categories of separation; for example, "native and naturalized citizens" or "Protestants and Roman Catholics."
On Prejudice	**1.** Social equality must be the result of a "mutual appreciation" and "a voluntary consent of individuals." **2.** Legislation intended to abolish distinctions based on race "can only result in accentuating [stressing] the difficulties of the present situation."	**1.** The "seeds of race hate" will be "planted under the sanction of law," and "permanent peace" between the races will be impossible. **2.** The Louisiana law targets only African American citizens, not other groups of citizens.

Name ______________________________ Date ______________

CHAPTER 20 Activity Sheet: (continued)

A. CLASSIFYING. Determine which side made the following points. Write **majority** on the line to the left if the statement refers to the majority opinion. Write **minority** if the statement refers to the minority opinion. Write **both** if the statement refers to both opinions.

__________ **1.** The 14th Amendment was not intended to guarantee social equality between the races.

__________ **2.** Racial distinctions had no bearing on the law's compliance with the 13th Amendment.

__________ **3.** The Louisiana law promoted public peace and good order.

__________ **4.** The Louisiana law violated the promises of the 14th Amendment.

__________ **5.** The Louisiana law created a category of separation.

__________ **6.** The Louisiana law followed established usages, customs, and traditions.

__________ **7.** The Louisiana law favored whites over African Americans.

__________ **8.** Congress had passed laws similar to the Louisiana law.

__________ **9.** Prejudice cannot be erased through legislation, but planting the seeds of racial hate under the sanction of law makes racial peace impossible.

__________ **10.** Social equality must result from the actions of individuals.

__________ **11.** The Louisiana law was obviously intended to promote inequality between the races.

__________ **12.** The law targets only African Americans.

__________ **13.** This law is similar to other laws promoting separation of the races.

B. CRITICAL THINKING. Use the knowledge that you gained by comparing the majority and minority opinions to help you answer the questions below.

1. List three reasons that the minority side believed the Louisiana law was unconstitutional.

a. ______________________________

b. ______________________________

c. ______________________________

2. The majority and the established "traditions of the people" made the Louisiana law a "reasonable regulation." Why do you suppose the minority side would disagree with this reasoning?

____

____

____

Name ____________________ Date ____________

CHAPTER 21 Activity Sheet: Analyzing a Political Cartoon: Booker T. Washington

A political, or editorial, cartoon is a primary source that conveys an opinion through a drawing and labels. It is usually based on an important issue of the day, and like a newspaper editorial it takes a definite stand on the issue. Political cartoons, for example, may point an accusing finger at a public figure or expose government corruption or folly. They may express outrage or praise, warn against a possible disaster, or raise a call for action.

The political cartoon below appeared in a Boston African American newspaper, the *Guardian*, in 1902. This newspaper was generally critical of Booker T. Washington and his policies. Study the cartoon carefully, noting especially any labels and the actions of Booker T. Washington in each of the two scenes. Then answer the questions that follow.

The Guardian, DECEMBER 13, 1902

1. What activity is Booker T. Washington involved in in the scene on the left? ____________________

____

2. What is Booker T. Washington doing in the scene on the right? ____________________

____

3. According to the cartoonist, what "real service to his country" has Booker T. Washington performed? ____________________

____

____

4. What does the cartoon imply are Booker T. Washington's motives for doing what he does in the scene on the right?

____

____

____

Name ______________________ Date ______________

CHAPTER 22 Activity Sheet: Analyzing a Bar Graph: Expenditures for Southern Schools

A bar graph displays information, usually quantities such as degrees, dollars, or population. When the scale runs across the top of the graph, the bars run from side to side. When the scale runs along the side of the graph, the bars run from top to bottom, or vice versa. A bar graph may also present more than one set of data so comparisons can be made. When you analyze a bar graph, begin by looking at the scale and the amount each section of the scale is measuring. Then study the graph to find out what is being measured against the scale. Finally, compare the heights of the bars to determine the highs and lows and any trends.

The bar graph below presents data relating to Southern schools about 100 years ago. Under the impact of Jim Crow policies, African American children had to attend segregated, underfinanced, and poorly equipped schools. Study the graph. Then answer the questions that follow.

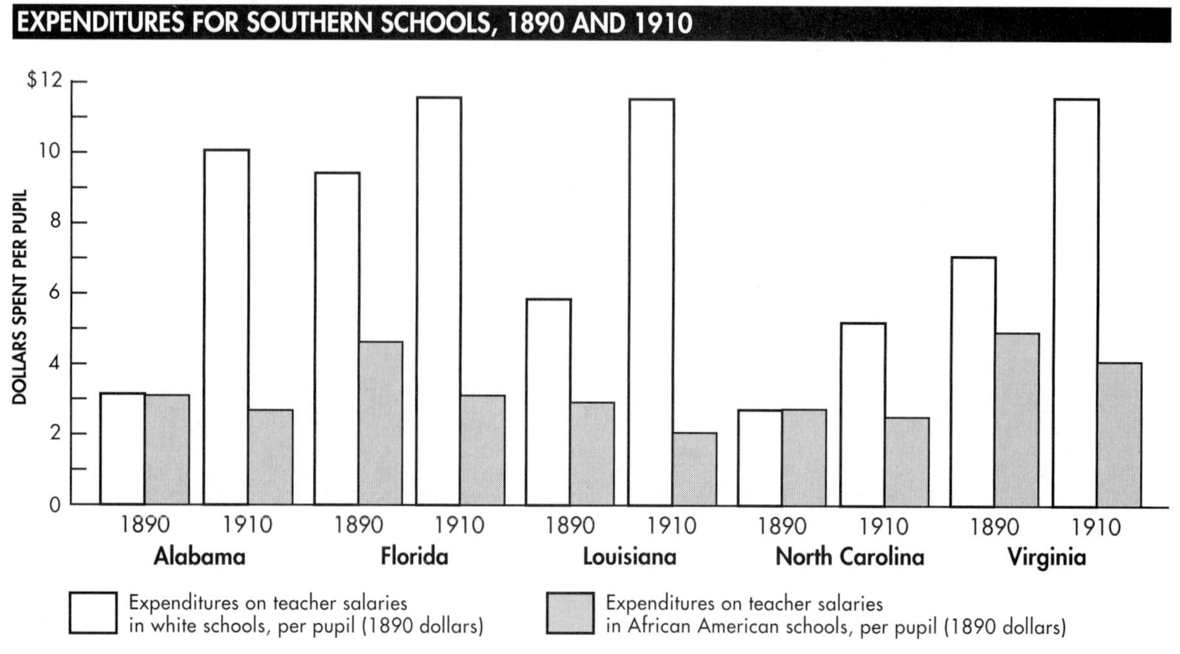

Source: Data from Robert A. Margo, *Disfranchisement, School Finance, and the Economics of Segregrated Schools in the U.S. South, 1890–1910* (New York: Garland Press, 1985), Table I-1, p. 9

A. INTERPRETING DATA. Write the answer to each question below.

1. According to the vertical scale and the graph's heading, what data does the graph display?

____

____

2. For what years is data given? ______________________

3. For what states is data given? ______________________

____

Name ______________________________ Date ______________

CHAPTER 22 Activity Sheet: (continued)

4. Into what two main categories is the data broken down?

____

____

5. In which states were expenditures for white and African American schools most nearly equal in 1890?

____

____

6. Which state in 1890 spent the most money on white pupils? ______________________________

____

7. Which three states in 1910 spent the most money for white pupils?

____

8. Roughly how much did Virginia spend per African American pupil in 1910? ______________

____

9. In which state in 1910 was the gap between expenditures for white and African American pupils the greatest?

____

____

B. DRAWING CONCLUSIONS. Circle the number of each statement that can be supported by the data shown on the graph.

1. The gap between teacher salaries per student in African American schools and teacher salaries per student in white schools generally decreased between 1890 and 1910 in all states shown on the graph.

2. The gap between teacher salaries per student in white schools and teacher salaries per student in African American schools generally increased between 1890 and 1910 in all states shown on the graph.

3. While very little difference in per pupil expenditures existed between white and African American schools in 1890 in Alabama and North Carolina, the gap in 1910 became greater in Florida than in North Carolina.

4. In 1910 the gap in teacher salaries per student between white and African American schools was $7.50 in both Alabama and Virginia.

5. If states in 1910 were ranked according to the gap between expenditures for white and African American schools, North Carolina would rank highest and Louisiana lowest.

Name ______________________________ Date ______________

CHAPTER 23 Activity Sheet A: Drawing Conclusions: Recorded Lynchings, 1889-1918

Reaching a conclusion is the same as making a decision after thinking about available information. Textbooks often present data on the same subject in such different ways, or forms, as the printed word in narration and captions or visually as in maps, charts, graphs, and photographs. In this activity, information about lynchings in a 30-year period of American history is provided in a map and a chart. Study the map, noting its key. Then study the chart, comparing its data with the map's. Finally, answer the questions.

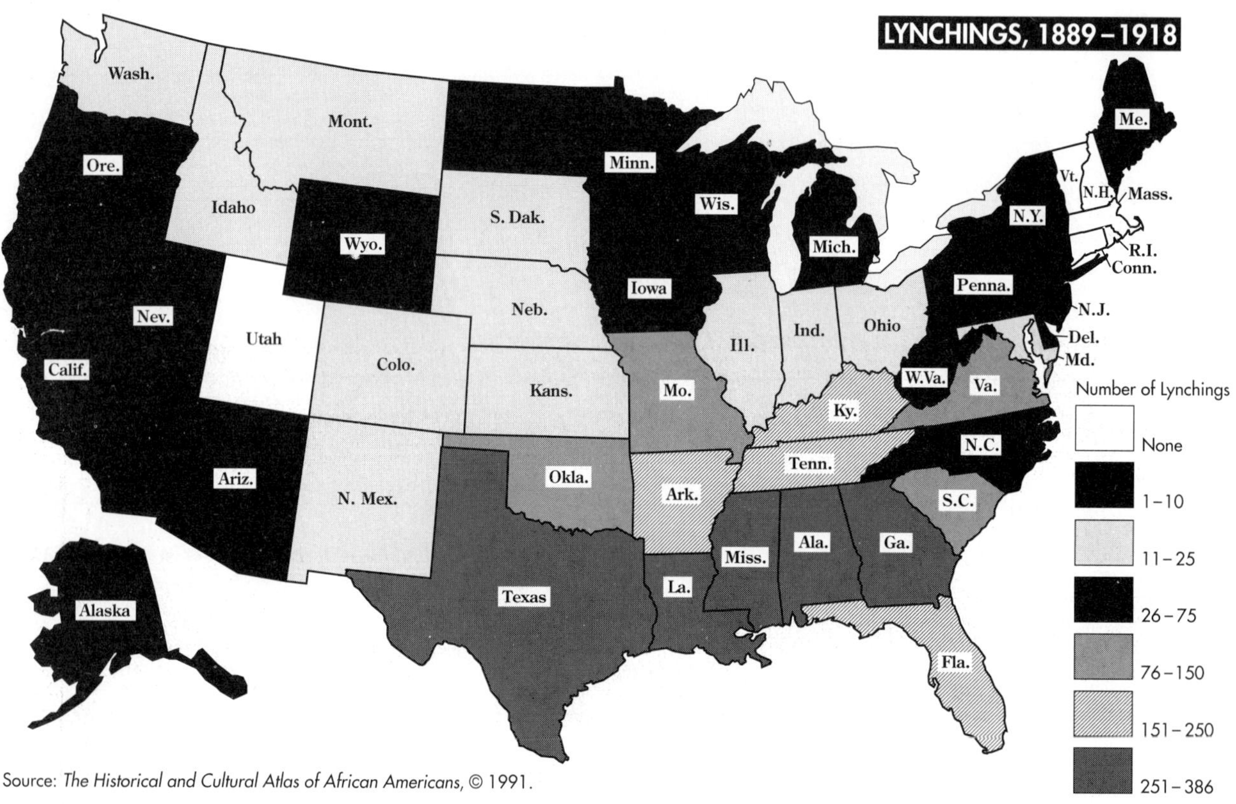

Source: *The Historical and Cultural Atlas of African Americans*, © 1991.

LYNCHINGS, 1889-1918							
New England States		**Former Slave States**		**Western States**		**Other States**	
Connecticut	0	Alabama	276	Alaska	4	Illinois	24
Maine	1	Arkansas	214	Arizona	8	Indiana	19
Massachusetts	0	Delaware	1	California	26	Iowa	8
New Hampshire	0	Florida	178	Colorado	18	Kansas	22
Rhode Island	0	Georgia	386	Idaho	11	Michigan	4
Vermont	0	Kentucky	27	Montana	22	Minnesota	4
Total	1	Louisiana	313	Nevada	4	Nebraska	17
		Maryland	4	New Mexico	13	New Jersey	3
		Mississippi	373	Oregon	4	New York	3
		Missouri	81	Utah	0	North Dakota	2
		North Carolina	22	Washington	16	Ohio	12
		South Carolina	120	Wyoming	34	Oklahoma	96
		Tennessee	196	Total	160	Pennsylvania	4
		Texas	335			South Dakota	13
		Virginia	78			West Virginia	11
		Total	2,604			Wisconsin	4
						Total	246

Source: *The Historical and Cultural Atlas of African Americans,* (c) 1991

Name ______________________________ Date ______________

CHAPTER 23 Activity Sheet A: (continued)

1. Name the five states that had the greatest number of recorded lynchings.

   a. ______________ d. ______________

   b. ______________ e. ______________

   c. ______________

2. Name the category to which these states belong.

   ____

3. Name the state with the greatest number of recorded lynchings.

   ____

4. Name the six states with no recorded lynchings.

   a. ______________ d. ______________

   b. ______________ e. ______________

   c. ______________ f. ______________

5. Name the only Western state to have more recorded lynchings than California.

   ____

6. Name the two former slave states that had less than ten recorded lynchings.

   a. ______________ b. ______________

7. Circle the letter of each conclusion below that is supported by the data shown on the map and the chart.

   a. More recorded lynchings occurred in the former slave states than in any other section of the United States.

   b. More recorded lynchings occurred in densely populated areas of the nation than in sparsely populated areas.

   c. Western states had a greater number of recorded lynchings than the New England states.

   d. The number of recorded lynchings in former slave states of the South declined after 1918.

   e. African Americans were the victims of all recorded lynchings in the United States.

Name ______________________________ Date ______________

CHAPTER 23 Activity Sheet B: Recognizing Points of View: Washington and Du Bois

One way of being sure you understand opposing points of view is to make a discussion web. For example, you might make a discussion web to show the points of view of Booker T. Washington and W.E.B. Du Bois about the question highlighted in the box below. As a first step, review material in your textbook on the two men, paying special attention to the Points of View feature that appears on pages 250-251.

With a partner, discuss the information that supports each man's position. Write key words and phrases for each man's point of view on the lines provided in the web below.

Then work with another set of partners. Discuss the information with them and reach a group consensus, or general agreement, on the question.

Next, decide which of all the reasons given on both sides best supports the group's conclusion. Write this reason at the bottom of the web.

Finally, choose a spokesperson to present the group's conclusion to the class. If differing viewpoints exist in the group, the spokesperson should mention those as well.

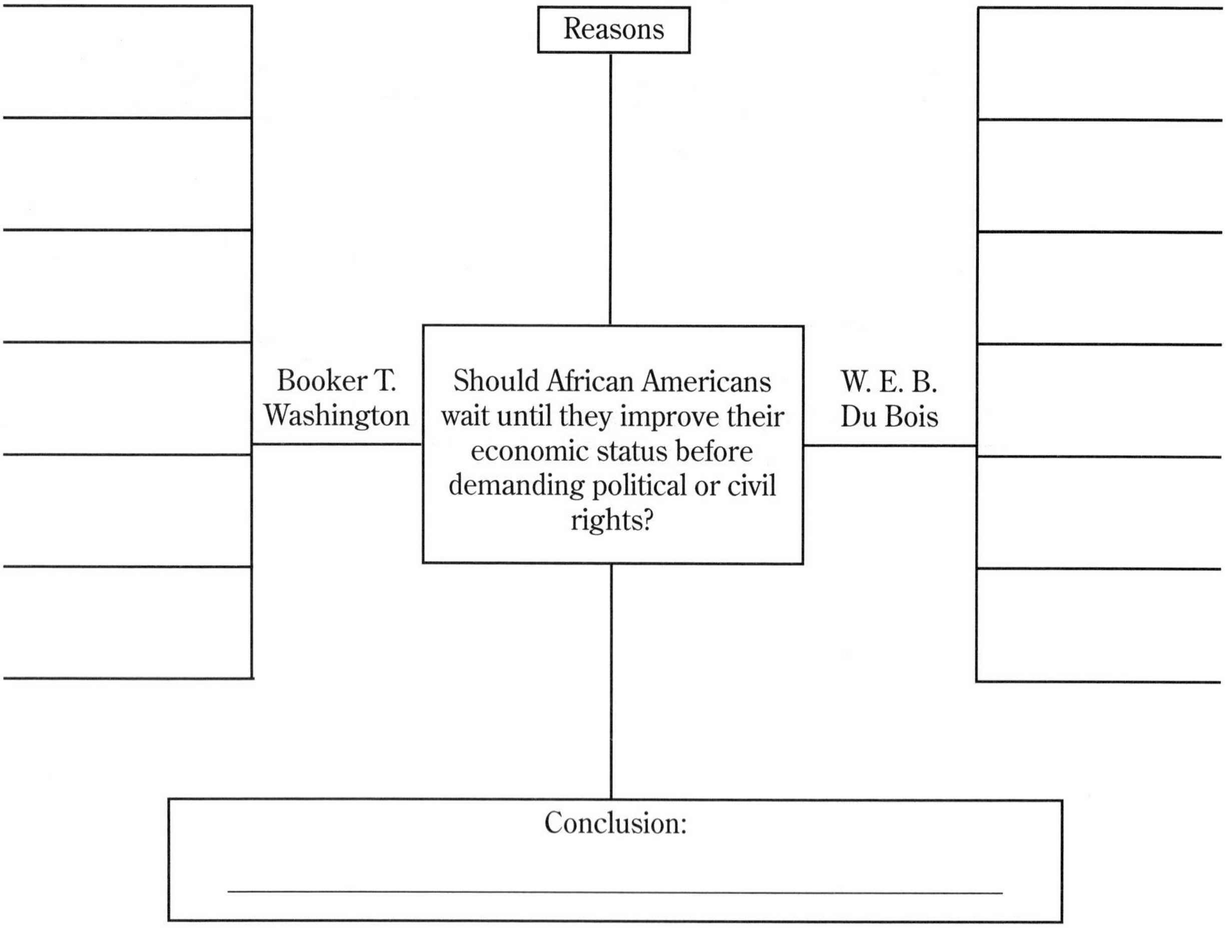

Reasons

Booker T. Washington

Should African Americans wait until they improve their economic status before demanding political or civil rights?

W. E. B. Du Bois

Conclusion: ______________________________

Strongest Reason: ______________________________

Name ______________________________ Date ______________

CHAPTER 24 Activity Sheet: Interpreting a Map: The Great Migration, 1915-1930

Maps are often used to give readers a quick visual summary of written data and also to add clarifying details. The map below presents information about the Great Migration of African Americans that occurred in the 1920s. Study the map, using the map key to unlock the meaning of any special symbols used on the map. Then answer the questions that follow.

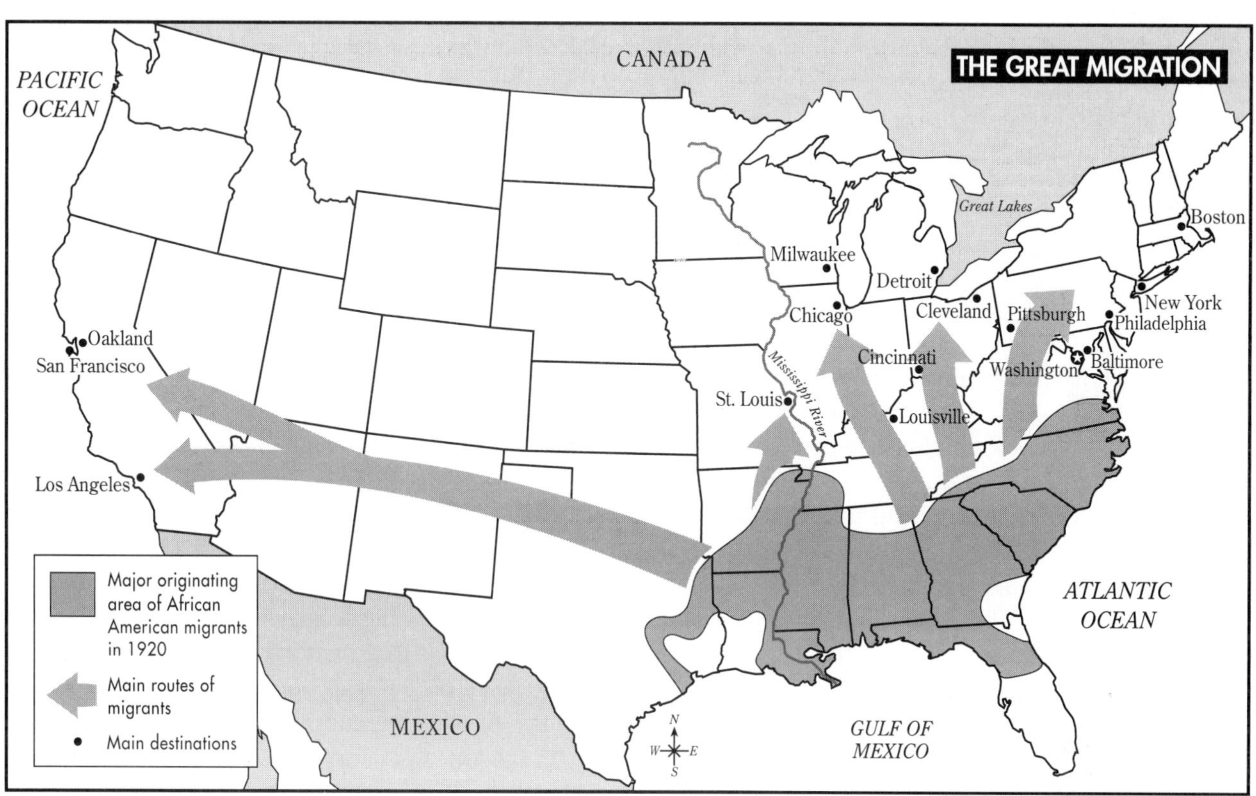

1. Which general region of the United States did African American migrants originate from in 1920?

____

____

2. In which two general directions did the paths of migration lead?

____

3. What characteristic do all the cities shown on the map have in common?

____

4. Based on the map, why do you think African Americans migrated to the cities shown on the map?

____

____

____

Name ______________________________ Date ______________

CHAPTER 25 Activity Sheet: Analyzing a Primary Source: Understanding Marcus Garvey's Nationalism

Historians often turn to primary sources to understand the views of people who helped shape events in American history. To understand these views they analyze the source, separating main ideas from supporting details. In the 1920s, Marcus Garvey became very popular by urging African Americans to establish a country in Africa where they could escape discrimination by being completely in charge of their own economic, cultural, and political lives. In the essay below, Garvey divides African American history into three stages and recounts how African Americans responded or ought to have responded in each stage. After reading the essay, complete the outline form as a way of analyzing it.

> I believe, as far as the Negro is concerned politically, that there are three stages relating to our contact with the white man:
>
> The First Stage in the life of the Negro in this Western Hemisphere was the stage when the white man shackled us in Africa and brought us here and kept us for two hundred and fifty years. During this period we worked and received no recompense, no pay for our labor, and we were satisfied because of the white man's Christian teaching "Learn to labor and to wait."
>
> The Second Stage was the thing called Emancipation, which we have enjoyed for fifty-eight years. This stage came when they gave us partial freedom, and a petty [small] existence by way of wages, and we were satisfied during that stage to do just what they told us to do. We worked for small wages and voted Republican Democratic and so forth, until after fifty-eight years we discovered that a change was necessary.
>
> Now we have entered into the Third Stage of our existence, wherein we say to the white man "After two hundred and fifty years of slavery and fifty-eight years of partial freedom under your leadership we are going to try but fifty years under our own direction." This new stage calls for all the manhood within the race and means that we must throw off all the conditions that affected us in the first and second stages, and go out and do—acquit [conduct] ourselves like men in the economic, industrial, and political arena.

Source: *Philosophy and Opinions of Marcus Garvey,* © 1968 by Arno Press

1. a. Description of First Stage: ______________________________

____

b. Response of African Americans: ______________________________

____

2. a. Description of Second Stage: ______________________________

____

b. Response of African Americans: ______________________________

____

3. a. Description of Third Stage: ______________________________

____

b. Response of African Americans: ______________________________

____

Name ______________________ Date ____________

CHAPTER 26 Activity Sheet: Analyzing a Primary Source: "Lift Ev'ry Voice and Sing"

Literature — poems, stories, and plays — can provide a better understanding of the concerns, goals, and values of a particular historical period and its people. By analyzing a piece of literature — that is, by looking at its parts and examining its details — historians and students of history can draw valuable conclusions about the past.

James Weldon Johnson, an important figure of the Harlem Renaissance, wrote the following poem, which his brother J. Rosamond Johnson set to music. As a song, first performed in 1900 in Jacksonville, Florida, by a chorus of 500 African American schoolchildren as part of a Lincoln's Birthday celebration, the poem was a hit. Johnson wrote, "Within twenty years the song was being sung in schools and churches and on special occasions throughout the South and in some other parts of the country. . . . Later it was adopted by the National Association for the Advancement of Colored People, and is now quite generally used throughout the country as the 'Negro National Hymn.'" Read the poem aloud, perhaps several times. Then analyze the poem by answering the questions that follow.

Lift Ev'ry Voice and Sing

Lift ev'ry voice and sing,
Till earth and heaven ring,
Ring with the harmonies of Liberty;
Let our rejoicing rise
High as the list'ning skies,
Let it resound loud as the rolling sea.
Sing a song full of the faith that the dark past has taught us
Sing a song full of the hope that the present has brought us
Facing the rising sun of our new day begun,
Let us march on till victory is won.

Stony the road we trod,
Bitter the chast'ning rod,
Felt in the days when hope unborn had died;
Yet with a steady beat,
Have not our weary feet
Come to the place for which our fathers sighed?
We have come over a way that with tears has been watered
We have come, treading our path thro' the blood of the slaughtered,
Out from the gloomy past, till now we stand at last
Where the white gleam of our star is cast.

God of our weary years,
God of our silent tears,
Thou who hast brought us thus far on the way,
Thou who has by Thy might
Led us into the light,
Keep us forever in the path, we pray;
Lest our feet stray from the places, our God, where we met Thee,
Lest, our hearts drunk with the wine of the world, we forget Thee;
Shadowed beneath Thy hand, may we forever stand
True to our God, true to our native land.

Name ______________________________ Date ______________

CHAPTER 26 Activity Sheet: (continued)

1. Analyze the poem's three stanzas and express the main idea in each stanza.

   Stanza 1: ______________________________

   ____

   Stanza 2: ______________________________

   ____

   Stanza 3: ______________________________

   ____

2. According to the first stanza, what two things should the singers' song be full of?

   a. ______________________________

   ____

   b. ______________________________

   ____

3. The first stanza urges people to "march on till victory." What precisely will the marchers win when victory comes?

   ____

4. Name at least two details in the second stanza that describe the marcher's "gloomy past?"

   a. ______________________________

   ____

   b. ______________________________

   ____

5. What two requests are made of God in the last stanza?

   a. ______________________________

   b. ______________________________

6. According to this poem, what four values have brought the marchers to the brink of victory?

   a. ______________________________

   b. ______________________________

   c. ______________________________

   d. ______________________________

7. Why do you suppose this work became so widely popular among African Americans soon after it was written in 1900?

   ____

   ____

Name ______________________________ Date ______________

CHAPTER 27 Activity Sheet: Interpreting a Chart: Detecting Patterns and Trends

Charts organize statistics so that they can be compared and studied more easily to detect patterns or trends.

The chart below compares percentages of whites and African Americans employed in 1940 in seven different categories of work. The chart gives these percentages for males, females, and for all workers in each category, excluding farmers and farm laborers. Study the chart carefully, then decide whether the statements that follow are true or false. Write true or false on the line to the left.

EMPLOYED WORKERS IN NONAGRICULTURAL OCCUPATIONS, 1940

Work Category	% Male White	% Male Black	% Female White	% Female Black	% All Workers White	% All Workers Black
Professional Persons	6.8	2.9	14.7	5.0	8.9	3.8
Proprietors, Managers, Officials	13.9	2.5	3.8	0.9	11.2	1.8
Clerks and Similar Workers	19.2	4.4	34.4	1.7	23.5	3.2
Skilled Workers and Foremen	20.3	7.5	0.9	0.1	14.9	4.3
Semiskilled Workers	23.9	20.0	30.6	15.9	25.8	18.3
Unskilled Workers (Laborers)	12.2	39.2	0.9	1.0	9.0	22.7
Unskilled Workers (Servants)	3.7	23.4	14.6	75.3	6.7	45.8

Source: *The National Urban League, 1910-1940* (c) 1974

TRUE OR FALSE. Use the chart to help you decide whether the following statements are true or false. On the line to the left, write either **true** or **false**.

_____ **1.** The highest percentage of employed African American males are unskilled laborers.

_____ **2.** The highest percentage of employed white males are semiskilled laborers.

_____ **3.** More African American females are proprietors, managers, and officials than African American males.

_____ **4.** In four categories white females have a higher percentage of workers than white males.

_____ **5.** In two categories African American females have a higher percentage of workers than African American males.

_____ **6.** The percentage of semiskilled African American males is higher than the percentage of semiskilled white males.

_____ **7.** More than 68 percent of all African American workers in 1940 were either unskilled laborers or servants.

_____ **8.** Less than 50 percent of white female workers held skilled jobs or better.

_____ **9.** Compared to African American males, a higher percentage of African American females held skilled jobs or better.

_____ **10.** While more than 58 percent of all white workers held skilled jobs or better, only about 13 percent of African American workers held such jobs.

Name ______________________________ Date ______________

CHAPTER 28 Activity Sheet: Interpreting Statistics: Using Circle Graphs

Circle graphs give a simplified view of complex situations. The circle itself represents the whole, or 100 percent. Each segment of the circle is a slice, which is why a circle graph is sometimes called a pie graph. The parts, or slices, of the whole are expressed in percentages.

In making a circle graph, the percentage that each section of the whole represents must be determined. The percentage of each part must then be "translated" into the percentage of the circle or 360° that it represents. For example, if a family spends $500.00 of a total monthly income of $2,000.00 on food, then they use one-fourth or 25 percent of their monthly income on food. One-fourth of 360° is 90°, or a quarter of a circle.

A. FIGURING PERCENTAGES Read the statistics below. Then, using the hints, figure the percentage of the whole and of the circle that each statistic represents and answer the questions that follow.

During World War II, approximately 891,000 African American men and women served in the armed forces. Of that total, 700,000 served in the Army, 165,000 in the Navy, and 26,000 in other branches.

1. What percentage of the total number of African Americans serving in World War II were members of the Army? (Hint: divide the total in the Army by the total number in the armed services to get the percentage)

____

2. What slice of the circle's 360° does this number represent? (Hint: multiply 360° by 0.785)

____

3. What percentage of the total number of African Americans in World War II were members of the Navy?

____

4. What slice of the circle's 360° does this number represent?

____

5. What percentage of the total number of African Americans in World War II served in other branches of service?

____

6. What slice of the circle's 360° does this number represent?

____

B. MAKING THE GRAPH Fill in the segments of the circle graph below by placing the correct number in each slice: **1)** Army membership; **2)** Navy membership; **3)** Other branches.

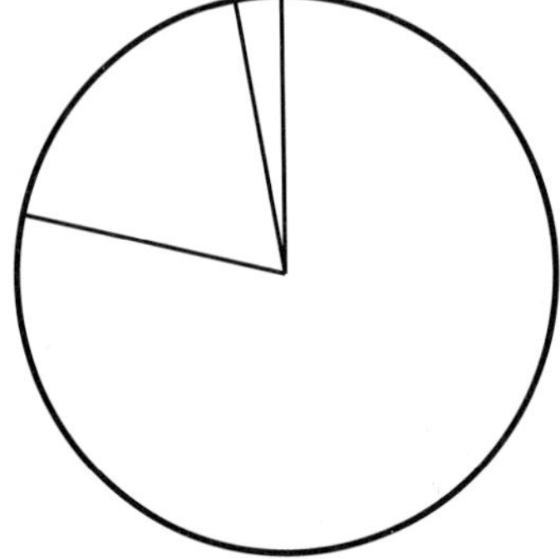

Name ______________________________ Date ______________

CHAPTER 29 Activity Sheet: Charting Data From Maps: Shifting Population Centers

Mapmakers and statisticians often use census records to compile maps and charts that help reveal the trends in an always shifting population. By plotting data in different ways, the direction of population shifts can be determined as well as which states in any two periods have gained or lost population. Study the two maps on the next page, which show the African American population in each of the 48 contiguous, or bordering, states of the United States. Then follow the directions below.

A. CHARTING POPULATION SHIFTS On a separate sheet of paper, copy and complete the outlined chart below, using the data shown on the 1940 and 1960 maps. After listing each state's data in the proper columns, place a plus sign (+) after any state that had an increase in its African American population in 1960, a minus sign (-) to show a decrease in its 1960 population, or a zero (0) for any state where the African American population stayed in the same range.

Less than 1,000		1,000-9,999		10,000-49,999		50,000-99,999		100,000-499,999		500,000-999,999		1,000,000 or more	
1940	1960	1940	1960	1940	1960	1940	1960	1940	1960	1940	1960	1940	1960

B. COMPARING POPULATION SHIFTS Use the data compiled on the completed chart to answer the questions below.

1. **a.** Between 1940 and 1960, how many states had an increase in their African American populations?

   ____

   b. How many had a decrease? ______________________________

   c. How many stayed in the same range? ______________________________

2. Between 1940 and 1960, what happened in states where the African American population was less than 1,000?

   ____

   ____

3. Between 1940 and 1960, what happened in states where the African American population was 1,000,000 or more?

   ____

   ____

4. Which state showed an increase in its African American population from 100,000 to 499,999 in 1940 to 1,000,000 or more in 1960?

   ____

Name ______________________________ Date ______________

CHAPTER 29 Activity Sheet:(Continued)

AFRICAN AMERICAN POPULATION CHANGES, 1940 – 1960

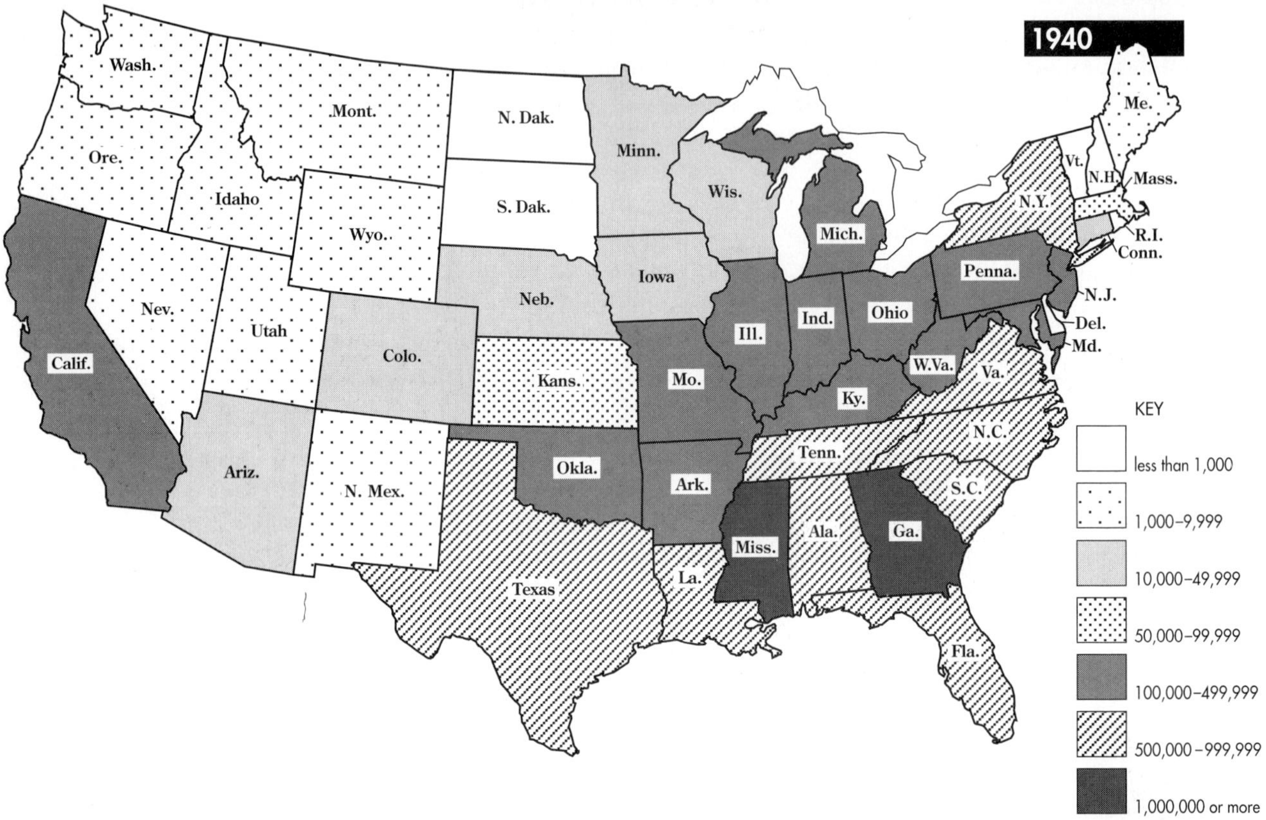

1940

Wash.
Mont.
N. Dak.
Minn.
Me.
Ore.
Idaho
S. Dak.
Wis.
Vt.
N.H.
Mass.
N.Y.
Wyo.
Mich.
R.I.
Conn.
Iowa
Penna.
Neb.
N.J.
Nev.
Utah
Ill.
Ind.
Ohio
Del.
Md.
Calif.
Colo.
Kans.
Mo.
W.Va.
Va.
Ky.
N.C.
Tenn.
Ariz.
N. Mex.
Okla.
Ark.
S.C.
Miss.
Ala.
Ga.
Texas
La.
Fla.

KEY

- less than 1,000
- 1,000–9,999
- 10,000–49,999
- 50,000–99,999
- 100,000–499,999
- 500,000–999,999
- 1,000,000 or more

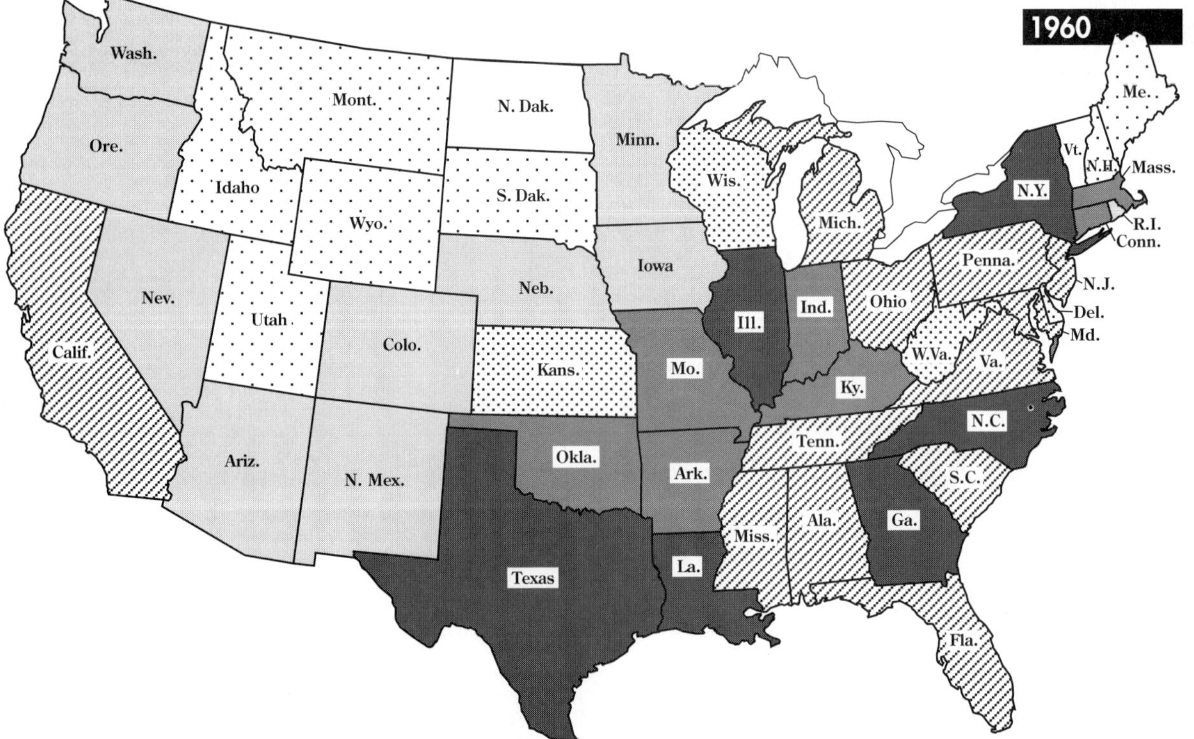

Name ______________________________ Date ______________

CHAPTER 30 Activity Sheet: Using a Primary Source: The Montgomery Bus Boycott

Boycotting turned out to be one of the most successful weapons in the fight for civil rights. Boycotting for African American rights began in Alabama when the African American community protested the arrest of Rosa Parks for refusing to give up her seat to a white person and move to the back of the bus she was riding. Martin Luther King, Jr., and other African American leaders wrote the leaflet below that initiated the boycott. Read the leaflet. Then answer the questions that follow.

> Don't ride the bus to work, to town, to school, or any place Monday, December 5.
>
> Another Negro woman has been arrested and put in jail because she refused to give up her bus seat.
>
> Don't ride the buses to work, to town, to school, or anywhere on Monday. If you work, take a cab, or share a ride.
>
> Come to a mass meeting, Monday at 7:00 p.m., at the Holt Street Baptist Church for further instruction.

1. Against what organization, institution, or person was this boycott directed?

____

____

2. Why was the boycott directed at this organization, institution, or person?

____

____

3. What action did the leaders of this boycott ask African Americans to take?

____

____

4. What do you think Martin Luther King, Jr., and the other leaders in Montgomery, Alabama, wanted to achieve by the boycott?

____

____

5. How do you think a boycott might help them to succeed?

____

____

6. For what would you be willing to boycott and why?

____

____

Name ______________________________ Date ______________

CHAPTER 31 Activity Sheet: Connecting History and Geography: Determining Regions

Social scientists often use the methods of both history and geography to analyze human experiences. History asks about the *when, who,* and *why* of an event, and geography asks about the *where, why,* and *significance of the location* of the event. By answering both sets of questions, social scientists develop better understandings about why things happen.

Geographers group areas together to help them analyze human experiences. Geographers call these areas regions. A region is an area on the Earth that has common characteristics. The characteristics may be physical or they may be human. For example, places with the soil and climate to grow cotton could be grouped into a physical region. Places that had Jim Crow laws (see Chapter 20, pp. 212–220) would form a region based on human characteristics.

The map below shows regions that existed in the United States after 1960. Study the map and use what you learned about African American history to answer the questions.

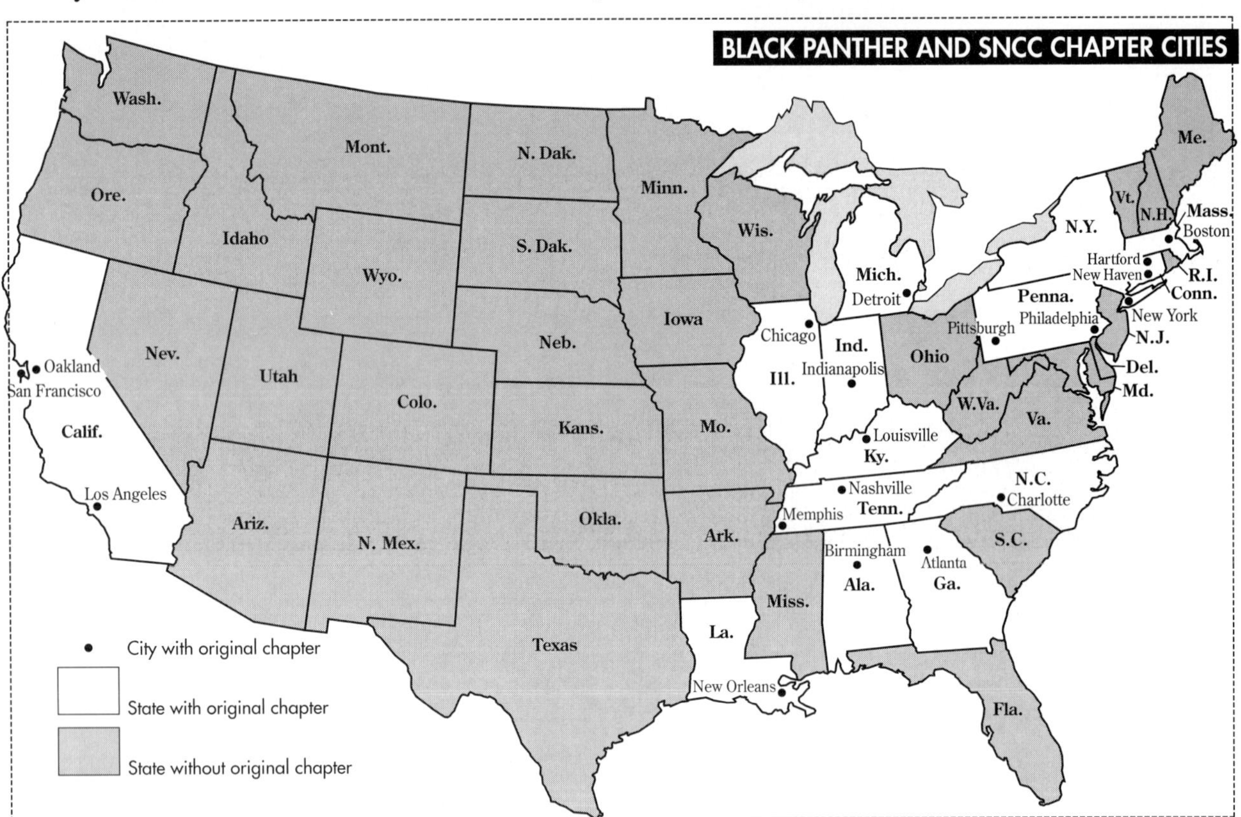

1. What is the chief human characteristic of the states identified by the lighter color?

____

____

2. Geographers define regions as areas that share the same characteristics. List two groups of states that could be called regions because they have the characteristic you identified in question 1.

a. Region: ______________________________

b. Region: ______________________________

Name ______________________ Date ______________

CHAPTER 31 Activity Sheet: (continued)

3. What are some historical facts that explain the common characteristics of these two regions?

4. Sometimes physical and human regions overlap. What physical region overlaps the two regions indicated by the lighter color?

5. What two states share characteristics with the two regions identified in Question 2 but are separated from them geographically?

6. What human characteristic unites the states indicated by the darker color?

7. In what physical region are most of the states indicated by the darker color located?

Name ______________________________ Date ______________

CHAPTER 32 Activity Sheet: Interpreting a Political Cartoon: Fighters for Freedom

A political cartoon is like an editorial because it expresses a point of view, or an opinion, about a person, issue, or event. Almost 280,000 African Americans served in the U.S. armed forces during the Vietnam War. At the same time, African Americans on the home front were continuing to fight for civil rights. The political cartoon below expresses an opinion about the relationship between these two circumstances. Study the cartoon to understand the cartoonist's point of view and the message it contains. Then answer the questions that follow.

'DEAR SON— I'M PROUD THAT YOU'RE DEFENDING THE FREEDOM WE'RE TRYING TO GET...'

1. Where is the African American soldier? How do you know?

____

____

2. What is the soldier doing?

____

3. What does the letter tell the soldier about what is happening at home in the United States?

____

____

4. Irony can be used to describe an outcome or situation that demonstrates an inconsistency between the actual and expected result. What irony is suggested in this cartoon?

____

____

5. As a comment on the progress of the fight for civil rights, is this cartoon optimistic (hopeful) or pessimistic (lacking in hope)? Explain your answer.

____

____

Name ______________________________ Date ______________

CHAPTER 33 Activity Sheet: Analyzing a Map: African American Businesses

An important part of the African American middle class is made up of business owners. Every year, *Black Enterprise* magazine compiles a list of the nation's top 100 African American owned businesses. To be eligible to be included on the list, a company must have been in operation for at least one full year and be at least 51 percent owned by African Americans. Businesses on the list must also manufacture or own the product they sell or they must provide industrial or consumer services. The *Black Enterprise* list is usually accompanied by graphic material such as this map. Study it carefully, then answer the questions that follow.

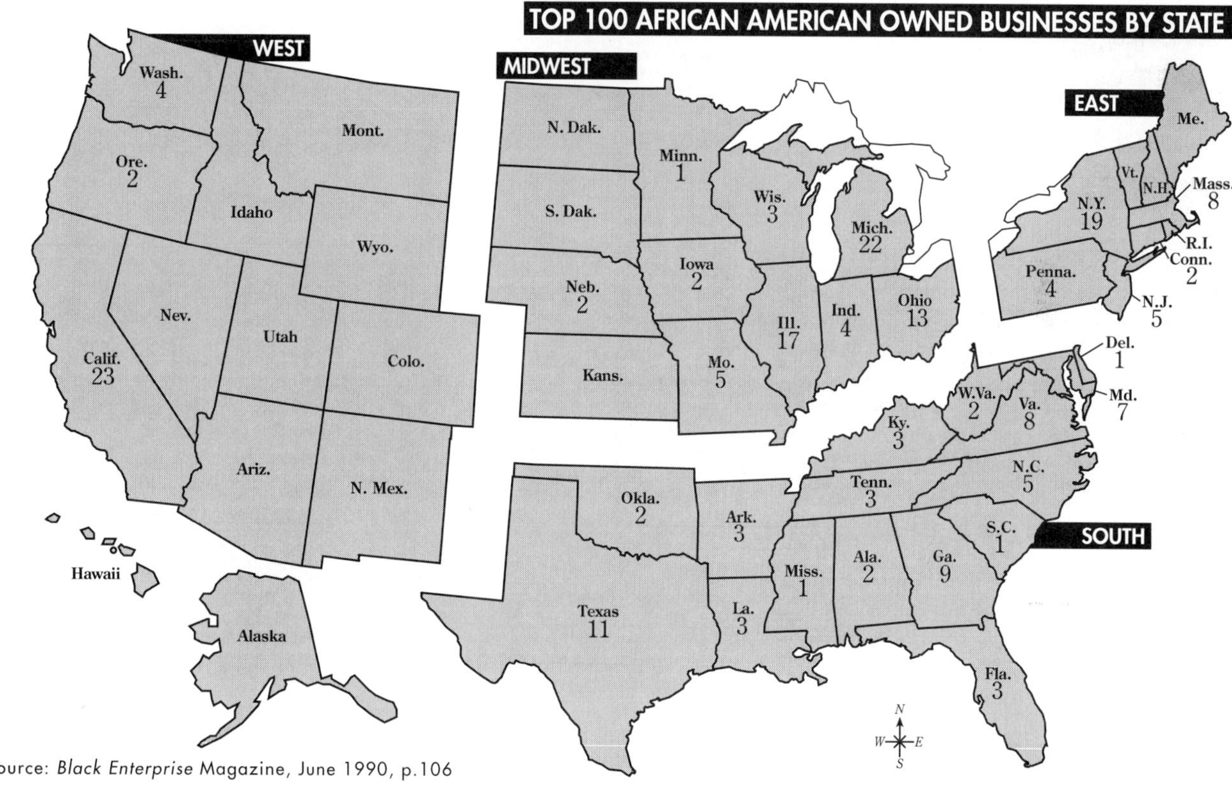

Source: *Black Enterprise* Magazine, June 1990, p.106

1. What does this map show? ______________________________

____

2. What state has the largest number of the top 100 African American owned businesses?

____

3. How many of the top 100 African American owned businesses can be found in the Northeast?

____

4. Which region of the nation has the largest number of the top 100 businesses?

____

5. Write a generalization about the geographic distribution of the nation's top 100 African American owned businesses.

____

____

Name ______________________________ Date ____________

CHAPTER 34 Activity Sheet A: Recognizing Points of View: Woodson and Lowery

Use a discussion web to help recognize and analyze points of view. In the Points of View feature on pages 380-381, Robert T. Woodson and Rev. Joseph Lowery discuss the question highlighted in the box below. Review the feature, and then follow the instructions below.

With a partner, discuss the information that supports each man's position. Write key words or phrases for each point of view on the lines provided in the web below.

Then work with another set of partners. Discuss the information with them and reach a group consensus, or general agreement, on the question.

Next, decide which of all the reasons given on both sides best supports the group's conclusion. Write this reason at the bottom of the web.

Finally, choose a spokesperson to present the group's conclusion to the class. If differing viewpoints exist in the group, the spokesperson should mention those as well.

Reasons

Robert Woodson

Is racism the main problem for African Americans today?

Rev. Joseph Lowery

Conclusion: ______________________________

Strongest Reason: ______________________________

Name ______________________________ Date ______________

CHAPTER 34 Activity Sheet B: Stating and Supporting an Opinion: Influential African Americans

An opinion is a view or judgment formed in the mind about a subject. People have opinions about a variety of subjects—about what is the best football team, who is the best rapper, what is the worst place to eat. An opinion is *not* a fact. But if you want to convince others that your opinion is sound, it is important that you be able to explain how you took facts about a subject into account when reaching your opinion. For example, if you think that your school's football team is the best in the conference, you should be able to support that opinion by pointing out the school's win-loss record, how many points it scores per game, and how few points it gives up to its opponents.

Each year, *Ebony* magazine runs a list of "The 100 Most Influential Black Americans." The African Americans on the list are those who, in the opinion of the magazine's editors, have had the greatest impact on the African American community. What kinds of things do the magazine's editors take into account when reaching their opinion? According to the editors, these are their standards:

- Does the individual transcend [rise above] his or her profession or position and command widespread national influence among Black people?
- Does the individual head an organization that commands widespread national influence among Black people, or whose individual members are influential in their communities?
- Is the individual unusually influential among those Blacks and/or whites whose policies and practices significantly affect the lives of large numbers of Black people?

Among the African Americans who have been on *Ebony's* list in recent years are General Colin L. Powell, Chairman of the Joint Chiefs of Staff; Bill Cosby, entertainer; L. Douglas Wilder, governor of Virginia; David N. Dinkins, mayor of New York City; Dorothy Height, president of the National Council of Negro Women; Oprah Winfrey, television host; Benjamin Hooks, executive director of the NAACP; Coretta Scott King, civil rights activist and widow of Martin Luther King; Thurgood Marshall, former justice of the Supreme Court.

Reread the standards that *Ebony* used in making its selections. Also, study the names taken from its list; note that many of these people have been discussed in your textbook. Then, answer the questions below.

1. Select one of the people the editors of Ebony named as most influential and explain why you think that person met *Ebony's* standards.

____

____

____

2. What three standards would you set for choosing today's most influential African Americans?

a. ______________________________

____

____

____

Name ____________________ Date ____________

CHAPTER 34 Activity Sheet:(continued)

b. ____________________

____

____

____

____

c. ____________________

____

____

____

____

3. What three African Americans do you consider most influential? Explain how each meets the standards you have described above.

a. ____________________

____

____

____

____

b. ____________________

____

____

____

____

c. ____________________

____

____

____

ANSWER KEY FOR ACTIVITY SHEETS

UNIT 1 ACTIVITY SHEETS

Chapter 1: Using a Timeline

1. 3200 B.C. **2.** A.D. 800 **3.** 4,000 **4.** 200 **5.** 500 **6.** the Middle Kingdom **7.** the building of the Great Pyramid **8.** the founding of Meroë **9.** 3100 B.C. **10.** the Hyskos **11.** six

Chapter 2: Reading a Map

1. to show West African trade routes, the products carried over them, and ways those products were carried
2. Lake Chad
3. (2 of the following) Benin, Djenne, Timbuktu, Gao
4. Gao **5.** north **6.** the Sahara Desert
7. about 1,200 miles **8.** Lake Chad
9. gold **10.** Songhai **11.** Niger
12. It was an oasis in the middle of the desert
13. caravan; route should show understanding of map

Chapter 3: Interpreting a Primary Source

1. Islam, because they learn the Koran
2. The reading mentions the presence of North Africans with substantial amounts of goods and treasure.
3. He probably approved, since he seems to approve of the other conduct he cites in his list.
4. It is favorable; he sees them as honest, religious, and clean.
5. It is probably reliable, since he spent some months there; however, because he is a Muslim he might be biased toward other Muslims.

UNIT 2 ACTIVITY SHEETS

Chapter 4: Explaining Illustrations

1. how a cargo of slaves is stowed on a slave ship
2. a lengthwise cross section of the whole ship
3. the platform area of the room where boys are kept
4. Men, boys, and women are kept in separate areas both on the deck and on platforms in each area.
5. view of lower deck from above
6. Students' descriptions will vary, but will probably range from overcrowded to inhuman.

Chapter 5: Interpreting a Circle Graph

1. It shows the percentages of enslaved Africans brought to each of six regions of the Americas between 1500 and 1870.
2. The United States and the Dutch, Danish, and Swedish Caribbean were tied for least imports at 6 percent.
3. It means that 17 percent of all enslaved Africans brought to the Americas between 1800 and 1870 were brought to the British Caribbean.
4. 17 percent
5. a. 101 percent **b.** all Africans brought to the Americas between 1500 and 1870 **c.** yes **d.** because the total number of slaves is over 100 percent

Chapter 6: Drawing Conclusions from a Map and a Table

1. economic activities and chief products in Britain's 13 North American colonies
2. New York, New Jersey, Pennsylvania, Delaware
3. naval products, timber, furs, cattle and grain
4. Maryland, Pennsylvania, New Jersey, Connecticut
5. cattle and grain
6. rice and indigo in the Southern Colonies
7. Massachusetts
8. South Carolina
9. the Southern Colonies
10. African population was largest where tobacco, rice, and indigo were the major products.

UNIT 3 ACTIVITY SHEETS

Chapter 7: Interpreting a Primary Source

1. Africans brought to the colonies, enslaved persons
2. violating the rights of enslaved persons
3. by fighting against the colonists who are seeking liberty for themselves
4. Jefferson makes no mention of them or their roles.
5. Answers should indicate that Northern and Southern merchants, shipowners and plantation owners played active and willing parts in the trade of enslaved persons and that acceptance of Africans as slaves was not forced on them.
6. Students should point out that there would be no justification for slavery after independence if the passage remained. Furthermore, many Southerners had no wish to see slavery abolished because it was an important part of the South's economy.

Chapter 8: Interpreting a Chart

1. false **2.** true **3.** false **4.** true **5.** false
6. false **7.** true **8.** true **9.** false **10.** true

Chapter 9: Explaining a Map

A. COMPLETION **1.** Spain **2.** Great Britain
3. Mississippi and Missouri
4. Plattsburgh **5.** New Orleans
B. MATCHING **1.** e **2.** b **3.** c **4.** d **5.** a **6.** f
C. TRUE OR FALSE **1.** false. **2.** true
3. true **4.** false **5.** true **6.** true
D. **1.** banned slavery in Northwest Territory
2. the state of Louisiana and the Missouri Territory
3. Many enslaved African Americans had run to Florida where Seminoles had given them refuge. The addition of Florida forced the return of many African Americans to slavery.

UNIT 4 ACTIVITY SHEETS

Chapter 10: Interpreting a Map

1. to show cotton-growing regions of the South and some of the climatic conditions that affect them
2. Kentucky, Missouri, Virginia, and Florida
3. Kentucky, Tennessee, North Carolina, and Virginia
4. Virginia, North Carolina, South Carolina, and Georgia
5. Alabama, Florida, Tennessee, Mississippi, Louisiana, Arkansas, Missouri, and Texas
6. Florida is bounded by ocean and gulf waters and is too rainy for growing cotton. It also lies in the path of hurricanes.
7. parts of Alabama, Mississippi, Louisiana, Arkansas, Missouri, Texas, and Oklahoma
8. because rainfall decreases to less than 25 inches a year and cotton growing becomes too risky
9. Students might notice that the best cotton-growing areas are in states settled after 1801. They might suggest that cotton growing had worn out the soil in areas settled before 1801.

Chapter 11: Recognizing Cause and Effect

1. the insurrection of Nat Turner
2. Possible effects include: panic in the slave States; the deaths of the "brightest and best men," and a crackdown on African Americans praying together.
3. Because Nat Turner believed that God had called on him to lead a revolt, white slaveowners feared that other enslaved African Americans might receive a similar message. Also, they feared that enslaved African Americans gathering to pray might really be planning an uprising.

Chapter 12: Making Inferences

1. legal status strengthened somewhat
2. daily fear of losing freedom due to false accusations, kidnapping or court action
3. in the city and county of New York on April 24, 1811
4. **a.** in Boston, Massachusetts **b.** in New York City, **c.** free
5. certificate of freedom
6. Any white person could accuse them of being slaves and there was little the free African Americans could do about it. They could be kidnapped into slavery.
7. Students' responses will differ but they might infer that free African Americans in the North were often safer than free African

Americans in the South. But they might also infer that free African Americans could be challenged by people who claimed they were really runaway slaves. They might also infer that the condition requiring free African Americans in Northern states to carry legal documents was similar to those in Southern states, which required African Americans to carry certificates of freedom.

UNIT 5 ACTIVITY SHEETS

Chapter 13: Comparing and Contrasting Primary Sources

1. The major argument against slavery is that it is a sin.
2. Reading A condemns all plans of expatriation as a remedy for slavery.
3. Reading A says that immediate freeing of the slaves is the main goal of the abolitionists.
4. Reading B argues that the emancipation is the main goal of abolitionists
5. The three major arguments against immediate abolition are: **a.** no thought has been given to the consequences of such a scheme; **b.** there would be no controls on the freed slaves; **c.** there would be no compensation for slave owners.
6. Possible arguments in response include; **a.** It is more important to do the right thing without thinking of consequences than to continue doing an evil, sinful thing; **b.** Individual states can pass laws to control the freed slaves; **c.** No compensation should be paid because slave owners never had a right to own human beings. The use of free labor will prove profitable in a way that would more than compensate for the loss of slaves.

Chapter 14: Recognizing a Point of View

1. He might be described as a runaway African American slave.
2. He is writing to his former owner.
3. He is probably writing from Canada, since he mentions that he fled because the way was open to Canada.
4. He seems to be writing in order to explain and justify his flight from the slave owner.
5. Bibb fled because his wife and daughter were being abused and he had no power to protect them while he was a slave.
6. He seems courteous and respectful, treating the former owner as an equal; he does not seem angry or resentful over the ill treatment his family received.

Chapter 15: Using a Map and Time Chart

1. a. Richard Allen and Absalom Jones **b.** because of discrimination against African American worshipers in white churches
2. a. 1861 and 1896 **b.** 449,000
3. a. 1856–1896 **b.** 1816–1826
4. a. The founding of the Mother Bethel AME Church and the formal organization of the AME Church took place in Philadelphia. **b.** The letter B represents Wilberforce, Ohio, where the AME founded Wilberforce University.
5. The chart notes that in 1822 an AME congregation fled South Carolina after the Vesey conspiracy was discovered. Possibly white reaction to AME members was so hostile that no attempt was made to reestablish the church there in the period covered.
6. a. The AME expanded into the South between 1857 and 1892. **b.** Students may mention that pre-Civil War laws in the South sharply limited African American church gatherings. Defeat of the Confederacy and the establishment of Reconstruction governments removed those laws, enabling establishment of AME churches in the region of the nation with the largest African American population.

UNIT 6 ACTIVITY SHEETS

Chapter 16: Summarizing a Primary Source

1. Union, Bell; Democratic, Stephen A. Douglas; Seceders, John C. Breckinridge; Republican, Abraham Lincoln
2. None of the parties are really trying to free enslaved African Americans.
3. They do not want to move quickly to overthrow slavery.

4. Lincoln was opposed to the repeal of the Fugitive Slave Law.
5. The South was entitled to the law and any modification of the law should not lessen its efficiency.
6. African Americans are citizens, and no party is entitled to loyalty from African Americans unless that party is willing to extend all the rights of citizenship to them.
7. a law that requires a white person to back up the statements of an African American when the African American is testifying against a white person
8. While African Americans are taxed for every conceivable purpose, they receive none of the benefits of that taxation.
9. They show no sense of urgency to end slavery. They do not support ending the Fugitive Slave Law. They fail to support African Americans in the struggle to secure freedom, rights, and the benefits of American citizenship in free states.

Chapter 17: Understanding Points of View

1. The volunteers approved of his actions and thought they were a good plan to save the Union.
2. "Old Abe" was Abraham Lincoln who feared that Kentucky, one of the border states that permitted slavery, might leave the Union if African American troops were used in the Union Army.
3. "Old Jeff" was Jefferson Davis. The song refers to Southern threats to treat captured African American troops as rebellious slaves and hang them.
4. The song indicates African American eagerness to serve, expressed in the final stanza.

Chapter 18: Comparing and Contrasting Maps

1. cotton
2. One of the major buildings is labeled "Cotton Gin."
3. probably, since the cotton gin is still there
4. the plantation owner's family
5. enslaved African Americans
6. Suggested responses: easier to keep order, could prevent secret meetings by enslaved African Americans, cheaper because cooking was done in a central kitchen and more people could be housed in fewer buildings
7. The African Americans lived in separate houses. The plantation's owner was now a landlord. The plantation was probably divided into small plots of land which were now worked by individual families and, instead of receiving all income from the sales of the crop, the landlord only received a share. Also, a church and a school had been built.
8. Suggested responses: The arrangement gave them more privacy, the chance to live as individual families, and freedom from interference by the plantation owner.

Chapter 19: Drawing Conclusions

1. July 1877
2. in Kansas, 240 miles west of Topeka
3. to attract settlers to the new town of Nicodemus
4. an abundance of such natural resources as good soil, water, building stone, some timber, possibly coal; also the challenge of starting over in a new place, of farming their own land
5. the federal government **6.** Students' questions will differ but they may ask what the costs of moving will be, how much land costs, if there is a railroad nearby, if there are other towns nearby, what crops can be grown there, what the weather is like, etc.

UNIT 7 ACTIVITY SHEETS

Chapter 20: Comparing Supreme Court Opinions

A. CLASSIFYING
1. Majority **2.** Majority **3.** Majority
4. Minority **5.** Both **6.** Majority
7. Minority **8.** Majority **9.** Minority
10. Majority **11.** Minority **12.** Minority
13. Both
B. CRITICAL THINKING
1. Students should cite any of the items in the Minority Opinion column.
2. The minority would argue that

perpetuating the separation of the races, one of the people's traditions, is the same as perpetuating prejudice and the idea that African Americans are not equal to whites. For example, slavery was once "traditional" and considered "reasonable."

Chapter 21: Analyzing a Political Cartoon

1. He is holding his hand out for money for Tuskegee from prosperous-looking white men and women.
2. He is burying a coffin.
3. The inscriptions on the coffin and on the grave in the front as well as the caption indicate that Washington's "service" has been to "bury" issues of equal rights and the franchise (voting rights) for African Americans
4. The cartoon implies that money from whites is what motivates Washington to "bury" the issues of equal rights and the right to vote.

Chapter 22: Analyzing a Bar Graph

A. INTERPRETING DATA
1. dollars spent per pupil for Southern schools
2. 1890 and 1910
3. Alabama, Florida, Louisiana, North Carolina, Virginia.
4. expenditures on teacher salaries per pupil in white schools and expenditures on teacher salaries per pupil in African American schools
5. Alabama and North Carolina.
6. Florida
7. Florida, Louisiana, and Virginia
8. Roughly $400.
9. Louisiana
B. DRAWING CONCLUSIONS 2, 3, 4

UNIT 8 ACTIVITY SHEETS

Chapter 23 Activity A: Drawing Conclusions

1. (in any order) **a.** Texas **b.** Louisiana **c.** Mississippi **d.** Alabama **e.** Georgia
2. former slave states
3. Georgia
4. (in any order) **a.** Connecticut **b.** Massachusetts **c.** New Hampshire **d.** Rhode Island **e.** Vermont
5. Wyoming
6. Delaware and Maryland
7. a, c, e

Chapter 23 Activity B: Recognizing Points of View

Responses may differ significantly but should demonstrate a careful reading of the text and understanding of the concept of point of view. Key words or phrases:
Washington—begin at bottom; agitation is folly; progress from struggle; no contributing race will be excluded; preparation before exercising privileges; earning is worth more than spending
Du Bois—rights won't come in a moment; rights not gained by throwing them away; voting is necessary; color discrimination is barbarism; blacks need education as well as whites; strive with Washington for Thrift, Patience, Industrial Training; no apologies for injustice; no opposition to higher training
Conclusions: Student conclusions may be in agreement with either speaker or suggest another alternative but should be clearly derived from their strongest reason.

Chapter 24 Activity Sheet: Interpreting a Map

1. South or Southeast
2. west and north
3. All are located on waterways, either oceans, lakes, or rivers.
4. These cities were important to the trade and economy of the United States and African Americans were seeking job opportunities.

Chapter 25: Analyzing a Primary Source

1. a. two hundred and fifty years of slavery **b.** work without pay; satisfied with Christian teaching of patience
2. a. fifty-eight years of partial freedom during Emancipation **b.** satisfied to receive petty wages and to do just what white people told us to do
3. a. self-direction **b.** must throw off all the

conditions that affected us through the first and second stages and must conduct ourselves like men in the economic, industrial, and political arena

Chapter 26: Analyzing a Primary Source

1. Stanza 1: Let's sing joyously and march on to victory. Stanza 2: Our march has been difficult, but we are now on the verge of victory. Stanza 3: God has been guiding our march; let us stay true to Him and to our native land.
2. a. "Full of the faith that the dark past has taught us"; **b.** "full of the hope that the present has brought us."
3. liberty
4. Students may mention any two of the following: "Stony road," "Chast'ning rod," "hope unborn had died," "fathers sighed," "tears," "blood of the slaughtered."
5. (in any order) **a.** "Keep us forever in the path"; **b.** "may we stand, true to our God, true to our native land."
6. (in any order) **a.** faith **b.** hope **c.** steadfastness of purpose **d.** Providence
7. Students should point out the poem's appeal to the enduring concerns, goals, and values of African Americans in the early twentieth century. They might also point out that its popularity was probably aided by the emergence of the civil rights struggle after 1900 and the founding of the NAACP in 1910.

Chapter 27: Interpreting a Chart

TRUE OR FALSE

1. true **2.** true **3.** false **4.** true **5.** true **6.** false **7.** true **8.** false **9.** false **10.** true

---

UNIT 9 ACTIVITY SHEETS

Chapter 28: Interpreting Statistics

A. FIGURING PERCENTAGES

1. 79% **2.** 283° **3.** Navy **4.** 19° **5.** Other 3% **6.** 10°

B. MAKING THE GRAPH

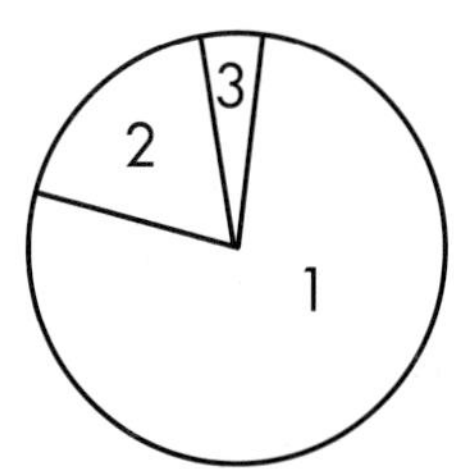

Chapter 29: Charting Data from Maps

A. CHARTING POPULATION SHIFTS

Less than 1,000		1,000-9,999		10,000-49,999		50,000-99,999		100,000-499,999		500,000-999,999		1,000,000 or more	
1940	1960	1940	1960	1940	1960	1940	1960	1940	1960	1940	1960	1940	1960
Vt.	Vt. (0)	Me.	Me. (0)	Wis.	R.I. (+)	Kans.	Kans. (0)	Calif.	Mass. (+)	N.C.	Calif. (+)	Miss.	Texas (+)
N. Dak.	N. Dak. (0)	Oreg.	N.H. (+)	Minn.	Minn. (0)	Mass.	Wis. (+)	Ill.	Conn. (+)	N.Y.	Mich. (+)	Ga.	Ga. (0)
S. Dak.		Nev.	S. Dak.(+)	Iowa	Iowa (0)		Del. (+)	Ind.	Ind. (0)	Texas	Ohio (+)		La. (+)
N.H.		Mont.	Mont. (0)	Nebr.	Nebr. (0)		W. Va. (+)	Mo.	Mo. (0)	La.	Md. (+)		N.C. (+)
R.I.		Idaho	Idaho (0)	Colo.	Colo. (0)			Ky.	Ky. (0)	Va.	Va. (0)		N.Y. (+)
Del.		Wyo.	Wyo. (0)	Conn.	N.M. (+)			Ark.	Ark. (0)	S.C.	S.C. (0)		Ill. (+)
		Utah	Utah (0)	Ariz.	Ariz. (0)			Okla.	Okla. (0)	Fla.	Fla. (0)		
		N.M.						Ohio		Ala.	Ala. (0)		
		Wash.						Penn.		Tenn.	Tenn. (0)		
								Md.			Miss. (-)		
								N.J.					
								W. Va.					
								Mich.					

B. COMPARING POPULATION SHIFTS
1. a. 22 **b.** 2 **c.** 24
2. the number decreased from 6 to 2
3. the number increased from 2 to 6
4. Illinois

Chapter 30: Using a Primary Source

1. the bus company in Montgomery, Alabama
2. An African American woman was arrested because she did not give up her whites-only seat on a bus.
3. They ask that no one ride the bus on Monday for any reason.
4. They wanted the buses integrated.
5. A boycott placed economic pressure on the bus company since many of its riders were African Americans.
6. Responses will differ but any logical answer is acceptable.

Chapter 31: Connecting History and Geography

1. These states were the first states to have charters for the Black Panthers and SNCC.
2. a. Region includes: Massachusetts, Connecticut, New York, and Pennsylvania
b. Region includes: Michigan, Illinois, Indiana, Kentucky, North Carolina, Tennessee, Georgia, Alabama, Louisiana, and California
3. All the states in the **b** region originally had a large African American population. The African American population of both the **a** region and the northern portion of the **b** region increased as the result of various migrations mentioned in the text. By 1960 there was a high concentration of African Americans in both these regions.
4. the Eastern United States
5. Louisiana and California
6. These are states without original chapters of the Black Panthers and SNCC.
7. Most of the states that are indicated by the darker color are located west of the Mississippi river.

Chapter 32: Interpreting a Political Cartoon

1. in Vietnam; written on the box **2.** He is reading a letter from his mother at home
3. African Americans still do not have equal rights and are continuing to fight for them.
4. Students' responses will differ. They may point out that African Americans are fighting abroad for freedom for others when they still do not have it at home for themselves.
5. The cartoon is pessimistic because it points out that African Americans are still not completely free in the United States and yet they must die in Vietnam for the country that will not grant them equality.

UNIT 10 ACTIVITY SHEETS

Chapter 33: Analyzing a Map

1. the states in which the top 100 African American owned businesses are located
2. California
3. 38
4. Midwest
5. Generalizations will differ in both form and content but students should demonstrate an understanding of the data shown on the map as well as the concept of generalization. Possibilities include: Most of the top 100 African American owned businesses are in the South and Midwest; The West has the fewest of the top 100 African American owned businesses; The top 100 African American owned businesses are not evenly distributed around the United States.

Chapter 34 Activity A: Recognizing Points of View

Responses may differ significantly but should demonstrate a careful reading of the text and a clear understanding of the concept of point of view. Key words or phrases include the following: **Woodson:**— some problems have nothing to do with racism; there is a crisis within ourselves; why are there more single parent families now; the destiny of black America is not determined by white people; white people are not responsible for black people's actions
Lowery—African Americans must develop a will to achieve; will in hearts and minds; opportunities for employment are needed; we have not developed a national will; U.S.

government is more concerned about rich Kuwaitis than poor Americans; elitist to say all can be self-starting; some need motivation; the opportunity must exist to fulfill that motivation; all who made it had help; must create environment to maximize opportunity
Conclusions: Student conclusions may be in agreement with either speaker or suggest another alternative but should be clearly derived from their strongest reason.

Chapter 34 Activity B: Stating and Supporting an Opinion

1. Responses will differ but should demonstrate an understanding of *Ebony's* standards and knowledge of the person chosen, whether derived from the text or outside research
2. A wide variety of standards will probably be suggested. In evaluating student's answers look for consistency, logic, and clarity.
3. Students may choose whomever they wish but should support their choices according to their own previously stated standards. In evaluating students' answers look for knowledge of the person chosen and a clear, consistent and logical argument in support of the student's choice.

THE WRITING PROCESS AND SOCIAL STUDIES

WHY WRITE IN SOCIAL STUDIES?

Writing is a skill that students need for success in virtually every academic subject as well as for success in the world beyond the classroom. Some people say that teaching writing is important, but that this task is the responsibility of language arts teachers. However, students must learn that the skills of writing apply to every discipline. By using techniques of the writing process in social studies classes, by requiring students to express themselves well on paper, and by holding them to the conventions of standard English usage, social studies teachers greatly add to students' overall proficiency. So the real question is "What can a social studies teacher do to develop writing skills in the classroom?"

WHAT IS THE WRITING PROCESS?

Today, teachers know that writing is a complex process that involves the application of a wide range of thinking skills and language abilities. Teachers recognize that the process involves a series of steps. Writers practice very different skills and undertake very different activities at each of these steps. By understanding the steps of the writing process and employing them in teaching, teachers can focus on the techniques and tools students need, the knowledge they must develop, and the choices they must learn to make at each step to become effective writers.

The first step of the writing process is called, **prewriting**. This is the discovery stage. Student-writers get warmed up, choose ideas, gather details, and sort through information. Students address issues of audience, voice, and purpose. Prewriting is a rich, productive stage that generates a flow of material and ideas for writing and focuses the writer's attention on the topic.

The goal of prewriting is for students to develop the content and to explore the possibilities so fully in their minds that papers will virtually write themselves. To facilitate prewriting, students can practice many techniques. The following strategies help writers get words on paper: journals, logs, reading logs, brainstorming, clustering, mapping, charts, oral activities, outlining, taking notes. Several of these techniques are employed in the Writing Workshops.

Writers need to get their ideas recorded in some sort of tentative, first-draft shape as easily and quickly as possible. This occurs in the **writing/drafting** phase of the writing process. After students have identified their ideas, they are ready to make choices as to what and how they will write. Students must be familiar with the options available to them to achieve their goal. At this stage, writers turn their prewriting ideas into coherent, organized writing.

At this stage students should try to get ideas down quickly, with a minimum of worry, expecting that changes can be made later. Choices resulting from audience, voice, purpose, and form are made at this time. Students consider diction, sentence structure, and connections in order to write what they want to communicate. The guidelines offered in the Writing Workshops help student-writers with problems of organization, diction, and form while keeping them focused on audience, voice, and purpose.

After students have generated the first draft, they are ready to move to the next phase of the writing process, **revising.** Effective revision almost always involves the positive, informed response of outside readers and rethinking and revising by the writers themselves. Writers look for places to improve content and sense, word choices, and sentence style. Peer response, while it can be utilized at any stage of the writing process, is especially effective during revision because it allows writers to receive feedback about the first draft. When students know their peers will listen to, read, and respond to their writing, they care about their work because they care about what their audience thinks. In every Writing Workshop, students are asked to respond to another's writing as they "Talk It Over." Armed with suggestions from partners, students are given the opportunity to "Make the Changes" that will improve their papers.

Editing is an important part of this stage. While formal correctness is not the only objective in writing, it is important because errors can impede communication. Therefore, after papers have been revised, students act as editors to edit and proofread. Proofreading is the job of cleaning up the manuscript, or eliminating surface errors. Students need to understand that proofreading is not revision but simply correcting errors in spelling, usage, and mechanics so their audience can easily understand their writing. At the editing stage, peer response can again be a valuable tool. The editing phase in the Writing Workshops gives students the opportunity to help one another eliminate surface mistakes. Fewer mistakes make a teacher's job less tedious.

A final step in the writing process is **postwriting**. This step gives credibility and value to the act of writing. Postwriting includes **evaluating** and **publishing** student work. This step goes beyond simply grading. Putting student work on display benefits the classroom because students work harder and learn from others' points of views. Publishing can range from simply posting work on the bulletin board to entering it in a national compctition where money and nationwide recognition are the reward. The goal of honoring student writing is to help students realize that they have something worthwhile to say and that they have the skills to communicate that message in an effective way. All the Writing Workshops present opportunities to honor student writing.

USING THE WRITING WORKSHOPS

The Writing Workshops are designed to help social studies teachers implement a structured writing program in their classes by taking students step by step through the writing process. Literary models written by African Americans from the time period that students are studying are presented for writers to analyze. Directed reading questions point students to important historical details and exemplary literary elements in the writing models. During the prewriting step, questions about topic, audience, and purpose focus the writers' attention on the task at hand. Students learn prewriting techniques not only by explanation but also through examples. As students begin their first draft in the writing stage, guidelines assist them in choosing linguistic options and determining organization. Before students begin to revise, peers respond to student writing and help writers make improvements. Editing develops awareness of proper English usage by teaching proofreading. Finally, in postwriting students present their writing to others. The publishing activities offer social studies teachers ways to honor students' work. Finally, the forms on the following pages assist teachers, or even students, with different techniques for evaluating the final product.

WRITING WORKSHOP EVALUATION

Writer________________________________ Title________________________________

Write comments about the content, organization, style, and spelling, usage, and mechanics in the space below.

Content

Well-done: ________________________________

____

____

Needs Improvement: ________________________________

____

____

Organization

Well-done: ________________________________

____

____

Needs Improvement: ________________________________

____

____

Style

Well-done: ________________________________

____

____

Needs Improvement: ________________________________

____

____

Spelling, Usage, Mechanics

Well-done: ________________________________

____

____

Needs Improvement: ________________________________

____

____

____

WRITING WORKSHOP EVALUATION

Writer________________________________ Title ________________________________

To evaluate a paper holistically, first read the paper. Then, with your first impression in mind, use this scoring guide as a basis for your assessment.

SCORE	CRITERIA
4	clear, concise sentences varied sentence structure specific or descriptive details special flair; uses imagination or makes thoughtful comments effective word choice good use of transitions writes to the topic well-organized excellent spelling, usage, mechanics other: ________________
3	clear, concise sentences some detail, imagination, or thoughtful ideas writes to the topic some use of transitions mechanical or usage problems do not interfere adequate organization appropriate paragraphing other: ________________
2	some incomplete sentences lacks organization partial development of the topic errors interfere with understanding faulty paragraphing other: ________________
1	little or no organization short and underdeveloped wanders from the topic many mechanical problems other: ________________
0	inappropriate illegible off the topic blank page

WRITING WORKSHOP EVALUATION

Writer______________________________ Title______________________________

Rating: 5 = highest possible rating; 1 = lowest possible rating

AREAS	RATING	COMMENTS
CONTENT		
Content Soundness. Is the content thoughtful, factually accurate, logically valid, and otherwise sound?		
Interest. Is the paper interesting?		
Appropriateness. Is the content appropriate for the audience and purpose?		
Topic. Has the topic been narrowed accurately to suit the length and purpose of the paper?		
Main Idea. Is there a clear main idea or thesis statement?		
Support. Is there enough supporting evidence? Are there enough details?		
Introduction. Does the introduction catch the reader's attention? Is it effective?		
Conclusion. Does the conclusion contain a reminder of the main idea or thesis statement? Is it effective?		
Title. Is the title appropriate?		
ORGANIZATION		
Order. Is the content arranged logically and effectively?		
Unity. Are all the supporting ideas and details relevant to the main idea or thesis statement?		
Coherence. Are transitions used to connect ideas clearly?		
USAGE, MECHANICS, AND STYLE		
Clarity. Are all statements clear? Do the sentences read well?		
Sentence Style. Are all sentences sufficiently varied in length and structure?		
Correctness. Is the paper free of errors in usage, mechanics, and style?		
Legibility. Is the handwriting or typing legible?		
Appearance. Is the paper neat and clean? Has it been written or typed in the correct form?		

Name ______________________________ Date ______________

Unit 1 Writing Workshop: A Paragraph

A famous North African scholar and traveler, Al Hassan Ibn Muhammad traveled along the Niger River in northeast Africa in 1513. He lived in the city of Timbuktu in the African empire of Songhai, a city that impressed him with its wealth and intellectual life. Here is a part of his description of Timbuktu's greatness.

Discover

- **how the writer uses facts to explain**
- **his informative tone**

Look at the Model

Here are many shops of artificers [people who make things] and merchants, and especially of such as weave linen and cotton cloth. And hither [here] do the Barbary [coastal area of northwestern Africa] merchants bring cloth of Europe. All the women of this region, except the maid-servants, go with their faces covered, and sell all necessary victuals [foodstuffs]. The inhabitants, and especially strangers there residing, are exceeding rich, in so much that the king that now is, married both his daughters to rich merchants. Here are many wells containing most sweet water; and so often as the river Niger overflowed, they convey the water thereof by certain sluices [artificial passages] into the town. Corn, cattle, milk, and butter this region yielded in great abundance; but salt is very scarce here; for it is brought hither by land from Taghaza which is 500 miles distant. . . . Here are great store [number] of doctors, judges, priests, and other learned men, that are bountifully maintained at the king's cost and charges, and hither are brought divers [various] manuscripts or written books out of Barbary, which are sold for more money than any other merchandise.

—Leo Africanus, The History and Description of Africa (London: Hakluyt Society, 1896)

1. What is the main idea of the passage?

____

____

2. List three facts that support the main idea.

____

____

____

3. Most expository writing has a topic sentence. Al Hassan Ibn Muhammad does not use one in the model. Write a topic sentence for his passage.

____

____

Name ______________________________ Date ______________

Prewriting

Choose Your Topic

The purpose of expository writing is to give information or to explain something to the reader. This purpose is often accomplished by providing facts and examples. Research an African civilization or empire to find details about its culture. Choose one aspect of the civilization that you find important or impressive. Then, write an expository paragraph, explaining why you were impressed with the culture.

Your primary purpose will be to inform your readers, but you will have a secondary purpose. Do you also want to entertain or amaze your audience? Write your secondary purpose

here: ______________________________

Who are you writing this paragraph for? Describe your audience here: ______________________________

____

Take Notes

Before you write your paragraph, make notes about aspects of the culture that impressed you. Record details about the culture to serve as evidence. However, be sure that you are using facts, not opinions, to inform your readers. Your notes do not have to be in complete sentences; just jot down the important information.

Some of Al Hassan's notes might have looked like this:

Shops — linen, cotton cloth, cloth from Europe

Women — cover faces (except servants), sell food

Value learning — doctors, judges, priests supported by king; books the most expensive item

Use the space below to take your own notes. After you have written your notes, number the facts from the least important to the most impressive. In that way, when you are ready to draft, your facts will be in order of importance.

____

____

____

____

____

____

____

____

____

Name ______________________________ Date______________

Writing

Your First Draft

Use this space to write a first draft of your expository paragraph. Do not worry now about errors in spelling or punctuation. You will have time later to correct any errors. As you write, refer to the guidelines on the left side of the page. Use them along with your notes to help you organize your draft.

Write a topic sentence that gives the main idea of your paragraph.

Give your first fact. Include details to make it interesting.

Write your second fact and all the important details about it.

Concentrate on explaining as you write.

Write your next fact and include details.

Continue with your facts, ending with the most important one.

Write a concluding sentence that restates your main idea.

Name ______________________ Date______________

Revising

Talk It Over

Choose a partner. Listen as your partner reads his or her work aloud twice. During the first reading, listen to be sure your partner has included all the information needed to explain the main idea to the audience. After the second reading, jot down the answers to these questions:

1. What is the main idea of the paragraph?
2. Is the main idea supported with factual examples, not opinions? Has your partner included any other inappropriate material? If so, what should be eliminated or clarified?
3. What facts and details could be added to make the explanation clearer or more informative?
4. How could the organization be improved? After the second reading, share your answers with your partner. Then read your own paragraph and listen to your partner's comments.

Make the Changes

Think about the comments your partner made about your paragraph. Make any changes you think will improve your paper. Write your revision on a clean sheet of paper.

Editing

Review these proofreading marks to help you correct errors.

∧	add something	❛❛ ❜❜	add quotation marks
⳼	delete something	¶	new paragraph
≡	capitalize	/	lower case
⊙	make a period	(sp)	spell correctly
∧,	add a comma	∽	transpose

Re-read your paragraph to check for errors in spelling and punctuation, or exchange paragraphs with your partner and proofread each other's work. Read your partner's paragraph for errors, making a small check in the margin where an error occurs.

Postwriting

Evaluate Your Writing

If your paragraph has many proofreading marks, copy it onto a clean sheet of paper before submitting it for final evaluation.

Publish Your Writing

Submit your paper to your teacher. The teacher will read several students' paragraphs to the class. Then you and your classmates will vote on which aspect of African civilization impressed you all the most, based on what you learned from one another's paragraphs.

Name ______________________________ Date______________

Unit 2 Writing Workshop: A First-Person Narrative

Writing that describes personal experiences is called first-person narrative. It is an account of an event told by a person who actually experienced the event, either as a participant or an observer. Such stories supply information to historians in their quest to understand historical periods, events, or persons. Olaudah Equiano, also known as Gustavus Vassa, used first-person narrative to tell about an incident that occurred on the slave ship on which he was a captive.

Discover

- **the events that take place**
- **the feelings that give the event meaning**

Look at the Model

> One day, when we had a smooth sea, and moderate wind, two of my wearied [tired] countrymen, who were chained together (I was near them at the time), preferring death to such a life of misery, somehow made through the netting, and jumped into the sea; immediately another quite dejected [very sad] fellow, who, on account of his illness, was suffered to be out of irons, also followed their example; and I believe many more would very soon have done the same, if they had not been prevented by the ship's crew, who were instantly alarmed. Those of us that were the most active were in a moment put down under the deck; and there was such a noise and confusion amongst the people of the ship as I never heard before. to stop her, and get the boat out to go after the slaves. However, two of the wretches were drowned, but they got the other, and afterwards flogged him unmercifully, for thus attempting to prefer death to slavery. In this manner we continued to undergo more hardships than I can now relate; hardships which are inseparable from this accursed [hated] trade.
>
> — Gustavus Vasa, *The Interesting Narrative of the Life of Olaudah Equiano or Gustavus Vassa, Written by Himself* (London, 1793)

1. From whose point of view is the narrative written? How do you know?

____

____

2. What event is the writer telling about? Where and when did the event happen?

____

____

3. What emotions does the writer associate with the event?

____

____

4. List three words and phrases that show the writer's feelings.

____

____

Name ______________________________ Date ______________

Prewriting

Choose Your Topic

Imagine you were an eyewitness to one of the events that are presented in Unit 2, and you have decided to write about it. Begin by choosing the event or events you wish to relate. If you decide to write about one event, you may be able to relate it in one paragraph. If you choose a series of events, you may need to write a longer narrative. Write down the event or events you will relate here: ______________________________

Who will read your narrative? What is your purpose for writing? Will you entertain your audience or inform them? Describe your audience and purpose here: ______________________________

____

____

Brainstorm

To get started, brainstorm, or quickly think up as many ideas as you can, about your topic. Write down what comes to mind. Do not worry now about the usefulness of your ideas. After you finish brainstorming, you can discard ideas that do not fit your audience and purpose. Gustavus Vassa's brainstorming notes might have looked like this:

When: day on ocean voyage from Africa to Americas — smooth sea — moderate wind
Where: on slave ship
What: 3 slaves tried to escape–jumped into water–2 men were chained together–other slaves put below–2 drowned–one rescued and whipped
Why: 3 jumpers preferred death to slavery–slave traders wished to make an example to discourage other jumpers

Use the following questions as springboards for your ideas.

When? ______________________________

____

Where? ______________________________

____

What? ______________________________

____

Why? ______________________________

____

Name ______________________________ Date ______________

Writing

Your First Draft

Use this space to write a first draft of your narrative. Do not worry now about errors in spelling or punctuation. Use your brainstorming notes for writing ideas. If other ideas occur to you, include them in your narrative. Use the guidelines listed below to organize your draft.

Begin by setting the scene and introducing the incident. ______________________________

____

____

Tell how the event began. ______________________________

____

What did you, as the narrator, do or think? Remember to express your feelings. ______________________________

____

____

____

What occurred next? ______________________________

____

What happened after that? ______________________________

____

____

Include descriptive details to help your audience "see" the event. ______________________________

____

____

How did the event end? ______________________________

____

Conclude with a personal observation. Write a sentence that tells what you learned or how you felt. ______________________________

____

____

____

Name ______________________________ Date____________

Revising

Talk It Over

Choose a partner. Listen as your partner reads his or her narrative aloud twice. During the first reading, try to imagine what the event was like. After the second reading, answer these questions:

1. Is the first-person point of view maintained throughout the narrative?
2. Does the writer make the time and place of the event clear?
3. Are enough details given to understand what happened and why?
4. Does the writer express feelings about the event?
5. What personal observations about the event does the writer make?

Discuss your answers to the above questions with your partner. Then, switch roles, read your narrative, and repeat the process.

Make the Changes

Reread your first draft. Think about the suggestions that your partner made. Make any changes you need to improve your first-person narrative.

Editing

Review these proofreading marks to help you correct errors.

∧	add something	❛❛ ❜❜	add quotation marks
℘	delete something	¶	new paragraph
≡	capitalize	/	lower case
⊙	make a period	ⓢⓟ	spell correctly
∧,	add a comma	∿	transpose

Re-read your narrative to check for errors in spelling and punctuation, or exchange narratives with your partner and proofread each other's work. Read your partner's narrative for errors, making a small check in the margin where an error occurs.

Postwriting

Evaluate Your Writing

If your narrative has many proofreading marks, copy it onto a clean sheet of paper before submitting it for final evaluation.

Publish Your Writing

Meet with other students who wrote about similar events. Collect all the narratives in a "book." Create a cover and a title for your collection. Display your book in the classroom.

Name ______________________ Date ______________

Unit 3 Writing Workshop: Writing About Geography in History

James Beckwourth was an African American slave who escaped west and became a mountaineer, scout, and chief of the Crow nation. In 1850, he discovered a pass through the Sierra Nevada mountains that still bears his name. The passage below, from his autobiography, describes the first time Beckwourth saw the pass.

Discover 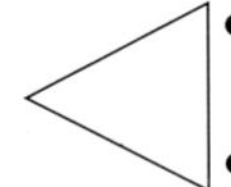

- **how Beckwourth uses specific, precise words to make his description of a place come alive**
- **how geographic themes are used in Beckwourth's description**

Look at the Model

> It was the latter end of April when we entered upon an extensive valley at the northwest extremity [end] of the Sierra [Nevada] range. . . . Swarms of wild geese and ducks were swimming on the surface of the cool crystal stream, which was the central fork of the Rio de las Plumas, or sailed the air in clouds over our heads. Deer and antelope filled the plains, and their boldness was conclusive [evidence] that the hunter's rifle was to them unknown. Nowhere visible were any traces of the white man's approach, and it is probable that our steps were the first that ever marked the spot. We struck across this beautiful valley to the waters of the Yuba, from thence to the waters of the Truchy. . . . This, I at once saw, would afford the best wagon-road into the American Valley approaching from the eastward.
>
> —James Beckwourth, *The Life and Adventures of James Beckwourth, Mountaineer, Scout, Pioneer, and Chief of the Crow Nation of Indians,* written from his own dictation by T. D. Bonner (London, 1892)

1. What specific words and phrases does Beckwourth use to describe the location of the pass he discovered?

____

2. Does the writer give exact or relative locations? Why would Beckwourth be concerned about the specifics of location?

____

3. What specific words and phrases does Beckwourth use to describe the characteristics of the pass's location?

____

4. What observations does the writer make about human presence in the pass both in the past and the future?

____

5. What is the overall feeling or dominant impression that Beckwourth creates of the pass?

____

____

Name ________________________________ Date________________

Prewriting

Choose Your Topic

You will be writing a description of a place that was important in U.S. history during the period from 1763 to 1850. Good descriptive writing requires that you use your powers of observation to make the place come alive for your readers. Choose a place that you find very interesting. Look through "The Big Picture" and the chapters in Unit 3. Review the timeline to find a location that appeals to you. Write your choice here: ________________________________

____

Your purpose is to communicate a dominant impression of the location by giving important characteristics of the place and details of people's contact with it from 1763 to 1850. Write the dominant impression you want to communicate here: ________________________________

____

Who will be reading this description? Will it be included in a letter to friends, will it be a part of an autobiography like Beckwourth's, or will it be included in a social studies report? The tone, or writing voice, you choose — friendly, amusing, serious — will be determined in part by who you are writing for. Identify your audience and tone here: ________________________________

____

Make a Cluster

Before you begin to write your description, it helps to gather and write down everything you know about your subject. One way to do this is to make a word cluster, or semantic map. To create a cluster, begin by writing the subject in the center of a sheet of paper. Then write down related facts and details. Do not worry about being neat or orderly in a cluster. Write anything that comes to mind anywhere on the page. If one thought relates to another, draw a line connecting the ideas. James Beckwourth's cluster might have looked like this:

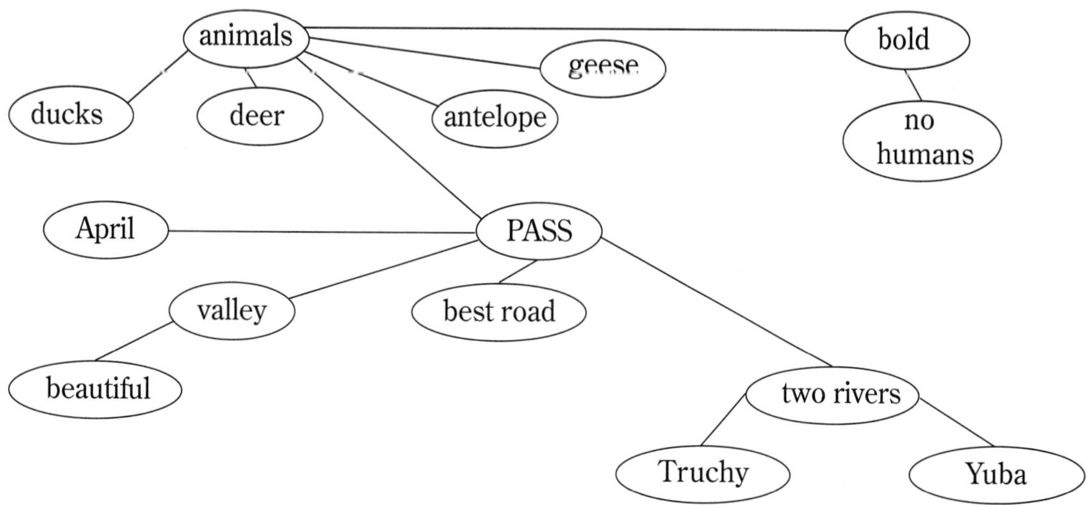

Follow the steps outlined above to make your own cluster. If you do not know enough facts and details, you may need to go to the library to find out more about the location you are writing about.

Name ______________________________ Date______________

Writing

Your First Draft

Use this space to write a first draft of your description. Do not worry about spelling mistakes or other errors now. You will have time to make changes later. Use the ideas from your cluster. You may also add new ideas or omit ones you think will not contribute to the strong impression you wish to create. Use the guidelines on the left as you organize your draft.

Identify the place you are writing about.

Add details about the physical and human characteristics of the place.

Use descriptive words to reinforce your dominant impression. Choose words that appeal to your readers' senses.

Think about your purpose. Will your readers be able to picture the place you are describing?

Add details in a logical order. Beckwourth described all the animals before he discussed human presence.

Write a final sentence or two summing up your impression of the place. Include a statement about its importance to the period.

Name ______________________________ Date______________

Revising

Talk it Over

Work with a partner to revise your description. Read your description to your partner. Ask your partner to close his or her eyes and picture the place you are describing. Read your description again, and ask your partner for specific answers to these questions:

1. Is it clear what place is being described? Is its location clear? What are the characteristics of the place?
2. What is the dominant impression conveyed by the description?
3. What words could be added or changed to make the description more concrete or vivid?

Now reverse the process and have your partner read his or her description to you.

Make the Changes

Reread the first draft of your description. As you read, look for ways to make your description better. Include any of your partner's suggestions that you think will improve your description. Write your revision on a clean sheet of paper.

Editing

Review these proofreading marks to help you correct errors.

Mark	Meaning	Mark	Meaning
∧	add something	❛❛ ❜❜	add quotation marks
℘	delete something	¶	new paragraph
≡	capitalize	/	lower case
⊙	make a period	(sp)	spell correctly
∧,	add a comma	∩∪	transpose

Re-read your description again to check for errors in spelling and punctuation, or exchange descriptions with your partner and proofread each other's work. Read your partner's description for errors, making a small check in the margin where an error occurs.

Postwriting

Evaluate Your Writing

If your article has many proofreading marks, copy it onto a clean sheet of paper before submitting it for final evaluation.

Publish Your Writing

Illustrate your description, and post the illustration and your description on the class bulletin board.

Name ______________________ Date ______________

Unit 4 Writing Workshop: A Letter to Persuade

How do you convince someone to change his or her mind? How do you get someone to see another side of an issue?

During the 1820s and 1830s, African Americans came to Indiana by covered wagon from North Carolina. They settled in Hamilton County and established an African American community there. Later, this settlement produced many lawyers, doctors, dentists, teachers, and ministers. However, life for the first African Americans in Hamilton County was not easy. Some questioned whether they should remain in Indiana. In 1830, settler Willis Roberts was considering returning to North Carolina. His cousin "Long" James Roberts wrote a letter to persuade him to think twice about returning.

Discover

- **what advice James Roberts gives his cousin Willis Roberts**
- **the reasons that support James Roberts's position**

Look at the Model

Dear Willis,

After leaving you on the 15th of February, 1830, I feel it a duty for me to write a few lines to inform you of my mind on what you are going to do. . .

It seems very plain to me that you are now going to make one of the worst mistakes that you ever made. . . . You are taking your children to an old country [North Carolina] [where the land] is worn out. . . . You may be taken away from them and they may come under the hands of some cruel slave holder . . . . You know that if they [slave owners] can get a colored child, they will use them as bad again as they will one of their own slaves . . . .

I would not this night, if I had children, take them to such a place [in which they would] not enjoy themselves as free men but be in a place where they are not able to speak for their rights. . . . This is from the heart of one who wishes you well.

James

— Letter from James Roberts to Willis Roberts, the Roberts Settlement Collection. (Washington: Library of Congress, Manuscript Collection.)

1. What does "Long" James Roberts want Willis Roberts to do?

____

2. What are three reasons James Roberts uses to support his opinion?

   a. ______________________

   b. ______________________

   c. ______________________

3. What powerful words or phrases does James Roberts use to make his argument more forceful?

____

____

Name ______________________________ Date ______________

Prewriting

Choose Your Topic

Imagine that you had a relative who had settled in Hamilton County during the early 1800s. That relative wrote to you expressing a desire to leave the territory and return to the South. What would you say to the person? Write a letter expressing your opinion about the decision to leave Indiana and support your position with facts.

Think about your audience. Who will read your letter? What do you want your letter to accomplish? How can you persuade the person to accept your point of view? Describe your audience here: ______________________________

____

State your purpose: ______________________________

____

Make a List

When you write to persuade, your position should be forcefully presented and carefully supported. You can state your opinion in a single sentence and then make a list of reasons that support it. After you have listed your reasons, number them in the order you wish to use them. Usually persuasive writing is most effective if you begin with your least important reason and build up to your most powerful argument. Cross out any item on the list that does not support your position.

If James Roberts had made a list, it might have looked like this:

Willis should not return to North Carolina

⑤ the trip is long

② slavery exists there

① the soil is poor and worn out

③ his children might be kidnapped and sold into slavery

④ his children will not be able to exercise their rights as free citizens

Make your own list here. Use facts and evidence from Unit 4 of *The African American Experience* to support your position. Then number your reasons and cross out unimportant ideas.

____

____

____

____

____

____

____

____

Name ____________________ Date ____________

Writing

Your First Draft

Use this space or a separate sheet of paper to write a first draft of your letter. Do not worry now about errors in spelling or punctuation. Use ideas from your list. If other ideas occur to you, include them in your letter. Use the guidelines listed below to organize your draft.

Write the date of your letter.

Write a greeting followed by a comma.

Begin by introducing the topic and giving your opinion.

State your first reason.

Be sure to be thorough in your presentation.

Use persuasive, powerful words and phrases to add force to your argument.

Continue supporting your opinion with reasons.

Remember your purpose. Do your reasons tell why the audience should think as you do?

End your letter by summing up your argument. If possible, end with a proposal, suggestion, or the consequences as a "zinger."

Name ______________________ Date ____________

Revising

Talk It Over

Choose a partner. Listen as your partner reads his or her work aloud twice. During the first reading, listen for the writer's opinion. After the second reading, answer these questions:

1. What is the writer's position?
2. Which reasons clearly support that opinion? Which do not? What other reasons could the writer add to the letter?
3. How convincing was the letter? What can the writer do to make the letter more persuasive?

After your partner has read his or her letter twice, discuss your answers to the questions above. Then read your letter to your partner and listen to his or her responses. Be sure to make notes of suggestions and ideas.

Make the Changes

Think about the comments your partner made about your letter. Make any changes you think will improve your letter. Then copy the revised letter on a clean sheet of paper.

Editing

Review these proofreading marks to help you correct errors.

Mark	Meaning	Mark	Meaning
∧	add something	∜∜	add quotation marks
℘	delete something	¶	new paragraph
≡	capitalize	/	lower case
⊙	make a period	Ⓢⓟ	spell correctly
∧,	add a comma	∽	transpose

Re-read your letter to check for errors in spelling and punctuation, or exchange letters with your partner and proofread each other's work. Read your partner's letter for errors, making a small check in the margin where an error occurs.

Postwriting

Evaluate Your Writing

If your letter has many proofreading marks, copy it onto a clean sheet of paper before submitting it for final evaluation.

Publish Your Writing

After you have turned in your letter, your teacher will distribute the letters to members of the class. Write a response to the letter you receive, stating whether or not you would follow the advice and why.

Name ______________________________ Date ______________

Unit 5 Writing Workshop: Taking a Stand

The Fugitive Slave Law of 1850 shocked and angered people who were working to end slavery. African American and white abolitionists vowed to defy the law in every way possible. Dr. Martin R. Delany, an African American physician and editor, took this stand:

Discover

- **the action that Martin Delany threatens to take**
- **the specific details that add force to his statement**

Look at the Model

> Honorable mayor, whatever ideas of liberty I may have, have been received from reading the lives of your revolutionary fathers. I have . . . learned that a man has the right to defend his castle with his life, even unto the taking of life. Sir, my house is my castle. . . . If any man approaches that house in search of a slave—I care not who he may be, whether constable or sheriff, magistrate or even judge of the Supreme Court—nay, let it be he who sanctioned this act to become a law [President Millard Fillmore] . . . if he crosses the threshold of my door and I do not lay him a lifeless corpse at my feet, I hope the grave may refuse my body a resting-place, and righteous Heaven my spirit a home. O, no! He cannot enter that house and we both live.
>
> — Frank A. Rollin, *The Life and Public Services of Martin R. Delany* (Boston, 1883)

1. What does Martin Delany state he will do if officials come to his house in search of African Americans who have fled from their owners? In what sentence does he state his course of action? ______________________________

____

2. The writer uses strong action verbs and vivid, powerful words and phrases to make his point. List three examples.

____

____

____

3. Do you think Delany would have carried out his threat? Explain your answer.

____

____

____

____

____

____

Name ______________________ Date ______________

Prewriting

Choose Your Topic

What is your opinion of the Fugitive Slave Law of 1850 (see p. 167)? What would you have done if officials had come to your door looking for escaped African Americans? Would you have defied the government of the United States, or would you have obeyed the law? Present your position in a newspaper editorial. State your position here: ______________________

____

Who will be reading your editorial? If you expect your audience to agree with you, you may suggest taking strong action. However, if your audience does not share your opinion, you must try to change their minds by presenting logical arguments and strong emotional appeals.

Describe your audience here: ______________________

____

Freewrite

Freewriting is a technique that can help you get your thoughts and ideas on a subject flowing. When you freewrite, you write down whatever comes to mind for a certain length of time or until you have filled a certain number of pages. You don't edit what you write or even stop to evaulate your ideas. Just write down your thoughts as they come. Use the space below to freewrite.

____

____

____

____

____

____

____

____

____

____

____

____

____

____

After you have finished freewriting, wait a little while, and then read and evaluate what you have written. Now add or eliminate ideas based on their suitability for your audience and purpose.

Name ______________________________ Date ______________

Writing

Your First Draft

Use the guidelines at the left as you write your editorial. Do not worry about errors in spelling or punctuation now. You will have time to make corrections later. Include ideas from your freewriting and any other ideas that occur to you.

Begin by addressing your audience.

Give background details to help readers understand your opinion.

Offer facts, evidence, and logical arguments to support your opinion.

Share your feelings and emotions about the issue with your readers.

Explain the actions you propose for yourself or others.

Use strong, action verbs and vivid, persuasive language to present your position convincingly.

Conclude by restating your position and the action you propose.

Name ______________________________ Date______________

Revising

Talk It Over

Work with a partner. Read your editorial aloud twice. After your partner has heard your editorial, ask these questions:

1. What is my opinion on the Fugitive Slave Law?
2. Have I made my chosen course of action clear? What could I add or eliminate to make my position easier to understand?
3. What words and phrases were the strongest and most vivid? What changes could be made to make my editorial more powerful or convincing?

Then switch roles and respond to your partner's editorial.

Make the Changes

Reread your first draft. Think about the suggestions that your partner made. Then any changes needed to improve your editorial. Copy the revised paragraph onto a clean sheet of paper.

Editing

Review these proofreading marks to help you correct errors.

Mark	Meaning	Mark	Meaning
∧	add something	∨∨	add quotation marks
ꝭ	delete something	¶	new paragraph
≡	capitalize	/	lower case
⊙	make a period	(sp)	spell correctly
∧,	add a comma	∿	transpose

Re-read your editorial to check for errors in spelling and punctuation, or exchange editorials with your partner and proofread each other's work. Read your partner's editorial for errors, making a small check in the margin where an error occurs.

Postwriting

Evaluate Your Writing

If your editorial has many proofreading marks, copy it onto a clean sheet of paper before submitting it for final evaluation.

Publish Your Writing

Volunteer to read your editorial to the class. After all volunteers have read their papers aloud, have a class discussion on which editorial was most persuasive. Be sure that you and others give reasons and examples to support your evaluations.

Name ______________________________ Date______________

Unit 6 Writing Workshop: Reporting Facts

One of the first concerns of newly freed African Americans in the South was education. Even before the Freedman's Bureau set up schools, thousands of freed African Americans were learning to read and write with help from African American and white teachers sent south by Northern missionary societies.

Charlotte Forten, one of the African Americans who went south to teach, reported her experiences in an 1864 magazine article, "Life on the Sea Islands." Notice how she uses facts to give a detailed report of her students on the Georgia Sea Islands.

Discover
- **the main idea of the passage**
- **the facts that are used to support this main idea**

Look at the Model

> . . . I never before saw children so eager to learn, although I had had several years' experience in New England schools. Coming to school is a constant delight and recreation to them. They come here as other children go to play. The older ones, during the summer, work in the fields from early morning until eleven or twelve o'clock, and then come to school, after their hard toil in the hot sun, as bright and as anxious to learn as ever. . . . Many of the grown people are desirous of learning to read. It is wonderful how a people who have been so long crushed to the earth . . . can have so great a desire for knowledge, and such a capacity for attaining it.
>
> — Charlotte Forten, "Life on the Sea Islands," *Atlantic Monthly* Vol. 13 (March, 1864)

1. What is the main idea that the writer communicates?

____

____

____

2. Where is this main idea stated? Write the topic sentence — the sentence that contains the main idea.

____

____

____

3. List three facts that provide evidence in support of the main idea.

____

____

____

____

Name ________________________________ Date ____________

Prewriting

Choose Your Topic

Imagine you were asked to give your opinion about an event or development that occurred in Unit 6. You might have an opinion about the Dred Scott case, the heroic 54th Massachusetts regiment, or the Ku Klux Klan. Write one paragraph that states your opinion and supports it with facts. Whatever topic you choose, you must state your position clearly in a topic sentence and use the rest of the paragraph to report facts that support your opinion. What issue in Unit 6 do you feel strongly about? Express your opinion on the issue here: ____________________

____

Think about your purpose. Why do you want to present your opinion? Write your purpose here. ________________________________

____

Think about your audience. Who will read your paragraph? Will your audience respond better to formal or informal language? Describe your audience here: ____________________

____

Take Notes

You may find that you need to reread parts of Unit 6 or do research in the library to find enough facts to effectively support your opinion. As you do your research, take notes. Use index cards and write each fact on a separate card. Then you will be able to try various ways of organizing your evidence by rearranging the cards until you have found the most effective presentation.

Two of Charlotte Forten's note cards might have looked like this.

<u>Young Children</u> school, a delight school, like play	<u>Older Children</u> work all morning still anxious to learn

Notice that the notes are written in phrases, not in complete sentences. Also note that each card has a title indicating the subject of the notes.

Use index cards or similar-sized paper to take notes for your paragraph. Then arrange your notes in the most effective order. You might organize them chronologically, by order of importance, or by parts of a whole — for example, battles of Civil War.

Make a list here of places you can look for facts.

____

____

____

____

____

Name ______________________________ Date ______________

Writing

Your First Draft

Use this space to write a first draft of your paragraph. Do not worry now about spelling mistakes or other errors. Use your notes and the organization you chose while prewriting. The guidelines below will help you write your draft.

Write a topic sentence that states your opinion. (You may wish to put your topic sentence at the end of your paragraph for greater impact.)

____

____

____

____

____

Write your first fact or piece of evidence. Be sure to include all the details.

____

____

____

Continue presenting the facts and details in the order you selected.

____

____

____

Where needed, use transition words such as: *first, next, on the other hand,* to help your audience follow the relationship of your facts.

____

____

____

____

____

Write a final sentence that brings your paragraph to a close.

____

____

____

Do you want to move the topic sentence to the end? If so, be sure that your paragraph also has an interesting beginning.

____

____

____

____

Name ______________________ Date______________

Revising

Talk It Over

Choose a partner. Listen as your partner reads his or her work aloud twice. During the first reading, listen for the main point your partner is making and for the facts presented to support the main point. After the second reading, try to answer these questions for your partner:

1. What is the main point of the paragraph? Where is it stated?
2. Is the topic sentence in the most effective place? If not, where else could it be placed?
3. Do all the facts support the main point? Could any facts be eliminated or added for greater clarity?
4. Are there effective transitions from one fact to the next? If not, how could these transitions be improved?

Then switch roles. Have your partner follow the same steps with your paragraph.

Make the Changes

Reread your first draft. Do you need to add facts or transitions? Think about your partner's comments and suggestions. Then make any changes that will improve your paragraph. Copy the revised paragraph on a clean sheet of paper.

Editing

Review these proofreading marks to help you correct errors.

Mark	Meaning	Mark	Meaning
∧	add something	∜∜	add quotation marks
℘	delete something	¶	new paragraph
≡	capitalize	/	lower case
⊙	make a period	(sp)	spell correctly
∧̦	add a comma	∿	transpose

Reread your paragraph to check for errors in spelling and punctuation, or exchange paragraphs with your partner and proofread each other's work. Read your partner's paragraph for errors, making a small check in the margin where an error occurs.

Postwriting

Evaluate Your Writing

If your paragraph has many proofreading marks, copy it onto a clean sheet of paper before submitting it for final evaluation.

Publish Your Writing

Exchange papers with a different partner. Read your partner's paper while he or she reads yours. Write one or two sentences that explain why you agree or disagree with the main point your partner has made in his or her paragraph. Discuss your opinions of each other's views after both of you have written your explanations.

Name ____ Date____________________

Unit 7 Writing Workshop: Stating Your Case

During the Jim Crow era in the South, thousands of state laws, city ordinances, and social customs kept African Americans from even the most basic privileges of citizenship. In some states, African Americans could not drink from the same water fountains as whites, use the same textbooks, or even bury their dogs in the same pet cemetery. Many African Americans resisted Jim Crow and demanded an end to discrimination. In 1886, African American businessmen from the South told white writer Charles D. Warner what rights they expected as citizens of the United States.

Discover

- **the demands of African American businessmen**
- **how each sentence relates to the main idea**
- **how the ideas flow naturally from one to the next**

Look at the Model

> We want to be treated like men, like anybody else, regardless of color. We don't mean by this social equality at all. . . . We want the public conveyances [transportation vehicles] open to us according to the fare we pay; we want privileges to go to hotels and to theatres, operas and places of amusement. We wish you could see our families and the way we live; you would then understand that we cannot go to the places assigned us in concerts and theatres without loss of self-respect.
>
> — Charles Dudley Warner, "The South Revisited," *Harpers New Monthly* Vol. 74 (March, 1887)

1. **a.** What is the main idea of the model?

   ____

   b. Where is it stated?

   ____

   ____

2. List the civil rights that the African American businessmen demand.

   ____

   ____

3. What do the African Americans say that they do not want?

   ____

   ____

4. How does the parallel structure of the sentences help tie the ideas of the passage together?

   ____

   ____

   ____

Name ______________________________ Date______________

Prewriting

Choose Your Topic

Imagine that you are a member of the group interviewed by Charles Warner. How would you respond to his question about what civil rights you want? What facts and reasons could you give for demanding these rights? List the rights you expect here: ______________________________

____

Who is your audience? Whom do you want to reach with your response? Describe your audience here: ______________________________

____

What is your reason for responding?

____

Make Lists

Before you write your response, make notes about what you will say. First, list the civil rights you expect to enjoy. Second, list reasons and facts that support your demands. Third, make notes on any additional information you want to convey. The African American businessmen might have made lists like this:

Civil Rights Demanded

— to be treated like men
— to have equal access to public conveyances, accommodations and places of entertainment

Facts and Reasons

We are men "like anybody else."
We pay same fare for public transportation as others pay.
Without equal treatment, we and our families cannot maintain our self-respect.

Use the space below to write your own lists.

____

____

____

____

____

____

____

____

____

____

____

Name ______________________________ Date______________

Writing

Your First Draft

Use the lines on this page to write a first draft of your answer to Warner's question. As you write, refer to the guidelines on the left side of the page. They will help you organize your draft.

Begin your paragraph by stating the rights that you expect as a citizen.

Explain in more detail what those rights include.

Give facts and examples that show what life is like for you without those rights.

Be sure that your paragraph has unity, meaning that all sentences relate to your main idea.

Also be coherent. Present your information in a logical order.

Conclude with an emotional appeal designed to move your audience.

Name ______________________________ Date______________

Revising

Talk It Over

Choose a partner. Listen as your partner reads his or her work aloud twice. During the first reading, listen to be sure that your partner has stated clearly what civil rights he or she expects. After the second reading, answer these questions:

1. Do all the facts and reasons support the main idea? What could be eliminated or added for clarity?
2. Are the facts and reasons presented in an order that makes sense? How could the organization be improved?
3. Is the conclusion a strong one? Is there an effective appeal to the emotions of the audience?

Share your answers to the questions above with your partner. Then switch roles, read your paper aloud twice to your partner, and listen to your partner's responses.

Make the Changes

Reread your draft. Are you satisfied with the case you have made for your rights? Think about your partner's comments and suggestions. Make only those changes that improve your response. Then copy your revised draft onto a clean sheet of paper.

Editing

Review these proofreading marks to help you correct errors.

∧	add something	∀∀	add quotation marks
℘	delete something	¶	new paragraph
≡	capitalize	/	lower case
⊙	make a period	ⓢⓟ	spell correctly
∧,	add a comma	∩∪	transpose

Reread your response to check for errors in spelling and punctuation, or exchange responses with your partner and proofread each other's work. Read your partner's response for errors, making a small check in the margin where an error occurs.

Postwriting

Evaluate Your Writing

If your response has many proofreading marks, copy it onto a clean sheet of paper before submitting it for final evaluation.

Publish Your Writing

In a small group, share your response with other students. As a group, create a list of civil rights demands. Read the list to the class and discuss other rights you might want to add to the list.

Name ______________________________ Date ______________

Unit 8 Writing Workshop: A Leaflet of Protest

On July 28, 1917, three months after the United States entered World War I, 15,000 African Americans marched in a silent demonstration through New York City. The parade was organized by the NAACP. The signs the marchers carried protested racial discrimination, race riots, and lynchings. The protestors distributed a leaflet containing the message below.

Discover
- **what the marchers are protesting**
- **what techniques they use to express their grievances eloquently and powerfully**

Look at the Model

> We march because by the grace of God and the force of truth the dangerous, hampering walls of prejudice and inhuman injustices must fall.
>
> We march because we want to make impossible a repetition of Waco, Memphis, and East St. Louis [anti-African American riots] by arousing the conscience of the country, and to bring the murderers of our brothers, sisters, and innocent children to justice.
>
> We march because we deem it a crime to be silent in the face of such barbaric acts.
>
> We march because we are thoroughly opposed to Jim Crow cars, segregation, discrimination, disenfranchisement, lynching, and the host of evils that are forced on us. It is time that the spirit of Christ should be manifested in the making and execution of laws.
>
> We march because we want our children to live in a better land and enjoy fairer conditions than have fallen to our lot.
>
> — *Why We March,* NAACP leaflet

1. The writer of the NAACP leaflet used a technique called parallelism. *Parallelism* is the repetition of key grammatical elements or sentence parts in a series of sentences or paragraphs. Where is it used here?

____

____

2. Why is parallelism effective in the leaflet?

____

____

3. What effect does the message have by being so short?

____

____

4. What and why are the marchers protesting?

____

5. Why do you think they chose to have a silent parade?

____

____

Name ______________________________ Date ______________

Prewriting

Choose Your Topic

Imagine that you are on an NAACP committee to publicize the struggle for civil rights during the early part of the 20th century. You decide to prepare a leaflet explaining the need for the civil rights struggle. What will you write about? Think of five practices common in the 1900s that you wish to protest. Write them here: ______________________________

____

Who will read your leaflet? Describe your audience:

____

What is your purpose for writing this leaflet? Write it here:

____

Make an Informal Outline

Make sure you have enough support in the form of reasons, facts, and examples to convince your audience of the validity of your statements. To evaluate your support, arrange it in an informal outline with the supporting material placed under the main ideas. In an informal outline, you do not have to worry about using Roman numerals or upper or lower case letters. An informal outline for the text of the 1917 NAACP leaflet might look like this:

End anti-African American riots
— Waco, Memphis, East St. Louis
— justice to murderers
— arouse nation
Need equal treatment
— Jim Crow
— lynching
— segregation
— discrimination
— voting
Better future for children
— better life
— fairer conditions

Look at the objects of protest you wrote down during the prewriting stage. List them in the space below. Then list the reasons, facts, and examples that support your call for justice and will make it a powerful one.

____

____

____

____

Name ______________________________ Date______________

Writing

Your First Draft

Begin to write the first draft of your statement here and finish it on a separate page if necessary. As you write, refer to the guidelines on the left side of the page. They will help you organize your draft.

Summarize what you are protesting and why.

State your first object of protest.

Give evidence in the form of facts, reasons, or examples.

Continue presenting your objects of protest and offering evidence of their destructive effects. Use parallelism to add emphasis.

Remember to keep your message short and powerful.

Conclude with your strongest evidence.

Name ______________________________ Date______________

 Revising

Talk It Over

Choose a partner. Read the text for your leaflet to your partner twice. During the first reading, the listener should simply try to understand the purpose of the statement. After the second reading, the listener should think about the answers to these questions:

1. What evidence supports the charges or protests made in the leaflet? Is this evidence strong enough to convince the audience or gain its sympathy?
2. What other evidence might the writer have included? Is any of the support given ineffective or unnecessary? What and why?
3. How effective is the writer's sentence structure? Would the use of parallelism make the message more effective? Where might the writer use parallelism?
4. What else might the writer do to improve the message?

Now reverse the process and have your partner read his or her statement to you.

Make the Changes

Reread the first draft of your statement. As you read, look for ways to make your message more powerful. Think about your partner's suggestions. Make any changes that you think will make your message more forceful. Write your revision on a clean sheet of paper.

Editing

Review these proofreading marks to help you correct errors.

Mark	Meaning	Mark	Meaning
∧	add something	❛❛ ❜❜	add quotation marks
⸍	delete something	¶	new paragraph
≡	capitalize	/	lower case
⊙	make a period	Sp	spell correctly
∧ (with comma)	add a comma	∿	transpose

Reread your statement to check for errors in spelling and punctuation, or exchange papers with your partner and proofread each other's work. Read your partner's text for errors, making a small check in the margin where an error occurs.

Postwriting

Evaluate Your Writing

If your text has many proofreading marks, copy it onto a clean sheet of paper before submitting it for final evaluation.

Publish Your Writing

Meet in small groups. After each member reads his or her leaflet to the group, discuss how to combine members' ideas into a group leaflet. Copy the text of the leaflet and include a title and graphics to make it eye-catching. Use the leaflet in a bulletin board display on the history of the civil rights struggle in the early 1900's.

Name ______________________________ Date ______________

Unit 9 Writing Workshop: A Position Statement

During the Civil Rights Movement of the 1950s and 1960s, conflicts arose over the best method of organizing to gain political power. Stokely Carmichael developed the concept of Black Power. Congressman Ronald Dellums, an African American from California, expressed a different view.

Discover
- **the different positions held by Carmichael and Dellums**
- **the reasons for each one's position**
- **the precise, powerful words and phrases each used to win the audience to his position**

Look at the Models

The point is obvious: black people must lead and run their own organizations. Only black people can convey the revolutionary idea — and it is revolutionary — that black people are able to do things themselves. Only they can help create . . . the basis for political strength. In the past, white allies have often furthered white supremacy without the whites involved realizing it. . . . The black politicians must stop being representatives of "downtown" machines. . . . Black power calls for black people to consolidate behind their own, so that they can bargain from a position of strength.

— Stokely Carmichael and Charles V. Hamilton, *Black Power.* (Random House, 1967)

. . . [when all minorities — women, Native Americans, Hispanics, Asians, even ecology-minded activists — unify] you have the majority of America. We can turn this country around. . . . But most important, we're standing side by side, unified; unified for freedom in this country in 1972. We may not be uniform, but we're unified. Because there's a strange, weird thing about freedom. Once you take that first step toward freedom, all slaves have got to be free. So when the black people stood up and said "Freedom," so did the Chicanos, the Indians, the Orientals [Asians], the young and the women. . . . That's the strange, weird thing about freedom.

— Ronald V. Dellums, speech at the *Third Annual Du Bois Cultural Evening,* sponsored by Freedomways (Carnegie Hall, New York City, January 30, 1972)

1. What is Stokely Carmichael's position regarding the organization of the civil rights struggle? Give two of Carmichael's reasons.

____

____

____

____

2. What is Ronald Dellums's position? Give two of Dellums's reasons.

____

____

____

____

Name ______________________________ Date ______________

Prewriting

Imagine you are an African American activist during the Civil Rights Movement of the 1950s and 1960s and you have been asked by your local newspaper to give your opinion on the best political organization for the civil rights struggle. Think about the views of Stokely Carmichael and Ronald Dellums. With which leader do you agree? Or, do you take another position? Write your opinion here: ______________________________

Who reads this local paper, and whom do you wish to convince of your position? Describe your audience here: ______________________________

____

Brainstorm

Before you write, you need to generate ideas. One of the easiest ways to start ideas flowing is to brainstorm. Start by writing a summary statement of your position at the top of a blank sheet of paper. Then jot down all the reasons, facts, and examples that support your position. Be open to all ideas. At this point, do not worry about whether or not what you write makes sense or is related to your topic. Put all your thoughts down on paper, and later you can choose what to use or discard.

If Stokely Carmichael had brainstormed before writing, his notes might have looked like this:

Position: A separate African American political organization is essential.
led by African Americans, run too
no more white machines from downtown
need to bargain from strength
economic power through organization
we can do it ourselves
white leadership undermines our goals
what about Malcolm X?

Write your own brainstorming notes here:

Your Position: ______________________________

____

____

____

____

____

____

____

____

Name ______________________________ Date ______________

Writing

Your First Draft

Use the lines below to write a first draft of your position statement. Do not worry now about spelling mistakes or other errors. Use information from your brainstorming notes. The guidelines on the left will help you as you organize your draft.

Write a topic sentence that summarizes your position. (Keep your audience in mind. Are you using language that they will understand?)

Give evidence to support your position. Start with your least powerful argument and build up to your strongest.

Use specific action words — for instance, *demanded* instead of *said* — to communicate clearly and add interest and strength to your writing.

Present your next piece of evidence.

Continue presenting evidence and conclude with your most powerful argument.

Wrap up your position statement with an emotional appeal to your audience.

Name ______________________________ Date______________

Revising

Talk It Over

Choose a partner. Listen as your partner reads his or her work aloud twice. During the first reading, listen for the writer's position on organizing for civil rights. After the second reading, try to answer these questions:

1. How logical is the writer's position? State your partner's position in your own words. Does it makes sense to you?
2. How well does the writer support his or her position? What evidence could be added? What could be eliminated?
3. How effectively does the writer use specific, powerful words to make the position statement clear and interesting? What words could be improved?

Discuss the answers to the questions with your partner. Then, reverse roles, read your paper aloud, and have your partner evaluate your work.

Make the Changes

Reread your first draft. Have you ended your position paper with your most effective argument and a forceful appeal? Think about your partner's comments. Make any changes that will strengthen your position statement. Then copy the revised statement onto a clean sheet of paper.

Editing

Review these proofreading marks to help you correct errors.

Mark	Meaning	Mark	Meaning
∧	add something	∨∨	add quotation marks
⌿	delete something	¶	new paragraph
═	capitalize	/	lower case
⊙	make a period	(sp)	spell correctly
∧,	add a comma	∿	transpose

Reread your paper to check for errors in spelling and punctuation, or exchange position statements with your partner and proofread each other's work. Read your partner's paper for errors, making a small check in the margin where an error occurs.

Postwriting

Evaluate Your Writing

If your position statement has many proofreading marks, copy it onto a clean sheet of paper before submitting it for final evaluation.

Publish Your Writing

Volunteer to read your position statement to the class. After all volunteers have read their position statements, ask class members to vote for the position they support. Then have individual voters discuss the reasons for their choices.

Name ______________________________ Date ______________

Unit 10 Writing Workshop: A Biographical Blurb

Since readers are usually interested in the backgrounds of the writers whose books they read, publishers often print biographical "blurbs," or brief accounts of the lives of the authors, on the covers or jackets of their books. The purpose of these blurbs is to give just enough information to entice readers to buy the book. Here is a portion of the blurb about Sylvester Monroe, the author of *Brothers, Black and Poor – A True Story of Courage and Survival,* a Newsweek Book published by William Morrow.

Discover
- **some important events in Sylvester Monroe's life**
- **the kind of specific details that add interest to a biographical blurb**
- **the techniques that make the reader want to read more**

Look at the Model

> Vest Monroe had taken the longest journey one could take in America, and now he wanted to go home. He'd come from the want and isolation of a black Chicago ghetto to the Washington bureau of *Newsweek,* but even with credentials in his wallet that gave him entry to the White House, he had trouble getting a taxi to stop and take him there. He'd arrived on the doorstep of the American Dream with his eyes open and his soul intact but, like any child of the ghetto, he had a contingent sense of life [saw life as unpredictable] and a persistent cause of doubt. There were no answers in Washington to the questions that troubled his reporter's mind and plagued his heart. He had to go home, to his old neighborhood and old friends.

1. List three facts about Sylvester Monroe's life that you learn from reading this blurb.

____

____

2. What reason is suggested for Monroe's leaving Washington?

____

____

3. What effect is created by the use of specific details such as "credentials in his wallet" and "the White House"?

____

____

4. What do you think is Sylvester Monroe's point of view? Why do you think so?

____

____

____

____

Name ____________________ Date ____________

Prewriting

Choose Your Topic

Imagine that your editor-in-chief has asked you to write a biographical blurb for a book by one of the people mentioned in Unit 10. Which person would you choose? Write your choice here:

____

Your job is to make the blurb interesting so that people will want to read the book. What type of reader do you wish to attract? Describe your audience here: ______________________________

____

____

The tone you choose will also influence the reader of your blurb. Will you be informative, mysterious, or amusing? Describe your tone: ______________________________

____

Ask Questions

Before you begin your blurb, you will need to gather and record information on your subject As you review Unit 10 or do additional research at the library, you may find it helpful to look for answers to a few key questions that you write beforehand. For example, when journalists are gathering information for a story, they often look for answers to the following questions: *who? what? when? where? why?* and *how?* Notes taken in this fashion for Sylvester Monroe's blurb might have looked like this:

Who? Sylvester Monroe, African American reporter for Newsweek

What? left successful correspondent's job to return to his beginnings

When? after professional acceptance in Washington, Monroe chose to return to his old neighborhood

Where? grew up poor in Chicago; later had a working journalist's access to the White House but returned to his Chicago neighborhood

Why? wanted to write a book exploring the future of African American men in U.S.

How? by retracing the course of his life and the lives of the friends he grew up with

Begin answering your questions here.

____

____

____

____

____

____

____

____

Name ______________________________ Date ______________

Writing

Your First Draft

Use this space to write a first draft of your biographical blurb. Do not worry now about errors in spelling or punctuation. You will have time later to correct any mistakes. Use the facts and ideas you gathered in your prewriting notes. The guidelines on the left will help you as you draft.

Begin with a catchy sentence that includes the name of your subject and a hint about the topic of the book.

Give some interesting and relevant background information about your subject.

Include specific details and incidents that are important in the person's life.

Add what he or she could have been thinking or feeling about the incidents you include. (Do not say too much; you want to intrigue your audience.)

Add a hint about the subject or theme of the book. Give clues about the motivation and point of view of the author.

Conclude with a reason why your audience should read the book.

Name ________________________________ Date ________________

Revising

Talk It Over

Choose a partner. Listen as your partner reads his or her blurb aloud twice. During the first reading, listen to see if the blurb makes you want to read the book. After the second reading, answer these questions:

1. Is there enough information about the author to satisfy readers' curiousity? If not, what other information might be added?
2. What hints are given about the author's motivation or the content of the book? What else could be done to interest and intrigue the reader?
3. What "dead wood" — dull words or phrases — could be eliminated? What language could be substituted to make the blurb more exciting?

Make the Changes

Reread the model and then go over your first draft. Can you borrow any techniques from the model to improve your blurb? Think about your partner's comments and suggestions. Make any changes that will improve your work. Then copy the revised blurb on a clean sheet of paper.

Editing

Review these proofreading marks to help you correct errors.

∧	add something	❛❛ ❜❜	add quotation marks
⸗	delete something	¶	new paragraph
≡	capitalize	/	lower case
⊙	make a period	(sp)	spell correctly
∧,	add a comma	∿	transpose

Reread your blurb to check for errors in spelling and punctuation, or exchange blurbs with your partner and proofread each other's work. Read your partner's blurb for errors, making a small check in the margin where an error occurs.

Postwriting

Evaluate Your Writing

If your blurb has many proofreading marks, copy it over on a clean sheet of paper before submitting it for final evaluation.

Publish Your Writing

Design and create a jacket or cover for your author's book. (Hardcover books often have paper jackets that are placed over the outside of the cloth covers. Paperback books sometimes print blurbs right on their back covers.) Add the blurb to the jacket for your teacher to display in the classroom.

Checklist for Writing A Research Paper

Writer ______________________________ Title ______________________________

Prewriting

Planning

_____ What are some subjects that might interest me? Which shall I choose as a topic?

_____ Is the topic narrow enough for one paper?

_____ Is the topic engaging enough to hold my interest?

Researching

_____ Where can I find information about my topic? Will a list help?

_____ What sources should I use (books, articles, encyclopedias, and so forth), and where do I find them?

_____ Do I have enough note cards to take down all important information?

_____ Have I made one bibliography card for each source I used?

_____ Do my note cards have complete source information?

- _____ Do I have the source title(s), author, and publication information as it will appear in my bibliography?
- _____ Have I recorded the library call number, if necessary, and page number where I found the information?

_____ Am I taking accurate research notes?

- _____ Did I use a new card for each new subject and source?
- _____ Have I placed a citation for the source and a page number on each note card?
- _____ Have I placed a subject heading on each card?

_____ Do I need to make an outline to organize my information?

- _____ What are my subtopics?
- _____ Have I organized my note cards by subtopic?
- _____ What is the best organization for my paper—chronological, spatial, order of importance, or developmental?

Writing

Drafting

_____ Do I have an introduction that includes my thesis statement?

_____ Is the body of my paper clear, unified, and coherent?

_____ Do I have a satisfactory conclusion where I restate my thesis and summarize my major points?

_____ Have I avoided plagiarism, presenting someone else's ideas as if they are my own?

Checklist for Writing A Research Paper: (continued)

Writer ______________________ Title ______________________

Citing Sources

_____ Have I used at least three sources?

_____ Have I footnoted all information I have borrowed from other sources?

_____ Have I created a bibliography that follows proper form?

Revising

Polishing the Introduction

_____ Does my opening statement arouse interest and include enough background information so my audience can understand my thesis statement and the body paragraphs that follow?

_____ Is my purpose for writing clear in my thesis statement?

Polishing the Body

_____ Does the organization of my body paragraphs develop my thesis and its subtopics?

_____ Are the facts and details in each paragraph organized logically?

_____ Do I need transitional words or phrases to make my organization clearer?

_____ Have I cited all direct quotations and any other borrowed ideas in a consistent manner?

Polishing the Conclusion

_____ Does my conclusion restate my thesis and summarize my major points?

Polishing the Style

_____ Have I made my writing style interesting by varying sentence lengths and structure?

_____ Would illustrations, diagrams, maps, or charts improve my paper?

Checking for Sense

_____ Does my research paper make sense?

Editing

_____ Have I corrected all spelling errors, usage problems, and mechanical mistakes?

_____ Is the revised copy of my research paper neat and easy to read?

Postwriting

Final Polishing

_____ Do I have a title page that contains my name, the title of my paper, and any other information the teacher requires?

_____ Would a folder or cover help me make a good impression?

Using Maps with *The African American Experience*

This chart lists mapping activities to give students practice with geographic elements in the study of African American history. Each activity is correlated to one or more of the themes of geography. and can be done by completing one of the four outline maps on pp. 305–308. Most activities can be completed using the text. Activities requiring additional research appear in italics.

	Map	Mapping Activity	Geographic Theme
Unit 1	Africa	African civilization and empires	location, movement
Unit 2	The World	Triangular trades	movement, place,regions
	Eastern United States	*Slave population of the colonies*	place, movement,human/ environmental interaction
Unit 3	Eastern United States	*Battles of the Revolutionary War*	location, movement human/environmental interaction
		Northwest Ordinance	region, place
		Slave and free states	region, human/ environmental interaction
	The United States	Louisiana Purchase/ Lewis and Clark Route	region, movement
Unit 4	Eastern United States	Slave rebellions	location
Unit 5	The United States	Routes of the Underground Railroad	movement
Unit 6	The United States	Missouri Compromise	region, human/ environmental interaction
		Compromise of 1850	region, human/ environmental interaction
		The Union and the Confederacy in 1861	region
		Battles of Civil War	location, movement
		Military districts under Reconstruction	region, movement
		Cattle drive routes	movement
	Eastern United States	Effects of the Emancipation Proclamation	region
Unit 7	The United States	Sites of African American colleges and universities	location, place
Unit 8	The World	*Battles of World War I in which U.S. soldiers participated* (save and add World War II battles in Unit 9)	place
	The United States	States gaining and losing population in the Great Migration	movement, region
Unit 9	The World	*Battles of World War II* *Vietnam* (add to map above)	place
	The United States	Sites of major civil rights encounters	place, movement
Unit 10	Africa	African nations today	location, region
	The United States	African American population today	region, movement

Name ______________________________ Date______________

OUTLINE MAP **The World**

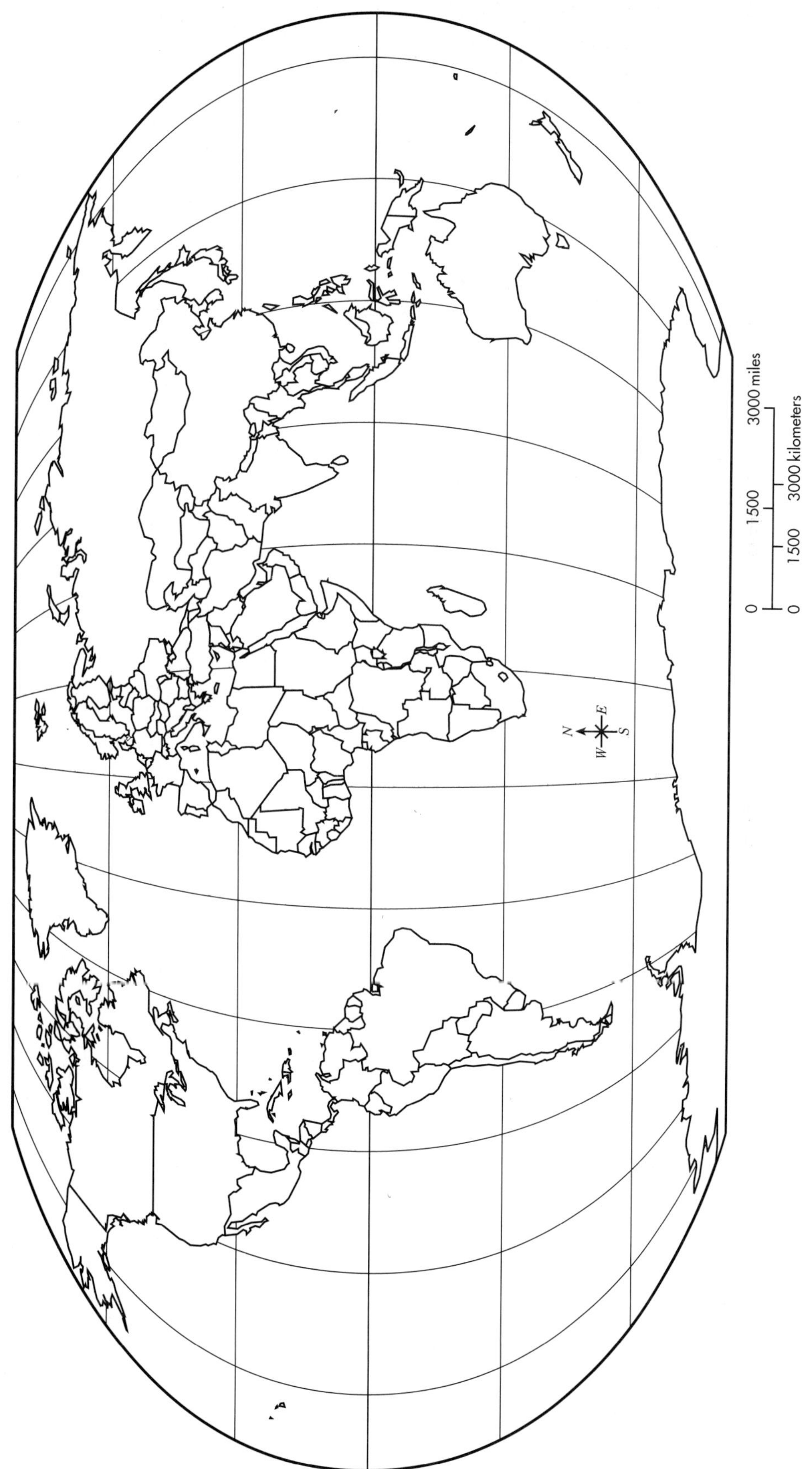

Name ______________________ Date ______________

OUTLINE MAP

Africa

Name ______________________________ Date______________

OUTLINE MAP

Eastern United States

Name ______________________________ Date ______________

OUTLINE MAP

The United States

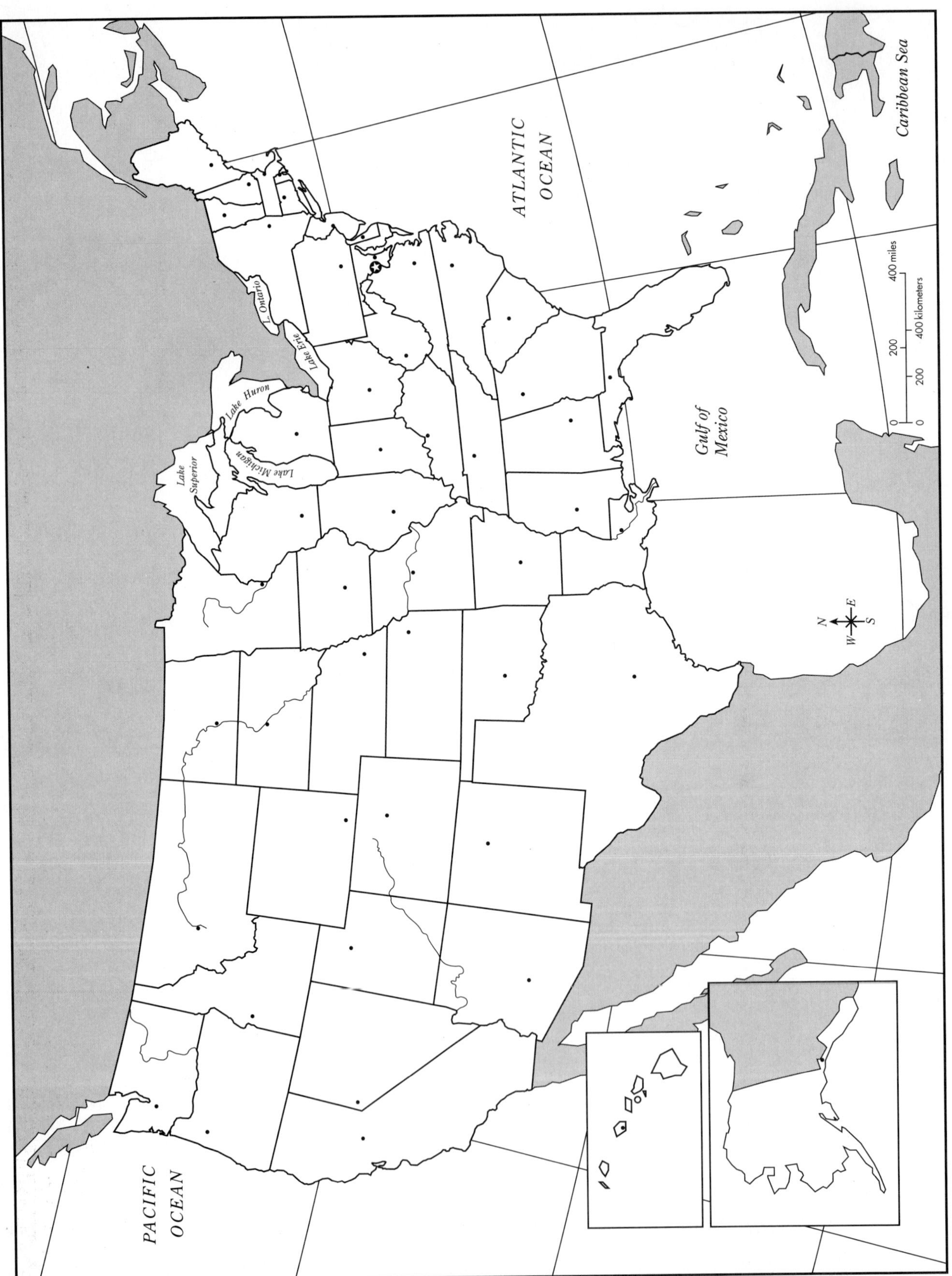